Indigenous Inhumanities

Indigenous Americas
Robert Warrior, Series Editor

Chadwick Allen, *Earthworks Rising: Mound Building in Native Literature and Arts*

Chadwick Allen, *Trans-Indigenous: Methodologies for Global Native Literary Studies*

Raymond D. Austin, *Navajo Courts and Navajo Common Law: A Tradition of Tribal Self-Governance*

Lisa Brooks, *The Common Pot: The Recovery of Native Space in the Northeast*

Kevin Bruyneel, *The Third Space of Sovereignty: The Postcolonial Politics of U.S.–Indigenous Relations*

Eric Cheyfitz, *The Colonial Construction of Indian Country: Native American Literatures and Federal Indian Law*

Glen Sean Coulthard, *Red Skin, White Masks: Rejecting the Colonial Politics of Recognition*

James H. Cox, *The Red Land to the South: American Indian Writers and Indigenous Mexico*

Karrmen Crey, *Producing Sovereignty: The Rise of Indigenous Media in Canada*

Brendan Hokowhitu and Vijay Devadas, *The Fourth Eye: Māori Media in Aotearoa New Zealand*

Daniel Heath Justice, *Our Fire Survives the Storm: A Cherokee Literary History*

Daniel Heath Justice and Jean M. O'Brien, *Allotment Stories: Indigenous Land Relations under Settler Siege*

Emil' Keme, *Le Maya Q'atzij / Our Maya Word: Poetics of Resistance in Guatemala*

Thomas King, *The Truth About Stories: A Native Narrative*

Valerie Lambert, *Native Agency: Indians in the Bureau of Indian Affairs*

Scott Richard Lyons, *X-Marks: Native Signatures of Assent*

Mark Minch-de Leon, *Indigenous Inhumanities: California Indian Studies after the Apocalypse*

Aileen Moreton-Robinson, *Talkin' Up to the White Woman: Indigenous Women and Feminism*

Aileen Moreton-Robinson, *The White Possessive: Property, Power, and Indigenous Sovereignty*

(continued on page 310)

INDIGENOUS INHUMANITIES

California Indian Studies after the Apocalypse

Mark Minch-de Leon

Indigenous Americas

University of Minnesota Press
Minneapolis / London

The University of Minnesota Press gratefully acknowledges support for the open-access edition of this book from the University of California, Riverside.

Excerpt from Dead Pioneers, "Bad Indian," copyright 2023 Dead Pioneers; permission courtesy of Gregg Deal. Excerpts from Deborah Miranda's "Correspondence," in *Indian Cartography,* copyright 1999; "Old Territory. New Maps," in *Zen of La Llorona,* copyright 2005; "San Francisco Bulletin, May 12, 1859" and "Los Pájaros," in *Bad Indians: A Tribal Memoir*; copyright 2013; used with permission from Deborah Miranda. Excerpts from Janice M. Gould's "Blood Sisters," in *Earthquake Weather,* copyright The University of Arizona Press, 1996; "Six Sonnets: Crossing the West," in *Doubters and Dreamers,* copyright The University of Arizona Press, 2011; "Ancestors," in *This Music: A Poetic Prose Memoir* (forthcoming); used with permission from the Literary Estate of Janice M. Gould.

Portions of chapter 5 are adapted from "Atlas for a Destroyed World: Frank Day's Painting as Work of Nonvital Revitalization," in *Native American and Indigenous Studies Journal* 8, no. 1 (Spring 2021).

Published by the University of Minnesota Press
111 Third Avenue South, Suite 290
Minneapolis, MN 55401–2520
http://www.upress.umn.edu

Available as a Manifold edition at manifold.umn.edu

ISBN 978-1-5179-1829-3 (hc)
ISBN 978-1-5179-1830-9 (pb)

Library of Congress record available at https://lccn.loc.gov/2025011004

Printed in the United States of America on acid-free paper

34 33 32 31 30 29 28 27 26 25 10 9 8 7 6 5 4 3 2 1

Contents

Prologue
(Re)Turning

Never does one open the discussion by coming right to the heart of the matter. For the heart of the matter is always somewhere else than where it is supposed to be.

—Trinh T. Minh-ha, *Woman, Native, Other*

There is no such thing as "Indian," but now there's no turning back.

—Tommy Pico, *IRL*

Turning

We turn toward the dead. Dancing in an open, and therefore infinite, circle, we turn toward them, because they turn toward us. Our close relationship to death has earned their attention. *Isn't this a turn away from the world?* Which? The diurnal world of settler colonial midday when all is flat and the sun is too bright and hurts one's eyes? The waking world of means and ends and its blunt cruelty? Certainly. Such a world foreshortens lives, murders and removes children, places on women the terrible burden of settler sexual futurity through rape and enslavement, undoes relations of all sorts, casts the rhythm of life and death into disarray until no sense of time is left. In the name of the law. In the name of progress. In the name of time, of the end of times, and the ends of time itself. And so we saw through the illusion of time. We left homes, jobs, relationships, all the work of living, to dream with the dead, to dance and sing until exhaustion carries us away, drops us into dream again, *fall down dead in the middle of the dance,* and then start over.[1] Dancing past exhaustion, with and through it. Like the return of the dead, we got up and kept going. Day and night. *I came back nine months later and they were still dancing,* says the surprised observer.[2] And it terrifies him. *Dancing among the Indians has been carried to that extravagant extent that the able-bodied Indians have been compelled to desist from . . . exhaustion; some of the most fanatical, dancing for several days and nights continuously . . .*[3] We showed up for this. *Indians, of their own accord, are gathering upon the reservations and many who have been absent for one or two years are there now. They are nightly engaged in war dances, and decorating themselves with paint and feathers . . . They urge and insist that everyone engage in these dances, and will not even excuse squaws . . . living with white men.* This fear led to pleas from Indian agents for help against the constantly imagined threat of Indian uprisings. But we have never stopped dancing because the dead dance slowly, ever so slowly, our way in an open circle. Where our circle meets their line; our line, their circle, *they said the dead danced in a round dance and singing,* yet they are returning, an open circle.[4] *They never arrived.* Who knows the time of the dead? If the dead even know time? Why such certainty? To turn toward the dead is to turn away from certain time, from knowing according to a timeline, a calendar, the workday schedule and rhythm. Yes, they have not arrived yet, or perhaps they keep arriving and will keep arriving, not stop arriving, for all of what the colonizer calls time. After all, the dead keep growing in number.

We turn away from the world, from the enforced *here* of property, labor, law, accumulation, reproduction, settler futurity, and the good. *They began arresting participants in the dance and those singing because it took the men away from their work.*[5] Doctor George got arrested because *he made all the people go crazy. They just camped around and listened to him instead of working.*[6] It was a work stoppage.[7] We gathered together, left everything of the white world behind, went on strike against the white world. Lucy Thompson said, *He-na Tom, dreaming after his wife died, had asked everyone to destroy everything derived from whites as part of the Ghost Dance.*[8] We told each other that the world was to turn over and end; this was our goal.[9] To bring it about, we refused individual wealth and accumulation. *All valuables which were secreted would be transformed into worthless objects, but valuables which were exposed would remain unaltered. As a result dancers carried their riches to the dance.*[10] It was a collective, popular response. Lucy Thompson said, *the poor were the first converts.*[11] Sixes George had lost his wife and son. *He wanted to die and go where his relatives were. That is why he started to dream and dance.*[12] The old ones *went crazy and began dreaming things and kept on singing.*[13] The dance became an affliction of the old, the poor, and the bereaved, who, in lieu of dying, as a form of dying otherwise, dreamed the most and danced the hardest. To dance in a circle is to embark on an infinite journey in place, to go nowhere but still away from place itself. To extend the turn toward the dead, the turn away from the world, to infinity. And it cannot be done alone. In the nonarrival of the dead lies a gesture to another world; it is a refusal of the arrival of a settler "here" and "now." Upending spatio-temporal relations and conditions, upending phenomenological groundings, together with the dead, we gesture toward an elsewhere-within-here that makes us dizzy, disorients all orientations, a dizziness that contributes to the turning over of the world, that protects our very movement of suspension as a pointing-in-the-direction of the dead in our turn away from "here" and "now."[14] *The dance was not prescribed to a particular spot, as are the native dances, but could be made anywhere,* and yet nowhere and nowhen.[15] An anticolonial response to your incessant encroachment and brutality, this was not tradition; we had not done this before, though it was simply a round dance that had been going for well over five hundred years. With gaze cast down, dancing in circles, the ground spins, ground itself spins. Disorientation of place, in place. Loss of horizon. Do not look up.

We turn to the dead whose names we are never supposed to mention. Breaking our rules, our laws (yes we had them, have had them for thousands of years). They are not *our* dead, but, most insistently, they do not belong to the settler. The dead cannot be owned; destroy all owning. We cannot even presume that the dead are human. How could they be? Why assume the dead arrive in anthropomorphic form? We were told by Weneyuga that *all the dead are coming back, even the wild animals, like bear, deer, wolf.*[16] Our relations have always been more than human, including that of the dying and dead world. We chose to follow our dying social world, our forms of interrelation into their death but through reinvented relations. To break protocols. To insist that everyone *bathe together without shame, but intercourse was forbidden on pain of having the genitalia turn to stone.*[17] To make new rules. Rearrange social relationships. Another doctor, Sambo, forbid fighting and "growling," encouraged married women to dance with anyone, said anybody could love anybody and married people didn't need to stay together, old women could have young men, one couldn't refuse sexual advances. He commanded people to eat only traditional food; for this, some people starved. But most importantly we chose to socialize with the dead despite powerful restrictions. *My uncle, who was Jo Tom, broke up the dance at Cottage Grove because he said it was an insult to mention the dead.*[18] Henry Joseph clarifies, *all the Indian stories which went way back never had anything in them about the dead coming back. Those stories were like school for the Indians. They told us how things were.*[19] It was Coyote, after all, according to some stories, especially those of Hanc'ibyjim, who introduced death into the world and made it permanent, something even he couldn't take back after the loss of his son, the first person to die.[20] In others, it is the creator who teaches the world about death: *it is the law of the Klamath that if you bury a man and hear him moving, you must pile rocks on him to keep him down. If the dead get up, they will kill the whole village. The Creator said not to let anyone out of the grave after burying him.*[21] What fortitude needed to risk communing with the dead! By dancing in a circle, the living have entered into the realm of the dead. Social death is death into the absolute social.

We turn away from the world through dreaming. We turn toward dreams. We dance, we don't sleep, and yet we dream. Some say dream is a day in the night, a strange light, but it is also a night that interrupts the day, fully nocturnal at noon.[22] The Destruction has already overturned the rhythms of life and death, night and day. To dream is to follow this turn even further, to go over *over-*, to turn over, a true continuity through discontinuity, following the curve of destruction, perhaps the only truth that isn't genocidal. Henry Joseph reports, *after Sambo's word came through, people began dreaming themselves. Dead persons told them songs and the next morning the dreamers would sing. They might hear a song for four or five nights. They got kind of crazy. They took one man, Pekirivriken, to the asylum and he died down there. His song was: uhu uhe he howia he. It had no meaning to it.*[23] Mass insomnia. There was no sleep left to be had, as the world where one could rest one's head was gone. Dream carries us past meaning, past the world itself. *The women let their hair hang loose all over their faces. In the old dances it should be parted in the middle and wrapped. Hair hanging loose was just for mourning.*[24] With their hair hanging loose in their faces in such manner, *about a hundred old ladies danced like young girls,* a collective form of mourning unbound.[25] A mourning that exceeds the terms of mourning, a pure form, incessant, exceeds the work of life and death in their rhythm, just as *the name taboo must have suffered infringement where the dead relatives were the main topic of conversation.*[26] To speak of the dead, to name them, to socialize with them beyond both settler and Native sociality is a pure form of mourning and an act of risk or desperation. Who decides? It is the purest name through unnaming. The dream and the name connect us to the vigilance of the dead, a permanent wakefulness past waking itself, past the wake, of the dead, who sing a song that cannot finish, can never finish, can only be performed in an unsatisfactory fragment, calling us to where the dead come from, their infinite departure and arrival. The dead no longer let us sleep. They make us move more than we can without going anywhere, nowhere, past exhaustion, in and through it we get up and dance. Perhaps there is no dream except of the songs the dead sing to us without sound and without end.

And you disappear, burn up *without even leaving ashes.*[27] A perfect disappearance. A perfect crime, so no crime at all, an end to crime itself. Set in motion, something that will only end when settler time has stopped. And even then it keeps going, turning around itself, infinitely ending. Who or what were you in the end, if you can disappear so completely? So perfectly. The circle open for us but closed, closing, for you. The Ghost Dance was never for you. You were collateral damage. And still we prepared for war. *A. B. Meacham credits the Modoc War to the Ghost Dance.*[28] Kintpuash and his warriors were all practitioners. *The band of Modoc who were to be involved the following year in the Modoc War received the doctrine from a fellow tribesman, called Doctor George (xelespiames), who had participated in the Paviotso dance at Beatty. These Modoc, under the leadership of the famous Captain Jack, danced at the mouth of the Lost River where it empties into Tule Lake.*[29] Alan David, dreamer and headman of the Klamath, has been credited by some with influencing the Modoc. The Karuk also painted themselves red for war.[30] And yet your disappearance is bloodless *without even leaving ashes.* An afterthought. An outcropping of our firm resolve to turn over this world, to associate with the dead. You are just in the way. But we did do terrible things. Weneyuga advocated the killing of all half-breed children, to thwart white settler futurity.[31] We even killed our dogs.[32] Our firm resolve. But the war was through dreaming. *Whenever you dream, paint your face red and white, do what your dream tells you. If you don't obey your dreams, you will turn to rock.*[33] We do what dreams tell us, sing the songs, dance, fall down dead, dream, get up and keep dancing; the dead return, the world turns over, and you disappear without remainder.

They had us believe *the Indians were surrounded like an island in a sea of whites,* but really it is the settler, on our land, who is surrounded by the dead.[34] "In a little more than a generation, Americans outnumbered Indigenous People in the state. The Ghost Dance promised to reverse these trends, with the return of the dead and the animals."[35]

Returning

Why, when survival was at stake, did so many of our ancestors turn toward the dead? This astonishing occurrence is difficult to understand much less interpret. Rather than seeking sociological, anthropological, or historical explanations or critical analyses of the phenomenon as so many have done before, this book turns to the conditions and characteristics of the dead in all their danger and distance, returns to the risks that our ancestors took, and maps their continued relations to contemporary knowledge and artistic production. It refuses to explain away the radicalness of this act and accumulate knowledge about it in order to tame it, to make it known, to make it safe, to institutionalize, discipline, or instrumentalize it. *Indigenous Inhumanities* engages in California Indian studies as a continuation of the Ghost Dance, our ancestors' collective anticolonial intellectual praxis in the face of destruction, and it performs alongside California Indian modes of study within a post-apocalyptic temporal and spatial orientation attentive to relations to the dead. In other words, *Indigenous Inhumanities* allows our ancestors to lead us astray on their errant paths (the open circle, the spinning, disorientation) away from the colonized world while we remain in place, and it takes time, destroys time, by waiting with them for the dead who are on an infinite journey back (without departure, without arrival). Without treating the Ghost Dance as a topic, this book continues the Ghost Dance's methodology, laid out by these outrageous ancestors: follow the turn away from the world and wait for return of the dead, two coterminous movements that subsist in the ambiguity of indetermination and hold open its radical nature.

These two movements are an anticolonial response to the Destruction (colonization, coloniality, genocidal violence, and their effacements of their own conditions). They challenge naturalized definitions of movement through erring, disorientation, and stasis—definitions that often undergird conceptions of subjectivity, value, and the human—opting instead for a stillness that moves more than any naturalized sense of motion. They refuse colonialism outright by leaving the world of its making, by failing to fall in line or take part, by riding the fraught energies of the Destruction itself. The Ghost Dance has been understood by settler logics to be an irrational act of "savagery"; it has more sympathetically been understood by settler historians and anthropologists to be a difficult response to an impossible situation, a more recuperative interpretation. Foregoing both evaluative tendencies, to reject or recuperate, throughout the course of this book we will stay with the difficulty the Ghost Dance presents in order to make available both impossibility—for which the dancers took responsibility in the name of a more fundamental irresponsibility—and the infinite arrival of the dead in their anticolonial suspensions of a spatial and temporal colonial order. This approach is meant to release anticolonialism from its capture and domestication by instrumental logics of colonial reality and their institutions, by the individualist colonial world of efficacy and action, to release decolonization from the snares of humanist and vitalist double binds in which it has been entangled.

The book is split into two parts. Part 1, "Ancestor," traces a process of humanization deployed in what we now call California to control Indigenous people by controlling our relations to the dead, thereby attempting to manage the power that the dead hold to disrupt the colonial order. In a context where settlers have interrupted California Indian death ceremonies through assimilation, stigmatization, and the violent targeting of ceremonies themselves during a genocidal campaign, this section looks to research related to repatriation, the archive, and the discourse on genocide as these processes have come to stand in for interrupted ceremony and the interdiction on mourning. Each of these sites is associated with a social scientific discipline that has largely held a monopoly over the interpretation of our ancestors in physical (archaeology), cultural and imagistic (anthropology), and remembered (history) forms. Responsible for some of the most racist and dehumanizing effects of representation, these disciplines—which roughly make up the colonial institutional formation of California Indian studies—have also self-reflexively asserted themselves as the site for the rehumanization of Indigenous peoples in California, if not, as some contemporary anthropologists and historians have asserted, as the site of decolonization.

Organized around the western colonial figure of the normative human, early iterations (and some lingering ones, as I discuss in chapter 1) of these intellectual formations created the conditions for the exclusion of Indigenous peoples and worlds from the invented category of the *human*, using these exclusions to sediment this figure in colonial institutional settings. This isolation of the human made possible the conditions for separating Indigenous peoples from their worlds and social contexts in order to conscript them into this humanizing process by determining the acceptable categories of human existence, action, and relation. Such a violent process of "settlement" at turns mutilated, killed, or assimilated Indigenous peoples based on their relation to the normative figure and their responses to colonization. Each of these humanizing disciplines has been confronted by strident critique from Indigenous scholars and communities and in turn responded by disavowing their institutional pasts and asserting themselves as the site of reform of the institution and knowledge production by taking on the project of promoting an Indigenous agenda. Each of these disciplines, as discussed in the chapters that make up Part 1, include a self-reflexive critique of western conceptions of the human but, in general, operate as a form of reconciliation with the state. Undergirded by a western colonial sense of vitalism or what Elizabeth Povinelli calls a "biontological enclosure," this process of humanization values and organizes relationships according to a privileging of western conceptions of Life against Nonlife, buttressed by the state and within colonial extractive systems that reach their apex in the state form.[36]

Rather than a systematic unveiling or historicization of this process of humanization, Part 1 proceeds through specificity by attending to how humanization arises in particular circumstances from an Indigenous standpoint (or lack thereof). The specific instances take the form of a controversy over the location of a Native American Graves Protection and Repatriation Act (NAGPRA) research unit on the UC Berkeley campus in 2007 (chapter 1); an encounter with images of my great-grandmother while doing research in the anthropometric photography archive of anthropologist Edward W. Gifford (chapter 2); and the historiographic case to recognize colonial violence in California as a genocide using the colonial archive as evidence (chapter 3). In each instance, research under colonial conditions, in the face of the Destruction, leads the way. In the context of Indigenous California, such research takes place in a postapocalyptic setting, whether this be Deborah Miranda's beginning her book *Bad Indians* after "The End of the World"; Cutcha Risling Baldy's use of Lawrence Gross's concept "Post Apocalypse Stress Syndrome" to discuss California Indian experiences of surviving genocide;[37] or Tommy Pico's ethical imperative to "give everything away" because, thanks to the prying eyes of colonial researchers, everything has already been revealed anyway (apocalypse means, of course, "revelation").[38] Embedded in the concept of the postapocalypse, this ethical and epistemological California Indian stance of endurance asserts that *we've already seen it, we simply keep going, but we also don't forget,* at work in the concept of the postapocalypse. Catastrophe is banality. Something to be navigated. But nothing dramatic. The always already revealed.

This approach of postapocalyptic research foregoes the types of revelatory logics that feed academic scholarship as a commodity as well as the critical project of reform that smooths over the rough aspects of colonization to make it palatable for the purposes of reconciliation. Critique reveals and corrects nothing, a desire and demand that rather operates as a force of alignment with the state. Institutionally, these processes of (re)humanization take the form of what Abigail Boggs and Nick Mitchell call the "crisis consensus," the uniform call to defend against right-wing attacks on the university—which is positioned as an inherent good with a progressive nature at its core and not as the intellectual arm of the settler state that it is. The crisis consensus operates, they note, as a "call for return to ideals of tuitionless university enrollment and noninstrumentalist liberal curricular breadth, [which] invokes right-wing salvos (administrative-managerial proliferation, debt-generating tuition levels, and overall ethos of privatization) as transparent evidence of the crisis-ridden nature of the now," eliding the settler and carceral logics of the liberal university.[39] Such a project as the crisis consensus operates in a self-reflexive mode, most notably as defined by critical university studies, one that seeks to know itself as both a gesture of confidence and "to attend to its crisis prone structural tendencies [in order to] manage their effects." Further, "consensus itself is normed by an analytical predisposition towards rescue and restoration."

The university and the humanities in particular are significant sites of such rescue. Not only has the humanities been centered, along with the interdisciplines, as particularly under threat (primarily due to the political nature of these fields), but the humanities have also been enlisted as agents of rescue at their critical intersections with the social sciences. Interpretive social sciences have taken up humanist critical practices and traditions and mixed them with critiques coming from the communities they have historically studied to produce a dual practice of rescue of the discourses of these communities and a self-rescue of the institution and their own disciplinarity through them. This serves the dual purpose of softening the colonial scienticity of the social sciences (humanizing them, which continues to create significant conflicts with the more science-based side of the "social" sciences) and "restoring" an aesthetic form of humanism and human liberation to Indigenous peoples, even projecting the idea that this is an Indigenous formation first and foremost. This book takes as one of its focuses this aesthetic humanism at work in progressive social scientific discourses and their forces of humanization, often in the name of Indigeneity.[40] It questions the generativity of this approach and instead turns to the inhuman conditions it seeks to disavow, the refusals and failures to contribute to institution-building and the colonial edifice of knowledge, that seek their undoing.

Part 2, "The Destruction," focuses on the power of the dead as they guide California Indian authors and artists in writing and representing destruction. Attending to works by Esselen and Chumash poet, theorist, and author Deborah Miranda and by Maidu painter and cultural leader Frank Day, Part 2 emphasizes how they each engage the powers of the dead and of the Destruction for the purpose of survival. Operating within a practice of transvaluation—or perhaps more accurately what Fred Moten calls "invaluation or antivaluation, *the extraction* from the sciences of value"[41]—both engage and employ difficult and often dangerous powers, including the negative representations of California Indian peoples and the husks or carcasses of discarded colonial knowledge forms, out of which they grow a form of Indigeneity like a fungus. As they illustrate, "For the native, life can only spring up again out of the rotting corpse of the settler."[42] Such an enigmatic violence extends from the refusal of violence performed by ghost dancers and seeks to disperse (as opposed to accumulate) materials, forms, and forces. Relinquishing authorial voice to platform the voices of ancestors and populating the text with difficult archival materials in an epic found poem, Miranda challenges colonial forms of literary studies and education through a minoritarian practice of writing with and through the Destruction, at The End of the World. Similarly, Day's inappropriate use of western realist painting to document a destroyed Maidu world, through an outmoded form of anthropological representation, engages an avitalist, weak power that employs and outdoes dangerous representational forces and modes of knowing, particularly art history, exacerbated through the ambiguity of his position in his community and the questionable truthfulness of his discourse. Together, Miranda and Day indicate a stream of California Indian studies antagonistic to the colonial institutional version that is both specific to their historical moments and material practices and connected to the long curve of our ancestors' studied responses to destruction.

Bad Indians

Along these lines, this book seeks to linger in, be complicit with, what Miranda has robustly called the "bad Indians": those who did whatever they had to do to survive—lied, burned down missions, assassinated priests, drank too much, fought colonizers and each other, fucked, kept secrets, gossiped, slacked off, refused to work, continued to perform ceremony despite restrictions, forgot how, became too white, were never white enough, lived and breathed resentment, wore government-issued shoes, ran away from boarding schools, didn't live up to colonial expectations to be less/more Indian, acted badly and were bad at being Indian. As Paiute artist and front man for the punk band Dead Pioneers, Gregg Deal, says/sings:

> My cheekbones aren't high enough
> I don't have enough beadwork
> Or turquoise
> I do my best to celebrate November like a month long birthday
> for Indians
> For those of you who don't know, which is probably most
> of you
> It's National Native American Heritage Month
> And unfortunately celebrating feels like I'm celebrating my
> birthday by myself
> No one seems to know it's even happening
> Even with the Facebook notices
>
> I'm a bad Indian
>
> My favorite movie genre is westerns
> My last name isn't a sentence
> I'm not patient
> But I am stoic
> Usually only when I'm mad
> Or just thinking really hard
> People don't know how to pronounce the name of my Tribe
> And that makes me tired

Can't and won't say prayers in Paiute
Mostly because I'm not fluent

. . .

And I would be justified in punching him
I would be justified in cursing him out
I would be justified in calling him racist

But that would make me a bad Indian
Which contradicts that old saying
You know the one:
The only good Indian is a dead Indian

But I'm a bad Indian.[43]

An impossible situation, through an often-unstated evaluation of Indianness, too many interpretations of our stories, behaviors, actions, and ideas have sought to tame them, make them palatable to colonial tastes and sensibilities. To know them by controlling them; to control by knowing. This book foregoes such pacification, evaluation, and translation by leaning into both the Indianness and the badness, into the very impossibility to be. By foregoing knowing or failing to be entirely legible, it lives alongside bad Indians in our rawness, past, present, and future, as a mode of study enacted by both Miranda and Day, without reservation and without judgment. Operating within an ethic of uncivil discourse, it seeks a certain indeterminacy, a refusal or failure to be fully known, staying bad because to be judged good is to be captured, rendered utilitarian. Not a matter of agency or will, this mode of writing is rather attuned to weak power, a California Indian conception of attenuated agency,[44] and operates by getting lost in the work, foregoing judgment, eschewing comparison as meaning-making, pushing against the increase in knowledge (identification and categorization), refusing national literatures and the assertion that works are part of the colonial humanist treasury that is the canon.

Miranda's conception of the bad Indian is also a manifestation of bad feelings in common, of the despair that grips hold of a people when confronted with overwhelming destruction, and it offers an (anti)social and affectively configured *angle of perception.*[45] Despair is a mode of endurance, perhaps counterintuitively. It approaches the neutral by letting go of control. Despair does not end with death as hope does, which is teleological and seeks a closed and bounded existence (see, e.g., Jonathan

Lear's misreading of the Ghost Dance as a form of hope[46]). Hope is, perhaps ironically, as Maurice Blanchot has shown, intimately linked to suicide, as both seek meaning through a certain humanness and a sense of closure.[47] In other words, they have a similar orientation toward death, a human end. Despair, on the other hand, is attuned to a death that never arrives and that it therefore outlasts, an inhuman continuity. And it does so without effort. In relation to writing, language, art, and knowledge, despair introduces a certain unmusicality, a dissonance without resolution, without reconciliation, as it unsettles emotions. An unresolved continuity, despair's unmusicality is not a movement (musical or otherwise) with a humanistic end, a harmonious whole, but the unending sustain of feedback, an unpoetic/poetics of noise, feelings of unrest, an inhuman voice—one that damages the eardrums, creates an anticolonial tinnitus that merges with the voices of the dead.

Bad Indianness is an affective perception from underground, when one is *down in it* and *going through it*. As Day describes in chapter 5, the Maidu went underground to survive. Such perception he equates with the Maidu relation to nonhuman beings such as ants, with whom they share kinship, but it is also a perception from earth dwellings as bunkers that comes out of the Ghost Dance's afterlives, going underground and waiting for the colonial world to disappear. In profound misery and humiliation, ghost dancers found ecstatic ways to outdo colonial violence and cooptation. Miranda makes a similar observation in her writing alongside the archival body of work of one her ancestors, Isabel Meadows, on the stories passed down from the time of the genocidal Spanish missions. Miranda notes that Meadows often relates tales deemed irrelevant by the anthropological recording machine she uses: stories about adulterers, deserters of spouses, children whose fathers cannot be identified, alcoholics, men who rape granddaughters, lecherous jokes by old women, women who blind husbands with hot coals. Deeming them a sort of anticolonial gossip, Miranda asserts that "such tales take up as much if not more space as the linguistic data, creation stories, and place names typically mined from her [ancestor's] materials."[48] Describing Carmeleños, Mission Indians incarcerated at Carmel Mission, who died of sadness, drunkenness, too many accidents, from fights, stabbings, and clubbings, so much drinking and sorrow, Meadows and Miranda also highlight the sexual promiscuity and gender and sexual fluidity of the incarcerated Natives through archival traces ambiguously etched (coded) in J. P. Harrington's anthropological notes.

This complex assemblage of Indigenous sociality under severe constraint (colonial, cisheteropatriarchal, white supremacist, Manichean), confronting imminent death, as the abundant necro-statistics in Mission archives show, is where bad feelings in common bleed into intense dreaming. Miranda instructs us to "push into the pain" in order to see its value (or antivaluation) as "the only way through that allows preservation of an Indigenous identity."[49] A hard truth, prepared by a colonial perception, it can be reappropriated for thinking Indigenous sociality with and beyond colonial Manicheanism. To paraphrase Frantz Fanon, the only truth is what ends colonization.[50] Even the most difficult and racially charged representations carry within them the refusal and failure of Indigenous people to participate in the system, a dangerous energy; in California Indian parlance *a poison.* For example, "'The Indians are instructed how to live as rational individuals . . . but . . . in these matters they behave like children of eight or nine years, who have not yet acquired a constant or steady disposition,'" writes Father Juan Amoros of the Indians at Carmel in 1814, adding that "'they are prone to anger . . . and a spirit of vindictiveness.'"[51] Bad Indians hold onto this vindictiveness as a way of holding onto their Indianness. It is an anger that is not recuperable for a productive agenda; it is, for example, the "incandescent" rage Vine Deloria describes after reading accounts of the ghoulish collection of Native bodies for research.[52] It is a refusal of and/or failure to become human, to be normed as adult through reproductive maturity.

Miranda describes the spatio-temporal disorientation caused by grief and anger and its distorting effects in the section of *Bad Indians* titled "Ularia's Curse."[53] This is a curse that killed Sargent, "The American [who] ran Estéfana and her children off the land at Rancho El Potrero." Telling of the exodus of the tribe from their land, Meadows by way of Miranda describes Ularia's final act before dispersing:

> sitting there on the banks of the river, her worn skirts heavy and wet with rain and mud, her hair burnt short in mourning. She didn't have much left to work with—no bundles of mugwort, no roots, no cocoon rattle, not even a clapperstick. She was just an old Indian woman, beaten by soldiers, chastised by priests, her last grown child hung from the big oak as a horse thief by the Americans. . . . But out of habit, Ularia leaned down, her spine crackling with age, and scooped a handful of Carmel's clear water in her palm, brought it to her lips, drank it down. She tasted the cold roots of mountains

> off to the north. She felt the sharp grit of river sand in her worn molars, sparkle of a stray flake of gold, scales of a little fish on her tongue. And Ularia remembered: the river would be here long after she was gone. . . . She reached down, plucked a smooth round stone from beneath the water, spoke to it in the old language. She gathered salt from the estuary to the west, a gritty sand mixed with ocean and fresh-water spirits. She added charcoal from that last fire built on the river's banks by the refugees, great oaks reduced to ashes. She smudged the curse in the scent of toasted chia seeds made for the journey away, the scorched redbud of the basket that held them. Ularia made that curse of mud, the decomposing body of our mother black and thick enough to trip even a strong stock horse; she made that curse from slick water weeds that can tangle a man's legs, pull him down beneath the surface; she made that curse out of a rainstorm's rage, conjured waves ten years hence into heavy walls that would fall like the stones of a church in an earthquake.

The river did not act immediately. It took ten years before it took revenge on Sargent, "drank him down, and cleansed itself of his greed," finishing what Ularia had begun. We don't know the temporality of the dead just as Ularia didn't know the time of the river. But we feel them in common. Revenge is a long affair and is the work of more-than-(just)-human coalitions. It develops affective communities around it; revenge is an Indigenous feminist orientation.[54] In the end, decolonization will not be human-led.

The antisocial sociality of vindictive bad Indians incarcerated at missions, organized around pain and pleasure, as detailed by Miranda, is not the same as the antisociality the practitioners of the Ghost Dance have of and with the dead, and yet there is something in common. This in-common is partially what makes the phrase "California Indian" mean something (beyond the facile and utterly arbitrary, thin, and temporary geopolitical border of the state of California and by extension the United States—already disrupted by Alta California, Baja California and Baja California Sur, and the imaginary "Island of California"). The commonality that links those subjected to the missions, to the fur trade, and to the gold rush, to settler colonialism and Spanish conquest (and the postcolonial nation state), and to their deep and wide-ranging onto-epistemological projects is a form of social history that undermines both the social and history with an Indigenous interrelational and experiential framework. In other words, despite obvious historical differences, this common social history links mission and digger Indians in a tenuous identity that began with ex-nomination of tribal names by government officials. This tenuous coalition is also an angle of perception from the nowhere and nowhen of "California" and the dead.

Failed Indians

Bad Indians are in a profound way *failed* Indians. They have failed at the impossible, contradictory demands of being Indian (being a "good" Indian), and they have, importantly, failed to be human in the way the settler colonial and western imperial projects demand in their conscription of Indigenous people. If having bad feelings in common is a form of sociality organized around a certain kind of despair that refuses the idealism of hope for a more difficult relation to the future, one that makes survival and continuance possible outside of state norms, failure is the mode through which despair manifests itself. An alternative to the dichotomy of pessimism and optimism, failure is an errant path that keeps going, fails even to interrupt itself, failing to stop, offers continuance in a way eclipsed by the call to be successful under the colonial system. Moving beyond even the success of sovereign subjects implied by certain conceptions of Indigeneity, to fail is to undo state-mediated and/or recognized (domestic dependent) successes under colonial occupation, to see these "successes" as failures and paths down an alternative path. In fact, in a settler state ruled by ideologies of success, positive thinking, and the gospel of prosperity, Native Americans are the original failures, the original losers. And surviving is failing but doing it well. Not as a mode of progress, failing and failing better means destroying the very notion of progress that has decimated Indigenous lives and worlds and means doing so by our continued existence. We fail to go away. We have failed to die. Failure is often seen as a perhaps unfortunate step on the path to success, but success is an end. Emphasizing failure for its own sake, outside of means-and-ends thinking, brings an end to ends, to successes. Failure freed from success as a value and goal is continuity through a sustained discontinuity, a radical break with the colonial world.

What does it mean to succeed in a settler colonial society? Sandy Grande urges that we should refuse the signs of success that wed us to the state and the western imperial humanist project in our ongoing attempts to hospice this brutal system into its demise. Grande advises,

"Refuse the perceived imperative to self-promote, to brand one's work and body. This includes all the personal webpages, incessant Facebook updates, and Twitter feeds featuring our latest accomplishments, publications, grants, rewards, etc. etc. Just. Make. It. Stop. The journey is not about self—which means it is not about promotion and tenure—it is about the disruption and dismantling of those structures and processes that create hierarchies of individual worth and labor."[55] This call to refuse success is also a cultivation of failure and its collectivity. To refuse to be an individual will always create an indeterminacy between refusal and the failure to achieve. The failure to become human and/or to be a good Indian is tied to the deepest structures of the colonial project, its alternatingly murderous and disciplinary core, the brutal process of humanization that operates through a desire for recognition. Failure offers a completely different way of thinking about how to contest these structures. Rather than a heroic narrative of direct confrontation or maverick disruption that would solidify the subjects who resist—offering a redemptive narrative and the horribly misleading, humanistic, and historically progressive "arc of justice" trajectory—failure has no individual heroes, undoes hierarchies not by toppling and then replacing them but by eroding the conditions that make hierarchies possible, is deeply acentric and nonlinear in its forces and "actions."

Failure is an Indigenous ethic, the very atmosphere of Indigenous worlds. What has been lost through colonization in different degrees are the millennia of practices Indigenous polities have engaged in to mitigate violence and prevent the accumulation of power and wealth, particularly in the hands of individuals. To encourage collectivity, Indigenous societies have organized to render impossible the types of success that motivate the western imperial project. Many Indigenous societies, California Indians included, have participated in pluralistic, antihierarchical, and decentralizing modes of governance. These are practices that include all sorts of beings in complex networks of relationships and meaning that exceed the bounds of goal-based human politics. Without romanticizing (conflicts certainly arise), California Indians created these more-than-human social systems to handle these conflicts in ways that are nuanced, textured, and to include often difficult interrelationalities and coalitional gatherings. Deeply anti-intellectual from the beginning, the colonial project and, particularly, the imposition of a western knowledge framework has sought to destroy these millennia of political and knowledge forms. Tongan and Fijian scholar Epeli Hauʻofa makes this point about the reduction of Oceanic ontologies, trade networks, social relationships, complex power structures, elemental and spiritual forces, intricate languages, and the sheer expansiveness of cosmological perceptions of what he calls a "sea of islands" to small, dependent "islands in a faraway sea," dominated and "developed" (read: exploited) by colonial powers.[56] Targeting human and more-than-human relationships, women and third-gendered people and their leadership roles, leaders and intellectuals more broadly makes clear the threat this world of Indigenous knowledge poses to the simplifying, brutal, extractive, minimizing colonial form. The disciplinary practices of the boarding schools, removal of children through adoption, the violently imposed rupture with the land, and the replacement of nonhuman kin and relations with a colonial production system based on extraction and exploitation show the means by which colonialism destroys the plurality and relationality, the capaciousness and expanse of Indigenous worlds. The supposedly most "primitive" of California Indian tribes, for instance, have the most complex languages, a linguistic capaciousness that is grammatically at odds with the subject-focused and action-oriented, instrumental coloniality of English.[57] Such is the colonial process of humanization, an enforced ontological hierarchy of relations with humans at the top, abstracted, replicated, and imposed at a global scale through homogenization.

From the colonial perception, Indigenous peoples failed at becoming human. Interpreted as savage, childlike, animalistic, and, importantly, unable to appropriately distinguish between categories of beings and therefore unable to appropriately assert mastery over the land through the invented category of "nature" as resource, Indigenous people have inhabited the threshold between culture and nature within this system. Such a figure of failure, neither fully cultural nor natural, is the conditioning force for the successes of the colonial humanizing project. But, Indigenous peoples are also essential for the continuity of the settler state, which manages its claims to legitimacy through Indigeneity. Indigenous failure, then, is an opening onto bringing about systemic failure of the settler project; by operating within this space of necessary, ongoing failure, Indigenous peoples sabotage and wreck the system from the outside/inside space of indetermination. When our ancestors refused the "gifts" of civilization, failed to be good Indians, they pointed the way. To do things in a good way is invariably to also do things in a bad way (seriously, fuck 'em).

As J. Halberstam writes in relation to queer conceptions of failure, "while failure certainly comes accompanied by a host of negative affects, such as disappointment, disillusionment, and despair, it also provides the opportunity to use these negative affects to poke holes in the toxic positivity of contemporary life."[58] The toxic positivity of enforced goodness includes the settler state and its western imperial project. In their book *The Queer Art of Failure*, Halberstam outlines a theory of failure, what they call "low theory," that has wide-ranging implications for thinking about failure as an errant path outside of western and colonial norms. As they write, "low theory tries to locate all the in-between spaces that save us from being ensnared by the hooks of hegemony. But it also makes its peace with the possibility that alternatives dwell in the murky waters of a counterintuitive, often impossibly dark and negative realm of critique and refusal."[59] Indicating or orienting us toward a form of study that is a "stroll" down uncharted paths, that enters the path the "wrong" way by eschewing seriousness and rigor and all the infrastructures of scholarship and the recognitions they imply and instead emphasizes the frivolous, promiscuous, and irrelevant, Halberstam seeks an unbecoming and a long detour outside the bounds of academic disciplines that are crumbling anyway. Foregoing the crisis consensus described by Boggs and Mitchell and its imperative to rescue and restore, Halberstam offers a loose framework for ecstatically riding academic institutions, and by extension the settler state, into their deaths as a way to continue, to ride the forces of failure into an uncertain future. And to do so, like the family of losers in the final scene of the film *Little Miss Sunshine*, by embodying a "neo-anarchistic credo of ecstatic losers: 'No one gets left behind!'"[60]

These forces of failure include being undisciplined away from the modes of training and learning that assert what is already known according to approved models of knowing; losing one's way as a particular practice of charting alternative pathways; refusing professionalization (being a critical academic) by joining what Moten and Harney have robustly defined as the undercommons of the university (steal for the collective; be in but not of); turning to local and subjugated forms of knowing that the state and the western imperial project seeks to delegitimate, erase, and/or conscript; being stupid by inhabiting the limits of knowing and resisting mastery; privileging the naive or nonsensical; and being suspicious of memorialization, to name a few attributes. Significantly, these all indicate a turn to the collective, caustically eating away at the infrastructures of individual achievement and meritocracy on which the successes of the colonial state depend. Understanding that everyone participates in intellectual activity and is a theorist in their own right, not just a small class of intellectual elites, as part of a social project, is imperative for reframing pedagogical as well as social and material relationships. For Halberstam, a turn to failure operates within the framework of counterhegemony, the competing set of ideas that work against the "rightness" of dominant perception, so-called common sense or the intuitive. In an Indigenous context, the refusal of rightness can be summed up in a word by asking: What is the settler "good"? Representations of the Ghost Dance, for instance, as disorganized, unpopular, deceptive (carried on by "con-men"), superstitious, apolitical, primitive, in other words, as a failure, is the commonsense version of a western civilizationist understanding. This book both refuses and revels in such interpretations by engaging in what Miranda describes as the struggle in the realm of story, of narrative, of gossip, and it insists on the collective aspect of the Ghost Dance as a pluralistic theory, on the importance of failure that it elicits, and on the Indigenous socialities that underlie it. While the Ghost Dance cannot be interpreted as a success (both definitionally speaking, as the dead have yet to return and also in the "minor" role it played in California Indian responses to destruction), it is undoubtedly an anticolonial political formation in the way it contests colonial social and material relationships and offers a profound discontinuity toward Indigenous continuity outside, and with and through, colonial frameworks. In a similar way, Day and Miranda chart a map of failure through the dangerous colonial archives and images, stories and discourses, through the failed realm of the unrecognized. A map akin to Moten and Harney's concept of planning as opposed to policy, which refuses the "compulsion of scarcity" for an "ongoing experiment with the informal, carried out by and on the means of social reproduction."[61]

Whereas Halberstam and other proponents of "low theory" promote a turn to pop/low culture as an intellectual resource for thinking in terms of failure, Indigenous studies offers its own sense of low or minor theory outside of and against a settler colonial conception of populism, as Jodi Byrd has argued. For Byrd, "there is no way to incorporate the Indigenous body or Indigenous nations into the United States without either a horrible physical erasure or a complete disavowal of the violent history of colonization."[62] In their essay "in the city of blinding lights: Indigeneity, Cultural Studies and the Errants of Colonial Nostalgia," Byrd reads unconscious eruptions within popular texts, often presented as the source of populist energies, for the incongruities and unresolved tensions of disavowed Indigeneity. This is particularly the case for texts that seek to include Indigenous peoples, such as the 2001 video of a dramatic reading of the Declaration of Independence by a multiracial and multicultural cast of celebrities, analyzed by Byrd. Byrd highlights the moment in the reading when Oneida actor Graham Greene, the only Native in the video, appears on the screen to read the infamous section: "He . . . has endeavored to bring on the inhabitants of our frontiers, the merciless Indian savages, whose known rule of warfare, is an undistinguished destruction of all sexes, ages, and conditions." For Byrd, Greene's reading indicates a core issue at the heart of any call for populism within a settler state. The very relation between a state like the United States and Indigeneity is conditioned by, while simultaneously disavowing, the necessity of a liminal Indigenous subject caught in a sort of half-life, conscripted and yet continually disavowed (Greene is represented as the "good" Indian who redresses the United States' racism by reading its racist doctrine in a show of multiracial and multicultural solidarity, bringing the "bad" Indian back into the fold). Such a formation of Indigeneity perhaps explains swings between liberal and conservative settler claims to populism, both based on a form of authoritarianism that seeks to shield itself from an incommensurable yet paradoxically necessary Indigeneity perceived as threat, a deep-seated anxiety at the core of settler identity. Bad Indians refuse inclusion and fail to behave in an inclusive manner, seek "the destruction of all sexes, ages, and conditions" as merciless Indian savages, and they exacerbate the anxiety of the settler as a form of weak power. For Byrd, then, "until the ongoing colonisations of indigenous peoples around the world are recognized and redressed, the project of liberal democracy, no matter how inclusive it becomes, will remain a lost cause."[63]

Failure operates within this irreconcilable and unassimilable space of Indigeneity, a repetition of these unconscious symptoms of settler anxiety and dread. Failure indicates a core weakness within the settler armature and structure that depend on success, action, inclusion. By tapping into this stress point, Indigeneity as failure offers an opportunity to, as Byrd argues elsewhere, "both stop the world of signification and force a continual grinding within the systems of enlightenment that produce the subject at the site of freedom, equality, and conviviality through genocidal dispossession."[64]

Ghost Dance

In such a way, the Ghost Dance goes wrong from the very beginning. The Ghost Dance went wrong and is what went wrong. It was and is a failure but of a very particular kind. A response to what anthropologist Robert Heizer dubbed "the destruction of California Indians," the dance began in Nevada and initially spread, like gossip, to Northern California and Southern Oregon through social gatherings of tribes (big times) and ceremonies, offering a speculative, contaminative, otherworldly (anti)sociality with and through death in its deferred departure/arrival. Taking place between 1869 and 1871 and lasting in various forms, gone underground in a sense,[65] much longer, it has three components: (1) the return of the dead; (2) the end of the world; and (3) the bloodless extermination of the whites, who would "burn up and disappear without even leaving ashes." Failing to bring about the end of the world (the world already having ended), seemingly only lasting a couple of years (though never really stopping), it nonetheless has bent time and space toward dance, song, and prophecy, toward the infinite arrival of the dead. It was and is a failure with a profound and lasting disorienting effect, connecting it to an original disruption or error, what some call prophecy. Such an angle of perception offers a reading of the Destruction as *inter*-relation, a relationality interrupted by the infinite distance of the dead's incessant arrival, the antisocial, that incites a new sociality and mode of resistance as refusal/failure.

The three elements of the Ghost Dance offer in/comprehension through: (1) socializing under extreme conditions (renewed relations with the dead, having bad feelings in common); (2) thinking within a postapocalyptic temporal and spatial framework (the end of the world as a certain kind of foreclosure of revelation or eschatological logics, in other words, history); and (3) a refusal of violence (grappling with genocidal violence as a form of Indigenous felt theorizing). Together these offer an anticolonial interpretive practice and a corresponding poetics in sync with—in discontinuous continuity with—Indigenous and other anticolonial forms of living together. Yellowknives Dene political theorist Glen Coulthard refers to these interrelational practices as grounded normativities: "the modalities of Indigenous land-connected practices and longstanding experiential knowledge that inform and structure our ethical engagements with the world and our relationships with human and nonhuman others over time."[66] Grounded normativity includes forms of governance, social and political relationships, interpretive positionings, modes of ethicality, artistic and cultural practices, coalitions, antagonisms, complicities, affective communities, and epistemologies and ontologies (and their indistinction), reassembled and reinvested by the infinite destruction. These renewed relationships obviously include the dead but also include relationships with other beings and media, technological and otherwise, introduced into Indigenous frameworks, as well as the (often forced, sometimes chosen, often undecidable) relationships created through what Byrd calls the "transit of empire" and Lisa Lowe "intimacies"—the difficult connections between survivors of white supremacist, cisheteropatriarchal, rationalist, developmental, civilizationist, imperial and colonial western humanisms as well as their political and social structures.

The Ghost Dance is often associated with the names of charismatic prophets, the Paiute Doctor Wodziwob in this case,[67] Wovoka (also Paiute) in 1890, Tsali (Cherokee) in 1811, and Tenskwatawa (Shawnee) in 1805. Seneca scholar Michelle Raheja, however, notes that prophetic form and content (as represented in and by Indigenous film) do not hinge on individual leaders but demonstrate prophecy to be a collective practice "from the ground up . . . Rather than relying on a messianic figure or divine intervention . . . film reads the Indigenous body itself as a prophetic text."[68] Extending the cinematic lens, what constitutes the assemblage of bodies and voices is something that has prophetic and proleptic force. The circulation of the prophetic message by specific actors is of course important but so are the grassroots, interrelational circulations of prophecy that can spring up anywhere and spread like wildfire. As seen in the Ghost Dance, dreaming is radically democratized and contagious, as everyone dreams and anyone can be a dreamer. Further, having so many die in such a short time span touched everyone; it rendered sociality in different terms and changed the relationship to time.

Such dreaming is hard, conditioned as it is by the complete dismantling and replacement of the Indigenous world. Under its thrall, terrible and seemingly nonsensical decisions can be made. There is no satisfactory explanation for killing or calling for the death of doctors, mixed-race children, or dogs, or for turning over Joyas (third-gendered people) to the Spanish.[69] Such things challenge comprehensibility. Foregoing explication and analysis, refusing, that is, to translate such difficult decisions into colonial knowledge forms, we at the same time confront the risk of falling into the trap of colonial metaphysics and a too-clean conception of the mystical. Dreaming is imperfect, antagonistic, a struggle, and deeply interwoven with complex and often tentative forms of sociality that include the living, the dead, and other beings. Dreaming is also often wrong, even detestable. To say it is immanent is a bit redundant as Indigenous relating and communicating incorporate all manner of beings, including the so-called spiritual. There is no such thing as "Indigenous mysticism." The phrase is an oxymoron. Indigenous onto-epistemologies are a step beyond the western split between positive science and mysticism. Dreaming is dirty, of the mud. Intense dreaming as prophecy is nonmystical and nonmessianic. Through it, we stay with the difficulty of interrelation and read and hear prophecy rhetorically (proleptically) and materially (collectively), in its grain, and in relation to its (anti)socializing force.

The Ghost Dance was also a significant Indigenous anticolonial response to destruction. Lakota scholar Nick Estes, in writing about the 1890 Ghost Dance performed by the Lakota, describes it as part of an anticolonial theory and movement that had been growing among Native peoples and which he links to the No Dakota Access Pipeline (NoDAPL) resistance over a century later.[70] For Estes, the dance, particularly the visions, were a utopian dream "that briefly suspended the nightmare of the 'wretched present' by folding the remembered experience of a precolonial freedom into an anti-colonial future."[71] This vision of the destruction of the colonial relationship, for Estes, fed resistance to the United States, along with an "unrelenting" oppositional spirit, by bringing the dancers into intimate relationship with the dead, as described by an unnamed Lakota man:

> The people, wearing the sacred shirts and feathers, now formed a ring. . . . All walked cautiously and in awe, feeling their dead were close at hand. . . . The leaders beat time and sang as the people danced going round to the left in a sidewise step. They danced without rest, on and on, and they got out of breath but still they kept going as long as possible. Occasionally someone thoroughly exhausted and dizzy fell unconscious into the center and lay there "dead." . . . After a while, many lay about in that condition. They

> were now "dead" and seeing their dear ones. As each one came to, she, or he, slowly sat up and looked about, bewildered, and then began wailing inconsolably.[72]

This inconsolable wailing is a clear manifestation of what Dian Million calls "felt theory," "the emotionally laden affective force" that "transcend[s] the individual's experience," an "affective force [that makes] it necessary that these stories become a collective story."[73] A material manifestation of the unmusicality of despair, the sustain of feedback, the wail is what Moten describes as the ambiguous entrance into and expulsion from society, a "music, which is not only music, [that] is mobilized in the service of an eccentricity, a centrifugal force, sociality's ecstatic existence beyond beginning and ending, ends and means."[74] The wail is, in other words, a performative gesture. While seemingly having the return of the dead as a goal, such wailing cannot be recuperated into the meaning-making systems and instrumentality of colonial life. These felt experiences function, rather, as communal knowledge, overcoming hierarchies that place such forms of knowing beneath those of western colonial institutions or delegitimize them altogether, particularly along gendered and material lines.[75] The gathering together to dance at the command of the dead demonstrates the collectivizing force of having such bad feelings in common. As the unnamed Lakota man further explains, "Waking up to the drab and wretched present after such a glowing vision, it was little wonder that they walked as if their poor hearts would break in two with disillusionment. But at least they had seen! . . . They preferred that to rest or food or sleep. And so I suppose the authorities did think they were crazy—but they weren't. They were only terribly unhappy."[76] An antisocial sociality based on broken hearts, a terrible unhappiness, for Million, is "not an act of accretion, but a strategic felt comprehension that has the power to change a paradigm, or reinvest a political movement with a new vision to act. This is the power of intense dreaming, of the felt intensification when boundaries shift and other views become available."[77] It is a condition for visuality as such; no such thing as an individual, purely rational sight. This other view is a new angle of perception created by disorientation, falling down dead, the dreams the dead offer, broken hearts, wailing, and a new collectivity, from nowhere and nowhen. *They had seen!* They see past comfort, food, and sleep, through and with exhaustion, starvation, and insomnia. Pushing seeing past the distinction between sight and its opposite, this is another opening onto the realm of the avisual I discuss in chapters 2 and 5.

As I mentioned, optimism and pessimism become indistinguishable through such failure. People danced out of despair for a certain kind of hope, with a frantic and desperate sort of joy, and yet it's only through the ambiguity of joining with the dead (do we meet in their world or ours?), making community with them, that another world seems possible. For Estes, this is because the Ghost Dance was both an understanding and a messaging of the fact that "Indigenous life could not be remade inside reservations, nor within a colonial system, but only through the complete destruction of both."[78] Indigenous conceptions of life evade the idea of scarcity imposed by both systems, a concept constructed and enforced by genocidal approaches to land acquisition (and production), resource extraction, individualistic capitalist economics and ethics and their concomitant civil order, the confinement of Indigenous peoples to open air prisons (reservations), and a produced notion of dependence based on a civilizing mission and the treaty system. Indigenous life resists such subjection. This concept of scarcity is completely anathema to Indigenous interrelations with each other and the world. The concept of an economics of abundance as opposed to scarcity is borrowed from Indigenous forms of sociality and material relations.[79] The abundance of a destroyed world took the form of direct resistance and a refusal of the destructive "gifts" of settler society and its system of recognition. Speaking of the Lakota's Ghost Dance movement, Estes writes:

> as a resistance movement, its tactics included complete withdrawal from reservation life; opposition to reservation authorities; the creation of resistance camps in remote areas far removed [from] the influence of the agency; the pilfering of annuity distribution centers (and sometimes white settlers' cattle and crops); the destruction of agricultural equipment; and the refusal to send children to school, to speak English, to participate in censuses, and to attend work, church, or agency and council meetings; their tactics also included the refusal to live on assigned allotments, to obey "agency chiefs," to cut one's hair, to quit dancing, to wear white clothing and attire, or to use metal tools. In short, the movement posed a comprehensive challenge to the colonial order of things.[80]

For Wovoka, who taught nonviolence and pacifism, a message of self-removal was due to the fact that, according to Estes, "under present conditions, armed Indigenous resistance was futile."[81] Such an impossible situation, emanating directly from a sense of abundance and prophecy and yet confronted with the impossibility of direct insurrection, explains the ambiguity around violence associated with the Ghost Dance and Indigenous anticolonial movements more generally, and it offers a hint as to the infrathin distance between refusal and resistance as strategies.

Estes describes how both settler public discourse and debate among the Lakota over the "alleged pacifism" of the Ghost Dance created a division in a people fighting to survive over their tactics of resistance, between "legitimate" nonviolent pacifists and "illegitimate" and "criminal" violent militants, echoing the long colonial legacy of dividing Indigenous people into a "savage"/"Native" dichotomy. As I discuss in chapter 4, the Spanish held a debate in 1550–51 over the most just form of conquest and absorption of Indigenous peoples into the Christian brotherhood and western civilizationist project, whether through enslavement (due to inherent irrationality and perversion) or by appealing to their human rationality and social sensibility, that hinged on this same divide. It is a divide that also undergirds the infamous sloganeering by Richard Henry Pratt for the U.S. boarding school project, to "kill the Indian to save the man," with the term "Indian" standing in for a constellation of attributes that constitute the "criminal"/extrajudicial "savage," attributes that salvage ethnographers were invested in preserving as the founding archive of many U.S. museums and universities. For Estes, settlers create moral categories to differentiate "good" and "bad" Indians in order to project criminality onto "bad Indians" and hide "the US's own criminal enterprise."[82] While this is certainly true, and the criminalization of the Ghost Dance itself (which, of course, led to catastrophic results for the Lakota) gives evidence of this—mobilizing the ambiguity of its violence—the problem, however, goes much deeper.

Indigenous people by our very existence pose a threat to the continuity of the United States even while our presence is needed for its coherence. Elizabeth Povinelli theorizes the conceptual and discursive gymnastics that settler modes of representation, policy, and law have enacted in order to mobilize Indigenous priority, a concept necessary for British and U.S. property law, while effectively debilitating Indigenous polities in order to make them manageable, thereby transposing Indigenous priority onto the settler as their own inheritance, what she calls "the governance of the prior."[83] Robert Nichols describes how this necessitates a paradoxical retroactive attribution of ownership onto Indigenous peoples in order to dispossess them of land transmuted into property and an entirely new relational form.[84] A complex process of Indigenization ensues through which the settler seeks to found/find a nationality, a logical impossibility for them, by appealing to western developmental conceptions of civilization while holding Indigenous people in a liminal space of limited sovereignty, neither fully inside nor outside a fabricated U.S. nationhood, as guarantee.

As I discuss in chapters 2 and 3, the discourse of nonviolence plays an important role in managing this liminality while also creating the conditions for founding. In brief, in the name of law, democracy, and nonviolence, the United States and its (often extrajudicial) agents (Patrick Wolfe's "settler horde"[85]) enacted extreme amounts of violence on Indigenous peoples, perhaps nowhere more directly than in what is now called California. This incursion into Indigenous worlds was a form of law-making through "illegal" occupation and genocidal warfare—sometimes held accountable as the force through which the law makes its way, makes itself, a movement ritualized by stochastic violence and then apology and such things as the Truth and Healing investigations currently underway in California. What follows is law-preserving violence, the creation of "legal" systems of violence through monopolization by the state, violence done in the name of the law itself, as described by Walter Benjamin.[86] By definition, the "savage" in this framework was understood to be lawless, hence all the mythologies about the lawless west; genocidal violence was committed by settlers, then, in the name of founding the law, in moving history and progress forward through territorial acquisition, and, it can't be forgotten, in realizing manifest destiny as the evangelical millenarianism of end times, God's law over the whole of the earth.[87] Law and lawlessness are then two sides of the same colonial coin and really have nothing to do with Indigenous ways of being. Lawless, godless, sexually depraved, unable to keep relations straight between each other and with all sorts of other-than-humans, the Indian "savage" was paradoxically both too natural and too unnatural for existence, too cultural and not cultural enough, and therefore needed to be corrected. An original error. What is perhaps needed is a theorization of violence and its refusal from an Indigenous standpoint, one made available in the Ghost Dance.

The Ghost Dance, in its profound refusal of violence, puts violence and the dead into conversation and calls for an exploration of this relationship at the moment of so-called founding, rejecting colonial violence for another world. The project initiated by the Ghost Dance operates in intimate proximity to what Fanon describes as the failure to be able to be: "I couldn't hope to win. . . . I wanted to be typically black—that was out of the question. I wanted to be white—that was a joke. And when I tried to claim my negritude intellectually as a concept, they snatched it away from me."[88] A profound double bind, this condition is one that Fanon devastatingly defines as being damned. "Without a black past, without a black future, it was impossible for me to live my blackness. Not yet white, no longer completely black, I was damned." Such a condition of ontology, a lack of being, is what Moten (drawing on Nahum Chandler's concept of paraontology) describes as pre-ontology, the anoriginal displacement of ontology or the very condition for ontology. "Ontology's underground, the irreparable disturbance of ontology's time and space"—in a word, *damnation*—marks the site of an intense investigation into nothingness, for Fanon as for Moten, as well as a counterintuitive condition for sociality and creativity otherwise in the very poverty of world.[89] "Poverty in this world is manifest in a kind of poetic access to what it is of the other world that remains unheard, unnoted, unrecognized in this one. Whether you call those resources tremendous life or social life in social death or fatal life or raw life, it remains to consider precisely *what it is that the ones who have nothing have*. What is this nothing that they have or to which they have access? What comes from it? And how does having it operate in relation to poverty?"[90] Inverting the sociality founded on continuation of the violent conditions of primitive accumulation, Moten and Fanon's respective theories of sociality, based in common abjection and poverty, have strong resonances with the Ghost Dance. Not the same as the Ghost Dance, of course (a relation that needs to be sussed out, particularly as it engages the ongoing conversation between Blackness and antiblackness and Indigeneity and genocide, as theorized by Jodi Byrd, Tiffany Lethabo King, Joanne Barker, Jack Forbes, Shona Jackson, and Sandy Grande, among others). While Moten's conception of a creative sociality coalesces around a common condition of having nothing, being nothing, a paradoxical abundance in nothingness, it likewise puts into conversation such nothingness with the relation to the dead in the form of remaining in the hold of the ship. This relation between nothingness and Blackness offers, as he notes, a perception from nowhere, no standpoint, a poetics of/from the very poverty of world, a fantasy in the hold. The perception from nowhere is a perception that he shares with Fanon. As Halberstam notes, "Fanon, according to Moten, wants not the end of colonialism but the end of the standpoint from which colonialism makes sense."[91] This absence of standpoint as an end to a certain kind of common colonial sense is, for Moten, the condition for belief in the world: "Eventually, I believe, [Fanon] comes to believe in the world, which is to say the other world, where we inhabit and maybe even cultivate this absence, this place which shows up here and now, in the sovereign's space and time, as absence, darkness, death, things which are not (as John Donne would say)."[92] Such a reframing of violence as the stuff of life, though a life lived otherwise, before ontology, outside and beside it, as absence, darkness, death—things that are not, in other words, "exhaustion as a mode or form or way of life, which is to say sociality"—calls for a return to Fanon's theorization of violence to understand this form of radical sociality, which I discuss in chapter 3 as grounding the conditions of research against the state.[93]

How does Moten's poetics without standpoint relate to Miranda's writing from The End of the World? How does Fanon's call for a new humanism from the position of the global south—a south-to-south relation of recognition outside of dominant cold war ideological positions, one initiated through a violent reclaiming of humanity—relate to Coulthard's refusal of recognition and call for a return to grounded normativity against the settler state? And how do these poetics and interrogations of the position of the human in colonial situations relate to each other? These questions help frame, give us an angle on, the project of this book: to bring the writing of disaster—representation in the ongoing aftermath of devastating violence and its destructive self-erasure—into conversation with the critique of the human—the questioning of the value and material systems organized and developed around the figure of the western liberal humanist subject as master of the world—as they each emanate from the socialities and refusals/failures of the wretched of the earth.

It is my contention that the Ghost Dance and the turn to the dead offer a way to think this conversation, especially as it bears on California Indian studies, which currently is at an inflection point. "California Indian studies" is a field and phrase that has always been in contention, but the stress of its reference is threatening to explode the whole thing; the container can no longer hold the meaning. New powers are at work, and they have begun to pull the threads that have tenuously held together a coherent field of study. The institutional, colonial version can no longer contain and manage California Indian people (as it was created to do), and the grassroots version of study as survival, of collective and agonistic anticolonial refusal, of opting out and failing, is a rising tide washing away the other. Not necessarily outside, within the belly of the beast so to speak, California Indian studies also cannot be positioned inside the imposed western humanist system. Such is the importance of the turn away from the world, while we wait for the return of the dead, the world to turn over, and the settler colonial system to burn up and disappear without even leaving ashes.

From this (absence of) standpoint, the Ghost Dance was an attempt to confront the violence of the law on prophetic terms, in anticipation, proleptically, terms that were completely incomprehensible to the settler, who could only understand it as either a threat (preparations for an uprising) in the most banal sense of a purely instrumental, lawless violence or as a product of cultural belief. "The most widely used text on the movement, *The Ghost-Dance Religion and Wounded Knee,* written in 1896 by armchair ethnographer James Mooney, for instance, distorted the meaning of the Ghost Dance. Pandering to the sympathies of a U.S. public in an attempt to make the Ghost Dance more palatable, Mooney used cultural relativism to justify its existence."[94] In this sense, Indigenous conceptions of power, violence, prophetic vision and interpretation, and their concomitant socialities are misconstrued by settlers as either culture in its rupture from politics, and thereby as a sign of Indigenous peoples' lack of historical temporality (if sympathetically received) or as manifestations of irrational savage temperaments, feelings, bodies, desires, and ideas, as *vindictiveness.* The first interpretation leads Estes to assert that the Ghost Dance is definitively not a form of cultural revitalization, which commits him to a purely political interpretation that casts violence entirely in ethical terms related to liberation and is often indirectly carried on through critical exposure. This is an understandable move that is very common in Native American studies, especially considering the seductive force of cultural representation and its long-standing destructive material effects. The approach has led Indigenous and allied scholars to make deep interventions into the ethics and politics of research, as well as to assert self-determination and sovereignty through representational practices. The approach, however, risks conflating critique with politics and historicity and only understanding a movement such as the Ghost Dance as a form of political resistance, translating it into contemporary terms.

But perhaps we should turn to the ancestors who participated in this fragile, outrageous attempt to bring about a different world, one that was doomed to failure, the same way they turned to their ancestors and relations (of all sorts): irreverently and with the best and worst intentions; indignantly in relation to the work; stubbornly against the light and goodness of the settler reality; and with all the rage and inconsolable sadness that carried them past exhaustion into the infinite (into a vision of profound joy at the indeterminate point of their "death"!). Perhaps we should follow them into this failure along a curve carried so far that it loses trajectory and becomes both a straight line and a circle, which would mean navigating the dangers of the waters of culture outside of the culture/nature and culture/politics splits. This would entail returning to Indigenous conceptions of power, violence, and the prophetic, according to their perilous paths through archival logics, interrelationally, such that colonialism is dragged into the abyss. One way to do this is by following the fraught and unproductive path of the savage.

Introduction
Researching

My great-great-grandmother, Susie Evans, wore a locket that contained an image of Kintpuash, a.k.a. Captain Jack, the insurgent leader of the Modoc who fought the U.S. military to a standstill in the lava beds of Northern California. Kintpuash was later convicted by a kangaroo court and executed, his skull stripped of flesh and shipped to the Smithsonian. She also wore a bullet on a chain around her neck. The bullet, the family story goes, was from a missed shot by a U.S. soldier who nearly killed Susie. Susie survived two massacres by the U.S. government: one when she was living with the Modoc (she herself was Achumawi/Pit River) and the other during the Snake War, a guerrilla war fought by a coalition of tribes against the U.S. invaders, at the so-called Battle of Infernal Caverns in northeastern California (near Likely, for those familiar with the area). Until the day she died, Susie insisted that Kintpuash was her leader. In that bullet lies existence for many California Indians: the luck of a missed shot. In the image of Kintpuash lies our future, an end to colonialism mediated by our relations to the dead (Kintpuash, as already mentioned, was also a ghost dancer).

The Infernal Caverns, to this day, are off-limits to California Indian people who might want to go pay respects to the dead—left to decay in the caves by the U.S. military—or to bury them; during the battle, U.S. soldiers pushed a boulder in front of the entrance to try to bury the survivors alive, but the surviving Indians escaped through an unknown outlet. The dead remain there. Today, the caves are surrounded by private land owned by ranchers who have a distinct anti-Indigenous agenda and refuse access. The "battle field" is, however, a California Historical Landmark, complete with a memorial to the soldiers who died, and anyone seeking to pay respects to the deceased settlers is allowed entrance. My cousin, Chag Lowry, has been working diligently to gain access to the caves to no avail.

I don't offer this story as an entrance to the personal. The weight of a boulder has made that impossible. After all, it is not my story. It is Susie's. It has been passed down through family but bears the marks of such a colonial, genealogical formation. Like the ancestors "buried" in the Infernal Caverns, the personal in me remains in deep limbo. Neither buried nor exposed, it is nonetheless off-limits. This relation to the dead depersonalizes us, brings us into their challenging company. There is also no folklore or ethnography here—merely the praxis of survival for those who escaped out the back door. This story is not for consumption or the accumulation of knowledge but undermines these things. What must remain of this story is a missed bullet and an unending resistance to the U.S. empire. Survival and a Fuck You until the end, until we surpass the end, into the infinite. Nothing more. Nothing less. Out of respect for Susie, that is what I hope my words are: a bullet and resistance/refusal/failure of the worst, most infinite kind. That is my family legacy, one that includes white settlers as well as other California Indian tribes (Mountain Maidu and Washoe) and other stories that I keep from you or, as in chapter 2, tell to intervene in the dominant discourses.

Ethnographic Refusal

Audra Simpson's well-known concept of "ethnographic refusal" plays no small part in how I position this story and in the politics of research it performs. Simpson's own performance of the concept, beginning with her essay "On Ethnographic Refusal" and extending into her book *Mohawk Interruptus*, operates as a chiasmus in the form of a refusal of ethnography and an ethnography of refusal (of the settler state). It is a tactical and textual response to the discursive situation of knowledge production about Indigenous peoples, which, as Simpson asserts, is an imperative of empire. Through techniques of knowing, the settler state's arms of knowledge production reduce the complex social and political formations of Indigenous worlds to consumable and knowable units of "culture" that stand in for territorial spaces and are easily abstracted from them. Anthropology, in particular, plays a material role in translating Indigenous worlds into imperial relationships, even going so far as to attempt to represent Indigenous peoples by proxy or to ventriloquize Indigenous voices. As Simpson says, "anthropology has imagined itself to be a voice, and in some disciplinary iterations, *the* voice of the colonized."[1]

Following in the footsteps of other Indigenous scholars such as Vine Deloria Jr. and Linda Tuhiwai Smith, with her concept of ethnographic refusal, Simpson crystallizes research and its writing into sites of significant anticolonial struggle. These sites of struggle put peoples' very existences and interpretive worlds on the line. Simpson describes a rupture that took place as peoples "left their own spaces of self-definition and became 'Indigenous,'" separating these new definitions from their embeddedness in their worlds.[2] This separation caused by being defined as Indigenous occurs because "'Indigenous' is a category that did not explicitly state or theorize the shared experience of having their lands alienated from them or that they would be understood in particular ways."[3] In other words, *culture*, as an imperial translational tool, depoliticized Indigenous social and political relationships, separating them from the newly minted category "nature/resource" against which the settler colony defines *human*. It also depoliticized the material practices of colonization and genocide, likewise naturalized and caught in the rationalizing and universalizing category of "Indigenous." These effects are made possible, for Simpson, by what she calls the "violence of form" of western knowledge production, which "might be an innocent tale of differential access to power, of differing translations of events, were there a level field of interpretation within which to assert those different translations."[4] A deeply destructive mode of colonial un/knowing, culture and the violence of form render the very interpretive worlds of Indigenous peoples nonexistent. Absent an interpretive field, Indigenous peoples' primary strategy is a refusal to participate in the translational process. This refusal operates at both the material and semiotic levels.

Whereas Simpson's use and analysis of ethnographic refusal as a strategy (and tactic) has been interpreted by many as asserting a strong form of agency by further separating the political from the cultural and reinforcing the sovereign subject, I prefer to read it as operating in the discursive entanglements of representation Simpson details, outside the political and cultural divide, in the ambiguous space created by the chiasmus—ethnography of refusal and refusal of ethnography—that admits its own failure from the beginning by its own strained logic. How can one write a refusal of one's own writing? And do so without it being recaptured in the dominant discourse as a mode of ethical reform of the discipline itself? Caught in the dilemma of what Simpson describes as "discursive wrestling" at the site of representational violence that enacts material dispossession, refusal becomes an opening onto absented interpretive worlds in a way that doesn't pass through the abstractive and extractive categories of culture and Indigeneity as conceived by western humanist colonialism, that outdoes both the cultural and the political and their mutual exclusions. In discussing the impact of the Indian Act on her Kahnawake community, their response to attempts to control the terms of membership/citizenship by the Canadian state, and the discursive struggle involved in creating an ethnography about the issue, Simpson asks, "How does one write about this or analyze what is so clearly offensive to the anthropological sensibilities of access, of replicable results, in some ways of 'fairness,' and reconcile all this with the plight of those who are struggling every day to maintain what little they have left? And when they are struggling so clearly with the languages and analytics of a foreign culture that occupies their semantic and material space, and naturalizes this occupation through history-writing and the very analytics that are used to know them?"[5] Noting, reflexively, that the Indigenous scholar's work relies upon empire as well, Simpson's refusal of/as research touches on failure and the impersonal in a way that resonates with a California Indian metaphysic of luck and weak power, as I discuss in chapters 4 and 5.

Refusal is not critique. In Simpson's ethnography, refusal is that which is "arrived at at the very limit of discourse."[6] It is the coming to a specific *territory*, which she locates in "the space of method, critique, and construction," yet not of it and certainly not for it. In this antagonistic representational space, the struggle is over "the making of claims and staking of limits," claims and limits that convey "a tripleness, a quadrupleness, to consciousness and an endless play" of positions that includes determinations of who or what gets to know certain things and how.[7] An obstinate freedom through a negotiated and yet determined drawing of limits, it is also a relational and often fraught play that takes place on the surface before your very eyes and in a confrontation without resolution: "I am me, I am what you think I am and I am who this person to the right of me thinks I am and you are all full of shit and then maybe I will tell you to your face."[8] Such a notion of refusal rails against recognition, which Simpson defines as "the political practice, rooted in philosophical formula of seeing, unencumbered, what and who is before you—seeing as one ought to be seen, in a way that is consistent with one's sense of self and property."[9] For Simpson, this notion of recognition operates conceptually and materially by enforcing dispossession and then granting a certain "freedom" through legal tricks: consent and citizenship. Simpson calls this maneuver "the ruse of consent," and it, like culture, operates through abstractive and extractive methods to separate out individuals from their embeddedness in worlds, subjecting Indigenous people individually to modes of legal violence through the signing of agreements and their being assumed to (passively) consent to the law as the only path to "justice." Along with anthropological representation, these are the conditions for the deeply unequal scene of articulation that Simpson confronts with refusal and its violence of form.

But refusal has many faces, as Simpson implies by engaging a politics without easy answers. In her essay "The Ruse of Consent and the Anatomy of Refusal," Simpson embraces the difficulty implied by her concept of refusal; notably, she puts the U.S. and Canadian border, which she discusses in terms of Indigenous border crossers, in relation with the U.S. and Mexican border through the work of Gilberto Rosas. Rosas's book *Barrio Libre* attends to the movements of youth who cross the border due to neoliberal conditions of capital, trade agreements, and the imposition of a colonial border, and who are confronted with militarized violence, passing through sewers, across brutal, life-ending deserts.[10] Simpson summarizes: "They are walking through indeterminacy, through pain, refusing to die or to let go of a sense of themselves as a collective that does this sort of thing. In doing so, they inhabit a posture of profound self-determination even in conditions of danger and precarity, where a state perceives them to be criminal in their very act of movement."[11] Simpson sees the assemblage of a collective sense of freedom found by these youth through pain and difficulty, the hard stories Rosas tells, and the "context and scene of the youths' articulation" as a mode of difficult refusal akin to the struggle with and through sovereignty she and her people face.[12]

The indeterminacy of refusal opens it up to other differential and imbricated understandings. Trinh T. Minh-ha, for instance, has theorized the complex interplay of refusal in relation to refugees as those who, having been refused, having been designated a tide of human refuse, refuse the terms of their recognition and incorporation into national and state institutions: "the only way to survive is to refuse. Refuse to become an integratable element. Refuse to allow names arrived at transitionally to become stabilized. In other words, refuse to take for granted the naming process. To this end, the intervals between *refuge* and *refuse, refused* and *refuse,* or even more importantly between *refuse* and *refuse* itself, are constantly played out."[13] Similarly, Moten and Harney offer two constructions that draw out this interval between refuse and refuse in order to differentiate, without necessarily separating, it from institutionalized critique. The first is to *refuse that which has been refused to you* in order to find/found a new sociality among all those who have likewise been refused, across and by way of the two refusals.[14] The second is to *refuse refusal* itself, that is, to refuse the choice to refuse *what has been offered as possible* by the state, akin to Simpson's ruse of consent. As they describe, "the first right" is "the right to refuse rights."[15] This exit strategy from the position of critique, through the interval between refuse and refuse, is a radical passivity and indifference toward institutions and the subjectivities they invest and depend on. The exit nullifies the meanings accreted through opposition, nullifies the play of recognition that necessarily determines the critical relation as one *against* and, therefore, stealthily *for.* What refusal is, then, is an ethics of disloyalty that attempts to outplay its own co-optation by the state in the form of critique and professionalization. Refusing to refuse seems to me to be an accurate description of the postapocalyptic conditions in which Indigenous and other communities offer anticolonial resistance, refuse to take part in a system that absorbs resistance, fail at being (intransitively), simply fail and continue to fail by failing.

The indetermination of the chiasmus—refuse research/research as refusal—opened up by Simpson as a response to the violence of form resonates with the Ghost Dance's refusal of violence as a collective mode of study, another chiasmus balanced on the preposition *of* (a refusal of violence/the violence of refusal). And it participates in the politics of a complete withdrawal from the colonial system (because, as both Fanon and Walter Benjamin have argued, the tempered use of such tactics, such as a limited workers' strike, falls too easily into the mode of reform and therefore of a critical operation that serves the state and its ends[16]). Ethnographic refusal, in this sense, is not a corrective of representational practices in anthropology but a refusal of the project of anthropology as the *handmaiden of colonialism,* part of the intellectual arm of the state, even in its most critical modes. For both Fanon and Benjamin, the instrumental strike (for better wages and such) is an expression of a certain violence wielded by the strikers but used in a way that fortifies the colonial legal system by redirecting revolutionary energies toward reform, hence its protected legality (similar to the professional critic). Like the ghost dancers before them, both Fanon and Benjamin advocate instead a totalizing and therefore noninstrumental undoing of the system. What needs to be worked out is what an absolute refusal of the colonial knowledge production industry looks like. Refusal in this sense isn't only directed toward the self (even a collective "self") in the sovereignty of the autonomous subject, an instrumental and oppositional relation, but facilitates the failure of the system that relies on such subjects—and therefore the failure of subjectivity in the western colonial humanist formation. It is an ongoing revolt and reassembling of the social through a more collective orientation outside of the system, with and through the destruction, in this case in the violence of form and the dilemma it presents. Research as a continuation of the destruction is a way to respond to this dilemma by annihilating the ends of the violence of form.

Story

I began this section on research with story, because story operates in the anticolonial space of interaction between oppositional research and interrelational space. It is also a significant site of Indigenous intellectual production, and has been since time immemorial. Story is not the colonizer's narrative and operates within the weak force of antivaluation described by Moten and offers a way to annihilate the ends of the violence of form described by Simpson. Outside of colonial and imperial formations, story is the path that research takes. Like the Ghost Dance, story has been ongoing. One is already in it. In many ways it can't be escaped. Story grasps at the point of the absence of power. It is not structured to allow for accumulation or centralization, whether in the form of the author's identity or ego, the edifice of truth, or the force of action. Story always operates in the Creator's absence, offering a weak *I* at best. Who tells the story? Who knows? It belongs to no one. Story is never complete; it is always a perpetual beginning, perpetually at midnight. It is nocturnal, in the dead of winter, even when uttered during the day or during other seasons or when it takes place in the daytime. It is a destruction that never arrives, always impending, leaves us on the edge of our seats, even when it is boring. The closest thing to story is prophecy. This is because story is untimely, always improper. Even when on the nose, it holds within it a certain inaccuracy, and when wrong a certain truth. It shifts our gaze, oscillating, never settling. Story doesn't belong or encourage belonging. It un-belongs us. Removes us from the here and now, from place. Story is without value. Stories cannot be compared, only told again and again, told differently. All the effort, skill, and knowledge that go into telling a story derive from ignorance. It is the nullification of knowledge, not its accumulation or overvaluing. It has a weak, improper form, *headless and tailless*.[17] It is the opposite of ownership, the need for security and stability, the need to know, to be sure, to take and give account. In the telling, it sweeps these away. It is impersonal. It connects the inside to the outside in a profound ambiguity. There's always something uncomfortable or even intolerable about story even while it connects us through its inherently collective form. It seethes. We can never know where it comes from. It forgoes the certainties of the empirical sciences that police the boundaries of truth and fiction, nor is it the critical overcoming of this division, which always carries the opposition within it. It is outside of this division, indifferent to it. While it is collective, it is not instrumental; it doesn't consider the reader or assume an established community of readers. It doesn't derive its force from preestablished language and its web of meanings. It slides by and under these. It doesn't assign places. It doesn't seek to be in the place of truth. It is the very force of communication itself, the communal; it does not communicate. Nothing gets done. It is a weak power that undoes the binary between power and impossibility, holding them together in their extreme separation and undoing them by their common meaning (through their opposition). Story operates as an enigmatic violence that acknowledges the violence of accumulation, of the center, and mitigates this violence through decentering, through distributing it among the listeners, the beings addressed and included in story, the very materiality of connection, as the very means of sociality and interrelation, to ensure that no power coalesces. This violent liberation from power through its suspension is both the means of communication and what is communicated in story, to be repeated again and again. It is the restoration of indeterminacy. While human power accumulates and builds, centers, is here and now, is in conformity with the laws of action, story has little force. Its force is a negation of this power of the human. It is, in form, nothing but refusal and thereby a failure, which is the greatest accomplishment. Story is the absence of here and now where what happens does not come to pass as an event. What happens does not happen, does not become past. It rather recurs unendingly, in both its and our horror, confusion, and uncertainty. The force of story is not just telling but also untelling what has been told and retelling in the wake of destruction, as destruction, pushed past its own limit.

Frameworks

The major frameworks of this book and the research it performs are the critique of the human and the writing of disaster as they intersect and relate to California Indian studies. Operating within the imperial logics described by Simpson and a politics of reconciliation with the state, the dominance of anthropological and archaeological research, alongside the institutional historiographic focus on California as a "case" of genocide (and to a lesser extent the domestication of California Indian art and literature), call for a dismantling of the field as it has been known and a turn to the communally determined modes of study that make up another stream that has always been here. This is a hard turn, as evidenced by the Ghost Dance as a mode of study that calls for an anticolonial absolute.

Indigenous Inhumanities engages the ongoing strategic and relational emergence of the Ghost Dance as an anticolonial and postapocalyptic response to the destruction. As a form of endurance and radical refusal/failure, the Ghost Dance indicates that our ancestors were not only well aware of this ending but sought to confront it with a refusal of its violence and continue after it and to do so collectively and in relation to the dead. This continuation has made its way, often surreptitiously, into our knowledge and artistic production, as well as into our political and social forms. As a practice of dying without death and therefore of exceeding the human, the Ghost Dance opens onto an expanded politics and a corresponding expanded literature and poetics. To trace these expansions, I attend to the figure of the inhuman, which I locate at the intersection of the critique of the human and writing disaster. A turn to the dead, the turn to the inhuman forces that lie outside of human control; it is an abdication of control that seeks a more difficult freedom, less human, less individual, less "alive." We do not and cannot fully know the extent of these forces.

Critique of the Human

The critique of the human in Indigenous studies has a line of continuity going back to time immemorial. It's a basic principle of Indigenous thought and relationality without necessarily being formulated, but, in response to the imposition of western humanism, Vine Deloria Jr. has more recently described what he calls an American Indian metaphysics, in which "the world, and all its possible experiences, constitute a social reality, a fabric of life in which everything [has] the possibility of intimate knowing relationships because, ultimately everything is related."[18] Vanessa Watts calls this principle "place-thought," the embodied "network in which humans and nonhumans relate, translate, and articulate their agency" and "a theoretical understanding of the world via a physical embodiment."[19] Place-thought as a form of knowing and theory is not limited to human beings but emanates from a "non-distinctive place where place and thought were never separated because they never could or can be separated."[20] The position of the human in each instance is mediated by the specific relations that more-than-human communities have with each other, so it is difficult (if not unethical) to generalize. Nonetheless, the violent imperial imposition of the western colonial process of humanization has brought together a coalition of Indigenous scholars from multiple communities and their nonhuman kin to contest this homogenization. In a humanist "reality," "the idea of 'society' has revolved around human beings and their special place in the world, given their capacity for reason and language," relegating Indigenous knowledge at best to a form of belief at odds with that reality.[21] In contrast according to Watts, "habitats and ecosystems are better understood as societies from an Indigenous point of view; meaning they have ethical structures, inter-species treaties and agreements, and further their ability to interpret, understand and implement."[22]

Marisol de la Cadena, writing about Indigenous social movements in Bolivia, describes how demands from these movements on states seem to short-circuit political discourse and understandings, whether progressive or conservative. This because the notion of politics that operates in most states is western humanist through and through. Building on the work of Bruno Latour, de la Cadena details how the social-political worlds of Indigenous peoples, occupied by "powerful earth-beings," as she calls them, were expelled from the concept of politics via a split in western metaphysics between politics—the realm of human sociality and governance—and science—the mode of knowing that humans applied to the nonhuman world to control its forces. Such a split rendered Indigenous social forms nonsensical and illegible and initiated the translational practice of researching Indigenous peoples through "culture" described by Simpson. As de la Cadena writes, "Ethnographic works were precisely where these practices belonged—not in politics."[23]

This translational practice through ethnographic representation has given western thought access to Indigenous ways of being and forms of knowing abstracted from material conditions. In the introduction to his book *Magical Criticism* titled "What Are Savages For?," Christopher Bracken describes the strange movement of suppression of and desire for the "savage" as a theoretical movement by which the figure of the "savage" through translation and sublation founds radical western critique. Summarized by J. G. Frazer as being "unable to discriminate clearly between words and things,"[24] the "savage" inability to appropriately order the world, all the inappropriate relationships, is simultaneously justification for genocidal violence *and* the hidden source of the west's *most adventurous thought*. Bracken's ironic psychoanalysis of western philosophy and its obsession with the "savage philosopher" exposes this ambivalence (intentionally ironic because Sigmund Freud is one of the main contributors to this discourse). For Bracken, the association occurs through a projection of Indigenous peoples' thought and ways of being into the past as fictional intellectual forebears of western philosophy, a project best realized by ethnography/ethnology, particularly of the salvage variety. The translation follows from Indigenous people first having been judged as diabolical: "Writing of his voyage to Quebec in 1608, Samuel de Champlain remarks that it is a fundamental principle among 'the savages' of Canada 'that all the dreams that they have are true.' Only the 'Divell' [devil], however, would cause mortals to confuse the recollection of images from sleep with the perception of objects by waking consciousness."[25] This diabolical interpretive system, based on dream, is understood to be a fundamental error, something that goes wrong from the very beginning, before the beginning begins, an idea taken up by several continental philosophers, perhaps most notably by Friedrich Nietzsche. "For Nietzsche, however, mistaking an ideal for a real connection is not an error that can be corrected by further study. It is the very 'precondition' of study."[26] One studies to go awry by following an original disruption. One plays Indian to become a "savage philosopher." And real Indians become a satanic scare.

Killed for their thoughts and ways of being or disciplined and punished into being "more human," the "Indian" and its savagery is distinct from the salvageable Native—transmuted through figuration into a "poetic logic" as alternative to and respite from the severe scienticity of western thought since the Enlightenment. The next stage in the developmental history of progressive enlightenment is a return to "magic," a new communalism, a reenchantment of the world through a violently suppressed thought and ontology, a new but now universal Indigenization, made palatable, tamed, by passing through and being refined by theoretical discourse, mobilized as critique (self-reflexive, no less!). Jodi Byrd makes a similar argument in relation to poststructuralists borrowing from ethnographic representation for alternative social, political, and theoretical formations. Byrd focuses in particular on two figurations of the Indian: Jacques Derrida's "tattooed savages," which become the signs of the play of presence and absence that haunts the project of deconstruction; and Gilles Deleuze and Félix Guattari's "Indians without ancestry," which mark the antigenealogical, asignifying, stateless war machine on a path without memory that operates rhizomatically on the edges of the frontier as site of becoming. Byrd notes the multiple functions of the Indian as a colonial and imperial referent that continues to produce knowledge as well as a theoretical sign through which new energy, "presignifying polyvocality," is reintroduced into the stale signifying regime of the west.[27] "The Indian sign is the field through which poststructuralism makes its intervention, and as a result, this paradigmatic and pathological Indianness cannot be circumvented as a colonialist trace."[28]

The ethnographic sign of the Indian travels through reading practices and colonial readerships, making its way into the history of western philosophy as a figure of radical alterity, a counterpoint to the Enlightenment and, as Bracken shows, the means through which it is revived. Along these lines, Byrd notes David Kazanjian's discussion of the figure of the Indian in the work of Immanuel Kant as one example among too many to list.[29] The Indian is the condition for western thought just as Indianness is the condition for U.S. empire. It is, as Byrd quips, "an undeconstructable core within critical theories."[30] The pathways through which western theories transcribe and translate, abstract and absorb Indigenous relations and forms of thought are apparent. Note Bruno Latour's assertion that actor network theory is a form of anthropology that seeks to know nonhuman actors in ways akin to how cultural anthropology describes Indigenous people;[31] the new materialist desire to "reenchant" the material world with a form of quasi-agency;[32] the displacement of the human from the central position in animal studies and posthumanism in general. The most explicit example is, perhaps, Eduardo Viveiros de Castro's posthumanist anthropology, which seeks to cut out the middleman, with de Castro claiming that anthropology is nothing more nor less than the transcription of Indigenous thought and transformation into concept for its circulation in theory.[33] The figure of the Indian serves for de Castro as a site for "the re-establishment of a certain connection between anthropology and philosophy via a new consideration of the transdisciplinary problematic that was constituted at the imprecise frontier between structuralism and poststructuralism during that brief moment of effervescence and generosity of thought that immediately preceded the conservative revolution."[34] This is a clear doubled trajectory of anthropological and philosophical reading of the Indian: "it is absolutely essential to recall what Taylor (2004: 97) has stressed are 'the Amerindian foundations of structuralism,'" which de Castro seeks to link to the "dissident structuralism" of Deleuze.[35] And if there was any doubt as to the orientation of this project, de Castro clarifies that it is in the end a disciplinary one: "But in the end, anthropology is what is at stake. The intention behind this tour through our recent past is in effect far more prospective than nostalgic, the aspiration being to awaken certain possibilities and glimpse a break in the clouds through which our discipline could imagine, at least for itself qua intellectual project, a denouement (to dramatize things a bit) other than mere death by asphyxia."[36] This last part about the discipline dying from asphyxia is in response to what de Castro sees as the threat of critique of the representational history of anthropology, one that caused the discipline to imagine its own death, which would have been an actual anticolonial movement.[37] Instead, de Castro envisions anthropology metamorphizing into the ideal of *anthropology* as "a permanent exercise in *the decolonization of thought*" and offers "a proposal for another means besides philosophy for the creation of concepts."[38] One wonders if Indigenous people ever get to create concepts on our own.

Any number of Indigenous scholars have recently pointed out the irony if not the audacity of this "nonhuman turn." This critical attention ranges from Zoe Todd's noticing the similarities between Latour's claim that climate is a matter of "common cosmopolitical concern" and Inuit cosmological thought and legal order (more strongly, her claim that "ontology" is just another word for colonialism) to Kim Tallbear's critiques of animal studies (for emphasizing a western biocentrism) and new materialism (for universalizing particular Indigenous thought and secularizing it; see chapter 5) and Watts's thorough analysis of how new materialists adapt Indigenous conceptions of distributed agency such that the epistemological-ontological divide that produces ontological hierarchies in western metaphysics remains intact.[39] For Byrd, this transit of Indianness operates as various iterations of Carlos Castaneda, the pseudo-shaman and peyote-tourist/anthropologist on whose writing

Deleuze and Guattari based much of their concept of becoming-Indian: "Carlos Castaneda represents the becoming-Indian as a pathological colonizing condition of faux-Indian, a pathology that haunts any left intellectual who steps forward to ventriloquize the speaking Indian by transforming the becoming-Indian into replacing."[40] This radical liberation through flow and lines of flight, in the work of Deleuze and Guattari, for Byrd, undergirds much of posthumanist thought. But the real Indians *with* ancestry continually break up the party, discomforting theorists who play theoretical Indian. "Every time flow or a line of flight approaches, touches, or encounters Indianness, it also confronts the colonialist project that has made that flow possible. The choice is to either confront that colonialism or to deflect it. And not being prepared to disrupt the logics of settler colonialism necessary for the terra nullius through which to wander, the entire system either freezes or reboots."[41]

Rather than a rigged conversation with the colonizer via colonial discourses that seek to transcribe, translate, and abstract in order to play Indian and keep up with new trends in theory, the critique of the human opens other conversations between Indigenous peoples and studies and other oppressed groups and their modes of research and writing. Black studies has a profound and incredibly rich critique of the category of Man and a discourse on other humanisms. This conversation is somewhat latent in this book, though I have addressed it briefly in another publication.[42] In part, this latency is because this book is very much about centering California Indian studies, a "minor" "regional" field of Native American and/or Indigenous studies, and reorienting the field away from the institutional version that has held sway within academia toward a mode of intellectual resurgence by, with, and for California Indian people. So, the book is already engaging certain "internal" differentiations and imbrications, from and with Native studies and Indigenous studies, which both have their specific discursive registers, geographical and historical imaginaries, positionalities, and horizons of intelligibility, and from and with the official (read: colonial) version of California Indian studies. Thus, my engagement with Black studies, similar to my engagement with queer theory on this topic, has remained in what Deborah Miranda and Tiffany Lethabo King have each differently described as the subterranean streams that nonetheless nourish the work.[43] To bring it out and into focus here in the introduction worries me that I am performing a kind of epistemic violence. I also don't want it to be an apology. In this book, there is not the sustained engagement, dialogical and otherwise, that is needed for this kind of work. It is not a book *about* Black and Indigenous relations or the intersections of Black and Indigenous studies, or Afroindigeneity. And yet, the Black and Indigenous relationship is all over this work; the imbrications, resonances, and differentiations give the book some of its shape, and I would be remiss to not address it.

I do so with a caution in mind that King, who has delved deeply into the relations between Black people and study and Indigenous people and study in their book *The Black Shoals* offers in a dossier that includes Black and Indigenous feminist scholars' responses to *Black Shoals*. King writes:

> Even when the academy finds it convenient to engage the "Black and Indigenous Studies turn," it is done with violence. So often the curatorial practices of non-Black and non-Indigenous scholars that attempt to stage a meeting between Black and Indigenous peoples (and the fields) are structured by an impulse to discipline, block, capture, and contain what is possible and potentially transformative (unsettling) about Black and Indigenous relation. Over the years, I have witnessed non-Black and non-Indigenous scholars demand that a Black and Indigenous gathering and or agenda give an account of non-Black and non-Indigenous positionality or use a language that speaks to their role in the relationship. While the language(s) of Black and Indigenous relations are not exclusive, the relation and it's grammars, idioms, and syntax are particular.[44]

Creating a speculative space for gathering outside of such violence with their title for this piece, "Where We Intend to Meet after the 'Turn,'" King does so with a deep suspicion of the institution. "Over the years, I have struggled to find academic spaces free of interlopers, saboteurs, and institutional blockades."[45] Considering the violence of academic institutions toward Indigenous and Black peoples, which has been both epistemic and very material, directly supporting genocide and slavery both past and present, as well as the failures by even the most progressive agendas at universities to substantially address these violences, suspicion is a mode of protection and survival. The gathering after the turn, then, looks proleptically ahead to conditions that would not reproduce the violences of antiblackness and ongoing colonization. King is clear that the horizon is not inclusion into the category of the human on its terms. This is an impossible task anyway as the absorption of Black lives into the category of the human would, according to them, cause, "the social order and the scaffolding that upends and holds together the human [to] collapse."[46] Concomitantly, as King asserts, were Native peoples to be fully incorporated into the human, the nation-state as political form would cease to exist: "practices of Native refusal and decolonization and Black 'skepticism/pessimism' and abolition argue that the U.S. police state can no longer determine the conditions of possibility for being considered human."[47] The horizon is the end of the western humanist imperial project.

In the meantime, while the Black and Indigenous studies turn is having its moment, it is important to understand that these types of gatherings have been going on all along: a conversation is happening, has been happening, keeps happening without needing institutional sanction or recognition. The turn of Black and Indigenous languages of interrelation is rather an infinite curve carried past the point of the settler carceral state, past the distinction between line and circle, outlasting; it is not the linear turns of fashion and commodification. The ongoing turn is an infinite conversation between Indigenous antihumanism and Black humanisms otherwise. As Jared Sexton has argued, we should approach this conversation from the position of the amateur, from a lack of desire for mastery and therefore through antidisciplinarity.[48] It should subsist in the refusal of colonial demands for intelligibility, inclusivity, and civility; in other words, it should fail to be good, the best path toward good feeling. It remains unruly, unassimilable, a rupture in the smooth workings of theoretical and knowledge production. Across this infinite interrelational form, conversation follows the paths of pleasure and comes to an understanding without knowing. It is story told collectively.

This turn to relation isn't to elide the difficulty of surviving the necropolitical state or the fraught aspects of this conversation and mode of relating. Indigenous studies, for instance, has been critiqued in turns by other critical fields as being too identitarian, ahistorical, historically focused, land focused, sovereignty focused, not secular, exceptionalist, exclusionary, relying on colonial tools and definitions, using "self-evident" or oppositional categories, to name a few. The infamous debate between Elvira Pulitano and Craig Womack over the "essentialism" of place-based Indigenous frameworks for producing and understanding literature marks one moment of disciplining/policing; Robert Warrior's necessary critique of the exclusion of Native "creative nonfiction" from the category of literature and from literary studies engagements, *and* the still-fraught position of Native art as either too cultural or not cultured enough in avant-garde art contexts mark two more.[49] The list could go on, but the disciplining of Native studies from the position of authority by non-Native scholars needs to stop. To King's point, staged conversations of Black and Indigenous studies by non-Black and non-Native scholars have often played these fields against each other, using one framework to critique the other. In many instances, Black studies in such contexts has been used as a disciplinary device to bring Native studies into alignment with this or that scholar's critical agenda, and vice versa. And while conversations between Black and Native or Indigenous scholars have also at times operated from their respective standpoints and commitments in a critical manner that seeks to shore up one discipline at the expense of the other, this is a more productive, agonistic engagement than the staged conversations critiqued by King. It does, however, raise the question of how the conversation can take place and where. Critical or agonistic engagements invested in the political form of the conversation are, of course, better. An acknowledgment of the infinite interrelation as a coalitional path toward ending western humanism as a project has my vote.

King's suspicion extends to discursive spaces as well, particularly that of the posthuman. The "post" of posthumanism marks a dilemma between the promotion of a reflexive mode of criticism that seeks the accomplishment of the Enlightenment through the dissolution of the human figured as exceptional (and universalizingly white, European), a project that has always had investments in the historical complications of Indigeneity and Blackness, and what King calls external pressure, which they describe as "specifically the kind of pressure that 'decolonial refusal' and 'abolitionist skepticism' as forms of resistance that enact outright rejection of or view 'posthumanist' attempts with a 'hermeneutics of suspicion.'"[50] This pressure is needed "in order to truly address the recurrent problem of the violence of the human in continental theory."[51] Posthumanism must be interrogated for its investments in whiteness in order to address the diminishment of and unspoken reliance upon Indigenous, Black, anti-racist, and anticolonial configurations of the human that have radical decolonial and abolitionist possibilities and which, under the current order, too easily get co-opted, domesticated, and pacified.

In the long-standing question and imposition of the western human, King finds common ground between Native, Indigenous, and Black scholars and scholarship. The human, and its overcoming, as a problematic operates within the commodified turns of western theoretical production and acts as a disciplinary force against Black and Indigenous scholars, students, and activists. As King observes, "I have watched graduate students of color experience this kind of stress, anxiety, and unease as they confront the pressure to 'take up' more contemporary impulses within Western 'critical theory' to move 'beyond the human' or toward the posthuman."[52] The demand to give an account of oneself and one's work in relation to such a theoretical edict ends up, according to King, centering whiteness, an identity that seeks to disappear its already universalizing force into nonrepresentation (subjectlessness and nonidentity). This discursive power structure, in its attempt to modify the category of the human, positions certain people (white, male, able-bodied) as materially central to the production of such knowledge and is, therefore, for King, already an identitarian project.[53]

Instead, King calls for an examination of how Black and Indigenous feminists, with attitudes of misanthropy and misandry, refuse and remain skeptical of systems, institutions, and orders of knowledge that "secure humanity as an exclusive experience and bound identity in violent ways."[54] This is not the same project as western posthumanism, which in certain iterations sees itself as the extension and completion of the imperfectly realized Enlightenment, a progressive and rationalizing project, one that often syncs seamlessly with the colonial institution. Rather than the universalization of white disappearance as a form of hyper-inclusion, King's approach is specific, dialogical, and relationally agonistic. Grounded in Black and Indigenous struggles, it remains antagonistic to the settler carceral state and, in line with the body of work of Sylvia Wynter, distantly suspicious of the turns of the western episteme. "In the work of Sylvia Wynter, one senses a general suspicion and deep distrust of the ability of Western theory—specifically its attempt at self-critique and self-correction in the name of justice for humanity—to revise its cognitive orders to work itself out of its current 'closed system,' which reproduces exclusion and structural oppositions based on the negation of the other."[55] Wynter, of course, has had a massive impact on Black studies and its investigation of the liberal human and its worlding systems and forces, including its persistent production of Black existence as sub- or nonhuman. For King, Black studies, in this sense, is a racialized and gendered project: "Both Black studies' distrust of the 'human' and Black feminism's distrust of humanism in its version as man/men (which at times seeks to incorporate Black men) relentlessly scrutinize how the category of the human and in this case the 'post-human' reproduce Black death."[56] From this angle of perception, one of suspicion, King looks to bring decolonial refusal and abolitionist skepticism into conversation around the ironic demand to move beyond the human when Indigenous and Black people cannot seem to escape death and have never been fully absorbed into the category of the human.

The Writing of Disaster

Some of the agonistic friction in this conversation comes from the frames of reference. As mentioned, Moten theorizes Black study from no standpoint, from the radical sociality of the hold of the ship, the very conditioning of being—or, for King, drawing on Wynter, the conditioning of human/Man. Indigenous studies, however, thinks both genocide and place together, which requires a different understanding of interrelation, one exemplified by the Ghost Dance. Genocide, for King, is one of the primary points of contact between Indigenous and Black scholars through the logics of conquest (a topic I take up in chapter 3), and they use it to counter the framework of settler colonialism as land-focused in a way that is bounded by U.S. territorialism and property logics and their discourses of historical trajectory. As a mode of agency that privileges the settler, both in the actions of colonization and in the reflexive analysis of this history, according to King, settler critique effaces both the relations of Black, Indigenous, and other peoples affected by empire and the continuing modes of conquest bound up in the figure of the conquistador human, which links the United States to empire and the broader western humanist project. How to think the relation to land and place, grounded normativity, in the wake of genocide and environmental destruction under empire is a significant project for Indigenous studies.

The figure of the human impacts the very archives and genealogies of thought and study as different peoples are understood only through their relations to the colonizer, creating siloed histories and archives of the oppressed and a narrow definition of "freedom" according to the western liberal human forged along the paths of this singularizing relation (from an abstract enslavement to freedom). Analyzed in *Intimacies of Four Continents,* Lisa Lowe discusses the hidden connections between the transit of European liberalism as colonial export, settler colonialism, the transatlantic slave trade, and the East Indies and China trades in the late eighteenth and early nineteenth centuries in order to show how the massive extraction of wealth from Indigenous lands and enslaved and indentured bodies was the necessary condition for the "rights of man" of the French Revolution in 1789.[57] As Fanon writes, "The wealth of the imperialist nations is also our wealth. Europe is literally the creation of the third world. The riches that are choking it are those plundered from the underdeveloped peoples."[58] This material substructure of Man/the human based in genocide, the production of property, and slavery and its liberal ideology of freedom shapes the archives, subsuming colonial violence in narratives of reason and progress, and divides knowledge into academic disciplines that foreclose knowledge of intimacies between oppressed peoples as well as alternative formations of sociality and relation. One thinks of the Oregon "lash law" or Black Exclusion law that allowed whites to keep Black slaves in the territory that we now call Oregon for a period of three years before freeing and forcing them to leave the territory (if they didn't leave, they would be whipped, hence the name "lash law"). The lash law passed in large part through the leadership of Peter Burnett who became California's first governor. In California, Burnett attempted unsuccessfully to pass a similar Black Exclusion law according to his vision of an entirely white western United States. California did pass a fugitive slave law a year after Burnett left office, and southern slave owners were allowed during his term to keep possession of their slaves when they brought them to California to participate in the gold rush. Burnett also oversaw the enslavement and genocide of California Indians; though taking an active part in it himself as governor, he credited the inhuman forces of history, progress, and fate: "That a war of extermination will continue to be waged between races until the Indian race becomes extinct must be expected. While we cannot anticipate this result but with painful regret, the inevitable destiny of the race is beyond the power or wisdom of man to avert."[59]

What remains underexamined is the relation between California Indians and Black people during this time, an effect of the siloing of history. This siloing, as Lowe has shown, impacts the material basis of research in the organizational forms and categories of the archive and makes its way through discursive procedures into narrowly focused disciplinary practices and field formation.[60] Other colonial relations between California Indians, Chinese, Mexicans, Hawaiians, and Filipinos have been examined somewhat more, though they still remain obscure due to that same siloing. An example of the effect of this force is the general exclusion of non-whites in the mid-nineteenth century from testifying in a criminal court against white people. This exclusion from legal representation usually gets narrated as affecting the specific peoples taken as objects of study from a disciplinary standpoint; texts in California Indian studies, for instance, often mention this law but narrate it as affecting California Indians without mentioning its effects on Chinese migrants. What is compelling is perhaps thinking about the well-known impromptu bands of raiders and mixed communities that developed outside the law and the developing settler society of California as a space of anti-law and anti-state coalition-building. These are groups marginally referenced in various histories of California but they fall outside the space of analysis due to their difficult fit in the siloed archives.

Along with the significance of California for the development of American anthropology and archaeology, genocide has become one of the discursively defining relationships between the state and California Indians. In chapter 3, I address the effects of the campaign to recognize that a genocide took place in California and the relationship between historiography and the international legal definition. The archives of both slavery and genocide rest upon founding violence that, as Lowe shows, makes its way into disciplined forms of knowing as well as into the law. How we narrate this story, through what criteria, and with what resources, matters. The official narrative, even when it recognizes harms done by the settler state, will always work in the service of ongoing colonialism, by default. To envision what California Indian studies can be outside such a centripetal force requires engaging genocide through the disorienting terms of the *Destruction*. More capacious than genocide, *destruction* includes the effects of colonial violence on non-human worlds (without recentering human life), the extra-definitional effects of genocide such as on culture, and, importantly, the narrow pathways of justice and knowledge that wind communities tighter into the Destruction itself, defining how we address and know it within the terms of the destruction. The field that has most profoundly developed such a discussion is a loose association of projects in a multitude of contexts that take up writing and research in the wake of extreme violence that can be tentatively termed, after Maurice Blanchot's seminal work, the writing of disaster. This mode of writing and research has important resonances with the current interest in discourses of catastrophe.

Rather than attempt to address or summarize the dizzying range of such work, here I note the importance for the approach of this book, and, for me, for California Indian studies, of the anti-historiographical and storied research and writing of Saidiya Hartman. Hartman's work provides one of the most profound meditations on the intimacies of present experiences with the lives of the dead, specifically the unrepresented and unrepresentable lives and deaths of Black girls and women, from the Atlantic slave trade to reconstruction and after, with the lives of those surviving the afterlives of slavery. It is an approach to story that I see as having a deep resonance with the storying practices and work with and against the archive of Deborah Miranda, though in the terms of "literature" in her case. It is also an answer in some ways to Simpson's implied question: what does it mean to write your refusal to write? And to do so from the non-standpoint of the poverty of world addressed by Moten, one exacerbated by the very structures of knowing and aesthetics formed around the western liberal figure of the human. California Indian studies, as I conceive of it in this book, is the struggle over this frame. It's not *about* California Indians, as the institutional version would have it, containing us with disciplinary knowledge procedures. Rather, California Indian studies is an anticolonial and antihumanist angle of perception on the humanized world against which it struggles toward that world's end. Such a collective struggle takes place, for me, in the vexed realm of the inhuman, which brings together the various refusals and failures of the human and the research and writing of destruction.

What Hartman highlights is the need to work within a representational practice of failure, a practice that Halberstam echoes in their call for a queer art of failure. This call to work with failure is in part a response to the dilemma of the archive described earlier. The dilemma is one where any access or lack of access to the lives of the dead are mediated through colonial and racialized structures of power, that is, the human. In California, as we'll see in chapter 3, the archival dilemma takes the form of the need to rely on the "voices of killers" in the genocidal archive to build a case for the recognition of genocide. Because of this condition and situation of impossibility, Hartman emphasizes the need for "an untimely story told by a failed witness," to counteract the received or authorized account and its stabilization of the "event" as event.[61] A form of study as failure acknowledges its own inability to replace or become the institutional version and leans into this inherent failure to turn away from such demands. For Hartman, the turn away takes the form of emphasizing the incommensurability between prevailing discourses and the "event," amplifying the instability of the archive, and refusing the realist illusion that dictates the institutional version of research.

This practice turns Hartman to the question of story. She asks, "how does one tell an impossible story?"[62] It is in the indeterminacy, at the limits of writing, history in her case, as narration that Hartman finds an inhumanist form of writing that approaches this question. And she does so by following the most difficult demands of the dead, the "existences relegated to the nonhistorical or deemed waste," who "exercise a claim on the present and demand us to reimagine a future in which the afterlife of slavery has ended."[63] It is an impossibility that requires submission to failure, beginning with the acknowledgment that the dead cannot be saved, the past cannot be changed, we are too late to avert the destruction, there is "no way to derange the archive."[64] Letting go of the desire to recuperate, to humanize the dead, to make them work for us, as a form of mourning that appeases the living, is the way to liberate the dead and to liberate the powers of the dead in all their inhumanist glory. This is a difficult mode of writing and research that must bear on those who perform it, who live with the images of destruction of ancestors, who either "emerge from the encounter with a sense of incompleteness" or give in to becoming with the dead in the absolute turn.[65]

The indetermination between emerging incomplete or turning toward the dead, a perhaps entangled dilemma, is where Hartman's critical fabulation bumps into the Ghost Dance. Following Stephen Best's slight reorientation of what he calls "melancholic historicism," rather than an initial desire for recovery that proves impossible, from the world to destruction, what if we begin with the full turn to the dead and all their powers of disorientation, with the destruction itself, and move from there toward the world, carrying us past the divisions between life and death, confusing refusal and failure? As we'll see in chapter 4, Deborah Miranda's *Bad Indians* does not seek a lost literature but the End of the World that cannot be contained in stories and the stories that acknowledge the impossibility of such containment and destroy attempts at making it known. Literature has often been understood to be the speech that confronts the disaster with the powers of mourning, which is perhaps why in California there is no literature of genocide. We forgo mourning, do not seek literature, especially the literature of the colonizer; rather we seek stories and their failure, their intimacy with the destructive powers of the dead.

California Is a Fiction

Indigenous Inhumanities doesn't perform an *intimacies of California*, or of the Western Seaboard, or the Pacific and Pacific Rim, a desperately needed project. And yet, the formation of California Indian studies it argues for, by, with, and for California Indian people is meant to make such modes of interrelation and shifted angles of perception possible. It is not a call for a closed project but an interrelational one. In this sense, this book prepares for a study to come by seeking the destruction of the modes of research that have forestalled its arrival and, in their destruction, the corpse from which it sprouts. This book bears all the marks of its limitations. It is also committed to weak formations such that it continuously pulls back from making strong theoretical statements even while it engages them (and sometimes makes them) and from canonical and disciplinary commitments and materials, though it sometimes engages these as well. To Eve Kosofsky Sedgwick's well-known pairing, it is equally paranoid and reparative, while remaining suspicious of both for their tendencies to attempt to "fix" the colonial system, to better it or at least live with it with the least amount of harm.[66] The angle of perception of this book is an inside/outside one that rather lets that system die and contributes to the process of its death and decay with a corrosive force, a bit of acid sprayed on the inflection points and joints. It takes up a minor position, a regional study, ambiguous and excluded texts and materials, in a cross- or a-disciplinary manner, and yet it also addresses the absolute. It turns to the dead and waits for their arrival, dancing, spinning, and singing until the world turns upside down, a radical disorientation, the intractable force of the void. Like a wounded index finger or a broken sign, it points toward an Indigenous inhumanities through the very force of its failure.

As Deborah Miranda writes, "California is a story." California is a fiction but one with real, material consequences. Situated as it is on the Pacific Rim, a palimpsestuous site of competing and layered colonialisms, of militarization, California is already betrayed positionally by the idea of settler colonialism as westward expansion (a west that is east, according to some renditions[67]), part of the completion of manifest destiny, which takes the United States, specifically the "contiguous forty-eight states," as the pre-concluded horizon, reifying its existence through its own eschatological and teleological narrative. California fits uncomfortably into the United States, also a fiction, as much as it fits uncomfortably into the dominant regional divisions of the "nation" state (the southwest). Relations to the Pacific and eastward, some made along colonial and diasporic pathways, pull California in other directions, as do hemispheric relations. California is not a container, and when it is it is a leaky one. The Ghost Dance is called the California Indian Ghost Dance to distinguish it from others, particularly the one began by Wovoka that made its way across the plains twenty years later. But the dance began in Nevada and moved to both Northern California and Southern Oregon, ignoring and refusing these geopolitical entities, disturbing the identity of it being specific to California Indians and of the name California Indian itself.

Native American studies, likewise, is a fluid field, but it does have its trajectories and tendencies. It tends to be closely allied if not at times indistinguishable from First Nations studies or Aboriginal studies in Canada, yet it has a more fraught or complex relation to Indigenous studies south of the U.S. border and in Oceania, not to mention other parts of the world, specifically the global south. At times, it has even privileged white settler colonial studies and made some sort of intellectual map that includes alongside the United States, Canada, Australia, and New Zealand. Israel has played a more ambiguous role in this formation. But, of course, this formation is nation-state-specific in terms of its geographical imaginary. What of the U.S. empire, which expands extensively outside the nation-state border? Jodi Byrd has, perhaps, asked this question the most rigorously in Native studies, putting critical Indigenous theory into conversation geographically and intellectually with the various intimacies produced through imperial expansion and maintenance, including the formations that have come to the United States along the threads of empire, constantly disrupting accepted territorial (geographic and intellectual) formations. And then, of course, there is the hemispheric approach that seeks to relate Indigeneity across the American Project of western humanist conquest. Each of these approaches is a fiction based in material reality with discursive and performative powers of its own to mold things.

Beginning with California is a way to choose not to choose, to acknowledge all these layers of Indigeneity without commitment. We were given this identity. It's a weak one that doesn't have the legal, material, or theoretical weight of the others. It is imbricated with them but also shakes the colonial foundations on which they continue to subsist. It has also long been a coalitional name for organizing California Indian communities.[68] Neither *American*, whether in the U.S. exceptionalist exclusionary use of the term or in relation to the continent-centric Western Hemisphere (Amerigo Vespucci never "found" us), nor a bounded political identity of its own. It is both more humble than these but, like Hau'ofa's Oceanic vision of the world and cosmos as a sea of islands, it is a capacious vision that moves outward from place. In friction with *Native American*, with its bordering framework, as well as *Indigenous*, with its basis in international human rights discourse and fraught relation to universalization and the Enlightenment,[69] *California* is a force of derealization of colonial form. Having taken many shapes through colonial demarcations, California remains somewhat boundless, though the force of colonization and genocide has produced a scarred shape that has been a defining identity for anticolonial action. This is to say, like any identity, it is *of course* an often violently realized fiction that undergirds the production of fact. As Deborah Miranda says, California is a story, and yet, California is a *story* and carries with it such force, the connections to place, the teeming worlds that have been decimated, the polyvocality, the indeterminacy and the dead. When each California Indian community says the word *California*, they mean the specific interrelationships to place, to other beings, to other communities, to ancestors, moving from their storied worlds to a more expansive view through what Ngũgĩ wa Thiong'o describes as *concentric rings of relevance*.[70]

Even in *California*, these are very different landscapes, often different histories, such as the relation between those who survived the missions and those the gold rush and those who survived both. *California* is not the state of California, part of the United States. It precedes its name, or, rather, the name improperly references this more boundless *before* as well as the boundless *after*, after the settler state falls. California is an improper name, imprecise, a catachresis, as is *California Indian*. And yet, California is a place, an Indigenous one first and foremost though it may be differentiated by those who underwent missionization, which connects them to the broad project of Spanish colonization across the hemisphere and then the postcolonial nation-state, Mexico in particular; and the tribes further to the north and further eastward who weren't subject to the missions but who were perhaps affected by the Russian fur trade, connecting them to tribes up the northwest coast and into Siberia, or the gold rush and its capitalistic, genocidal fervor; or those with ties across the high desert and mountains through what is now Oregon, Nevada, Utah, and Idaho. California leaks and bleeds, spilling across the land and into what the Maidu painter Frank Day calls the great mystery, the Pacific Ocean, Mon•dow•wi [big water].[71] These are the colonial movements as well as the transit of empire. The movements of Indigenous peoples prior to and during colonization strain the limits of a bounded container.

And yet we have always been here. For ten millennia or since time immemorial we have been related to these lands, even as these lands change, and we change along with them. We relate to them still even in the most recent moment of colonialism that, though temporally shallow, has caused the greatest changes. Even after California has been terraformed more than any other place on the planet, we relate to it with and through the destruction. We tear down dams, take back land, carry our ancestors home. *California* and *California Indian* have no stable referents and yet because of this, they have become powerful sites of collective, anticolonial organizing.

Indigenous Inhumanities is interested in the inhumanist mode of study by California Indian peoples that have confronted destruction. Written over a long decade, the chapters take different forms and voices in response to the materials discussed and in relation to my thinking at the time of their creation. The choice of materials is largely a matter of luck or happenstance, as research would have it. This is to say, the reader will not find a smoothly developing and continuous mode of argumentation and writing. The consistency lies elsewhere, along with the heart. Each, though, refracts something of this heart in their commitments to ending colonization and ongoing anti-Indigenous genocidal logics. They also each engage the legacy of California Indian studies and brilliance by appealing to the thought of our ancestors, placing Indigenous ways of thinking and doing at the center. The knowledge has always been there; it's just a question of how we refract the long inflection of its troublingly prophetic orientation.

Most important, perhaps, this book is a response to the Destruction, and coming to understand something of the Destruction has been the guiding principle. To say something about it is both of a wholly other order and also cannot be disentangled from the process of understanding, of unlearning learning. That California Indian studies is the space from which to try to say something about destruction has been the slowest of realizations for me (not unusual in my case, to be honest). I am both thankful for it and must at the same time apologize for taking so long to those who have long been doing the work much better than I ever could. I must count my blessings that I find myself in the company of such amazing California Indian scholars, past, present, and future. The goal of this book is to attend to various points of inflection of our shared field, California Indian studies, with respect for the longer turn that has been ongoing and destroys the very notion of it being contained as a "field." This book is, in this sense, a modest offering to them and to the brilliance of our people.

Part I
Ancestor

Chapter 1
The California Indian Bone Game

"There will be an authentic disalienation" of the colonized subject *"only to the degree to which things, in the most materialistic meaning of the word, are restored to their proper places."*

—Frantz Fanon, as quoted in Glen Sean Coulthard (Yellowknives Dene), *Red Skin, White Masks*

Why is it that in this country we have to have a law passed to ensure we get remains of our ancestors back?

—Theresa Pasqual (Acoma Pueblo), panel at The School for Advanced Research in Santa Fe, "Forging New Landscapes in Cultural Stewardship and Repatriation"

In 2022, *Inside Higher Ed* published an article about a lawsuit filed against San Jose State University by professor of archaeology Elizabeth Weiss, in which she claims the university retaliated against her for her controversial views on repatriation and violated her First Amendment rights.[1] Rehearsing tired arguments regarding the virtues of osteological research, in the article Weiss asserts, "I'm against reburying bones. I think they can tell us a lot about the past. . . . I think they can be used to train forensic anthropologists. I think that they are a key resource for young anthropologists, for archaeologists, forensic anthropologists, and I think that we still have a lot to learn from skeletal remains. I also think that a collection is not something that you study once and then it can be repatriated, because as you build knowledge on the collection, it helps you ask deeper questions as you learn more about the collection." This statement echoes comparisons made by archaeologists during the height of the debate about repatriation, about human bones being like books in a library—*you never know which book you're going to need*—upholding research and education as thin veils that cover over the power dynamics that are enacted by western institutions possessing the remains of the ancestors of colonized peoples.

That debate has been settled, as made evident by both Weiss's unceremonious resignation from and settlement with the university[2] and, in 2020, the nearly immediate retraction of a statement made by the Society for American Archaeology (SAA) sent to the UC Office of the President (UCOP) voicing similar concerns as Weiss's, specifically regarding updated repatriation policies, along with the recent release of a statement by the SAA acknowledging harms done by the association.[3] Weiss and the small group of leadership in the SAA who penned the statement were the last holdouts in the turned tide away from colonial archaeology and its investments in white supremacist scientific epistemologies. The SAA retraction and more recent statement about harms act in accordance with demands made by the Indigenous Archaeology Collective, "a network of Indigenous and non-Indigenous scholars within archaeology, heritage preservation, Cultural Resource Management, museum studies, and related disciplines working from Indigenous epistemologies in engaged ways with Native American Tribal Nations and Indigenous and descendent communities."[4] These demands were made in an open letter to the SAA, published in *News from Native California*, in response to the SAA's initial statement sent to the UCOP and are as follows:

1. The SAA must support the UCOP draft Policy and issue a public retraction of its June 19th [2020 statement to UCOP].
2. The SAA President and board must make all attempts to communicate with and apologize to CalTHPOs [California Tribal Historic Preservation Officers] and the Native American Heritage Commission.
3. In demonstration of the SAA's commitment to addressing structural inequalities and promoting anti-racist practice in our field, the society will undertake a racial climate survey; increase funding for the participation of Native American and Indigenous peoples in archaeology; provide meeting registration and membership waivers to Native American and Indigenous meeting attendees; highlight the Indigenous history of host meeting cities; and formally request and receive permission of local Tribal Nations to host SAA meetings in their traditional lands and territories.

4. The SAA must formalize its commitment to consulting with the Committee on Native American Relations on any and all matters related to NAGPRA and repatriation.
5. Convene a Task Force to develop a revised policy on repatriation that supports the rights of Indigenous peoples "to the use and control of their ceremonial objects; and the right to the Repatriation of their ancestral Human Remains" as articulated in Article 12 of the United Nations Declaration on the Rights of Indigenous Peoples (UNDRIP).[5]

What I'm interested in in this chapter is the force of humanization that operates within this turn in repatriation politics and what other possibilities exist for liberating our ancestors from colonial institutions or perhaps in following their own liberatory movements. I'm interested in the disorientation of the colonial project toward its death, as opposed to the humanization of Indigenous peoples and our ancestors. To understand the force of humanization and its alternatives, I track it through the power dynamics and structured conditions of voice as they shift in new policies and laws, a rhetorical project.[6] Thus, in the next section, I follow some of the struggles of NAGPRA's implementation, beginning with a case study at UC Berkeley from 2007, through subsequent attempts to fulfill what Joanne Barker describes as a human rights promise deferred. The question of human rights in relation to the Native American Graves Protection and Repatriation Act (NAGPRA), and repatriation politics more generally, often takes the form of either metonymic or metaphoric relations to the discourse on genocide. This resonance with genocide through human rights frameworks has resulted in a complete reformulation of the discipline of archaeology away from bioarchaeology, the evolutionary and population science–based research belatedly practiced by Weiss. The discipline has moved toward the hybrid formation of a more communally engaged and Indigenous epistemology-centric forensic archaeology, specifically in this case interested with identification of the remains of Indigenous peoples subjected to colonial violence or toward contributing to land claim cases. This is a shift that Weiss herself attempts to make in the quote by asserting the study of Indigenous remains as a necessary component of more current forensic archaeological practices, tying together colonial possession and redress.

This chapter is guided by a single question: Would our ancestors have wanted to be considered human in the way we use the term today? It's a question without an answer, but, in order to approach it, in the second half of this chapter, I return to an ambiguously failed—or perhaps tricky—proposal made by Gerald Vizenor in 1986 to create a federal bone court that would hear the bones' own testimonies. Essentially silencing the repatriation debate before it even begins, replacing the voices of "human" actors with those of bones, Vizenor's proposal operates subjunctively within the "*past conditional temporality* of the 'what could have been,'" as described by Lisa Lowe (in the context of the colonial archive): What could have been if Vizenor's proposal had been realized instead of NAGPRA? As a force of narration that anticipates its own failure, Vizenor's proposal also operates in the speculative and subjunctive narrative space of fabulation, described by Saidiya Hartman as writing alongside the impossible narration by/of those without a voice, an absence in multiple registers. Further, it draws into question the juridical nature of Indigenous representation, legal personhood, and humanity as part of a humanizing, western liberal, colonial force. It does so by situating itself within the failure to be human, the ambiguity of the humanity of both living descendants and ancestral remains, and by calling directly on U.S. colonial domination through law—specifically Congress's plenary power to create federal courts, to expose the Indigenous aporia of what Elizabeth Povinelli calls "the governance of the prior" through an appeal to the prior of the prior.[7]

The Limits of NAGPRA

Since the passage of NAGPRA in 1990, there has been a lot of pushback by Native and allied scholars and activists due to its shortcomings, which has led to the passage of additional legislation to correct various oversights or ensure enforcement—to put teeth into it.[8] In California, for instance, CalNAGPRA was passed in 2001 to ensure enforcement and close loopholes. While much of this new legislation has focused on cleaning up ambiguity, imprecision, and perceived loopholes in the language of the law, the discourse surrounding these criticisms tends to focus on NAGPRA's promise and subsequent failure to protect or enforce some sort of right, whether civil, human, natural, or cultural. NAGPRA, it has been argued, was (to be) a major achievement in the rights for Native American peoples; its weakness is an abnegation of these rights, in this case the right to tend to our own dead and maintain ownership of essential cultural and spiritual items. But what if the "weakness" that these criticisms have registered is not merely a weakness in the law's drafting and execution but rather an aspect of rights discourse itself as it relates to Native peoples, or of perhaps the law itself as it subjugates and subjectifies us? What if the condition of the law's fallibility isn't a condition to be diagnosed and perhaps cured but rather the conditioning of certain subjects in conjunction with such fallibility, ones that are made to desire a perfect/perfectible law that recognizes (more and more) fully their rights?[9] This is to say, what if it's the wrong kind of weakness, one conditioned by an evaluation of individual and subjective strength?

I am one of those subjects, and I desire a more perfect law. This, I confess, is my strongest and perhaps only claim to authority here. It is also what makes me an inappropriate grammatical subject—first, second, or third person—through which to voice concerns for something as sensitive as the final resting place of our—my, your, their—ancestors. "I" am too compromised from the start. As Kahnawake Mohawk anthropologist and political theorist Audra Simpson puts it, "The work of Indigenous scholars rests upon Empire as well, and through the vocabularies and analytics [and, I would add, grammar] it put into play."[10] To briefly position myself in relation to this text and some of the others with which I will be engaging, I must state that I (biographically) am not a legal theorist, but, as anyone who works on Native issues knows, one has to do a little bit of legal theory to address them, so my position is as a community member when it comes to doing legal theory, an amateur and not an expert, but one with a distinct vested interest. At the same time, I am also an academic with quite a bit of training in words. To borrow Anishinaabe theorist, writer, and trickster Gerald Vizenor's phrase in terms of meaning created from conflict, I am familiar with "The Word Wars."[11] Tactics like naming, unnaming, and renaming; looking for the intransitive motion in fixed phrases; moving away from or otherwise disturbing subject and object positions; teasing out irony; paying attention to the interval, the neutral, the cracks and fissures in oppositionally produced identities—in other words, paying attention to nonoppositional difference—are all part of the serious play of textual production in what has quickly become less of (and maybe never really was) a "war" and more of a *disaster* of world-destroying proportions. Think of the postapocalyptic status of many Native languages in relation to the naturalized colonial and settler colonial ones, such as the colonial English in which I am writing. As Tommy Pico writes about Native people:

> being sprayed
> on like roaches by cap-
> italism, by metabolic dis-
> ease, by team sports names,
> mascots, by general invisibility
> Being a function of the
> past, being a feature
> of the land, by forced Indian
> boarding schools with
> 20% mortality rates,
> by the English fucking
> language with its high
> beams in my face[12]

This chapter, then, is made up of spare parts articulated with various forms of discursive, and sometimes gestural, glue and linkages, parts drawn from "The Word Wars" and their genocidal aftereffects in the ruins of representation. The anthropological archives, oral traditions and song-stories, legal discourses and transcriptions, community emails, scientific treatises, traditional games, personal conversations, historical narratives, and bits and pieces of theory will all play their part, hopefully toward the goal of destabilizing the usual hierarchization of textual authorities and relations of commentary. After all, like René Descartes's suggestion, more recently echoed by Bruno Latour, that everyone spend a few hours a year practicing philosophy, Native community members, while often not having the luxury of such a choice, must do a little bit of legal theory, because we are *Homo legalis*, the legal person to an extreme point, a point that I will be approaching and perpetually missing throughout this chapter. This point is missed altogether in the question of what kind of right NAGPRA represents (whose? mine, yours, theirs?) and how well it does this. Yellowknives Dene political theorist Glen Coulthard (paraphrasing Kahnawake Mohawk author and educator George Taiaiake Alfred) writes, "The dominance of the legal approach to self-determination has, over time, helped produce a class of Aboriginal citizens whose rights and identities have become defined solely in relation to the colonial state and its legal apparatus."[13] Amateur legal theory can never be divorced from the settler colonial-induced *Word Disaster* and its difficult textuality because it is a form of self-making, even when that "self," that Native self (almost an oxymoron, right?), remains intractably unknowable. "We must be mindful . . . that in its theoretical and analytic guises 'culture' is defined in anthropological terms most consistently by its proximal relation to [oppositional] difference. And that difference was to be defined against the sameness and omniscience of a stable ontological core, an unquestioned 'self' that defined that difference and thence 'culture' for a readership, one that corresponded to a metropole and to a colony, a self and an other to define oneself proximally against."[14]

In order to approach the problem of Native subjectivation under these conditions, through the desire for a perfectible law and the enactment of rights, the first half of this chapter takes as a case study an event that occurred at the Phoebe Apperson Hearst Museum on the University of California Berkeley campus in 2007. Taking place during my second year of graduate school, this event drew me into the politics of knowledge production and the history of studying Native peoples in California. Revolving around a then-proposed and eventually implemented bureaucratic reorganization of the museum's daily functions, it involved issues of mis/identification (the slash between the prefix *mis-* and the root *identification* marks this as a deconstructive case, as to misidentify is still to identify in a way, just as to identify must necessarily risk misidentification) in relation to both the well-critiqued NAGPRA categories "culturally unidentifiable or unaffiliated" and the ambiguous position of the research unit in charge of collecting evidence toward repatriation at the Hearst Museum. Instead of immediately attempting to solve the problem by asserting a more true identity or a more apt mode of identification—processes that have been underway ever since—my procedure in this chapter is to hold open the suspension of meaning as much and as long as possible in order to give breathing space to the opacities and silences created by the various failures.

Primitive and Visual Accumulation

Much of the controversy around Elizabeth Weiss began when she posted a picture of herself on social media holding the skull of an ancestor (likely Ohlone). The expected outcry from California Indian communities and others resulted in Weiss losing her position as curator of the university's collection of remains and being banned from entering the research facility. *Inside Higher Ed* made the "brave" choice to republish the image in a story it ran about the situation, causing further outcry about the public display of Indigenous remains. Both instances participate in a legacy of conspicuous power long enacted through collection and exhibition. Weiss's posting of the image and *Inside Higher Ed*'s decision to republish it are not anomalous. Such images are tied to a long history of the possession and display of Indigenous remains and body parts. They gesture to genocidal settlers' proprietary claims to Native land and bodies, and the discourse from both, with their attempts to justify these actions, seeks to turn a vulgar display of power into an intellectual "debate." Tony Bennett, in *The Birth of the Museum*, writes, "The institutions comprising 'the exhibitionary complex' . . . were involved in the transfer of objects and bodies from the enclosed and private domains in which they had been displayed (but to a restricted public) into progressively more open and public arenas where, through the representations to which they were subjected, they formed vehicles for inscribing and broadcasting the messages of power . . . throughout society."[15]

Historically, in the case of Native American burials and other interred objects, grave digging wasn't just a pastime of the elites but extended to all parts of society. An estimated one million Native American remains were held in private and public institutions by the late twentieth century.[16] This number doesn't include the innumerable personal collections—such as those held by Thomas Jefferson, who employed his slaves to excavate the burial mounds on his property, and Henry David Thoreau, who spent his summers digging for Indian objects and remains—that we are familiar with because of their literary and physical traces and proximity to the settler public sphere. Along with the identificatory project by which U.S. citizens seek to indigenize themselves to the land through their excavation and collection of Native remains and objects, another facet of Weiss's posing with the skull—asserting an identity—the collecting of such remains acted as a replacement for the Native peoples who were being removed, killed, or forced to assimilate and understood to be on a path of disappearance.

The collecting practices of Ralph Glidden parallel the transition from such individual practices to a distinctly nationalizing project. Born in Lowell, Massachusetts, Glidden moved to Avalon, California, in 1896 at the age of sixteen. In 1915, while working as a carpenter, Glidden began to excavate sites on San Nicolas and San Miguel Islands, part of the homelands of the Gabrieleño-Tongva and the Chumash peoples, amassing a large collection that the *Los Angeles Times* wrote "would make any curator in this nation envious."[17] In 1918, he sold his collection to the Heye Foundation of the Museum of the American Indian in New York. The following year, the chewing gum magnate William Wrigley Jr. purchased Catalina Island and closed the island's interior to the many amateur collectors who were raiding grave sites and confiscating human remains. Wrigley's goal was to ensure that the "archaeological specimens" became the property of museums and the subject of serious research. The Heye Foundation received an exclusive contract to conduct all digs with an agreement to split the objects equally with the Chicago's Field Museum of Natural History. Ralph Glidden was hired to do the excavations, which included over eight hundred grave sites. Glidden accumulated the largest collection of human remains and artifacts related to the Gabrieleño-Tongva, the Indigenous peoples of Catalina Island and the Los Angeles Basin. In 1924, the Heye Foundation cut their funding, and Glidden's only other source of income was a small museum that he had established in 1922. He based his idea for a new museum on a mortuary chapel on the island of Malta, which had walls decorated with motifs formed from the bones of monks, and the Capuchin Crypt in Rome, which contains the skeletal remains of over three thousand Capuchin friars buried by their order.

Utilizing Native American skeletal remains as a form of decoration, the interior of his museum was a popular stop for tourists. Shelves displayed rows of human skulls, femur bones were used as supports for shelves, and windows were decorated with an assortment of smaller human bones, including those from fingers and feet. As a sort of remainder of the more "serious" scientific collecting practices with which he was earlier engaged, Glidden's display of Native American body parts participated in the larger exhibitionary realm of Wild West shows and World's Fairs. As an excess, it rode the line between archaeological practices protected and supported by the Antiquities Act of 1906, which set aside areas of public land in order to protect significant natural, cultural, or scientific features, and the raiding of grave sites by amateur collectors. As such, it starkly exposes the primitive accumulation of scientific materials and data and personalized and fetishized objects that continue to mark the distinction between Natives and settlers across the divide of such collections.[18] The mode of visuality is also telling: it unearths the hidden past for the sake of a power of display that stakes a claim on the land itself as property at the same time that it sets the conditions for the more fine-grained visuality of osteological research outside of public view, defining the relation between settler and Native alike. Weiss's pose with the skull performs a similar function.

Another high-visibility case is that of the Ancient One (a.k.a. Kennewick Man), which suspended for a moment the power of discursive practices to identify human remains. Washing out of a Columbia River bank in Washington state in 1996, the remains were first collected by a forensic scientist, who was brought in to determine whether there was any foul play. After asserting that the brutalized remains were "caucasoid" and included a stone point lodged in the bones, the scientist sent out samples for radiocarbon dating and was shocked to receive a report that the remains were over ninety-five hundred years old. This dissonance of two different scientific findings, forensic and archaeological, set off a racist and nationalizing media storm over the true narrative of America's past and the politics of belonging, with some using the opportunity to question whether or not Native Americans were the Indigenous people of the land. At the time, the bones were too mineralized and too old for any DNA testing to settle the issue of race. In 2015, the remains were identified as Native American by a scientist using new DNA testing technology, which in some sense put the controversy to rest but also strengthened the argument for a reliance on scientific technology to settle such disputes.

A Case of Mis/identification

What is a case? Gayatri Chakravorty Spivak answers in a very useful way. "But let me tell you first why I think of these slippery things as cases. Because I do not want them to prove a theory by becoming postdictions and making the theory pre-dictive metaleptically; but perhaps they do? I do not want them to be illustrations of our arguments. But perhaps they are? At any rate, these case reports inevitably produce a series of failures, working analyses and descriptions, in other words, that seem to lead somewhere."[19] She also responds to the question of how she knows a case is a case with the following:

> I cannot say, for I see a shaped outline in a fragment, it begins to make sense, and it fits into a case. And then, what is it a case of? This has not yet been a thing I have worried about in my project of unlearning learning in order to ask: What is it to learn? But, for the moment, since a question generates an answer, let me say cases of

> subject-ing, cases of agent-ing, thus cases of identifying, cases of the staging of culture as the originary synthesis with the absolute other; everything that we leap over when we start with the object of cultural studies or the politics of culture. But the real answer is you tell me, when you have read these pages.[20]

Keeping both the clarity and the difficulty of these responses in mind, I turn now to a case of mis-identification. In the wake of the passage of NAGPRA in 1990, the Phoebe Apperson Hearst Museum at UC Berkeley was required to survey its vast collection of human remains, upward of twelve thousand individuals, and over a million artifacts to determine any cultural affiliation to existing tribes and to repatriate any remains and implicated cultural items identified. A series of failures by the museum in this task led to an ambiguous situation and a controversy in 2007 regarding the location and enunciative position of the research team responsible for collecting evidence to make cases for identification and cultural affiliation. The initiatory details of this case are derived from a one-way email correspondence that occurred at that time between Larri Fredericks, an Athabascan Indian and the former interim coordinator for the UC Berkeley NAGPRA research unit, and the chancellor of the university, Robert J. Birgeneau, as well as a subsequent state senate hearing in 2008, from which the chancellor was also absent. The correspondence concerned the location/position of the unit in charge of overseeing and ensuring the Hearst Museum's compliance with NAGPRA. On the occasion of the first message, Fredericks wrote to the chancellor informing him of a recent decision by vice chancellor of research Beth Burnside, to integrate the formerly semi-autonomous NAGPRA research unit into the overall functions of the museum, a message that Fredericks sent simultaneously to both the Chancellor and the American Indian Graduate Student Association listserv, which is how I received it, as well as to the Native community more broadly. Seemingly a minor and internal matter of administration and museum organization, it is precisely "the minor" and "the internal" that are at stake in this case.

When it was passed, federal NAGPRA required institutions that received federal funding to create a summary and an inventory of their entire "holdings or collections of Native American human remains and associated funerary objects," sacred objects, and objects of cultural patrimony, and, using "evidence based upon geographical kinship, biological, archaeological, anthropological, linguistic, folkloric, oral traditional, historical, or other relevant information or expert opinion" to identify their "cultural affiliation."[21] The initial deadline was 1995. Once affiliation was determined, request by a lineal descendant, affiliated Native American tribe, or Native Hawaiian organization required the "expeditious return" of the "cultural items." Berkeley's research unit was founded in 1999, one year prior to the (already extended) deadline to be in compliance with the federal law and nine years after the law's enactment, a last-minute and last-ditch effort to summarize, inventory, and gather research for cultural identification of the massive collection. In this exceptional situation, due both to the egregiousness of Berkeley's procrastination and to the fact that Berkeley's collection was the largest one subject to NAGPRA, the research unit was created with a certain amount of autonomy, including separate funding. In essence, it was created to fix a mistake, a mistake made through intentional foot-dragging by a number of prominent social scientists. The NAGPRA unit was not responsible for determining which remains were to be deemed culturally affiliated. That decision was and remains the responsibility of UC Berkeley NAGPRA Implementation and UCOP's systemwide Native American Repatriation Implementation and Oversight committees (nominated by the state's Native American Heritage Commission), which are made up of UC personnel and tribal consultants. The unit's job was simply to provide the evidence upon which the committee would base its decision.[22] At the time, Fredericks writes, "By disbanding the unit, the University avoids forcing the committees to make these decisions."

The story from administration was that the unit was never meant to exist in its exceptional position beyond the timeline needed to produce the inventory, but, in 2001, an economic downturn and the need to hire a new museum director delayed the intended reorganization. The story from members of the unit, however, "reads a bit like a murder mystery."[23] At the California Senate Hearing, member of the research unit Lalo Franco (Tachi Yokut) gave the following testimony:

> All this for us started, this whole problem, it didn't start for us at UC Berkeley. It started at UCLA. When we repatriated human remains from UCLA, we got 12 of our ancestors back from UCLA. The case was called the Tulare Nightie Case. Now, the two people that voted no against the repatriation was Philip Walker and Mr. Bettinger. So the vote was 5–7. Now, when we started working

> with Dr. Fredericks, almost during that same course or period of time, we believe that that is when all of this started happening. That Dr. Bettinger and Philip Walker which were also going to be overseeing the decision on the repatriation for Berkeley did not want to see a floodgate of human remains coming back to the tribes, because what we got from UCLA were remains that were culturally unidentifiable. You know, the culturally unidentifiable rule that is being proposed that's going to be in addition to NAGPRA and so it's going to require an entirely new set of regulations for declaring things culturally unidentifiable. Well, U.C. Berkeley's human remains that are there, I believe are 80 percent of them are classified as culturally unidentifiable. So it's no mistake to me that within six months of the rules being proposed and the final set of draft regulations hitting the tribes that all of a sudden, UC Berkeley decides to reorganize their museum and put the NAGPRA staff out and the rest of everything back into the museum to make it easier for them to botch those culturally unidentifiable objects.

Walker and Bettinger were brought in as "outside consultants" to assess the research unit and ultimately made the recommendation to "fold" the unit into the museum's daily functions and to redistribute the NAGPRA funds within the museum's operations, because they found the unit to be "unacceptably dysfunctional." This integration of the unit into the museum meant, among other things, that Larri Fredericks was to be demoted from interim coordinator, semi-autonomous supervisor of the unit, to herself being supervised by two of the museum's staff, and the other members of the unit were to be spread out among a variety of departments across the museum. Consider that, as Franco mentions, due to the time constraint written into the law, the museum had identified 80 percent of its collection of the remains of over twelve thousand individuals and over a million objects as culturally unaffiliated or unidentifiable, which interrupted the process of repatriation.

A result of the ongoing primitive accumulation by the settler state of a Native past it claims as its own, *culturally unaffiliated* and *unidentifiable* remains and cultural items at the time were generally defined by one or more of the following: (1) insufficient information existed to make any determination of cultural affiliation; (2) they were associated with Native American tribes that were not federally recognized and therefore lacked standing under NAGPRA; (3) they were associated with tribes historically known but without living descendants; or (4) they were of considerable temporal and cultural distance from contemporary Native American tribes. Fredericks writes, "It is crucial to understand that many inventories fall under the latter category [of culturally unaffiliated or unidentifiable] simply because the Museum would have been out of compliance with the Federal mandate to have the collection inventories for NAGPRA completed by June 2000." The immense size of the collection, together with procrastination on the part of the museum's administrators and a limited time frame (one year), made a comprehensive review of the documentation for thousands of archaeological sites impossible and led to such a large percentage of the collection being labeled unaffiliated and/or unidentifiable. This failure shifted the burden onto the tribes to contest the classification. "Folding" the NAGPRA unit into the museum's daily functions, according to Fredericks, amounted to shifting the burden of proof to the tribes to make claims "on a case-by-case basis," as opposed to an ongoing active process of collecting evidence for cases by the unit, the mode that it transitioned into after outliving its initial inventory phase. This negated the original shift in power enacted by the law, which placed responsibility in the hands of the scientists to identify "in good faith" the cultural items and remains and gain permission from the tribes to perform research. The inclusion of the research unit into the overall functions of the museum amounted to a shift in "voice."

It was precisely the failure to identify the remains, and the subsequent foreclosure of the ability to identify with the remains, that troubled recourse to the law. Further, identification, relying as it does on scientific discourse as a form of justice, merely redoubles the assumed crime (for which the law was needed as corrective to begin with). The bones, then, are caught between identification and misidentification, as to be unidentifiable and to be identified both fall into the realm of the continuing disaster began in the encounter with Europe five hundred years ago. Mis/identification and silence are the points of articulation between a shattered speech and the remains of a shattered past in the form of material culture. In such a relation between the fragmented word and the thing as fragment, who or what can speak? And what (kind of) voice could this be?

A Quick and Dirty History

Written into the state constitution at California's inception, the 1868 founding of the University of California, a settler colonial and western humanist institution, coincided with the genocidal war waged against California Indian people, against our bodies, collectivities, interrelations with all sorts of beings, and fundamentally against our worlds. In the midst of the gold rush, it was four years *prior to* the beginning of the Modoc War in the lava beds of Northern California, an insurgent resistance movement led by Kintpuash, a.k.a. Captain Jack. It was also parallel to the Ghost Dance, the Indigenous anticolonial movement based on grassroots collective forms of knowledge through dreaming and ceremony and organized around collective feelings and relations to death and colonial violence, discussed in the introduction. The two movements are, of course, not just temporally and spatially contiguous but indicate two parallel meanings of what comes to be called California Indian studies and two different lines of development and thought.

There's a seedy story about the development of the University of California (UC) that includes investments, deception, land deals, shell educational institutions, and all the usual shenanigans of settler colonial arrogance that people uncritically celebrate as "history" and "pioneering" that I'm not going to get into here.[24] What is important is that the UC system was created with Morrill Act or land grant funding.[25] From the early to mid-nineteenth century the federal government, through 162 violence-backed cessions, expropriated roughly 10.7 million acres of land from 245 tribal nations and divided it into roughly 80,000 parcels to be sold. This is the material basis for many universities and colleges throughout the United States. It is also part of what Robert Nichols more appropriately calls the *production* of property (and not just its expropriation) because it attempted a wholesale replacement of Indigenous modes of sociality with western humanist and property-based ones through education, with all the attendant effects of such an ontological reorganization.[26] This undoubtedly affected the forms of education, or, in other words, the reproduction of western humanist settler subjects. The Organic Act, which established the University of California, was signed into state law in 1868, and the University of California was formed, which included at the time a College of Mines, a College of Agriculture, a College of Mechanical Arts, and an Academic College (the classics).

These respective colleges fundamentally map the coordinates of the western conception of the human. The College of Mines was, of course, for the institutionalization and development of resource extraction, which, as seen with the gold rush, had direct genocidal effects for

California Indian people. The College of Agriculture also had genocidal implications, considering the role that ranching and farming had in developing property systems, which led to starvation through replacement of food sources and so-called punitive raids, the indiscriminate killing of Indigenous people in protection of property. It also turned California into one of the most terraformed landscapes on the planet through the development of its infrastructure, public works projects, and real estate, which directly connected to the massive collection of Native remains. The College of Mechanical Arts focused on development of technology and the sciences of labor, replacing Indigenous conceptions of abundance with an economics based on scarcity, exploitation, and strict social hierarchy. And the academic college sought to humanize in very explicit ways what were understood to be unpredictable settlers whose direct violence, it was beginning to be understood, had largely served its purpose.

This is the context in which then-governor Frederick Low attended the College of California's commencement exercises, a precursor to the University of California, at which the main speaker, famed chemist and founder of the American oil industry Benjamin Silliman, chastised the state of California for starting a polytechnic school instead of a "real university" with a liberal arts education like those in the East. The demand had little purchase at the time among what Patrick Wolfe calls the settler horde, and this jovial chiding over the need for the humanities between white male elites in the midst of a genocidal campaign must be understood within the discourses of the time. Against those calling for extermination or removal of California Indian people—a popular discourse in both the media and in government documents—other voices were demanding the assimilation of California Indians who were being brutally and forcefully dragged into California's material and sexual economies through written and unwritten laws that criminalized Indigenous freedom, structurally silenced California Indian voices, and legalized rape, murder, and child abduction. These softer and more enlightened voices were part of an established process humanizing both the Indian savage and the settler savage through educational missions that linked immigration policy to Indian policy through state security and the concurrent development of an aestheticized national/normative culture as white-oriented. The figure of the savage haunted Silliman's call for a humanist education as a way to tame what in his imagination was a lawless frontier, a wildness that, of course, existed only in the feverish dreams of a white imaginary. California Indian peoples had place-specific governance and social structures that had been the order of the world for millennia.

The humanizing process created the conditions for the "inclusion" into the university of, first, California Indian cultures, knowledges, and bodies—through the extractive practices of anthropologists and archaeologists—and eventually—California Indian academics, through inclusivist and diversity frameworks, what Roderick Ferguson describes as the betrayal of the student and civil rights movements.[27] Of this force of inclusion, Vizenor writes, "Now, the tribal survivors are summoned to the universities and museums, roused to be proud, cited to abide by the monologs, the dubious splendors of neocolonial tropes in tribal cultures, invented narratives, and aboriginal remains."[28] Of course, both of these "moments" were conditioned by the humanizing logics invested in the continuation of the colonial relationship to Indigenous land and over Indigenous bodies. California Indian studies began as research done by mostly white academics *about* California Indians, and the knowledge systems and frameworks continue this general orientation, even when they are supposedly sympathetic to Indigenous people.

Aporias of Recognition

Hiding the Bones: in the California Indian gambling game known alternately as Hand Game, Bone Game, Grass Game, or, in Maidu, Tep We (marked/unmarked), across a fire one of two opposing teams hides two pair of bone playing pieces in their hands (made from the leg bone of Pah-koo-nee, mountain lion). Two of these bones are marked. Two unmarked. They are hiding the pattern from the gaze of the opposing side.

"What other group in America does not have the right to speak for their dead?"[29] Because of the mass interpellation of UC Berkeley's collection as culturally unidentifiable, the remains and cultural items were placed outside of the discursive and recognitive powers of federal authority. Becoming the neutral objects of scientific discourse (thereby naturalizing this notion of object), they were identified and thereby contextualized, recognized, and interpellated but in a different way. To go unrecognized by one code is to slip immediately into another, as one is always preceded by a system or network that sets the terms for recognition and for action. Such a model is familiar to Native peoples, who have been subjected to the oppositional dichotomy of legal rights-bearing citizen and natural object/inhuman being across the divide of sovereignty. It has historically been a model of confinement either way, in this case confinement to the museum's storage rooms and laboratory. In this sense, mis/identification is a form of misrecognition: inclusion and exclusion from the political sphere is dependent upon being recognized as someone or something to which rights can or cannot attach. Joanne Barker has made this connection: "These relations of power and knowledge are instanced by the transposition of the unrecognized for the culturally unidentifiable—the recasting of 'unrecognized' as 'culturally unidentifiable.'"[30]

Such a contested space of mis/identification is the site of a split in cultural identity for contemporary Native Americans and our ancestors, effectively making identification a laboratory not just of "neutral" scientific identification of "objects" but a political laboratory of identification. This split is part of a legal discourse that expressly distinguishes between—while at the same time intimately connecting—the ethnographic enunciation *Indian*, defined primarily as cultural evidence in an anthropological discourse, and the politico-legal enunciation *Indian*, through which subjects are defined and enacted in the complex space of sovereignty. To be Indian in the politico-legal sense is to be called, addressed, and outlined according to at least thirty-three separate definitions of *Indian* used in federal legislation, a number that expands exponentially when tribal enrollment statutes are included. This multiple codification produces complex networks of mis/recognition/identification across the same individual and/or collective body. As Native Americans, in this sense, are primarily defined by inclusion in a social scientifically recognizable tribe and through eligibility for various types of governmental aid (codifying dependence). In other words, inclusion in a political system based upon redress and multicultural inclusion through the management of culture creates a heavily layered map of institutionalized recognition that falls on bodies in a variety of ways. The situation of Native remains, as well as cultural items, falls as well into an evidentiary discourse through mis/identification.

As I discuss in the introduction, the term *culture* is designated by settlers as the passage out of nature for Indigenous people, a thoroughly western concept (see chapter 2). The term in this context indicates politically and legally defined tribal affiliation based upon the very scientific processes that arose from practices of studying sites such as those excavated by Glidden and collections like those held at the Hearst Museum. The rhetoric resides in the designation "unidentifiable" being based on a legal definition of "culture" in conjunction with past and present identification procedures practiced and collected at the same site. This rhetoric has informed policy through the administrative procedures of such places as the Hearst Museum and in the role of scientific consultants in jurisprudence and policymaking. Here that particular mis/identification holds a certain power to cover over in the continuing interests of the scientific. Barker indicates the intimacy of this articulation: "Natives charged empiricism an inherently political ideology, discourse, and research practice aimed at denying its own motivations and cultural influences in the name of objectivity and neutrality even as empirical scientists sought positions within federal policymaking processes as administrators, staff, and consultants on such politically charged matters as native governance and territorial rights and the nation's cultural heritage."[31] What is done to our ancestors and cultural items seemingly transposes onto us, because scientific forms of identification and legal forms of recognition are intimately interconnected. What's tricky about this situation is that there are two countertendencies: one is to push for equal rights before the law as citizens, and the other is to assert one's humanity through universal (international) human rights. As Barker notes, "Native peoples rejoin with the inalienability of their human rights, reclaiming their standing as human within the legal terms of their international rights to social justice and equality."[32] These tendencies correspond to two different though not mutually exclusive forces of the inhuman or, perhaps more appropriately, humanizing violence: technical/rational control and inhumane/violent treatment.

The social and political action our ancestors have induced in us by their confinement—through exclusion from the political and inclusion in the natural—risks opening up the powers of control. One avenue is the requirement of federal recognition for repatriation to take place—for the culturally affiliated during the time of the UC Berkeley case and for the unidentifiable and unaffiliated since the rule adoption in 2010. Like NAGPRA's institutionalization of empirical methods through policy-writing and internalized organization, the Bureau of Indian Affairs (BIA) established the Office of Federal Acknowledgment to administer the regulations for federal recognition cases, stocking their bureaucracy with empirically based disciples and instituting the criterion of a preponderance of anthropologically determined cultural evidence. Culture was thereby naturalized; this is the objective of the power of technique: "The mandatory criteria assume that a tribe petitioning for recognition possesses the qualities that the procedures identify as characterizing an existing Indian tribe. The Indian tribe is not taken to be configured as such within the law or through the processes of petitioning to be recognized."[33] What kind of split is necessary to apply both objective techniques of identification and recognitive forms of subjection in the same instance? In other words, what kind of right is it that requires one to be adopted in both the community of humans or citizens and the inhuman world of "objects" at one and the same time? There was a long moment in theoretical time when thinkers fantasized overcoming the subject-object divide, but Native and Black people in the United States have been living the material horror of the imposition of this grammar and the vacillations of its overcoming for quite a long while.

Absence of Stories

Singing the Songs: in the Bone Game, the side hiding the bones sings songs of power to tease and distract the guessing team. These songs come from animals, trees, rocks, streams, anything that might whisper their song to you, giving you the power to hide.

Simply being in compliance with the law was not enough for Fredericks. Instead, she called for representation of a storytelling epistemology that would speak for the remains, including the culturally unidentified and unaffiliated, in a different way, a way that the external review committee deemed "dysfunctional." As I mentioned, NAGPRA has provisions for using Native American epistemological and traditional forms of evidence. Again, the evidentiary standard to show cultural affiliation is defined as "a preponderance of evidence based upon geographical kinship, biological, archaeological, anthropological, linguistic, folkloric, oral traditional, historical, or other relevant information or expert opinion." This inclusion of Native-specific forms of knowledge has caused some legal theorists to point to NAGPRA as an exemplar of legal pluralism. But, in practice, stories haven't carried the same weight as scientific physical evidence. To paraphrase archaeologist Tim White, a major opponent of NAGPRA and a significant part of the reason that Berkeley remained out of compliance for so long: science is hard work; making up stories is easy.

The lack of stories is no surprise if we consider the narrative that Fredericks herself recounts in 2007. It is a story of leaked correspondence and hushed voices. Take for instance this accidental forward from the vice chancellor at the time, originally intended for the assistant vice chancellor, who was the primary contact for Fredericks regarding the review process that ultimately led to the vice chancellor's decision. About it Fredericks writes,

> What is telling about this email is that she sent it to me by mistake; she thought she was emailing Price to give him guidance. I quote the email in its entirety:
>
> > "Bob, In a worst case scenario, you might address her issues by asking for a list of the last several months tribe visits and taking a random sample for the reviewers to interview by phone. That would give them input but not go near the idea they should be on the review committee. That's an absolute no. Maybe better to stonewall altogether but I see blackmail here that she's threatening to stir them up if we don't do what she wants. We should definitely not go there. Beth"
>
> So, should Native Americans be represented on a review committee affecting their ancestral remains and sacred objects? "An absolute no." What is the "worst case scenario"? Ask Walker and Bettinger to conduct some random "interviews" by phone. But watch out! The uppity blackmailer might "stir up" the Indians (sounds like a bad Western). "Maybe better to stonewall altogether." Price decided to stonewall.[34]

This is a message in excess. Fredericks was not meant to read it and certainly not supposed to send it along the channels of communication (just as I was never intended to show it to you). It is revealing through bungling because it concerns an issue of ongoing settler colonial politics. Here is a clear issue of representation. Again, the makeup of the committee created to assess and make recommendations regarding the role and location of the research unit—whether it should be under the management of the museum, who would distribute the funds allocated to it as they saw fit, or housed outside of the museum at the Center for Race and Gender, as Fredericks advocated—is seemingly a minor issue. The committee, as Fredericks notes in her message, was made up of two white anthropologists. This committee and the UCB and UCOP committees that ultimately decide the fate of the remains and cultural items housed by the museum were at the time, according to her, top-heavy with anthropologists and archaeologists. They didn't include any linguists, historians, or oral history specialists who might have countered the hegemonic process of a scientific identification of the bones. As Barker notes, "In each case, the aim has been to exclude the unrecognized and dismiss the veracity of native oral history and experts as politically biased, invented, and uncorroborated."[35]

A question arises, though, as to the effect of including oral tradition in the series of forms of evidence. If the issue remains one of a preponderance of evidence, a quantitative and legal western metric for determining truth, how much has the process really been affected by Native epistemology? Can a story be merely evidence in this sense, or would its inclusion require an overhaul of the entire structure of verification and the relationship between speaking and that of which is spoken? How does one work with story? Salish poet and theorist Lee Maracle has asserted the need for a form of research that would not simply be applied to Native stories or take Native stories as evidence or means of another kind of truth but would rather itself take on the form of story as research. For her, this is a Salish as well as a First Nations perspective, in which "the light must be bent in a direction that is not obvious, that is in the shadow. In shadow land we experience the discomfort of the unknown. Healers are present to ensure that this discomfort is processed and pushed past, and that we don't make fear-based, discomfort-based decisions about the unknown."[36] This is a practice of training the ear, even when the visual is sought; it is a matter of understanding the visual as that which is conditioned by the avisual and the concomitant heightening of sound. "In its possession of force, it may draw us to look again, to re-search, to play, to fiction ourselves in dreams of transformation or to escape the very force of looking."[37] At the same time, it is respect for both opacity and that which does not get said, in such a way that one does not want immediately to make silence speak or bring what is in the shadows into the full light of day. Even more strongly, it is the night present at midday: "We are listening—our imaginations fully engaged—to what is said, what is not said, and what is connected to what is not said."[38] The known, then, is always conditioned by the unknown, and this demands that we treat the unknown as an authority with all the enigma that this implies.

The absence of stories within the museum is certainly a subjugating of knowledges and of representations, allocating the bones solely as sources of information. In scientific representations, bones are things to be studied, found, sought out, for the sake of a rational knowing that has its roots in the Enlightenment's distinction between Man (the subject of politics) and Nature (the object of science), a split that organizes what are considered appropriately political subjects as well as the material conditions of knowledge and social reproduction. Fredericks's message seeks a re-membering of this divide by politicizing the processes of identification in the form of recognition. She imagines a unified Native political body, on behalf of those for whom she works, the tribes (an employment relationship that led to the label *dysfunctional*), and there is the not-so-spatially-distant past that seeks to speak through her about the colonial silences of identification, the fragments calling for a return to an imagined wholeness. But we must go further. Just adding Native ways of knowing is not enough. To accumulate a list in a preponderance of evidence is antithetical to a storied form of research. To follow Maracle along this detouring path, "We need to draw upon the tangled web of colonial being, thread by thread—watch as each thread unfurls, untangles, shows its soft underbelly, its vulnerability, its strength, its resilience, its defiance, its imposition, its stubbornness."[39] It's stubbornness. Including the stubbornness of silence.

Native Silences

Calling the Bones: the performance of the side that is hiding, the language of the body, past experiences, a lifetime of developing intuitions, as well as hidden or secret deformed charms all help in calling the pattern of the bones. One does not just look, one experiences, listens for the call of the bones, which speak through the hiding, a different type of seeing.

"Native silences highlight the unsaid and the unspeakable,"[40] notes Marianne Constable in her book *Just Silences*, where she further establishes the connection between positivistic research and positive law by describing contemporary law as being based on sociological and empirical information. In this sense it is only knowable sociologically, an epistemology that privileges efficacious power or control. The most apparent form of control would be discourses that correspond to a sociological worldview.[41] The affinity between the research agenda of the scientists and the management policies of the museum—an affinity based on technique—is supported by and supports in turn this notion of law. The alliance of these three levels of discourse—(1) scientific description and method, (2) institutional management of representation, and (3) legal recognition as control—further complicates the narrative that Fredericks recounts.

Constable specifically addresses NAGPRA and the Native American Languages Act (NALA, also passed in 1990) as two moments in legal jurisdiction that exemplify the "sociologically discursive and rule-like character of law." She states, "language and religion, speech and the sacred, become objects of well-intentioned social studies that articulate the conditions for preserving culture."[42] The mass interpellation of the collection in the museum as "culturally unidentifiable," then, is based entirely on a sociologically created notion of legal recognition, one that makes possible aporias such as the created category *culturally unidentifiable,* aporias that become the conditions for further control through their correction. Constable focuses on language preservation and cultural definition of artifacts and remains to show the manner in which the Indigenous subject is encoded in current politico-legal discourse. As a counteraction, she highlights the silences of Native peoples as pointing to a different type of subject and, therefore, a different type of law and voice. She writes, "In the silences that US law does not hear, there lie possibilities of law—as of language and of religion and of justice—that positivist jurisprudence and sociological society do not acknowledge and whose truths they cannot accept."[43] This sociological grounding of Native legal claims manifests in the discourse that subtends the NAGPRA research unit dispute in the form of evidence that is used on both sides. To make claims for the absence of ethnographic and linguistic evidence is to accept the basic ground, what she calls "the pervasive privileging at law of the kind of discourse that corresponds to a sociological worldview . . . In the transformation of the first person, who may not have spoken, into a third person about whom facts are known, and then into a presumed second-person 'you' who will have been presumed to be addressed as such, lies the legal positivist and social scientific misrecognition of other ways."[44] Here the complex process of providing evidence, within the frameworks and intersections of legal positivism and social/biological science, as Constable shows, by grammatically normalizing subject positions through subjection to the law, makes the terrain incredibly difficult to navigate, but it also makes the emergence of voice outside of such a grammar, in the form of difference, all that more powerful. As the mediator between the tribes and the museum (collections, researchers, archivists, administrators), the research unit, in its *dysfunctional* approach, revealed the ambivalence of such a position.

Constable writes, "Whether law is God-made or man-made, text or behavior or something else or both, law tells—gestures (to), indicates, shows, reveals, states, describes, threatens, or commands—its addressee or subject what must be done."[45] Recalling Barker's discussion of the role of experts in creating Native American policy, the sociological grounding of law means that law takes on social science discourse as its own (mirroring the inverse when a scholarly discourse takes on legal discourse as its own, such as in the historiography of genocide, which I discuss in chapter 3) and thereby becomes indistinguishable from social policy. It is a social policy grounded in a social scientific episteme, which only recognizes speech and actions identifiable according to its terms. This is a clear, performative force of humanization through social control and delimitation, developing the technical concepts and tools that allow the settler human (writ large) to master and mold the world to *his* own ends. "In starkest terms, is law other than a tool of social self-constitution, a social policy produced by social knowledges that gauge the social options in, and social preferences of, a society governed by social policy? What else could law be?"[46]

And what is the social policy of the museum, the university, the state, the country? In all cases, it is settler colonization and imperialism at ground and to the core. All laws and policies serve to reproduce this colonial and imperial social order, whether through force, reform, inclusion, exclusion, representation, or erasure. In the context of another settler state and its attempts to redress colonial violence, Dian Million, in her book *Therapeutic Nations*, describes the shift in Canada from hard power, directed at Indigenous communities in the forms of assimilation and direct social control and governance, to softer forms of control through therapeutic "human development"-oriented economic and social policies and the neoliberal reorganization of "self-government." The hinge for this shift, according to Million, is the codification of human rights in international law: "The creation of a legal framework for human rights also begat an 'advocacy revolution' that in turn recognized humanitarian 'victims' and those who would 'represent victims.'"[47] For Million, this legal turn constitutes an ambiguity such that a human rights framework acts as either or both an oppositional framework for contesting the forces and world devastation caused by global capitalism and/or a convenient cover for the extension of these same powers through a more subtle form of hegemonic, imperial control. It is, in Million's terms, "a field of hegemonic maneuver and its accompanying and constitutive violence and counterstruggles to obtain relief and justice for losers" that also marks the space of a humanitarian struggle over life and death.[48]

This struggle leads to uneven implementation of this policy of humanization. Humanitarianism also often acts as the justification for immense violence in a logic that Samera Esmeir describes as the "violence of non-violence," which calls on humanitarian powers to decimate peoples and polities for the sake of global "security," national and international "self-defense," "liberation," and the forced implementation of western-style "republican democracy." When, for instance, Israel, in its continuing settler colonial and genocidal assault on Palestine and the lives and worlds of Palestinians, not only ignores human rights—or at best seeks the threshold beneath which an act would be considered a "war crime," definitions that it actively seeks to manipulate—but also has its genocidal actions upheld as *war* or *self-defense* against an occupied people for its "self-protection" and is therefore operating within the human rights framework, we must understand what we are relying on when we call something "a human rights issue." The use of crises in many humanitarian interventions depoliticizes and naturalizes violence through the misnomer "war" or even "reprisal." Such mechanisms are extensions of and intimately and materially entangled with settler colonial policies toward Indigenous peoples who since the 1970s, and more recently with the passage in 2007 of UNDRIP, call upon this humanitarian regime for our rights.

This rights dilemma impacts the conditions for speaking and the registers in which speech is heard, especially as regards the shifting relations to international law and between domestic law and the international. These relations constitute a complex and often contradictory weave of the techne of rights. Million highlights how the need to appeal to the international human rights regime gives shape to contemporary power dynamics and hierarchies. "As Indigenous peoples, we are now called on to use instruments of truth-telling: international forums, reconciliation, and reparations as part of a formal trauma ethos as it gives shape to relations between the weak and the strong in our age."[49] In settler colonial contexts, the nationalist project of reconciliation and the demand to speak one's trauma toward this end often become the driving force of the implementation of rights. As an example, Million notes that "funds attached to residential school healing were provisional to the communities while their 'trauma' was relegated to a site for the national reconciliation of the nation."[50] Settler interventions and the bestowal of rights amount to a "politics" that is in some ways returned to communities but devoid of social and political content and form. Emptied of sociality by neoliberal state and international corporate interests, "politics" returns "in the form of individual morality, organizational responsibility, and ethical community."[51] The frameworks for recognizable speech are thereby determined by these narrow categories and according to neoliberal conceptions of the wholistic individual.

This erasure of Indigenous voice and relation is in part because both the United Nations and settler states generally recognize no other polities than anthropocentric ones. Consequently, Indigenous political and social worlds eradicated by violence are further destroyed through the means of redress and the demand to speak and be recognized as narrowly political in the western neoliberal sense, both at the national level and internationally. Making determinations about what constitutes "human development," healing, and life itself, settler management of Indigenous peoples is a vast biopolitical, humanizing, and vitalizing project that is, in the end, without a politics in any real sense, without any acknowledgment of what Joanne Barker calls "a polity of the Indigenous," the plural and "unique governance, territory, and culture of Indigenous peoples" in "related systems of (non)-human relationships and responsibilities."[52] The neoliberal and imperial form, both national and international, Barker and Million contest with an Indigenous framework that depoliticizes by destroying Indigenous polities, replacing them with a brute mode of exploitation and the illusion of a humanist "politics." It puts to use Indigenous claims for attending to past atrocities, acknowledging self-determination, healing from intergenerational trauma, and returning our ancestors, toward the renewal of settler domination and the continuing destruction of Indigenous political and social worlds in the figure of a becoming-human. "While we may celebrate the long, hard work that is represented in this landmark declaration [UNDRIP], the site wherein Indigenous peoples officially become subjects of 'human rights' must also be seen as a volatile place in a volatile time."[53]

At the same time, international human rights has the potential to open the space of a fourth world outside capitalist and socialist economic development, indicating other inhuman forces than developmental ones. In the context of repatriation politics, like the Kennewick Man controversy, what seems like the end result—the return of our ancestors as a form of reconciliation—is only the beginning of a deeper anticolonial, world-making process. In the pause of uncertainty, the question gets asked: what home do our ancestors come back to? (This is a question for both repatriation as well as the Ghost Dance and implicates and moves us differently.) This moment of stasis creates other ways of thinking and doing, as "to enact any actually practiced Indigenous self-determination threatens any nation-state's imagined homogeneous territorial sovereignty" and mode and imaginary of worlding—as it should.[54]

In large part, for both Constable and Million, it is the injunction to speak before the law that actually harms the unspeakable or the unspoken, as it cannot be heard. Some silences have yet to be said, and some silences are not unsaid. What kind of law can be inaccessible to articulations of policies grounded in empirical evidence, one that could hear silence as something other than what has yet to be said, that isn't an injunction to speak and to speak in narrowly recognizable ways? Can a silence speak without becoming recognizable speech and yet still be effective?

Ancestor: Voice of the Inhuman

In the first half of this chapter, I considered the relation between NAGPRA, cultural identification, and voice. This relation revolved around the enunciative position of a NAGPRA research unit on the UC Berkeley campus and the role of Indigenous storying practices as evidence. In this section, I turn to a proposal made by Gerald Vizenor to create a bone court that would hear the testimony of the bones themselves. Made before the enactment of NAGPRA, this proposal requires us to adjust our understandings of what constitutes a voice, our relation to the dead, and what effect NAGPRA has had on these two sites. Before addressing Vizenor's proposal, I turn to the current situation of NAGPRA and CalNAGPRA.

Two California Indian scholars, Brittani Orona and Vanessa Esquivido, detail extensively the current situation of NAGPRA in California in their article "Continued Disembodiment." In it, they analyze the series of loopholes that continue to trouble NAGPRA's implementation: culturally unidentifiable human remains; NAGPRA's narrow application to only institutions that receive state and federal funding, which excludes, of course, institutions in other countries that hold Native remains and ceremonial items as well as private collections, both individual and institutional; tribal recognition continuing to be the primary mode for repatriation; the "issue of funding, time, and organization on both Tribal and [nontribal] institutions to figure out logistics"; and, profoundly, the settler logic that requires tribes to seek recognition from these institutions and governments to have ancestors and ceremonial items returned that often were "collected through dubious circumstances and genocidal acts of violence."[55] One could add to this list the lack of land bases for many California Indian communities. Defining CalNAGPRA as "an Indigenous human rights law with little to no funding behind it,"[56] they attend to some of the recent attempts to address these issues and their uneven implementation, especially among the UC campuses. In line with my argument thus far about the catch-22 of speaking through the law, they ultimately conclude, "Rather than looking to laws and regulations to define Indigenous people's human rights in California and beyond, it is fundamentally important for California Indian people to assert their inherent sovereignty and self-determination."[57] Such sovereignty is against, in their view, the ongoing forms of white possession, defined by Aileen Moreton-Robinson "as a regime of power that derives from the illegal act of possession" and that produces "a generative sense of belonging and ownership [through] a possessive logic action."[58]

They also address similar difficulties with UNDRIP, which remains unenforceable and definitionally vague, and, resonating with Million's critique of international law, requires state mediation for the enforcement of a human right, relying on the same state mechanisms that created the situation to begin with. Following Hupa scholar Jack Norton, they turn to another international human rights law as another path forward: the United Nations Convention on the Prevention and Punishment of the Crime of Genocide (see chapter 3).[59] This relation between repatriation and genocide not only takes international legal form but also operates through communal and collective discourses, artistic practices, and literary tropes. It is an ambiguous connection. They ask, "can international law such as UNDRIP and the Genocide [Convention] be used to successfully return ancestors, sacred objects, unassociated/associated funerary objects, and objects of cultural patrimony?"—a deeply practical question.[60]

That NAGPRA fails is no surprise. As Indigenous people, the question we need to ask is: What is to be done with this failure, with and perhaps through it? What is to be undone? This question opens up the space of the inhuman. Pheng Cheah, in his book *Inhuman Conditions*, defines the inhuman as the "finite limit of man," a defective feature that the western liberal human, in its search for transcendence and freedom from the constraints of unfreedom—in this humanist taxonomy, therefore, from "nature"—fails to control.[61] The inhuman is what is "improper" to the human and yet supposedly reducible to it as what must be overcome for the sake of freedom. What I want to hold onto from this definition is this space of failure as an opening, one that stubbornly holds back the forces of humanization and universalization. The human, in this framework, is defined by the drama/dialectic of control and loss of control. The inhuman—when not subsumed within this drama, when taken as a detour without departure and without arrival, in the dialectic's suspension—opens another pathway.

It is this other orientation that makes possible the connection of osteology to genocide, when taken outside the terms of the human, as part of the rupture of the colonial archive, the archival powers of archaeology and genocide historiography to classify, collect, document via liberal forms of governance over Indigeneity. The connection couldn't be more material as the physical evidence of genocide, as noted by most genocide scholars and historians, is largely absent in California (with certain exceptions such as mission and boarding school cemeteries, as discussed earlier). The time frame of waiting nearly one hundred seventy years for the "official" recognition of this history; the repression of all forms of representation of California Indian people in the midst of genocide, including outlawing legal testimony against white people; the suppression of ceremony and forms of mourning; and the general erasure of Indigenous presence have created a vast abyss of material absence that the collections of our ancestors in institutions have come to fill through metonymy. When our ancestors danced for the return of the dead, they maybe didn't realize the form in which the dead would return and how long it would take.

Voice is a mediated structure, and to enact it in the context of the dead, one must read across these various repositories, histories, and modes of knowing and do so with equally cross-contaminated tools. To follow the term *ancestor* into this space of the inhuman, that which lies outside the forces of control, is to unsettle discretely bounded things, methods, times, and places. It is to engage what Lisa Lowe calls "intimacies" across otherwise siloed archival formations.[62] In this case, the siloing is done by Constable's notion of technique and the sociological grounding of law as what pre-comprehends humanity as the bearer of dignity, freedom, sociability, culture, and political life, an ideal project that must be actualized through processes of humanization. The inhuman path of the ancestor is also the turn to human rights as what places limits on the sovereign violence of nation-states, "seen as particularistic, oppressive, and even totalitarian," placing two different forms of the inhuman in conflict.[63] In each case, the inhuman remains in its various, troubling, uncontrollable forms: the "savage" that is being eradicated and humanized as "Native"; the field of techne and instrumentality; the realms of affect and emotion, opposed to reason; the inappropriate relations (sexual and otherwise) with kin of all sorts, including "inanimate" kin; and, of course, the dead.

Million's conception of the fourth world, as a movement beyond the global limits of capitalist and socialist (both humanist) social and political organizations, attends to nonanthropocentric modes of governance and calls us to reimagine what an inhuman form of anticolonial politics might be. It calls us to a different politics or perhaps toward a return of politics itself outside of the depoliticizing forces of the western humanist project. And it does so by operating within the interval of these two different registers and their respective forms of the inhuman, what in other words can be understood to be an Indigenous form of self-determination attentive to more than human socialities. To begin to sketch what such an imaginary might look like, in relation to the voices of our ancestors, I turn now to Gerald Vizenor's proposal to create a bone court to hear their testimonies.

The Proposal

While a professor at the University of California Berkeley, Gerald Vizenor developed a proposal to create a federal bone court that would hear the testimonies of Native bones. Vizenor initially delivered the proposal in 1986 as a resident scholar at the School of American Research (SAR, now the School for Advanced Research) in Santa Fe, New Mexico. The paper was later published in his book *Crossbloods* (dated 1989, though the publication date is January 1, 1990). Of the reaction to the proposal, Vizenor writes, "The response from other resident scholars, archaeologists and anthropologists, was tolerant; the idea invited some humor as critical abatement, but a discourse never matured at the seminars."[64] I'd like to now take up this discourse as, in the wake of NAGPRA's successes and failures and particularly the failure of human rights as a promise deferred, it has likely had time to mature.

That Vizenor delivered his proposal to a room full of archaeologists and anthropologists, working on such projects as "The Human Ecology of an Amazon People," "Interzonal Agrarian Economics and the Development of Complex Society in South Central Andes," and "Ecology of Social Evolution: Woodland Systems in the Prehistoric Midwest," indicates the trickiness of it. Meant to be a disruption of or intervention into not only the discourse of that year's resident scholars and their advanced seminars but also the ongoing project of the SAR, it seeks both to (re)politicize the neutral scientific discourses dominating the discussion but also to fail from the start.[65] Significantly, the proposal delivered in this context also makes visible the condition of *being the Indian in the room*, a well-known dilemma for many Native scholars and artists, especially resident ones including throughout the history of SAR; this being a question of minor discourse or what Vizenor calls "shadow survivance," more than of "representation."[66] Through such "shadow" visibility, Vizenor invokes the voices of ancestors absent from the discussion without directly speaking for them, ventriloquizing, or acting as a medium.

Founded in 1907 as a center for archaeological research in the Americas, SAR's institutional history tracks with the humanizing projects of anthropology and archaeology's collaborative, if distinct and uneven, recuperative, self-reflexive critical reformations (see chapter 2). About the impetus for its founding, SAR's website notes, "The unveiling of the treasures of Troy, Ephesus, and the Valley of the Kings held the world spellbound. But as the United States expanded westward, a new science sprang up in the native soils of the New World. Explorers, cowboys, missionaries, settlers, and entrepreneurs became fascinated with the remains of early Indian civilizations in the American West."[67] Expanding from a strictly archaeological venture, in 1967 SAR began to include anthropology and southwest Native art in its research agenda. Since then, each year the institution has hosted a resident Native scholar, through the Katrin H. Loman fellowship, and sponsored collaborative work with Native artists. Echoing Benjamin Silliman's call for the inclusion of the humanities in the UC system, this deployment of the arts as a critical humanizing apparatus to reform a colonial, technical science needs greater investigation, but it generally falls within what David Lloyd describes as the anthropologizing regime of aesthetic philosophy through mechanisms of representation: "In the late Enlightenment, a discourse on aesthetic experience emerged that finishes a decisive account of the conditions of possibility for universal human subjecthood."[68] It is an aestheticizing and humanizing apparatus captured in SAR's current mission statement: "SAR advances understanding of humanity through a unique alchemy of creative practice and scholarly research in Native American arts, anthropology, and related disciplines."[69]

Vizenor's proposal, on the other hand, plays literary and legal theories off each other in an inhumanist manner, in what he calls "a postmodern language game with theories on narration and legal philosophies to direct the discourse."[70] In this game, "narrative theories augment the proposition that bones have the right to be represented and heard in court; moreover, tribal bones would become their own narrators and confront their oppressors in a language game, in a legal forum—the proper person, mode, and perspective in narrative mediation."[71] The proposal itself is simple enough. Congress has the power to create federal courts with its plenary jurisdiction. Congress should use that power to create a federal bone court to hear cases in which "sovereign tribal bones" would "be their own narrators." According to Vizenor, "this new forum would have federal judicial power to hear and decide disputes over burial sites, research on bones, reburial, and to protect the rights of tribal bones to be represented in court."[72] For him, this is an appropriate path forward as federal judicial power has jurisdiction particularly in cases that arise under constitutional definitions, "such as human and civil rights, treaties, and tribal sovereignties."[73]

The rest of the proposal lays out the justifications and conditions for the speculative bone court: narratology to attend to voice and how to hear it; racial science as condition for the current situation in which "white bones are reburied, tribal bones are studied in racist institutions"; a robust conception of legal standing that pushes the limits of the concept of legal personhood; an interpretive theory of law and rights that creates cracks in and flexible understandings of settler law; and "an agonistic discourse on *anthropos* or humans and their real narrative remains" or a theory of discursive power that intervenes in knowledge production and evidence as presented in a forum with the power to make move.[74] Such an approach moves outside of colonial divisions between literary analysis, the performativity of legal edicts, and the constative statements of scientific discourse via a rhetorical reassemblage of voice outside the terms of humanist agency, interiority, and individualism and without a recuperative impulse as often found in institutionalized forms of *interdisciplinarity*. This eccentric movement, through rearrangement/derangement of the discourses, prepares a forum for the bones to finally speak.

Vizenor made a career poking fun at the humorless seriousness of academia and, particularly, scientists. In this sense, he continues in the grand tradition of Native communities who tease if not outright mock anthropologists. Vine Deloria's satirical and scathing sketch in his chapter "Anthropologists and Other Friends," from his seminal work of Native studies, *Custer Died for Your Sins*, perhaps most famously represents this tradition: "Into each life, it is said, some rain must fall. Some people have bad horoscopes, others take tips on the stock market. McNamara created the TFX and the Edsel. Churches possess the real world. But Indians have been cursed above all other people in history. Indians have anthropologists."[75] Vizenor adds his own contribution to this communal genre in his book *Earthdivers*, in discussing anthropologists' overly analytical, self-replicating, and proliferating interpretations of fecal and anal themes in Native American creation stories. "Some anthropologists seem to have little appreciation for sacred games in tribal creations. Their secular seriousness separates the tribes from humor, from untimed metaphors, and the academic intensities of career bound anthropologists approach diarrhetic levels of terminal theoretical creeds. The creation myth that anthropologists never seem to tell is the one where *naanabozho*, the cultural trickster, made the first anthropologist from fecal matter. Once made, more were cloned in graduate schools from the first fecal creation of the anthropologist."[76] But, as with Deloria, Vizenor's humor is deadly serious, if not downright dangerous (in the best/worst sense, that is, with best/worst intentions). Despite a cultivated uncertainty about the authenticity and effectiveness of his proposal, Vizenor seems to put at risk the discursive and juridical edifice of settler law, its fictitious plenary power and self-justification, through the law's reliance upon racialist science and civilizationist logics. In other words, Vizenor teases out and risks the western liberal humanist subject because the power held by the settler state and its institutions and actors to define our ancestors, to possess their bones while we remain an occupied people, to control the narrative of the past, is the assertion of the modern liberal human and its universalization as European Man, supported by the differentiation of race, culture, and temporal designation.

The racist possession and study of ancestors was an attempt both to control the narrative of history and thereby to claim possession over the land, as well as to control death itself, a settler colonial vitalist project in the form of a vacillating necro- and biopolitics, manifested in the scene of Weiss's handling of an ancestor's skull as a grisly trophy. The shift from amateur collecting practices (described earlier and coincident with the traffic in body parts that were simultaneously a gory market of colonial trophy hunting and part of a bounty system based on body parts tied to colonial extermination projects) to the "professional" and "scientific" knowledge production predicated on the transport of Indigenous body parts from murdered people to institutions for research makes clear the metonymic function of ancestors' remains for the settler colonial state. The stories of militias and U.S. cavalry members wearing the body parts of Indigenous people and of skulls displayed on the desks of prominent politicians represent the "victory" over "savages." The literal beheading of Kintpuash figured a political and cultural triumph; that his stripped skull was shipped to the Smithsonian—later repatriated—made his death scientific. For Indigenous peoples, this practice of collection and research subverted two relations to death for us: one the destruction, as it has come to be called in California (which I discuss in chapter 3), and the other our relationships to our ancestors.

An ancestor, by definition, is someone who has died. An ancestral relation invites death into the conversation. The many ways we have to control this relation to death (genealogy, identity, legal personhood, biological conceptions of life, assertions of agency, a meaningful existence, religion, spirituality, reason, finitude, and being human), to make it safe for our consumption, are here swept away. Letting go of the attempt to control death, Vizenor's proposal and its intended failure invites an intimacy with death and refuses a closed and bounded and therefore meaningful existence separated and/or protected from contamination with death. Vizenor's bone game isn't a willful refusal of the future à la Lee Edelman's *No Future*, which is merely another assertion of control.[77]

Rather, it is a cultivation of the indeterminacy between refusal of and failure to participate in western colonial temporal organization, to embrace this "lack of time," including the sense that we are *out of time*, and to find in this expression an impatience that opens onto a more radical patience. *Bring them home now! To what home do they return?* Such is the void opened onto ancestral time. Yes, the proposal is a tease but one with a dark turn, more sardonic than satirical. Following the ancestral relation outside the narrow frameworks of religion, spirituality, and political identity is an empty pragmatics that challenges "justice" as a type of "truth" (Rawls). It is, rather, an embrace of indeterminacy, of the bones (do they speak? do ancestors? do I?), not as a choice but as an inhuman impossibility that sweeps us outside the political, legal, and other frameworks of the western human. To propose a forum for the bones to speak is to desire death, to be in relation to death, the absolute inhuman, to desire the return of the ancestors by losing the will to die, to give in to continuing to live (by continuing to live), to continue with contempt for the false choices laid out before us. To continue with and because of contempt. It is intimacy with and intimacies created by the dead. Repatriation, rather than a closure to an episode or an end in itself, is an opening onto the interminability of death.

Vizenor's proposal, paving a path of return by way of bones speaking, is a disorientation of colonial relations. It places within the system of rights an ambiguous figure that puts pressure on weak and inflection points. By insisting that "human rights continue after death," Vizenor extends the form of the human as constituted before the law into the realm of death itself, daring the colonizer to ask *how far does it go?* "Human" remains that were not "human" in the sense we know when they died: do they become human through reburial, disposition, categorization? Are they ancestors? Bones? Remains? Fragments? Absences? Presences? Whole in their partiality? Which speaks? What kind of voice? Singular, plural, or something besides? Such an extension rebounds and draws the entire system of rights into this disorienting realm of indeterminate death, taking it on an infinite detour through thoroughly scrambled concepts and language that threaten the very foundations of settler possession. "Tribal bones are sovereign, a moral measure of properties, and an agonistic continuation of Native rights in a postmodern language game."[78] Vizenor plays with their categories, asserting that bones are in a "natural disposition," in "communion with the earth," and are to remain undisturbed in their slumber, a suspension both of their use for settler scientific and nationalist narratives and of our demands on them to be part of a political cause that often draws on humanist settler categories and underpinnings. They "cannot be taken for public use without legal consideration and compensation."[79] Bones have the same standing as "corporate bodies, ships at sea, church, state, and municipalities."[80] They are not "salvage," as in a wrecked ship or "treasure hunting." Stirrings of the abolition of property, these uses of *public* and *standing* anticipate Coulthard's critique of recognition and Nichols's analysis of the production of property, drawing the political and legal terminology of the settler state into the deep waters of ancestral time and letting it drown.

The Forum

Eyal Weizman, in the context of war crime investigations into Israel's genocidal actions in Gaza, writes, "The primacy accorded to the witness and to the subjective and linguistic dimension of testimony, trauma, and memory—a primacy that has had such an enormous cultural, aesthetic, and political influence that it has reframed the end of the twentieth century as 'the era of the witness,' is gradually being supplemented (not to say bypassed) by an emergent forensic sensibility, an object-oriented juridical culture immersed in matter and materialities, in code and form, and in the presentation of scientific investigations by experts."[81] The forensic, for Weizman, is threefold. It references the use of scientific methods and techniques in criminal investigations, the courtroom or forum as site of speech, and the rhetorical conditions of speech itself. Hearkening back in some ways to Constable's notion of technique, the forensic also disrupts technique by opening the door to in- and nonhuman matter and materialities as well as their mediated voices. Moving outside (or supplementing, perhaps prosthetically) the humanist episteme of the witness (testimony, trauma, and memory), Weizman goes forward and backward in time in order to understand the rhetorical assemblage of this seemingly new conception of the forum. Noting that the rhetorical concept of prosopopoeia, a mode of speaking on behalf of inanimate objects, has its roots in ancient Greek and Roman law, Weizman details the conditions of the scientific expert in the courtroom as akin to being a translator, interpreter, or perhaps an organizer of a set of technologies that mediate between the thing and the forum. Together these make up an assemblage that is "an entangled rhetorical technology."[82]

Going further, Weizman describes "a class of Athenian judges [who] presided over a special court in charge of cases brought against unknown agents and inanimate objects."[83] He mentions a case brought before this court regarding "a curious incident in which a statue of Theagenes made after the athlete's death was beaten by one of his rivals by way of revenge, until the statue fell and killed him. The statue was put on trial for murder, judged guilty, and thrown into the sea, only to be reinstated years later."[84] (Perhaps Weiss should have sued the ancestor/skull instead of the university! In a bone court, she could—and the ancestor could have their say about being handled.) The focus of Weizman's account of the forum is on the "political plastic" of the built environment in relation to social forces; the entangled performances of an ensemble of materialities, including states and some humans; and the forum that emerges from these conditions. The role of prosopopoeia is both to "evoke the dead" or give "voice to things to which nature has not given a voice," as the rhetorician Quintillian notes, but also to push voice outside of the human through its entanglements in the multiple materialities and positionalities of the forum.[85] Indeed, nonhuman objects, in Weizman's account, could not only be represented in court but could be themselves judged and condemned just as (one would assume) they could themselves judge and condemn. The question of the role of the human voice as the locus of representation in this account, though, still remains up in the air.

As with much new materialist discourse, Weizman's account of the forum seems to put a too-positive spin on the distributed networks of agency, reason, and vitality in its move away from the "era of the witness." The focus on the witness, with its emphasis on what Jean-François Lyotard calls the "differend"—an injustice that arises because the discourse in which the wrong might be expressed does not exist—considers the differential power structures of voice in a way that Weizman de-emphasizes, though not fully glosses over. Constable's discussion of the sociological ground of law falls squarely within the concept of the differend and her turn to silence as what is both harmed by the biopolitical demand to speak—speak or be spoken for, speak to the recording machine of society and the law or be counted as acquiescent, present in such a way that is understandable, or be silenced through the performative command of the law itself—opens other ways of thinking about what a nonperformative law might be, a law without violence that is attentive to hearing and seeing otherwise. Vizenor's proposal splits the difference between Constable's latent humanism and Weizman's posthumanism with attention to the voice of the inhuman.

Voice of the Inhuman

For Vizenor, the forum is a theater in which, he argues, legal pragmatists would act "as if" tribal bones had rights to their own narratives.[86] It is akin to living "as if" the dead are returning, living in the dizziness that disorients the certainties of colonial reality: a minor but rigorous way of being. Such a claim haunts the performative force of law with a certain inaction or emptying, a gestural quality. Repatriation, the return of our ancestors, cannot be a *legal action*—with all the meaning and recuperative energy this entails, humanizing us and them via the western legal tradition—but must be a different kind of movement altogether: illegal or, better yet, a-legal or lawless. What is emptied is the museum (as meaning-making machine), the discourse of capture, and the force of the law.

Beth Piatote, who wrote her play *Antíkoni* while also a professor at UC Berkeley, has captured this "criminal" aspect of the destruction of the law with her adaptation of Sophocles's *Antigone*. Her Antíkoni proclaims:

> I will commit this sacred crime, for I am true
> To the Order of the world, the eternal laws, set in motion
> Long before this time now, this time that will someday end.[87]

Piatote restages the confrontation between Antigone and her uncle and head of state Creon over the burial of Antigone's brother, Polyneices, whom Creon left unburied on the battlefield and forbid to mourn as punishment for leading an uprising. Piatote rewrites the confrontation as between a Nez Perce–Cayuse woman, Antíkoni, and her uncle, Kreon, the director of a museum, over Kreon's refusal to return the remains of two Native brothers who died in battle, one siding with the U.S. military and the other with Native insurgents. Antíkoni ultimately steals the remains to repatriate them but is captured. Both Antigone and Antíkoni end up alone or keeping company with the dead, suspended between life and death, one entombed in a grave, the other in a projected image.

> **CHORUS** Oh, Antíkoni, Poor Little One,
> We see you in your tomb, suspended
> Between the living and the dead.

ANTÍKONI And here I shall remain, along with the dead
My life as theirs suspended, just as that of my kin

Who find no comfort in grief, whose grief can never begin

And thus will never end.
In this world in-between, my voice and visage live on
To those not-yet-human what human laws may do

to interrupt time, to stop the Earth
From turning and turning around itself, how such laws disturb

The Order of the world.[88]

Sophocles's *Antigone* has come to be representative of the interdiction on mourning for those subjected to state violence and cast as subhuman as well as the possibility of another order of law that would allow such mourning to occur, a dilemma that hinges on the figure of the human. The play is oft-cited and analyzed within the discourse of the witness, the politics of mourning, and in the context of the differend. It is also often referenced in discussions about the differences between positive and natural law, between human and divine law. Piatote's play addresses the interdiction on mourning through the museum collection, once again connecting settler colonial genocidal actions with the scientific practices of archaeologists and the institution of the museum. The suspension between life and death that holds Antíkoni connects her directly to the status of our ancestors who lie between scientific object and ancestor, "Who find no comfort in grief, whose grief can never begin/And thus will never end."[89] This suspension goes to the heart of the dilemma, the double bind in which Indigenous peoples are positioned as prior to the existence of settler claims in settler narratives and legal recognition only for the sake of relinquishing our own claims and remaining in a state of suspension and nonthreatening half-life, to found perpetually and symbolically the state through obsolescence and assure its continuation. Antíkoni's actions invoke this dilemma by challenging the state directly and, according to Kreon, thereby threatening tribal survival, and yet tribal persistence for Kreon requires reconciliation with the state, which is another kind of death. Such is the destruction.

The ambiguity of the play's ending raises the question of the human from the different perspectives of the characters, Antíkoni, the activist, anarchist, and insurrectionist; Ismene (her sister), the traditionalist; Haimon (Antíkoni's betrothed), the collectivist; Kreon, the tribal leader, nationalist, sovereigntist, and upholder of settler law, to preserve tribal nations; and the Chorus of Aunties, elders, and guides, as they all face the screen that holds Antíkoni and speak.

ANTÍKONI Oh, to confound Justice with Laws!
What is denied the Dead is denied the Living ten times again.
We remain captives with them.

ISMENE Elder Brother set the Earth in motion, turning it to the right
We must care for the body this way
From time immemorial, for eternal time.

HAIMON You remain an Indian.
And an Indian is no one without his Tribe.

KREON This is how we've survived,
and how we've undermined
The United States of Surveillance.

CHORUS The humans are coming soon
Already they are coming this way.[90]

What does it mean that "the humans are coming"? Is this a process of humanization through a fuller reflection of Indigenous community? One that combats reductive or stereotypical representations? Or a deferral of humanity through the mechanism of prophecy? What kind of prophecy do the Aunties offer here? And how do we understand it in relation to Antíkoni's seeming sacrifice? Noting the Chorus's collective voicing of prophecy's resonance with the Ghost Dance: Are the dead the humans? When will they arrive? Will they?

Piatote's adaptation and Vizenor's proposal can both be understood through Vizenor's use of the grammatical construction fourth person. Fourth person generally refers to indefinite or generic referents, such as the *one* in "one would like to think" or the *many* in "many have tried." But Vizenor expands this notion to include hearsay in a court of law. Describing a scene from the transcription of a court case addressing the rights of the "Chippewa or Ojibwe" to regulate the manoomin (wild rice) harvest on the Rice Lake National Wild Refuge in Minnesota against the federal agents who had assumed authority, Vizenor focuses on the testimony of Charles Aubid (a.k.a. Zay Zah). Aubid, who was eighty-six years old at the time, claims to have been present as a young man when federal agents told Old John Squirrel that "the Anishinaabe would always have control of the manoomin harvest."[91] Aubid asserted that the Anishinaabe understood their rights by such stories. The judge for the case agreed with the objection by the federal attorney that Aubid's testimony was hearsay and therefore not admissible. "'John Squirrel is dead,' said the judge. 'And you can't say what a dead man said.'"

Against this manifestation of the differend, which echoes the question of what counts as evidence and through what form, Aubid, as Vizenor relates, "turned brusquely in the witness chair, bothered by what the judge had said about John Squirrel. Aubid pointed at the legal books on the bench, and then, in English, his second language, he shouted that those books contained the stories of dead white men. 'Why should I believe what a white man says, when you don't believe John Squirrel?'"[92] Aubid here asserts the fourth person, like Antíkoni's actions for the sake of the ancestors, to contest the second person of the law's command, the cycle of first person turned third person through evidentiary discourse become second person through the force of the law, described by Constable. The fourth person equalizes and upends the well-known distinction and power relation between the archive and repertoire (Taylor), neutralizing the force of law through indirect discourse (hearsay) and story. As Vizenor says, "Charles Aubid created indirect linguistic evidence of a fourth person by visual reminiscence. His stories were intuitive, visual memories, a native sense of presence, and sources of evidence and survivance."[93] And, like the other resident scholars at SAR, the judge in this case "was deferential, amused by the analogy of native stories to court testimony, judicial decisions, precedent, and hearsay. 'You've got me there,' he said, and then considered the testimony of other Anishinaabe witnesses."[94] Colonial humor is critical abatement as opposed to Native humor's deadly serious play.

Piatote's cacophony of perspectives, assembled around the bones/ancestors, understood through the grammatical position of the fourth person, does not act as a humanizing force. In relation to the creation stories, seeming non sequiturs woven throughout the play, this collective voicing rather prophesizes the conditions of the arrival of humans who, in most Native creation stories, are the youngest and least wise of all beings and in need of the most help. Told by the Aunties, these stories of violence, betrayal, metamorphoses into animals, ghosts, and cannibals present themselves as preparation for humans, a clearing of the ground, as if for a dance or ceremony.

> **AUNTIE #3** There's a story I know.
> Not so long ago, there was a woman
> And she had powerful medicine. She was the best gambler
> Of anyone around. No one could beat her at Stickgame
> Though many, many tried. Her power was known all around
> And when she died
> One of her rivals, a man from her mother's band
> Took two finger bones from her hand
> And made a pair of gambling sticks.
> This man became the most powerful then, virtually unbeatable.
> People came from all around to lose to him.
> His luck was fantastic.
> He had those gambling bones, you see.
> But at night
> The ghost of the dead woman would appear
> And insist that the man sleep with her.
> Night after night, she bothered him. She seduced him.
> She would not let him rest.
> Finally he gave up. He returned the bones
> And the ghost went away.
> This is a true story.[95]

Giving up, unceremoniously returning the bones, relinquishing the accumulation of power. The treacherousness of luck, the impersonal force of nature (see chapter 5). The indirectness of these stories, their impossible closure into meaning, into forms of evidence, informs the position of the fourth person in the multiple perspectives, the impersonal voice, the indirect discourse that does not offend the dead who will now haunt others. Or rest. Or return. To be one or many or both but only in the generic fourth person. *They said the bones should return.* Who are you to disagree?

This unfurling of the coloniality of being, exposing its soft underbelly, is neither ideology nor critical revelation of its mechanisms but follows in the very material footsteps of Creator, who left the world when bested by Coyote. In Creator's absence are only footsteps. As detached codes of expression, the voices of the dead do not restore or recover (sense or sociality) but disorganize, relate, and translate with and through interruption, forming an interrelational and therefore infinite space. In Vizenor's bone court, it is the dead who speak (of the destruction), it is not, it is the bones who speak (of their confinement), it is not. It is an assemblage, a singularity. The one, the many, *they* said it was so, they said it *would be* so. *They said.* An equivocal voice, the voice of the inhuman turns juridical power inside out (like a glove). The exterior. Vizenor's theater, evidenced by his many literary representations of courtroom scenes, contests the drama of western power. Western legal power's petty, humanizing, individualizing, interior drama, which has had such devastating effects, is teased, mocked, neutralized. Vizenor invokes absolute (plenary) power, Congress's absolute jurisdiction over tribes, as a way of grasping toward power's absolute absence. And if there is any doubt, note Vizenor's quotation in the proposal from Roland Barthes's essay "The Death of the Author:"

> writing is the neutral, composite, oblique space where our subject slips away, the negative where all identity is lost . . . As soon as a fact is narrated no longer with a view to acting directly on reality but intransitively, that is to say, finally outside of any function other than that of the very practice of the symbol itself . . . the voice loses its origin, the author enters into his own death, writing begins . . . Narrative is first and foremost a prodigious variety of genres, themselves distributed amongst different substances—as though any material would fit to receive man's stories.[96]

With all its problems, the "death of the author" discourse indicates, relying as it does on anthropological representations of Indigenous political and social forms, the mitigating power of the collective to forbid power's accumulation in a monologic voice.

Rights of Control

It seems to be the case that, rather than simply imposing values of stable objectivity, NAGPRA and federal recognition have inaugurated social action along with an imperative to do research. As Robert McLaughlin notes, "In practice, NAGPRA consultations often amplify . . . knowledge or, as anthropologists often regard it, knowledges. Indeed, since 1990, NAGPRA has served to enhance and renew Native American cultures and cultural identities. Native histories, too, have undergone renewal and change both in form and content. Many tribes, for instance, had no cultural provisions for the reburial of ancestors."[97] One should question this idea of progress through adaptation to settler law. This adaptation also describes the fact that Native peoples are given a certain kind of freedom along with our rights, but we must ask what kind of controls come along with it. In what ways are we put in the position to police ourselves through such rights, drawing new lines of inclusion and exclusion? The management of Native forms of culture and life have been outsourced to Native peoples. How we handle this new power will determine what kind of future we are condemned to.

We already know what the effects of Native Americans being put into a system of greater and greater (technical) knowledge is: Natives were always considered to be units within the system. Hence the need for various forms of documentation, from anthropometric photography and its complementary numbering systems for the body to ethnographic surveys of various types and data reporting to government agencies. Native Americans, because of this split identity, between nature and citizen in one sense and between unit and individual in another, are still in large part under an anthropological regime. From object-human to data-human lies the liberal path of progression and governance.

While the government was busy attempting to eradicate Native Americans and then confining them, the social sciences were already at work documenting them. This confluence set up the conditions for the desire for a future. We imagine that the shameful values of anthropology of the past were about authenticity and were imposed on us, but what if this were a ruse? What if all along it was about borrowing our own forms of authority, encoding them, and then offering them back to us through the form of rights, an authorization for us to be Native again? An authorization to which we have been given the code words. Perhaps the new task should be decryption of the codes we live (again) by and then their neutralization. Taking a storied path and being attentive to silence are two forms of such decryption. This is nothing more nor less than a bone game.

> Birds were people one time. Two birds went around the world.
> One bird
> Was over here. And [they] talked back and forth with the other
> bird, over
> there.
> When they came to a place where they couldn't just get through
> (like the white

man has a place you cannot get through, such as a gate—it's closed), they had
to stay there and gamble and beat their way through. If they won they could go
on . . . Those birds beat all the different animals. They sang like this:

one bird went over the blue
sky it's blue as far as you can
see
nobody knows what's behind the
sky [they] went over the sky
just to show the others what [they] could do.[98]

Chapter 2
The Postapocalyptic Imaginary

What do we see that is Native, and how do we create identities in the imagic moments of pictures? How can there be a sense of Native self, *a discoverable identity, in a picture of someone else?*

—Gerald Vizenor, *Native Liberty*

The lives of Native Californians had changed immensely since contact, especially in such crucial aspects of material culture as clothing and houses. Even their bodies had changed, with significant degrees of intermarriage. The camera could be of little use in documenting "the appearance they presented on discovery." It could not record a vanished culture.

—Ira Jacknis, "Alfred Kroeber and the Photographic Representation of California Indians"

What does a composite image of an Indian look like? Is it a racialized anthropometric set of photographs of the face and head superimposed to make a general image? An atlas or collection of an array of cultural types as represented in portraits of Native people wearing tribally specific regalia or field photographs posing with cultural items? Is it a series of action shots documenting practices of various sorts (basket weaving, flint knapping, dancing, singing, pounding acorns)? Is it still or moving? Posed, fortuitous, or some kind of any-instant-whatever? Gendered? Two-dimensional or more? Silent or auditory or otherwise sensed? Sedimented and realized over time? Is the composite image abstracted from context or bound to tribal and family histories, stories, historical and ethnographic data, material culture? Must it be explained and categorized? Is it relational to all other images (differential)? Would it be presented on paper, metal, screen, projected, a holograph? Immersive (VR), networked? Distinct from reality (and thereby upholding it) or indistinguishable from it (thereby either documenting or destroying it)?

Should it be made by Natives? Is the composite image of an Indian even visible at all?

There is, of course, no composite image of an Indian, much less of "the" Indian—but not for lack of trying. As I detail in this chapter, amateur and professional anthropologists dedicated labor and fiscal resources to compiling an archive of images of Indians, a representational complement to the bones and artifacts I discussed in the previous chapter. Part of the reason I begin this chapter by asking these questions is that something like the composite image of the Indian continues to motivate the settler, colonial, and racialized imagination of Indigenous people in the lands we only recently have been forced to call California and more broadly the United States and North America. This image also motivates many of the forms of critique that address this colonial imaginary.

Another question that puts the above one into relief: *what does a composite image of a "human" look like?* This question has been worked out aesthetically, discursively, and materially according to the western humanist attempt to gain mastery over the world, a project that seeks to have the world reflect back a humanized, rational order, subject to manipulation at a global scale. The produced image is part of a logic that sees the human liberated through reduction of nature—meaning all that lies outside of human control—a logic that works through the co-constitutive process of shaping the world that in turn shapes the human in a reciprocal dialectic. This humanizing image ranges across classical painting and aesthetics, universalist ethics and epistemology, political theory and subjectivity, legal rights discourses, political economy and physical and environmental sciences, satellite images and global positioning systems, and photography as used in nineteenth-century criminology, to name a few areas. Along these lines, Allan Sekula has discussed the intersections of statistics, aesthetics, and photography in criminology in English statistician and founder of eugenics Francis Galton's peculiar project of materially and visually producing a composite portrait of the "average man," as well as of "criminal types."[1] Materially speaking, Galton's composite portraits are a bit of an oddity, never really practically used in criminology, but symbolically they are indicative of a general trend in western thought to reduce difference and specificity toward supposedly greater powers of discernment and action through abstraction. Based on the bell curve distribution chart famously produced by Carl Friedrich Gauss (and its use by Adolphe

Quetelet to statistically and anthropometrically chart an "average man" as a mathematical expression of a social law), Galton sought in this logic of average measurements a "truer likeness" of certain essences (both criminal and human), in order to bring into view the ideal. This image appears as a sort of apparition, as made clear by his analogous project of making composites of ancient Greek and Roman portrait coins and medallions to find in the blurred images a vanished "physiognomy of a higher race."[2] "Thus conceived, the 'average man' constituted an ideal, not only of social health, but of social stability and of beauty."[3]

This question of the composite image of the human is a performative one in the sense that it both offers the question itself as a form of research and inquiry and guides the movement and the forms through which inquiry takes place (methodologies) as well as the answers (the knowledge-image as it takes shape). It is performative because it has real effects in the world, enacting a form of research and knowledge production that seeks to shape things according to the image it seeks, to selectively bring the human into focus through rigorous material realization. In this sense, it is a tautology—though not in any strict or straightforward logical manner. In fact, it operates at times along seemingly meandering or arbitrary paths, while fortuitously arriving at certain destinations. Specific and situated humans defining what it means to be human is always a treacherous and violent endeavor, especially when those specific humans have the power to impose their definition on others. The "happy accidents" of research have a way of gravitating into specific but fuzzy forms, like Chladni sound figures, which symbolically and sometimes physically resemble Galton's composite portraits, many taken of incarcerated individuals who likely had no choice in the matter. What is not generally seen are the soundwaves and vibrations that produce the visible shape.

The question of the composite image of the Indian makes this invisible shape-making clear. Consider the way that the early anthropology of Indigenous peoples, such as that found in the work of racial scientist/proto-anthropologist Lewis Henry Morgan, sought a normative scale of civilization based on a progressive notion of time from primitive to civilized. Here, Morgan and his contemporaries understood western civilization to be the mean while judging other cultures according to their perceived distance or proximity to this mean, by how far into the fuzziness they descend. It is a form of research motivated by the ghostly composite image of the human. This form of thinking, widespread among racial scientists and colonial societies of the nineteenth century, had devastating consequences for colonized peoples, who were losing their lands, cultures, and lives due to perceived inferiority, a picture of aberrant humanity.

Mohawk scholar Audra Simpson has analyzed the intricate entanglements of anthropology, colonialism, and indigeneity, specifically as represented in the work of Morgan and then in that of later anthropologists, as what she calls "a kind of discursive wrestling" between anthropologists and Indigenous people over these terms.[4] For Simpson, Indigenous people have long been confronting the colonial work of representation that seeks to materially expand imperial power. This power is "part of specific technologies of rules that sought to obtain space and resources, to define and know the difference that it constructed" in order to better govern colonized peoples who, inevitably, push back.[5] Such governance requires more than just direct forms of colonial power, violence, and control. What is needed are "methods and modalities of knowing, in particular: categorization, ethnological comparison, linguistic translation and ethnography," which together produce an image of Indigenous peoples deeply desired by a colonial viewer and readership who may then project themselves onto and compare themselves to colonized peoples, coming to know themselves intimately and reflexively through colonial entanglements and differentiation. Eventually even presenting themselves as Indigenous.

Simpson notes the development of the concept of *culture* as just such a translational colonial tool that helps produce "the conceptual and necessarily essentialized space that stood in for complicated bodily and exchange-based relationships that enabled and marked colonial situations in Empire: warfare, commerce, sex, trade, missionization."[6] Through the lens of culture, difference and containment become units of analysis, and colonizers are able to more clearly see themselves reflected back. Culture becomes a detachable product, one that can be slipped on like a jacket. The settler's unknown and unseen "past" is seemingly projected onto the cultural image, obscuring both the lives of Indigenous peoples, who get reframed through culture, and the actual past of white settlers, who become inheritors of Indigenous identity and material existence. Morgan notoriously played Indian himself, founding a fraternal Grand Order of the Iroquois, whose members "celebrated" Native culture by wearing costumes (as opposed to regalia) and performing "Native" ceremonies. Less direct than the "Improved Order of the Red Man," a fraternal order that had at one point 500,000 members, depicted in Figures 1–4, Morgan's playing Indian nonetheless functioned according to the same logic of inheritance.

FIGURE 1. Rappahanock Council No. 25, Meriden, Connecticut, year unknown; image courtesy of Red Men Museum and Library, Waco, Texas.

FIGURE 2. Chetuthutlie Tribe No. 6, Eagle, Alaska, year unknown; image courtesy of Red Men Museum and Library, Waco, Texas.

FIGURE 3. Minnetonka Council No. 24, Marion, Ohio, 1925; image courtesy of Red Men Museum and Library, Waco, Texas.

FIGURE 4. Wah-Wah-Tee Council, No. 15, Waco, Texas, 1929; image courtesy of Red Men Museum and Library, Waco, Texas.

Morgan's racialized social order, in this sense, became a sort of threshing machine whereby certain Native peoples who were understood to be capable of "advancement" based on armchair anthropological analyses of cultural artifacts were to be absorbed into "the white race" and into western civilization, both of which were perceived to be inevitable and virtuous. In this sense, Simpson's conception of culture echoes Edward Said's in his profound analysis of the effects of discourse and representation in the colonial construction of the image of the "Orient." The nefarious aspect of this weaponized notion of culture is that it becomes also the image taught to colonized subjects about themselves through educational and disciplinary procedures.[7] All the while Indigenous institutions, practices, ways of knowing, and, of course, lands are absorbed by the new settler society. Others, such as African Americans and "less civilized" Native tribes, were placed outside of the western human order into a state of inevitable decline, a state often pursued through violence, at the fringes of the image of the human. Note, of course, in either case, Native people were set on a path to forfeit land to settlers, and African Americans were barred from owning.

This cultural image of the declining *savage,* like Galton's vague composite portrait, is an imminently flexible and adaptable one that can be used for multiple purposes and has multiple facets. In an article on "the culture concept," Tony Bennett details the development of the concept of culture in the shift from a racialized social hierarchy model, such as Morgan's, to a Boasian cultural relativity model.[8] Part of a genealogical and archival argument that traces *culture* from elitist aesthetic notions of culture, especially in nineteenth-century Europe, to contemporary notions of culture as employed in the critical field of cultural studies, as the study of an everyday way of life (not that of the elite), Bennett's approach locates the origins of its more critical functions in the cultural anthropology of Franz Boas and his students. Rather than a celebration of this critical aspect, Bennett shows how the move from a single social evolutionary model of cultural development to a more pluralistic notion of cultures as harmonious, complex assemblages—which should rather be judged according to their own rules and forms of interpretation—holds within it a racialized mechanism for developing an assimilative, multicultural settler national culture. In this case, it is not the racial inferiority of Indigenous people that leads to a more advanced civilization inheriting their land and cultural products but rather the "borrowing" of Indigenous creative energies through a representational translation process comes to serve a developing "settler nationality" (an oxymoron if there ever was one).

Boas redefined culture as what "can be understood only as an historical growth determined by the social and geographical environment in which each people is placed and by the way in which it develops the cultural material that comes into its possession from the outside or through its own creativeness." However, according to Bennett, this revision still hides the fact that Boas (and especially his students) was deeply influenced by an aesthetic modernism that, rather than developing culture away from an elite aestheticism, carried within it an already aesthetic sensibility that, Boas believed, would generate (and regenerate) anthropology's creative capacities along differential lines.[9] Bennett locates this aesthetic sensibility as the source of authorization for anthropological expertise. Turning to the collaborative work of Alfred Kroeber and Clyde Kluckhohn, two students of Boas, Bennett notes how the two anthropologists sought to develop a notion of culture disconnected from earlier European humanistic traditions, a notion of culture both available to scientific study and uniquely American. As is typical of attempts to develop a uniquely "American" voice, identity, or method, the well, the stolen resource, is Indigenous ways of doing and thinking.[10] Working against the social evolutionary model of someone like Morgan, Kroeber and Kluckhohn also sought to separate the concept of culture from ruling-class associations, evidenced in T. S. Eliot's definition of English culture as "sport, food, a little art," which gives it a much more democratic appeal.

In this way, *culture* emerged as the unique creative energy of specific and specifically located people in their everyday lives. A "patterning of values that gives significance to the lives of those who hold them," this pattern is "instinctive"; it is also "aesthetically harmonious" and expressive of "a richly varied and yet somehow unified and consistent attitude toward life."[11] Through the creative capacities of people who are part of a culture, the aesthetic enters into this new conception. "The distinctive shape of a culture was re-interpreted in modernist terms as the result of form-giving activity [by Indigenous people] modeled on the work of art which, whether performed by individual or collective social agents, broke through inherited patterns of thought and behavior to crystallize new social tendencies."[12]

As I discuss in the introduction, Eduardo Viveiros de Castro's recent call to arms to the discipline makes clear the continuation of this translational process in (aesthetic) anthropological thought: "Accepting the importance of and opportunity presented by this task of thinking thought otherwise is to incriminate oneself in the effort to forge an anthropological theory of the conceptual imagination, one attuned to the creativity and reflexivity of every collective, human or otherwise."[13] De Castro makes clear anthropology's relationship to Indigenous thought:

> The aim of Anti-Narcissus [a shadow book anticipated but not yet or perhaps never to be written in some Borgesian way], then, is to illustrate the thesis that every nontrivial anthropological theory is a version of an indigenous practice of knowledge, all such theories being suitable in strict structural continuity with the intellectual pragmatics of the collectives that have historically occupied the position of object in the discipline's gaze. This entails outlining a performative description of the discursive transformations of anthropology at the origin of the internalization of the transformational condition of the discipline as such, which is to say the (of course theoretical) fact that it is the discursive anamorphosis of the ethnoanthropologies of the collectives studied.[14]

And even more clearly, "the styles of thought proper to the collectives that we study are the motor force of anthropology."[15] What is at stake for anthropology is a reflexive critical mirror image for western society. "Amazonianists have also perceived certain theoretical implications of this non-marked or generic status of the virtual dimension or 'soul' of existents, a chief premise of a powerful indigenous intellectual structure that is inter alia capable of providing a counter-description of the image drawn of it by Western anthropology and thereby capable, again, of 'returning to us an image in which we are unrecognizable to ourselves.'"[16] This reflexive image of translated Indigenous ways of being and doing is absorbed into anthropology, which becomes a tool for refashioning the west: "this transversalization of anthropology and philosophy . . . is established in view of a common objective, which is the entry into a state (a plateau of intensity) of the permanent decolonization of thought."[17] It is unclear what "decolonization" means when mediated by a colonial discipline, though it certainly bumps up against Eve Tuck and K. Wayne Yang's mantra *decolonization is not a metaphor!*[18]

Boas's (and by extension de Castro's—though he wouldn't use the same term) notion of culture is instinctive, unconscious. While indicating certain creative energies, it is wholly wrapped up in a judgment of authenticity and in the complete absorption that excludes a distanced or self-reflexive critical position. This turns Indigenous people into their own living archive without the critical distance necessary to interpret, a framework that imposes onto them a precarious position of inexorably disappearing knowledge and existence—unless translated and preserved by anthropologists. This formation of the critical position is reserved for the anthropologist who is understood to have the unique ability to distinguish the quality of cultures. This position is also racialized and deeply colonial, as Denise Ferreira da Silva's distinction between self-reflexive white subjects and affectable non-white others makes clear.[19] The anthropologist's judgment is a technical discernment that requires special methods of collection, analysis, and organization to understand the interrelations between things, stories, ceremonies, and languages, a form of rationality and aesthetic taste in their combination that only the anthropologist claims to maintain as cultural expert (and, absurdly, in de Castro's argument, as the site of the permanent decolonization of thought).

Bennett notes two distinct effects of this new aesthetic notion of culture: first, no longer required to account for a coherent and singular humanity (the composite image of the human that motivated Morgan), the anthropologist becomes an expert in manipulating cultural difference as a reflexive form of social critique. "Their fieldwork amongst others—most notably the Native Americans of the western seaboard and the Plains Indians—provided the anthropologist with privileged access to principles of alterity which, echoing modernist conceptions of the work of art as a defamiliarizing device, could then be used to make the distinctive properties of American culture and society perceptible in new ways."[20] Aestheticism and a scientific conception of culture wedded together produce a new, more flexible, and critical conception of the human at the expense of Indigenous peoples. Second, it gave anthropology and the anthropologist authority over a newly perceived object of scientific study, one held together by the creative energies of Indigenous peoples. Importantly, despite the more classical notion of aesthetic harmony that motivates Boas's conception of culture, another one of his students, Ruth Benedict, drawing on Boas's own notion of cultural diffusion, asserts that cultures are always fragmentary, assembled of "diverse and unlike" parts, thereby giving new powers of interpretation to the anthropologist who sees hybridity and diversity where Indigenous people, enmeshed in the culture, supposedly only experience wholeness and unity.[21] The ability to see hybridity and transformation as opposed to the whole and unification contributes to the temporal divide between a "modernizing" western subject caught in the flows of history and the timeless image of the Native, not in actuality but in perception. This new approach emphasized the ability to interpret culture but claimed to equalize the relationship between cultures. Offering a new sense of flexibility, an egalitarianism that nonetheless upholds racial and cultural distinctions among intellectual work, it created the conditions for producing a center of white management over the development of a democratic, multicultural nationality and citizenry. This tendency should draw caution whenever one engages in aesthetic critique.

Two types of image and their aftereffects illuminate (and at times cloud with shadow) these questions of imag(in)ing the human and the Indian. The first is the metaphorical image produced by the salvage ethnography of Boasian anthropologists who sought to capture timeless images of peoples presented as teetering on the brink of disappearance, producing what some have referred to as the (eternal) ethnographic present, the image of which is captured by the phrase *the salvage snapshot*. The second are the field photographs produced during the ethnographic salvage survey, especially the anthropometric photographs of racialized (and measured) Indigenous bodies. Rather than seeing these images simply as fixed, static, and dehumanizing (though they may be!), my purpose in this chapter is to try to understand their generativity: how they have been used to create the conditions of visibility for California Indian people and how this visibility, this having been made visible according to a certain imaginary and with specific techniques and media, is founded on a logic of disappearance that continues to organize even recent gains in visibility. And, further, I ask what anticolonial Indigenous work with light, shadow, visibility, invisibility, and the image looks like outside of the terms of western aesthetic humanism and its modes of critique and reform.

> Then Lizard put on his cap and began to dance. His cap was made of a grizzly-bear's head. Rabbit was talking, singing, while Lizard was dancing near the house-post. By and by it began to grow light. Lizard made daylight come by dancing.[22]

A-visuality and the Apocalyptic Imaginary

To understand this problem of visuality requires understanding the dynamics of a colonial apocalyptic imaginary that undergirds both the salvage snapshot and the anthropometric photograph. The apocalypse is a light that destroys, opening the images and the critical positions that have been developed through and against the images onto the Destruction (in this case, as anthropologist and archivist Robert Heizer defines it, *The Destruction of California Indians,* a theme that ironically describes his own archival project, a recursive destruction that I discuss in chapters 3 and 4 of this book). Queer Kumeeyay poet Tommy Pico engages this imaginary in their epic poem *IRL,* in the context of the perpetual (doom) scrolling of social media and internet hookups, in the conditions of socializing in a settler colonial context and having sex in the aftermath of genocide. He writes:

> I
> don't have the option
> of keeping my God
> alive by keeping her name secret
> The word for her
> is gone Keeping secrets is not possible So I give
> everything away
> and
> I'm saying my land was jam-
> med with brawny English,
> and I'm still single.[23]

In relation to the destruction of protocols, in the absence of secrets (the structuring device of Indigeneity, as I establish in the introduction), there's an ambiguity between having been revealed and having been destroyed, which leads to a kind of ecstatic openness and vulnerability. It's an ambiguity that queer Chickasaw theorist Jodi Byrd describes in the conclusion to their book *Transit of Empire,* beginning with an epigraph from French theorist (and white savage philosopher!) Jean Baudrillard: "The apocalypse is the end of secrecy. Literally, it is the discovery, the revelation when everything is said. It is the end of metaphors and secrets. The nuclear bomb is the Sun cast on the Earth, of the end of the Sun as a metaphor, as distance. It is the Sun materialized on Earth: the end."[24] Pico sets their poem in a postapocalyptic space after this end in which things begin anew—but under the most horrific circumstances and intimately entangled with other times:

> And I know I'm not supposed to use real
> Names—Where I'm from, in the valley I lived in
> for thousands of years,
> once someone has passed
> or pushed or pressed
> into the next life that I don't
> believe in, their name
> is forbidden. Reference them,
> but don't use the name bc
> it distracts them from
> heaven Sullies the peace
> they rest in. I don't want to be
> a sullier. I'm terrible
> in trouble.[25]

And yet, in whose company do California Indians find themselves? In the aftermath of genocide, in the throes of an ongoing demographic war,

> It can't always just
> be me, stumbling alone
> head first into these bright
> things—Lead me back
> to the water
> Mina, Guadalupe, Geo and Beam,
> Stoney, Ricky, Berto,
> Dessy, Woody, George,
> Lula, Reya, Robin, Bunty
> Beebee, Tina, Lucky
> Why am I the one left?
> Why do I have to know
> so many dead?[26]

This turning to the dead for sociality echoes the Ghost Dance in directly undermining protocols, and is shattering. It is also an everyday occurrence in this new metaphysics. The easy accessibility of information, the data-driven settler society in which Pico finds themself, is uncannily similar to the apocalyptic imaginary that sought to destroy/reveal Indigenous lives:

So
much info is disclosed from
the jump—profile pages,
light Googling . . . It's kind of exciting,
having a thing
to hide in the age of knowin
everything all the time.[27]

This space of revelation opens up a new/old economics of abundance, one that destabilizes any relation to the individual:

for fifteen
years I give all of myself to every
man I meet, mostly bc
I have nothing Worth holding. I want
to get lost, to merge and b
someone else . . .
Kumeeyays knew
a rounded Earth based
on the curve of stars
or didn't, I'll never know.
It's a dark part inside me.[28]

This last phrase about the dark part inside touches on a more profound sense of disappearance, of the invisible, and negative feelings produced by the intensity of light, including "the English fucking/language with its high/beams in my face."[29] Force-fed a language, tongue cut out and tied, light shining in one's eyes all the time, the dark part is made by the ambiguity between revelation and destruction, enlightenment and the savage (and its shadow), the light that marks the body and the Indigenous subject as known and yet always a secret revealed and thereby destroyed. In this way, darkness is both absence and refuge. It is exciting to have a thing to hide. It is disorienting to get lost, to merge and "b someone else"; devastating and disorienting to not know if one's ancestors knew the curve of stars. Moving erratically from muse/lover to muse throughout *IRL*, desire pulsing like light, Pico describes precisely the conditions of what Akira Mizuta Lippit calls *a-visuality*, the unseen that conditions what is visible and what is invisible, which marks and creates relations between an inside and an outside, the racially and culturally marked and the unmarked.[30] The intense light of culture made clear and imposed creates a new surface on which the image of the Indian gets projected, forming a dark part inside. The apocalypse, the Destruction, is the unseen structure that a-visually conditions these signified relations of visible and invisible, inside and outside. The rest of this chapter is devoted to trying to understand how the two images described above, the salvage snapshot and the anthropometric photograph, are conditioned by the apocalyptic imaginary and condition, in turn, its continuation in the political imaginary of visibility. At stake is the question of what Pico's postapocalyptic project of giving everything away means for the image and what it would look like to follow them into it.

The Salvage Snapshot

It has been noted many times how contradictory the ethnographic image is, collected from "informants" who usually had no direct experience of a time *before the coming of the white man.* Drawn from second- or thirdhand memory, collected, organized, and edited, this image was constituted by such a profusion of materials that it required slow, painstaking labor to gather, document, and sift. And today much of it still feels like an arbitrary, baroque jumble of things. The reconstruction of an image of peoples who were supposedly poised on the threshold of disappearance was a monumental effort destined to fail, but it carried within it the essence of the snapshot, with its mediated immediacy, its hurried temporality and ability to capture an instant before it is lost forever. This essence constitutes the foreboding image of an arrested moment before apocalypse, taken (paradoxically) after the event has already occurred. An image of memory and fantasy illuminated by apocalyptic light, this project of producing such an image delineates the destruction. In the delay, caused by the unwieldiness and misbehavior of beings, having always missed the event (strung out by structure), this mediated immediacy captures something of the form of the apocalypse. Poised on the threshold of destruction, it removes from the series of moments, from causality and history, from the flow of time, an image of a world as a fiction cloaked in fact. And it makes of the entire time of "prehistory" (Indian time) this impending scene gathered in a flash.

Beginning in the late nineteenth through the early twentieth centuries, amateur and professional anthropologists in California embarked on a project to document and collect as much cultural information as possible from California Indians. This project resulted in private and public collections and archives of untold size, an immensity of materials that is truly hard to comprehend. (UC Berkeley's warehouses alone hold upward of a million objects, not including documents and audio and visual recordings.) Simultaneous to this attempt to salvage an image of the "Indigenous past" (the temporal formation of the image conveniently cast Indigenous peoples as permanently of the past), government-sponsored assimilation projects sought to humanize the "savage" by removing everything Indian about them. The recordings of languages, stories, and songs, the documentation of cultural and spiritual practices, the collections of baskets, deer toe and cocoon rattles, and hunting and fishing tools constituted precisely the figure of the Indian that was being disciplined out of children in federally run boarding schools.

The frenzy of salvage collection—because it certainly was that—coincided with what Patrick Wolfe refers to as "absorption," whereby Native Americans were subjected to biopolitical and humanizing institutions and legislation (boarding schools, health and wellness policies, adoption, prohibitions on ceremonial practices, legalized slavery/indenture cast as apprenticeship, as well as legal and political subjecthood).[31] In this light, Richard Henry Pratt's infamous imperative to "kill the Indian to save the man" was also carried out by the ethnographic snapshot as a form of preservation that activated the murderous capacity of the image as knowledge-about-the-Indian—preservation as destruction. Separating out *the Indian* as by-product through the creation of an ethnographic image, killing the Indian through preservation in imagistic form, was a necessary condition for rehabilitating the savage into a liberal human subject aligned with a (expressed but failed) multicultural state imperative. The project of separating the Indian from the human is also a premise of western neoliberal-multicultural-settler colonial subjectification. As seen in the image of the "Improved Order of Red Men," Indigenous subjectivity is evacuated to allow a white gaze, and indeed white bodies, to fill and intermingle with the subjective space of Indigenous culture. This approach to the image creates the conditions for multicultural forms of subjectivity through proposed mutual recognition, a framework rigorously critiqued by Glen Coulthard in his book *Red Skin, White Masks*.[32]

Though the "era" of salvage ethnography is generally understood to have ended after World War II, like settler colonialism and its genocidal actions the salvage survey was never purely institutional, orderly, or representative of a consensus in its methodologies and goals. California, for instance, on top of being an epicenter of the project, led by the famed anthropologist Alfred Kroeber, was also flooded with amateur ethnographers, with anthropologists and archaeologists working outside the academic mainstream and in regional educational institutions, with private collectors, and with a number of niche publishers who blurred the line between academic and popular markets, many of whom were interested precisely in creating a salvage ethnographic image. This vascularized representational power became as much a part of California settler identity as that of California Indians' and continued the active processes of salvage at least up until the 1970s. Such a more flexible sense of the ethnographic snapshot also shows the ways that the California landscape was encrypted by an archival sensibility in conjunction with the settlement of the land.

The type of image most closely, if metaphorically, associated with this form of representation is the photograph. Its importance is evident by the amount of critical energy that has been expended analyzing this relationship. Associated with mourning, death, the uncanny double, technological and spiritual inhumanity, and the crime scene, the photograph has come both to emblematize and to materialize an itinerary of thought (distinctly progressivist and civilizationist) concerned with the destructive power of the image, summed up by Jean Baudrillard as "the murderous capacity of signs."[33] The image kills that which it represents by replacing it, being better than it, fixing it in a moment out of time and place, appearing as "more beautiful, more imposing" than it, thus exposing the absence subtending what is present.[34] Like a cadaver, the photograph undoes identity by showing what self-resembling looks like: it is what it is and it also isn't. "It is as if the photograph always carries its referent with itself, both affected by the same amorous or funereal immobility, at the very heart of the world: they are glued together, limb by limb, like the condemned man and the corpse in certain tortures."[35]

The image became a document. Salvage ethnography, which attempted to capture a totalizing view of a people who were understood to be poised on the threshold of disappearance, and photography, which captured a moment out of time with so realistic an image that the referent and the sign were glued together in a pure document, came together in the ethnographic imagination of the salvage snapshot. This photographic imagination took the form of a reconstruction. The California Indian world and its peoples, according to this view, were disappearing, and the image of that world was now stored in the material culture, languages, performances, and memories of survivors. The salvage operation sought to extract this image from catastrophic ruins through what we can anachronistically describe as data mining or, from the ethnographer's salvational view, a rescue mission.

Aesthetic Critique

But Native Americans have had a long love affair with their self-images. Despite rumors of the fear of photography's soul-stealing abilities, the accurate depiction and externalization of one's image was readily accepted and appropriated by many Native peoples. Describing a dialectical relationship between Indians and the proliferation of externalized photographic images, "from the Curtis stills to our own Kodachrome slides and Polaroid prints and Camcorder tapes," Paul Chaat Smith states that "the question isn't whether we love photography, but instead why we love it so much."[36] His answer is that the camera helped shape who Indians are today (post-1890, according to Smith); in fact, "everything about being Indian has been shaped by the camera."[37] Gerald Vizenor personalizes and develops this notion further by describing the introduction of the Kodak Brownie, an inexpensive cardboard box camera, to Native uses in 1900. He writes, "the spare meniscus lens captured natives in ordinary scenes and in common, untouched poses at home and at work, gathering wild rice and berries, curing hides, and preparing maple sugar. The Brownie scenes of friends and family were almost always casual; at times they were fortuitous in contrast to the studio photographs a generation earlier."[38] Documenting the shift from the expensive, mounted studio camera (in which Natives were predominately objects) to a cheap, mobile one (in which Natives were also photographers), he notes its effects on Native community, particularly regarding the vitality of the image. "The box camera . . . inspired a new perception and consciousness of the real, of humans and nature, a new expressive, wondrous world of black, white, and gray eyes and hands in distinctive, arrested motion."[39] Vizenor draws a hard line between images produced by non-Native photographers, which he links to *the pose*, and those produced by Natives, which he associates with the snapshot. In both, however, it is precisely such a mirror-stage type of relation to the image, a narcissism that Smith attributes to Natives and non-Natives alike, that makes the uses of evidentiary technology and their produced images for the reproduction of cultural knowledge and practices so important. "They're fables told to shape the future"—fables with exactitude and precision.[40]

Vizenor produces a semiotics of the photograph that squarely puts the ethnographic imagination on the side of the pose. These ethnographic photos, for him, are frozen, static images that capture their subjects "dead in camera time," bringing about their "extinction."[41] Interrupting relationships with the past, they are "discontinuous artifacts in a colonial roadshow" that allow the past to be consumed, rendering it *unreal*.[42] "This obsession with the tribal past is not an innocent collection of arrowheads, not a crude map of public camp sites in sacred places, but rather a statement of academic power and control over tribal images, an excess of facts, data, narrative interviews, template discoveries."[43] The photograph as document and evidence becomes one of the means of colonization, rendering the Native (the *real*) into a metasavage (the *Indian* as simulation of the Native).

The emblematic creator of the ethnographic pose, for Vizenor, is Edward Curtis, who famously employed a pictorialist aesthetic for the purposes of documenting a "vanishing race." For Vizenor, Curtis's manipulations of the images he produced, both in terms of his construction of dramatic scenes to be photographed and his post-production techniques, editing out signs of contemporaneity, indicate clearly Curtis's ideological project, which led to distortion and, ultimately, the "invention of tribes." Pauline Wakeham in *Taxidermic Signs* further elaborates on the complexity of Curtis's images, which, like taxidermy, present a certain semiotics and appearance of liveness through practices of preservation that ultimately signify death: "Curtis's photographic salvaging perpetuated the nostalgic pathos of American imperialist discourse by aestheticizing the death of the native other via the project of photographic preservation."[44] Locating Curtis's project in the history of museum display, particularly those of natural history, Wakeham argues that the process of taxidermizing animal corpses, within the evolutionary displays of "species," transfers certain signs to the racialized body of Natives. This transference indicates the attempt to master nature that continues in Curtis's vast survey of Indigenous peoples, one that spanned forty years and produced over forty thousand images. In fact, Curtis began his career as a self-taught nature photographer, taking the aesthetics of presenting the settler landscape, one created as "natural" and untouched despite thousands of years of Indigenous presence and relationality, and turning it toward Indigenous peoples.

Describing the material and imperial foundations of Curtis's project, Wakeham notes his governmental work with the BIA and the funding he received from railroad tycoon J. P. Morgan, who established the corporation The Native American Indian Inc.: "by working in conjunction with the Bureau of Indian Affairs on the one hand, and by forming alliances with the railroad industries of Morgan on the other, Edward Curtis developed his salvaging project within a powerful matrix of white imperial interests in turn-of-the-century America."[45] Curtis's project relies on an oscillating sense of life and death, as Wakeham's use of the imaginary of the taxidermic makes clear. This shifting movement and ambiguity extends to the interpretation and continuing popularity of Curtis's images. Wakeham quotes Chris Lyman: "If pictorial photographs go out of vogue, Curtis's images sell as anthropological documents. If anthropological documents are not in fashion, his images still appeal to fans of pictorialism and devotees of popular imagery of American Indians. Even those who cannot afford to buy original photographs and photogravures can choose from a remarkable array of reproductions of Curtis's work; in posters, books, portfolios, slides, and magazines."[46] Between the imperial ambitions Curtis advanced with his photographic survey, his conflation of Native people with nature through aesthetics, the ideological projection of the images into a future tense "what will have been," and, particularly, the ambiguity of Curtis's images between art and document, Curtis created a powerful, flexible, and durable node in the humanizing project using images of Indigenous people.

Curtis produced a hybrid image in the form of ethnographic portraiture. In this sense, Curtis wasn't simply attempting to photograph a people before they disappeared in order to create a lasting record in memoriam. He was, rather, enabling the process described by Patrick Wolfe as "the elimination of the native" through the production of a material imaginary.[47] But, unlike the apparatuses of absorption described by Wolfe that sought to separate the native as biopolitical excess from the becoming-human potential citizen of the state, Curtis was—more like John Collier and his promotion of Native self-governance through economic development during his time as Commissioner of the BIA—intent on humanizing the Native *as native*, through celebration and memorialization of the Native subject, a form of elimination through positive reinforcement. This is a much more nefarious project. Understanding it requires careful attention to our work within the ruins of representation, the figures of life and death at play, and, in particular, our relationships to images.

The question of the image draws us right into the dilemma of ideological critique. Vizenor's reading of Curtis's pose seeks to expose a false or produced truth, but in order to do this Vizenor creates several strong dichotomies: ethnography and aesthetics, simulation and the real, the Native and the indian, representation and creativity, camera time and mythic time, motion and stasis, modernity and the past, facts and "imagic moments." The invention of the indian, in this sense, becomes something like what Roland Barthes refers to as a mythology, a parasitic meaning that feeds vampirically on the vitality of the sign, freezing it into place, a distinct effect of the power of the image.[48] Ideological critique is, then, about recuperating or reviving what is left of that originary vitality by exposing the frozen image that conceals it, feeding off its energies and distorting it. "Today, the natives in [Curtis's] pictures, but not the simulated indians of his photographic missions, await the recuperation of visual analogy."[49]

As many have already noted, such a notion of critique relies upon western figurations of life that are problematic, something I address more directly in chapter 5.[50] The complications of critique can be seen in the "striptease" performed in a number of his texts by a fictional character, Tune Browne, as a form of what Vizenor calls socioacupuncture. Like acupuncture, it is the piercing that releases blocked energies, flows, in order to restore balance. Tune Browne enacts such a drama by first becoming the photographic pose: "in search of our past and common memories we walk right back into these photographs, we become the invented images."[51] Running for political office, Tune Browne goes out of his way to become an *indian* to garner votes, "a dreamer who lost his soul for a time and found his families in still photographs."[52] Piercing through to reality, past the dead images, he strips off cultural attire, all that is indian, in order to reach the Native beneath. This unveiling isn't, however, to achieve identity, as there is no bedrock there. The Native, for Vizenor, is embodied, temporally mythic, storied, visionary, and constitutes an "ontic sense of presence."[53] Vizenor's conception of the Native is in direct contrast to the "simulations by separation" that "modernist constructions of culture" produce by excluding the Native as an absence and replacing it with the strange presence of simulation that is an indian, the tragic victim, the savage who becomes present only by disappearing.

As a "release from captured images," the striptease is an ambiguous metaphor, especially as Vizenor relates it to Roland Barthes's description of the "myth" of mid-twentieth-century Parisian striptease by women and its heteropatriarchal nationalization. Barthes, in his piece, reads the semiotics of the movements, gestures, and costumes, claiming that the moment the dancer is naked, she is desexualized, returned to a natural state of "perfectly chaste" flesh. There are many things to take issue with in Barthes's text, not least of which is the decision to perform a semiotic analysis of sex work without any discussion of gender, sexuality (really), or capitalism (beyond references to the petit bourgeois), but in order to understand Vizenor's use of Barthes's analysis, it is necessary to follow the line of Barthes's (and Vizenor's) argument while marking the deficiencies of the text. It is an odd choice to transpose onto the semiotics of simulation of the indian. But it is central to Vizenor's analysis of the image, as it is in the final moments of Tune Browne's striptease—transposed also in terms of gender—when the ambiguity of the metaphor occurs and we get a sense of Vizenor's performative notion of the Native. His celebratory description of the striptease as a "release," as liberation from the fixture of the indian, is a reversal of Barthes's more critical reading of the dance as a national myth. Vizenor's transversal could be read as an appropriation, which would be in keeping with Vizenor's use of a "trickster hermeneutics," which also includes the fluidity of gender embodied in many of Vizenor's characters, but the impulse to recuperate Vizenor's reading as a queer Indigenous strategy passes over some of the more sticky aspects of such a liberatory narrative.

One of the more important facets of Barthes's analysis is the idea that the "petrified eroticism," the cliché embodied in props, costumes, and gestures, acts as an inoculation of the public in order to "plunge it afterwards into a permanently immune Moral Good."[54] Moving from separation through spectacle (a male-dominated sphere of seeming sexual transgression through the gaze, which is, of course, depressingly normative) to liberal humanist progressive incorporation of striptease as a way of life (a career), Barthes documents the shift from magic show-esque spectacle to an everyday household property of the bourgeois, thereby becoming part of the national myth. This becoming myth is effected through the art of technique, the props, the costumes, which all contribute to the "meticulous exorcism of sex," so that the dance, and those who dance, can reenter the public sphere, reassuring it of its inherent goodness.[55]

Vizenor cites the first line of Barthes's text, which lays out the problem of the striptease as a dialectical contradiction in which what the dance seems to be doing (offering up sex to the male gaze) is not what it is really doing, conjuring the idea of sex like a magic trick. The ideological structure is apparent. Which is why, when the revelation occurs, Barthes makes the problematic claim that the dancer's body is desexualized as it is caught in an act of disappearance of both the props that hold up sex and the body itself, which disappears through naturalization. It is an act of revelation that is in some ways the inverse of the exposure enacted by ideological critique. The question becomes: What is *the real* for Barthes in this context? Is it sex outside the gaze, liberated from this false liberation? But this answer still centers the male gaze in opposition, hence the dialectical problem of a semiotics of the real. The answer, for Barthes, must be, in the end, the sign *sex*. Ideological critique of myths must pierce the fictional real to find the source of their meanings in a first-order semiotics. Following Marx, this piercing through is the recuperation of a language of action that eludes the second order of myth by recourse to a notion of the performative, like a woodcutter's use of the word *tree*.[56] But its recuperation also draws the sign *sex* into an economy of action that is distinctly vitalist. The vitality of signs here is akin to Friedrich Nietzsche's description of first-order metaphors as a "hot magma" of images, vital and creative metaphors which slowly individualize and deaden over time with repeated usage and become concepts that take on the stability of truth and fact and contribute to the construction of massive edifices of knowledge.[57] This knowledge is an imposition of human mental constructs onto the world, through which the world gets assimilated. The critical answer for many who ascribe to such a notion is a return to the aesthetic, the originary metaphors, or signs, in Barthes's case.

Gerald Vizenor's emphasis on the snapshot (which is Native) as contradicting the pose (of the indian) uses this strategy, but in relation to the moment of revelation when Tune Browne strips, the snapshot takes on a different valence. With the removal of his "tribal vestments," the images disappear, "the inventors and the colonialists vanished," the separation of the past from the present dissolves, and, in a dim light, naked, Tune Browne tells a story about how he and Ishi (the so-called "last of the Yahi"[58]) received honorary degrees from the University of California Berkeley as "intuitive scholars." The audience has become populated with ghosts, animals (totemic and otherwise), dream beasts, and trees, and Tune Browne addresses them in a vision, telling a story about the ceremony in the Redwoods where "morning ghosts ride with our dreams over the tribal stories from the past, dark waves, slow waves, water demons under our ocean skin waves, trickeries and turtle memories under the stone waves, under the word gates, through the earth where we hold our origins with the trees and the wind, creation myths with ocean roots. . . . The ghosts dance roundabout in our dreams, clouds dance and burn free in the rituals of the morning sun."[59] Vizenor links the story to a transvaluation in which "the despised and oppressed" are turned into "symbols of salvation and rebirth."[60] The ceremony ends with Tune Browne and Ishi both dancing in a round dance, echoing the prophetic Ghost Dance, in breechcloths and academic sashes, "a striptease, deep in cultural revolution."[61] A final call from the crowd to "take it off" brings the ceremony and the text to a close with a "word striptease. Silence . . ." followed by what can only be a postscript: N. Scott Momaday's most quoted phrase, "We are what we imagine. Our very existence consists in our imagination of ourselves . . . The greatest tragedy that can befall us is to go unimagined."[62] To which Tune Browne, in a perhaps tongue-in-cheek way, responds ambiguously, echoing Ishi, "Evelybody hoppy?"

The striptease performed by Tune Browne was an entry into "mythic time," represented by the visionary quality of the images and the playfulness of the turns and various resistances enacted. The ambiguity of Tune Browne/Ishi's final phrase, whether it is an entreaty in the form of a question or a stinging, sarcasm-laced jab—"evelybody hoppy?"—echoes its complexity. Are these representations romantic images of indians performed for a non-Native audience? But who is the audience, overlaid as it is by the denizens of mythic time? Is this the Native real beneath the fictions of representational truths? But what is to be made of the reference to transvaluation and for whom is the Native a symbol of salvation and rebirth? Are all of these just feints to draw us in? Lures promising a new turn in the obsession with the mysteries of the Native (theorist, in this case, offering a resuscitation of theory)? Yes, because it references the end of the world in the form of the Ghost Dance that promises the disappearance of the colonizers. And Tune Browne understands the desire that the colonizer also has for this end by accepting the spurious honorary degree (the colonizer, after all, came up with the concept of their own death drive, engaged manifest destiny as part of an apocalyptic strategy of revelation, and continues to push global environmental collapse). The text/ceremony, at the same time, performs this disappearance of the colonizers through the return of the dead as told in prophecy, syncing with an Indigenous intellectual tradition and response to destruction.

Photography and the Image

Photography has been both disparaged and admired for its lack of critical power, its own and what it calls for. In either case, this lack lies in the ambiguity of the photograph in terms of its identity as either a scientific tool or an aesthetic object, as well as its resistance to discourse or meaning making, its flatness or matteness as a document that simply asserts *the referent was there*. In terms of its aesthetics, while there are certainly powerful and/or beautiful photographic images as well as masters of the art, the photograph always implies something of an accident, a fortuitous moment caught as part of a series of less compelling images that end up not being developed or thrown away. The most amazing image still implies that the photographer was lucky they were there to catch it: among the proliferation of any-instant-whatevers, the photograph was simply the one that stood out. In this sense, photography is more a practice of proliferation and art of curation. The photographic image, because of its mechanical nature and documentary quality, also resists in-depth critical analysis, offering not much in the way of intervention into the image. This is to say that the photographer, subject, and viewer are connected through their respective limited agencies. Roland Barthes, for these reasons, famously lauded the passivity of the medium, finding in this passivity something of its phenomenological essence.[63]

And yet, the image is also connected to the increasingly powerful agency associated with the technomediation of the human sense of sight and power to know. Rey Chow has detailed how a totalized image of "the world," as made possible by certain imaging technologies, syncs up with Paul Virilio's insight that vision and war are intimately linked: "For men at war, the function of the weapon is the function of the eye," an expansion of the familiar analogy between the gun and the camera through the homonym *shoot*.[64] Chow notes how the same technologies are used both to extend the powers of human sight and to increase the accuracy of targeting. In this sense, the world itself, grasped as a picture/target, is no longer simply an object of knowledge but a condition for sight: "the process of (visual) objectification has become so indispensable in the age of modern scientific research that understanding—'conceiving' and 'grasping' the world—is now an act inseparable from the act of seeing—from a certain form of 'picturing.'"[65] This world picture is also a maximal target, the object to be destroyed. According to Chow, this total image with its conditioning of sight is a co-constitutive subjectivation that brings the world picture before "men" who struggle to conquer it, activating an "unlimited power for the calculating, planning, and molding of all things," in their image, a clear process of humanization.[66] Such an apocalyptic vision of unveiling, through the wedding of image and material constitution (unveiling as making a permanently unveiled world), takes the form of scientific and technological mediation, which become necessary conditions for establishing a self in a world that has become a picture/target.

To speak of the photograph in relation to the current conditions of the image makes photography seem quaint. The new total-image is understood to be embodied, dialogic, multimediated, reflexive, more supple and live, often based on acts of critique and resuscitation of the supposedly fixed and dead images of the past by perpetually self-correcting colonial forces in their updated technological, scientific, and aesthetic modes. In fact, this new image isn't an image at all but rather seeks a step beyond the regime of representation through the intricate wedding of image and materiality. As Jean Baudrillard succinctly put it (during a time when this seemed less true than today), "we have swallowed the mirror."[67] Representation has been consumed and assimilated by the forces of production. "What characterizes the so-called advanced societies is that they today consume images."[68] Multiple and with new powers drawn from its mutation, the image now functions at a cellular level, locally, and dispersed uniquely into each and every identity as an internalized and thereby erased caesura. The well-known mirror-stage dialectic between one's identity and externalized images, discussed earlier in relation to Native photography, has become a general condition of life with social media such that the effect is largely invisible. The very darkness of matter now shimmers with an infinity of opaque reflections. Almost seen. Almost there. Going a step further, as I noted, the anthropologist Eduardo Viveiros de Castro recently declared the age of anti-Narcissus, ushering in various forms of posthumanism that have left both the image and signification behind.[69]

In the proliferation of small screens, a genuinely atmospheric swarming of any-instant-whatevers, in the further eroding of the difference between still and moving images (digital), and the democratizing (?) of the aerial view, in the expansion of simulation through artificial intelligence and the deepfake, the outsourcing of memory to databases, and reliance upon real-time mapping from a global perspective using the same technology as missile guidance systems, in the materialization of the "copy" through cloning technology, *we* are reaching a point where the image hasn't simply replaced the real but the image itself has disappeared. The image no longer holds any fascination as it has become coterminous with reality; the two have become confused and their lack of distinction spells their end. The idea that there was a sense of unmediated reality now seems distant and certainly irrelevant to many contemporary experiences. This is the event that Baudrillard placed as the culmination of the drama of western metaphysics, the completion of a puzzle created twenty-five hundred years ago near the Mediterranean Sea, one materially carried out by the turns of progressive technomediation: the apocalypse.

In the Baudrillard quote about the apocalypse being the end of secrecy and the sun manifested on earth, cited by Byrd, the material conditions of this apocalypse, whether in the form of atomic destruction or the indiscernibility between screens and nerves, is mirrored by the conditions of knowledge. Just as the image has disappeared through its oversaturation and the murder of its own referent, knowledge has disappeared into various forms of telecommunication, intelligence, and data, which, thanks to increasingly complex computations carried out by machines, have become largely inaccessible to humans, even while humans still operate them.[70] And yet the database and artificial intelligence are, for Baudrillard, the end of mystery, the unveiling. Positivism has prevailed. The world has been en/decoded, or so they say.

In relation to the anticolonial project of revitalizing Native ways of being, this should give pause. While practices of representation have moved in directions that seek to disavow their own pasts—dematerializing in some cases (moving away from collections as sources of knowledge), textualizing, performing, and seeking new, sometimes experimental, but more flexible and reflexive forms of representation, even moving beyond the regime of representation entirely to the agency of things—Native peoples have become the inheritors of the dangerous, abandoned images and objects of past knowledge-production: the collections and archives. Considering these conditions, what does research in the colonial archive, a.k.a. the ruins of representation, look like for California Indian people? Through an uneasy habitus of visual and political ambiguity, California Indian communities have been engaged in such research as part of cultural revitalization efforts, which have their source in earlier prophetic movements such as the Ghost Dance and the Bole Maru. These range across language reclamation,[71] revitalization of women's coming of age and other ceremonies,[72] renewal of traditional burning practices and other forms of care for the land,[73] destruction of dams and protection of and reconnection to salmon and other nonhuman relatives,[74] resurgence of boating and other societies, and an increase in basket weavers in relation to the LandBack movement,[75] land stewardship relationships, and the development of Native gardens, among many other things. These practices often have complex relationships to the archive and the colonial visual regime.

The complex relationship is in part because the ruins of representation take many forms thanks to the multimedia approach of anthropologists—which created the salvage snapshot image, "including texts (primarily in Native languages), ethnographic observations, sound recordings, artifacts, as well as photographs. All were discrete objects in some way, and all could ultimately be preserved in a museum or archives."[76] Such a separation of the senses and bodily imaginary into differentiated media—and thereby disciplines, fields, and knowledge products—locates and materializes colonial discourses of separation into discrete objects. In order to hear a recorded song, see the instruments with which it was played, read the ethnographic notes, make sense of the words or vocables, or view a video recording of the performance requires one to move through multiple partitions, visiting different archives and collections, organized and governed by different disciplinary and institutional forms, with different rules of access and rationalized through different intellectual discourses and systems of notation. It also places the location of culture squarely within the realm of the human separated from relations with other beings, the Indigenous world translated into belief, an image, captured in archived stories. In the western sense, both ethnographically and aesthetically, culture functions to separate *humans* from *nature*—two concepts that either don't exist or don't mean the same thing in Indigenous frameworks. The work of humanization has sought to disturb what Coulthard calls grounded normativity (an interrelational sense of governance, connection, and reciprocity, what Indigenous peoples generally mean by *culture*), through both representation and, materially, through removals, terraforming the land through private and public development (including public works projects such as dams, national parks, and creation of agricultural spaces), replacing Indigenous species and food sources with large-scale agribusiness and landscaping, a settler population explosion, and destroying species through environmental devastation.[77] These colonial ruins have become a solely human imaginary, projected onto and realized through the disrupted Indigenous world.

So what does photography offer to this situation of the image for California Indian people? Speaking about the ethnophotographic collections at the Phoebe Apperson Hearst Museum on the UC Berkeley campus, Ira Jacknis, former curator of the Hearst Museum, states, "Native people are now the most interested and dedicated users of these ethnographic collections."[78] Add to this the work of California Indian photographers such as Cara Romero and Dugan Aguilar; photography collections such as *First Families: A Photographic History of California Indians,* edited by Tongva-Ajachamem artist L. Frank and Kim Hogeland, as well as the role photography has played in California Indian–centric news publications, such as *News from Native California,* and one begins to get a sense of the significance of this question. The colonial disturbance of the Indigenous world is, as I have been arguing throughout this chapter, a struggle over land and territory, including the territory or space of the image. Both paintings and photographs, from the inception of California as a settler geopolitical construct, have sought to create an image of inhabitable space for settlers. This progressive and then seemingly inexorable imaginary operates in line with the changes in the California landscape.

Barthes has also noted that photography is related to death; for him, it is the *eidos,* the distinctive expression, of the photograph.[79] Calling it a "microversion of death," like the taxidermic for Wakeham, Barthes understands that it is precisely the production of a sense of the lifelike that associates photography with death. But, as I discuss earlier, this liveliness will open up a certain power of passivity that allows photography to slip outside of discourses that seek to capture and make meaning from its images, to turn its referents into objects. Further, its elusiveness aligns the photograph with the prolixity of materiality through its very mediatory quality and materials (light, paper, chemicals), which allows for an immediate connection between viewer and viewed across time and space. Photography's destructive power has possibility for depleting the vital energy reserves upon which colonialism feeds.

Before I can begin to discuss the significance of this insight about the passivity of the image and its possibilities for California Indian people, anticolonial work, and the relation to the archive, though, I need to address Barthes's explicit proclamations of his desire to become "a primitive" as a way to evade the trap of culture.[80] A thread that runs throughout his book *Camera Lucida,* and indeed throughout the rest of his body of work, this impulse depends on the problematic separation of anthropology and history and the assumption that Indigenous people are absorbed into knowledge immediately without the possibility of critical reflection, part of nature in fact, and therefore a resource for the thoughtful critic to see, experience, and know otherwise. Barthes variously desires to be "a primitive, without culture" while looking at the photographs he loves, senses that photography is a "primitive theater" offering an opportunity to meditate on masks and death, proclaims that he is "a primitive, a child—a maniac" in order to assert his irreducible and intractable individuality, and draws on the figure of the primitive philosopher (discussed in the introduction).[81] In all these gestures, he asserts that, materially speaking, photography is a form of magic and not an art; he is, like the salvage ethnographers, using culture to adapt Indigenous ways for western critical projects. He takes these positions in order to develop his "subjective science" in the name of a universal truth as opposed to the general. What Barthes perhaps does differently, by drawing on a more difficult aspect of Indigenous conceptions of the image and reality and emphasizing their ambiguity, is offer a possible way to repatriate stolen Indigenous ideas and begin to grind the colonial project to a halt. This is in part because he does so with an explicit adisciplinary orientation: he is not trying to salvage a colonial mode of knowledge production; in fact he is attempting to neutralize the role of the professional critic.

The Ethnophotographic (Re)Turn

In 1993, my mother, a basket weaver, was awarded a Native arts grant to study the vast collection of California Indian baskets housed in the UC Berkeley warehouses. While there, she was informed by the curator that many of their archived ethnographic photos had recently been digitized and uploaded to the Online Archive of California. The curator offered to use the search engine to see if any of my mother's family members had their photos there, and, in the collection titled "Guide to the California Ethnographic Field Photographs, 1900–1960," in the subsection "Northeast California Achumawi," there were two images of my mother's grandmother: a slightly blurry facing head shot and a more focused profile.

When I arrived on campus for graduate school in 2006, I had heard

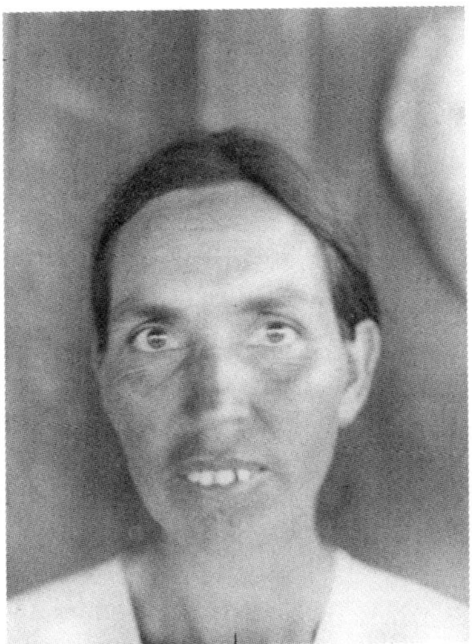
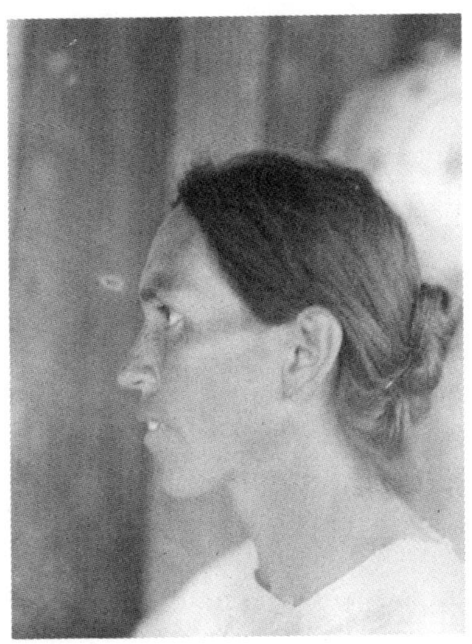

FIGURE 5. Edna Lowry, photograph by Edward W. Gifford as part of the anthropometric survey of California Indians, Modoc County, California, 1922; University of California, Berkeley, copyright Phoebe A. Hearst Museum of Anthropology and the Regents of the University of California, catalog nos. 15-7056 and 15-7057.

of the existence of these images. I had never seen them, and, to be honest, I had half-forgotten them. But it had become part of the family narrative, a complicated mixture of colonial encounters in itself. While doing research (really just drifting) in the online ethnographic collections of the curator and anthropologist Edward W. Gifford, I came across the images of my great-grandmother. Taken by Gifford, they were entitled, "Edna Lowry August, 1922" and "Edna Lowry (profile) August, 1922." Having been made aware of them, I was only half-surprised. In many ways, I was confirmed. The "oh, there you are" confirmation of family story mingled, uncomfortably, with the ethnographic and racialized evidence of one branch of my Native descent—a question of authenticity that gets raised for many mixed Native people, especially in California due to its violent past.

Part of the salvage ethnographic survey of California Indian cultures, these images were contained in a subsection of that project, as Gifford was interested in the racial science of anthropometry—the measurement of the body to try to understand and make arguments about social and racial essences. Of the 2,500 photographic negatives that have been digitized in the guide, 565 were taken by Gifford. The rest were portrait-style images, people posing in regalia, images of dwellings, ceremonial houses as well as ceremonies, certain features of the land (some sacred), and different implements. Taken by a number of other anthropologists, they represented forty-four tribes across California, organized geographically: Northeast California, Northwest California, Southern California, South Central California, and North Central California. What marks Gifford's images as anthropometric is the pairing of the facing head shot and the profile (echoing the mugshot). It is this turn away from the camera in two stilled moments that unequivocally racializes them. Resonant with Wakeham's argument about the role of taxidermic signifiers in ethnographic images, Gifford began his career as an assistant curator of ornithology at the California Academy of Sciences—a connection that is both consistent with the colonial archive and oddly echoes the complex relation of many California Indian ceremonial practices to birds; this relation to birds is at least a reprieve from the animalized language of genocidal discourse that generally used the nomenclature for deer to reference California Indians, a reference directly linked to hunting, the fur trade, and the intentional decimation of Indigenous animal species. Gifford's work as a museum curator propelled his career and informed his practice of salvage ethnography, placing his anthropometric work clearly within the logic of racial types.

The coincidence of anthropometry with salvage ethnography is, of course, not an accident. Boasian anthropology supposedly sought a distinctly pluralist and nonhierarchical understanding of cultures (in opposition to the more clearly racial and Eurocentric civilizationist discourses that he sought to critique); his notion of culture created a racialized conception of knowledge that extracted from but didn't formally address Indigenous forms of knowledge. Through this racialized conception of culture a distinction is made between the development of westernized "American" culture, founded in a modern aesthetic feeling, often adopted from Indigenous people, and that of Indigenous people themselves, an attitude which one of Boas's other students, Clark Wissler, crystallizes by calling Indigenous peoples "slackers in culture."[82] As Bennett notes, "Boasian anthropology played a key role in detaching Native Americans from the realms of American history and assigning them to a timeless anthropological present that was in America, but not of it."[83]

Boas's own interest in anthropometry makes most clear how Native cultures functioned as defamiliarizing devices for a white settler nationalizing project. Alongside his work in salvage ethnography, Boas was also engaged in studying the bodies of immigrants in U.S. public schools, which provided him with anthropometric data about the effects immigration had on the bodies of children.[84] Seemingly indicating an interest in culture's impact on the plasticity of the body, with odd resonances to the implicit hierarchization of culture and the racialization of non-white bodies, highlighting the dialectical tension between the two, Boas relied upon the racial scientific categories that generally inform anthropometry: biologically differentiated stocks of humanity named Caucasoid, Mongoloid, and Negroid. Jenny Reardon and Kim TallBear, in their article, "'Your DNA Is Our History,'" note how "in the interest of promoting 'European' knowledge, moral claims to access indigenous lands and bodies get made."[85] This construction of race, particularly whiteness as property, proceeds through genetic sciences and genographic projects that seek to map racialized populations globally in their origins and movements, an undercurrent of the culture concept. This mapping project both asserts a singular humanity and simultaneously sediments essentialized differences, making other races the property of European knowledge and yet differentiating them according to complex historical, scientific, and evolutionary calculi and narratives.

Boas conveniently left African Americans and Native Americans outside of his anthropometric science of assimilation, arguing that both groups physioanatomically would eventually disappear through interracial mixing or, in the case of Native Americans on reservations, being too distant from the centers of "culture" to become part of "American" stock (with the usual exclusion of any discussion of genocide).[86] For Bennett, this exclusion was an analogous project to and part and parcel with Boas's larger vision for anthropology to provide the guiding frameworks for white settler nationalization: "the plasticity and conjunctural mutability of inherited cultures was translated into the enculturation of [people of color] into white culture."[87] Boasian anthropology was part of the assimilative energies of the development of a national identity that was at one and the same time flexibly inclusive while centralized around whiteness. Bennett notes the historical conjuncture of a 1790 Act of Congress that limited citizenship to white land-owning persons and the immigration and citizenship laws passed between 1840 and 1924 (the year that Native Americans became citizens) as together making a laboratory for redefining whiteness. Undergirding Boas's anthropometric project was a dialectic of installing national myths and memories into descendants of Europeans—to help them forget their European ancestry—through purposeful population sciences linked to the subsidized settlement of small towns throughout the United States, a force of absorption into white nationalism using Indigenous land.

The above is one context for understanding the images of my grandmother. It is buoyed by a textual and metric supplement to the images (or vice versa, depending on how one looks at it). "Grouped under the respective California groups to which one parent belongs," the archive locates my great-grandmother under the titles "Hybrids" and "Achomawi"; alongside her images is a list of numbers and code:

> Edna Lowry. F 37 St 1710 Hsh 1405 HMF 640 Str 1760 HS 900 WSh 360 LF 450 LH 190 BH 144 LFH 186 LFN 123 BF 135 LN 52 BN 35 LE 66 BE 32——RI 102.9 CI 75.7 FI 91.1 NI 67.3 EI 48.5 (half white)——U (lighter than) 24 E 25 (ruddy on cheek bones).[88]

Measurements of her age, body (primarily), and skin tone (Gifford attempted to document the racial disappearance of California Indians in shades), these numbers insert themselves into the metrical space between the two photographs. Like all metrical units, they both facilitate connections and infinitely separate. Simply facing the camera, the image could be read as a pared-down document of humanity exposed, similar to Dorothea Lange's or Walker Evans's work (though, significantly, not Edward Curtis's), minus the aesthetic composition or even steady hand. (The images are a bit blurry, a testament to the frantic nature of the survey as a snapshot of supposedly quickly disappearing peoples.) But adding the complement of the profile, the turn away from the direct gaze of the camera with its capture of the soul in the subject's eyes, turns the affect away from humanism toward scientific meter. The turn here is both a metrical step and a step into meter. The anthropometric form connects her images to the use of anthropometry and statistics for the development of criminology, as Sekula describes, as well as the colonial and imperial use of the form to control colonized subjects around the world, especially the medicalized images of indentured workers by medical doctors on colonial plantations.[89] Different uses, perhaps, but the same form illuminates the figure of the human organizing these images.

Another more complicated context is the series of images of Edna Lowry and her family—my family. Many of these are part of private collections, including the photograph of her with her husband, Robert Lowry, that hangs on the wall in my parents' home. These images fulfill the typical sociological function of family rite. They are forms of remembrance and record family ties. Copies exist in multiple households, connecting us across these images. What is complicated about these connections is that they operate within a reformed notion of the extended nuclear family imposed by colonial conceptions of kinship. This imposition of family form is part of the "straightening" of the Native family in line with the development of private property and the destruction of collective forms of ownership, as detailed by Mark Rifkin, Scott Lauria Morgensen, and others.[90] While I have *a sense* of what social and familial relationships looked like for California Indians prior to contact, like Pico, it is a dark part inside of me.

The family as a unit has come to define my Indianness in many ways (as connection to community and ceremony, through the ubiquitous genealogical chart and ancestral ties, in the extended narrative of my family that has spilled into the public realm due to the important work many of my family members are doing),[91] and yet the blurring between family and tribe has significant historical and social complications. The federally recognized rancheria I belong to (Susanville Indian Rancheria)—because Edna and Robert Lowry became early members—is made up of four distinct "anthropologically defined" tribes—Paiute, Mountain Maidu, Pit River, and Washoe—but it was initially solely a federally recognized Paiute tribe. During reorganization, in order to not lose status, the tribe was forced to open their rolls to Native people from other tribes living in the nearby community because the Paiute were considered to be a family and, according to the federal government, a family could not be recognized as a tribe. This is how Edna and Robert became members. (Some unrecognized California Indian tribes have unrecognized status because they refused this model of reorganization.)

And yet the family form materially supports the tribal and has been an important part of survival for communities who have undergone relentless devastation and direct attempts of genocidal extermination, outside the terms of federal recognition. Speaking about the photographs of my mother's cousin, Dugan Aguilar, in the foreword to a collection of his work edited by Theresa Harlan that presents Dugan's decades-long project of documenting the endurance and resurgence of California Indian communities, founder of Heyday Books Malcolm Margolin notes:

> These are portraits of our friends and neighbors, of people we know or think we know, people glowing with the fullness of being, people whose survival in this world is nothing short of amazing. . . . Look closely at the people here. Think about who they might be, about what their parents, grandparents, and great-grandparents experienced. Imagine who their children and grandchildren might be. Look with your eyes and with your heart. *She Sang Me a Good Luck Song* is a record of a people who, against all odds, have survived. The volume you are holding in your hands is, in essence, nothing less than a Book of Miracles.[92]

Recoiling a bit from the romanticized notion of Indigenous people as "miraculous" (I prefer something more hard-edged; see chapter 4), I am nonetheless in agreement with Margolin's insight that Dugan's photography captures something of the force of survival and, I would argue, thereby necessarily something of the Destruction, of luck, both in its form of documentation and in the subjects he documented, including his own family members, my family members.

In the introduction, Harlan expands on this idea by noting the ethical and processual aspect of Dugan's work:

> There are no "stolen" moments in Dugan's photographs: he doesn't use photojournalist tricks to photograph a person without his or her knowledge, and his approach is not intrusive. Instead, through Dugan's photography, we become witnesses to intimate moments between friends and family who knowingly share their presence with him. In turn, Dugan presents each person in the light of their accomplishments and contributions. He solidifies his relationships with his subjects by presenting them with large, high-quality prints of the images. His photographs are an extension of the relationships that hold a community of individuals together; relationships that are familial, tribal, and contemporary.[93]

This last point emphasizes the significance of family and community in the photograph and of photography in the family and community. It also emphasizes the role of the photographer in offering a relational and reciprocal method. Dugan presents Indianness as part of the family form and extends it through community beyond the connections between humans. "Living in an Indigenous Light," the title of one chapter, atmospherically and materially makes communal and familial connections through the medium of photography and sight, while the chapter "In Song and Dance, We Embody the Dreams of Our Ancestors" challenges the purely visual aspect of photography. The chapter "Wa'tu Ah'lo: We Are Connected to the Earth Through Our Umbilical Cord" interrelationally connects the family to the more-than-human world and an Indigenous sense of place and land. There is no figure of the western "human" to be found here. There is no composite image but rather a collective and collectivizing one by, with, and for California Indian peoples. It is an angle of perception from gathering spaces and ceremony, a light touch that upholds and makes connections. And this perception reflects back onto the form of the family. Dugan was, after all, the one who took the family photograph every year at our family reunion, standing on a ladder to capture us all. This took place on our family's land, an allotment where the tribe of my great-great-grandmother, Julia Lowry (Mountain Maidu), Robert's mother, had a village site.

Edna Lowry's anthropometric photographs need to similarly be put into relation not only with the method of making images but also with the realm of research. In *First Families*, Two Spirit Tongva-Ajachamem artist and activist L. Frank and Kim Hogeland also emphasize an Indigenous approach to the family and photography.[94] Constituting a massive research project to present and contextualize family photographs of California Indian people across the state, Frank lays out a method that is the inverse, or perhaps shadow, of the photographic survey project of salvage ethnography:

> At the beginning of this wonderful immersion in our California Native lives, we asked if we could enter Indian homes and meeting places to look at people's personal family photo albums and record them talking about their pictures. My job was simply to look and listen. . . . People opened their lives to us. Many times they thanked us for listening instead of telling them what was important. Most of the people we listened to were elders. The images were chosen by the interviewees with no direction from me other than "Choose what is important to you and your family for whatever reason. Define yourself for yourself." What emerged was no less than incredible.[95]

The images people shared range across historical portraits (individual and family), a contemporary picture of a Tongva grindcore band, images of significant and sometimes devastating historical moments (such as "the last photo taken at Warner Springs before the Cupeño removal to

Pala, May 1903"), babies in baby baskets, Native people in regalia (both traditional and powwow style), photos representing different eras of clothing, people at work, images of revitalized cultural practices such as ti'at societies, and a prison photo.[96]

For Frank, this research is a work of exhaustion, thoughtful suspension, and reticence, even failure:

> I've talked about my journey into the real California to my friends and a few strangers, and I have tried to write about it, but only drawings came out until now. And even now, the shared emotions of more than one hundred elders' voices are really to be absorbed and pondered more than written about. Marina said to me one day something about how exhausted we were after interviewing only two families in one day (we would spend about three hours with each person). When I heard her say this, I realized I was exhausted not because three hours is a long time, but because these generous people took us down a very long path, paved deeply with timeless emotions connected to some creator or some act of magic or one particular spot on earth.[97]

The photographs become an occasion for storytelling, for beginning a journey "down a very long path" (Frank covered more than just the fifty-five thousand miles physically). The collective feelings of elders open up a certain passivity before them, perhaps onto the interminable, translated here as timeless, magic, a particular spot on earth. What accumulates are not just the fifteen hundred images collected or even the hours and hours of stories told, but the exhaustion itself, a passive action that connects the project to the exhaustion of ghost dancers in their collectively felt emotions.

Unlike Dugan's book, which emphasizes the images and spares explanation, Frank and Hogeland's tightly weaves words and images, echoing at times the ethnographic in drawing abstract geographic boundaries (for organizational purposes), explaining the images with cultural and historical contexts presented as information, flat facts. There are also profound moments of analysis in the stories of the people who offered the photographs, such as Richard Stewart's description of his grandfather, Louie Stewart, buying the camera in 1919 that produced the images present in the book as well as a compact recorder to tape himself telling stories and explaining the Paiute language shortly before he died. "He carried on with himself because there was no one else around. And he kind of like fell in love with the machine. . . . So you're kind of moving with the time and staying with it. . . . And the interesting thing was, when he died is when I found out he couldn't read or write."[98] *Moving with the time and staying with it,* using the recording device to archive what can't be read or written. I discuss this art of preservation in the last chapter of this book because it resonates with Maidu painter Frank Day's similar project. It is a project that was seemingly widespread, a generalized singular response to the destruction. The self-recording of stories, songs, and language is part of the deep personal archives of California Indian families, mapping what Frank calls "the real California."[99] This auditory map obliquely is the soundtrack for the family photographs.

First Families is another place where I ran across images of my great-grandmother, this time intentionally; I went looking for them. Frank interviewed Dugan and his mother, Virginia Aguilar, and they provided two images of Edna Lowry, Virginia's mother. The first was taken sometime in the 1890s and shows her as a very young woman or an older girl. The photo is cropped, as elbows of seemingly two men seated and wearing jackets are visible resting on a table on either side of her. Edna stands, staring directly into the camera, her right hand resting palm down on the table. She is wearing a white dress, wrinkled with poofy shoulders and a sash for a belt. A shawl of some sort made of a darker material is clasped tightly at her neck and drapes unevenly down her torso. Her expression, to me, is inscrutable. I don't know if this is the oldest image of her, but her youth renders her nearly unrecognizable to me in relation to the other images of her I know. I have seen this image before, in my mother's collection. I have also seen the second one, taken in 1910, of my great-grandmother seated with three of her young children and a small dog, the youngest child on her lap. Here to me she looks much more like her. Her features, ones that I see in certain members of my family, are much more defined. What is perhaps striking about this image is that my great-grandmother is the only one, including the dog, who isn't looking directly into the camera; she looks slightly off-center/out of frame.

In Frank and Hogeland's book, the images of Edna Lowry are surrounded by images of her family, her daughter Virginia and son-in-law Robert Aguilar, her grandson Dugan and granddaughter Judith Lowry, her husband Robert and his brother Wyatt Lowry, her son Leonard Lowry, and her mother Susie Evans. These are the images one finds in a family photo album; many of them are in my mother's album. What aren't included in these or any other albums are anthropometric photographs. They are left in the museum and under the sign of a now-outdated racialized science. What would it take to bring them home?

Edna Lowry's anthropometric images are caught between the form of the images, the context of anthropometry, and the content, in this case, my great-grandmother, the context of family photographs. Her images are also caught between the cultural image of the salvage snapshot and the racialized image of a disappearing Indianness. Perhaps the approach shouldn't be one of trying to critically analyze all these contexts, using them to explain the images, causing the images themselves to in a sense become more real, to take or develop, becoming more ensnared in the various discourses and their attempts to make the images mean something. Returning to the point about the lack of photography's critical power, perhaps the answer is to lean more heavily into the ambiguity of the images themselves, an ambiguity that coincides with the ambiguity of the medium, offering a different sense of what is real. The power of the photograph as a mechanically produced document is, after all, to say that Edna Lowry was there, a proof without meaning. In a very real way, these documents are my great-grandmother. Despite the violence of the image, what I know is that my grandmother was there when these images were taken and a photographer, seemingly Gifford, was there taking them. I also know that the light that emanated from her and into the lens, captured on celluloid and then developed through a chemical process then digitized, also emanates from the screen into my eyes. Her eyes emanate directly into my eyes, connecting us materially through the medium of light. This is a profound suspension of time. Having been there to the question of her return home, raised by the violence of these images, is truly a question about the return of the ancestor, the return of the dead.

A different real, the real California, is realized in the image in the way it awakens the passive in me. This real lies somewhere between the generality of the composite image (the mean) and the universal that Barthes seeks in his subjective science and is neither of them, being far too antihuman. The images as indexicals point to Edna Lowry without pulling her into the powerful whirlpool of meaning making, without making her work for us today (absorbed into culture, aesthetics, or politics and our everyday affairs). She is here before me, one hundred years later as I write this, and she is there in the past. She is also, of course, not here as it is her image I see, and not there any longer. Photography was

FIGURE 6. Rick Bartow, *CS Indian*, 2014, pastel, tempera, graphite on paper, 44.5 × 44.5 in. Bartow Trusts.

already, as an obsolete medium, suspended between the referent that is there and the return. It is a medium made for a postapocalyptic imaginary. But the complications of genocide, colonialism, and scientific racism and its images heighten the force of revelation and its destruction, the light of camera lucida, creating a conundrum for California Indian people: What is the postapocalyptic relation to death? Does it have something to do with the complicated Indianness that passages (camera obscura) through all these images?

Wiyot painter Rick Bartow has created an image with paper, paint, and graphite that, to my mind, captures the essence of this real, between mean and universal and neither of these, as it relates to resemblance, ancestral relations across time, and the ambiguity of the image

FIGURE 7. Byron Lotches, photograph by Samuel A. Barrett as part of the anthropometric survey of California Indians, Klamath Reservation, Oregon, 1907; University of California, Berkeley, copyright Phoebe A. Hearst Museum of Anthropology and the Regents of the University of California, catalog no. 15-4087.

awakening the passive within it. *CS Indian* in its resemblance to a face and head, seemingly morphing into one of the bird people that Bartow is known for painting without actually taking shape (a whiff of a suggestion), the two-dimensional fracturing of features without distinct breaks (even smeared), the multiplication and absence of perspective, recognizable eyes (too many) and a partial mouth, in the disorientation of the face with merely implied coordinates such as ears, the resonance with his proliferation of self-portraits in the form of animal-humans and other inhuman things, smudging of bright colors jarringly juxtaposed, and the hues of grayscale that seem to stretch the mind, has collapsed the postapocalyptic structure of time, of before and after destruction, of the sense of the apocalypse as light and destruction, of the *there* of ancestors before the creation of photography with the here and there, the nowhere and nowhen after it, into a density of an interminable moment. If there is a composite image of an Indian, I wager this is it. This is an other generality that opens onto the avisual conditions

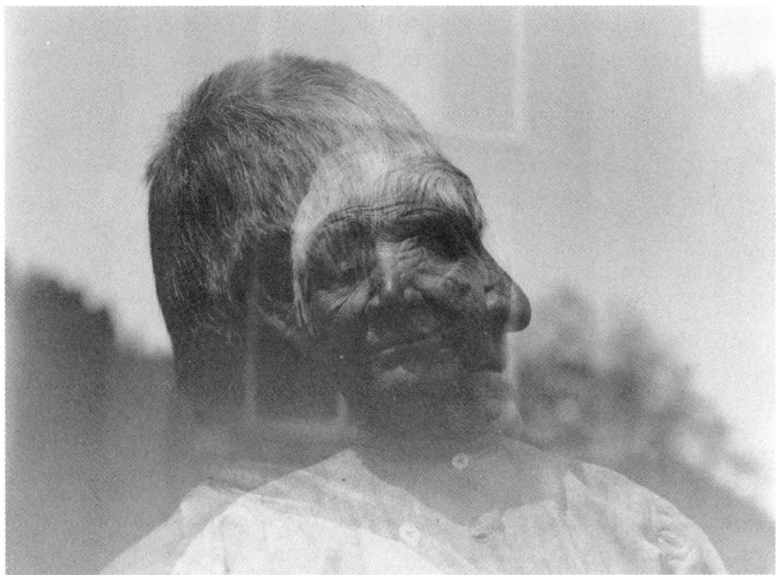

FIGURE 8. Old Woman Becky, photograph by Alfred L. Kroeber as part of the anthropometric survey of California Indians, Hoopa Valley Reservation, Humboldt County, California, 1907; University of California, Berkeley, copyright Phoebe A. Hearst Museum of Anthropology and the Regents of the University of California, catalog no. 15-3755.

of the image. Bartow has said that the eyes in this painting are the eyes of ancestors that have moved across time (CS is a reference to one of Bartow's ancestors). I say these eyes have destroyed time and also move across it, changing the relationships to the face that here seeks to hold, but cannot, all that is specific and general, resembling and distinct. It asks *what is Indian* about the face? Indianness in an image. The ethnophotographic turn is here turning in the partial and suggested angles, profile and forward-facing head shot collapsed in the same image/face. It says, *we were always here.*

When my mother first saw the anthropometric images of Edna Lowry, she saw sickness. My mother had told us that Edna Lowry must have been dying when the images were made due to her drawn-in face, accentuated by her protruding, crooked teeth and large, glossy, and etherealized eyes. She did die of tuberculosis but not until 1938, sixteen years after the photo was taken. Yet my mother was not wrong: she was searching for a language to respond to the destruction evident in the medium and the images. In the image of sickness lies the resistance to language caused by the colonial disturbance. It is a story that was made in a moment or made on the drive home. The image lingers, it comes forward with a certain truth when one actually looks away from it and drops the scrutiny. My great-grandmother is caught in a moment of dying by the very technology that makes the image both a death and the deferral of death, a mourning and the deferral of mourning. As Sontag observes, "These early technologies stage the vanishing 'now' to construct a past that can be accessed (and mourned) at some later time."[100] When do we get to mourn her? "Whether or not the subject is already dead, every photograph is this catastrophe."[101] Barthes was inspired to write this statement by a photograph of a young man, Lewis Payne, waiting in his cell to be hanged, in relation to a photograph of Barthes's recently deceased mother as a child, whom Barthes was still mourning when he wrote *Camera Lucida*. But in the photograph of my great-grandmother, the apocalypse is ongoing in a different way. It's not simply a moment or an individual is risked and lost by technologically produced nostalgia, but the world itself for entire peoples.

What the colonial disturbance caught/caused in the photograph is the disturbance of the relation to death. This direct disturbance takes shape as suppressing and outlawing ceremonies, lessening of the use of burnings to mediate death due to assimilation, targeting gendercide of third-gendered people who often were the caretakers of the dead (chapter 4), digging up and absconding of the bodies of ancestors (chapter 1), and destroying and replacing the world of the dead and our forms of relationality with a humanist theology (both secular and religious). In this postapocalyptic relation to death, the archive and the images of our ancestors stand in for the relation to death, with the form of destruction, and research has become a sort of ceremony. In the interdiction on mourning produced by the colonial disturbance is found a grief deferred, one that cannot transform into mourning and be thereby resolved. It is an infinite grief that finds no direct expression. The ethnographic image produces death while trying to preserve life, an asymbolic death outside of mourning, outside of the usual rhythms of life, of ceremony usually conceived. In this sense, perhaps the project of turning to our ancestors and of their returning to us is one not of giving back their humanity but their ambiguity, before us.

I close my eyes and see Edna Lowry's teeth, chin tattoos, and eyes. What I see is the destruction captured in those eyes. In the frontal image, the process of becoming death through objectification itself gets objectified in the distinct reflection in her eyes of the light source. The absolute inseparability of the referent from the medium exposes the violence that the medium enacts on the referent through its very act of preservation. "The Photograph belongs to that class of laminated objects whose two leaves cannot be separated without destroying them both."[102] One cannot separate the referent from the medium, my great-grandmother from the anthropometric image of her, without destroying both. The photograph sticks, like a flypaper made of light. The gluing together itself, as act, has been captured in this image. In the moment of encounter between a technology that perhaps lay outside of my great-grandmother's image-repertoire *and* her image-repertoire proper—the object of ethnography—which gets eclipsed in the articulation caused by the light source, by the two lines of reflected light slicing across the irises of her eyes, objectification gets objectified, opening onto the disorientation of the destruction itself. The reflected light is the invisible glue holding together the seemingly inseparable referent and medium, a seam in the otherwise translucent lamina. It is also an image of what connects us materially across time. Appropriately, the reflection interrupts her gaze, obscuring the pupils, a gaze that, if left uninterrupted, would be, like the technologically limited early ethnomusicological recordings of songs of mourning, unbearable. The glossy eyes show the effects of lamination. This irruption of the medium into the flattened distance between lens and eyes raises questions: What did she see when asked to pose before the camera? What infinity did she stare into, knowing that the condition of her being photographed was her and her people's assumed disappearance?

> In the beginning it was always dark. Darkness was a woman, who had two daughters, and came from the eastward to gamble with Wildcat. She reached Wildcat's house at night, and after supper began to talk about gambling, saying, "I never came here before. I came to gamble." The others present advised Wildcat to play: so all the preparations were made, and, sitting on either side of the fire, they began to play. Darkness bet her two daughters against all the people which Wildcat had. Darkness wanted Wildcat to bet her husband, Chicken-Hawk, but she did not wish to. Finally, on Coyote's advice, she bet him as chief first. Then they began to play, Coyote helping to sing. He thought the game was going favorably, and that Wildcat would win the two girls, and that he would get

them for wives. But just as she almost won, Darkness beat her, and, taking Coyote, broke him in two and threw him outside. Darkness then threatened to "stay dark all the time" unless Wildcat would bet her husband, as Darkness wanted him for a husband for her daughters. Wildcat refused, and bet other people in the house. All but three offered themselves to be bet. These were Rabbit, Lizard, and Caterpillar. Finally all were lost to Darkness but these . . .[103]

Chapter 3
Refusing Genocide

Of course, they will never admit—or perhaps they will simply never understand—what I have just written here: that the essence of genocide is the destruction of the archive. But they are historians. One cannot ask them to understand a world grounded on the destruction of that which is their very essence, and not only their profession: the archive.

—Marc Nichanian, *The Historiographic Perversion*

We're the evidence of the crime. They can't deal with the reality of who we are because then they have to deal with the reality of what they have done. If they deal with the reality of who we are, they have to deal with the reality of who they aren't.

—John Trudell, *When Columbus Got Off the Boat*

As I finish up revisions for this chapter, South Africa has brought charges against Israel for committing genocide in Gaza, while the five-year project of the Truth and Healing investigations into California's violence against Indigenous peoples nears its end. These two occurrences are not unrelated and, in fact, operate like a crystallized node of temporal and spatial collapse. Without intervention, Palestinians can see their future, decades or centuries later, in a forthcoming investigation by the state of Israel into its own current and future past atrocities refracted through California, if they so choose, with the apologies and tentative recognitions of "past" violence (always past). This isn't to imply a carbon copy of settler colonial violence that proceeds without difference. The temporality and narratives that Palestinians maintain in relation to settler colonialism, genocide, apartheid, segregation, and mass incarceration—to name only a few of the colonial situations they confront—are specific and inevitably change the relation to the state and any possible future. Just like Israel, with its advanced weapons and "security" apparatus, Palestinians have tools at their disposal that California Indians did not have at the height of U.S. genocidal violence.

Nonetheless, the connection between Israel and the United States is a powerful one that is both material, in terms of the entangled interests of Israel and the United States and the latter's support of genocide in the form of weapons and capital, and discursive, in the logics used by both to justify violence against an Indigenous population they each seek to displace.

Watching the genocide of Gaza unfold in real time on social media, as someone who has spent an inordinate amount of time reading about genocide in California and growing up hearing the stories, is both uncanny (as was my time spent in the West Bank and East Jerusalem a few years back) and also viciously defamiliarizing. The speed and horror of the decimation of Gaza and its people has ripped the world open and exposed its viscera in a way that no other event has done before.[1] I've read and heard the stories of U.S. soldiers and militia's treatment of California Indian children: the archive is full of body parts, but I have rarely seen the images. Gaza and its children, on the other hand, have their meat, intestines, organs, and torn and burned flesh exposed before the world. The bluntness of official Israeli dehumanization of Palestinian life—Netanyahu's invocation of Amalek and that story's call for the total destruction of a people and their world, the Israeli prime minister's Twitter account dividing up of the colonial world into children of light and darkness, Israel's defense minister Yoav Gallant calling Palestinians "human animals"—to name just a few incidents, echo the language used by U.S. officials to reference Indigenous peoples, as well as other colonial situations around the world in the generalized call to *exterminate the brutes* in the name of western civilization, the western humanist project. (Though U.S. officials were sometimes a bit more cagey, less blunt.) Even the sadistically playful social media posts by Israel Occupation Force (IOF) soldiers echo the casual cruelty of U.S. soldiers and militia in their treatment of Indigenous peoples. It is both all too familiar and so disorienting as to knock the world off its axis.

The South African case against Israel before the International Court of Justice (ICJ) will continue, as will the other cases being brought by other nations, including before another international tribunal, the International Criminal Court (ICC). What powers Israel has to disrupt or ignore any outcome will likely be determined by the position of the United States and its privileged status and effective immunity, which it has extended to Israel until now. Thanks to radical shifts in international power, that may no longer be the case. What is important for this chapter is how the stories of Palestinians, their deaths, and the destruction of their world have made their way out of Gaza. Through a combination of on-the-ground reporting by some of the bravest people that have ever existed—a situation that Israel is using to directly target journalists and their families, who have died in numbers that exceed any other conflict—and social media, which has become a site of intense struggle against censorship, Palestinians through popular control of the narrative have been able to combat the dominant state discourse and mainstream media propaganda in a way never seen before. Not only do we get testimonies, but bodies themselves speak: destroyed and mutilated bodies, exhumed bodies, bodies in action trying to dig other bodies out of the rubble or amputating limbs. The land speaks, tells the story of its decimation. It is a form of gestural communication through which the very destruction itself speaks. The other side of this communication is that Israel and its actors have consistently incriminated themselves through the same medium. The juxtaposition of taunting Israeli soldiers committing atrocities and Palestinian bodies is stark. And the power of these images and their circulation on social media has not been lost on those bringing the charge of genocide against Israel who have crowd-sourced social media information, images, and stories, for their case, bringing these as evidence before the ICJ.

Such a turn in the archive from official to popular, from a war of words without a commensurate forum to the world itself as witness, is important because, in its destruction of Gaza, Israel has targeted universities, libraries, memorials, religious architecture, as well as cemeteries and recent mass graves. It has targeted educators, authors, journalists, and international witnesses. Israel has, of course, also targeted Palestinian life and bodies that act as archives and witnesses, including the basics of the maintenance of life, infrastructure and hospitals. Despite flimsy arguments about Hamas tunnels and infiltration into civilian life, the logic is crystal clear. As Marc Nichanian notes, "Conquerors have always destroyed the archives of conquered peoples. Colonizers have always managed so that the archives would reflect their perspective on history rather than the perspective of the colonized. One has always converted, massacred, annihilated, while also annihilating the very memory of the conversion and annihilation, erasing the monuments, the tombs, the funerary stones, the traces of the sacred, the sites of life and the sites of death, of mourning."[2] Setting aside for now discussion of the efficacy of the ICJ or even of the charge of genocide (a topic

I discuss throughout this chapter), the turn to the popular archive is a powerful shift in the rhetorical situation of combatting mass violence and colonialism. While Palestinians remain physically at the mercy of a more powerful and heavily funded military, undergoing massive death and destruction, the destruction is never limited to just a body count.[3] Palestinians are fighting a successful war over the symbolic realm, what they call (ongoing) *catastrophe*, the *Nakba*. Moving from the traditional spheres of the archive and testimony and even from the post-witness forms of architectural and other material evidence employed by human rights groups such as Forensic Architecture (both of which take time to amass), they have instead used popular forms of media to archive instantly their deaths in the devices and minds of people all around the world, to turn everyone into an archive and witness, to turn the world itself into a witness. They have woken people up.

This chapter addresses the limitations of the discourse on genocide, its relation to historiography, and the disciplinary role History has played in California Indian studies (including especially the specifics of the archive of violence), and how the destruction registers or not in these discourses. I begin with Gaza in part because I cannot imagine revising a chapter on genocide right now and not beginning with it—Gaza has broken me—but there are lessons to be learned between the contexts of California and Gaza that perhaps go both ways. One is the relation between how both the United States and Israel have each sought to make sense of their respective violences against Indigenous peoples, a making sense that requires rendering Indigenous conceptions of and responses to violence nonsensical or a threat worthy of more violence. It has taken the state of California a hundred and seventy years to "recognize" its foundational violence in an official manner. This time lag already significantly dampens the impact of such acknowledgment, but the discursive modes of making sense of the violence negate unofficial, collective, and popular discourses such as story—a general condition of the historiographic control of and reliance on, and therefore destruction of, the archive. The lesson from California: don't let them turn your death into history. A lesson we share with Palestinians: fuck western civilization. This is what is so powerful about the collective, grassroots form that the documentation of genocide in Gaza is taking. It moves against historiography and western colonial forms, including the law (I'll say more later).

One of the intellectual frameworks somewhat adjacent to this chapter is genocide studies, a largely comparative project for historians that I discuss and refuse. It is a field haunted by a comparative dilemma that has affected both Native Americans and Palestinians—though by no means in an equal manner. This dilemma is the narrative of the singularity of the Holocaust, which has been upheld as a paradigmatic case of genocide and also as unassailable in both its singularity and inapproachability. That is, it is perceived by some to exceed any attempt at knowledge of it. Explanations, particularly historicist material ones, have been understood to be denialist in essence, an insult to the event. It is both normative and an impossible threshold, like the white western human. This problem crystallizes in Israel's defense of their actions in Gaza, their description of Hamas's jailbreak and incursion on October 7, 2023, into Israeli territory as a "second Holocaust," already weakening the singularity through its faux-repetition. According to Israel's logic, this "second Holocaust" justifies all their actions after October 7 (and before!) as being nongenocidal, drawing on the powers of Holocaust memory to claim immunity. The instrumentality of *defense*, a "defense" that has been the motivation for decades of occupation; the building of illegal settlements; mass incarceration, detention, and torture; an embargo; an apartheid system to commit mass violence and destruction, marks these more extreme measures by Israel as somehow a lesser violence sheerly due to its supposedly instrumental nature—and, of course, marks Israeli lives as worth more than Palestinian lives, as more human, through an unbearable calculation.

As I argue in this chapter, these distinctions form part of a humanizing logic that continues to subject colonized and racialized peoples to self-disavowing violence through logics of instrumentality. This logic is two-pronged: according to colonial logics, colonial violence is less significant because they do it for a reason—economic, defensive, territorial—and colonized peoples are lower on the humanist ontological hierarchy due to using instrumental forms of reason, despite being the ones subjected to instrumental violence. I'll address this in more detail later, but the Holocaust as the paradigmatic *crime against humanity*, according to this humanist logic, marks a division between a supposedly noninstrumental violence that exceeds comprehension (where, as Nichanian has shown, its meaninglessness is the meaning attributed to it[4]) and other forms of mass violence, particularly colonial, which are supposedly explainable and even reasonable. The irony, of course, is that Israel's continuing instrumentalization of Holocaust memory to justify state violence works directly against its own project of asserting the Holocaust's singular noninstrumental force. Like with their faux-charges of antisemitism against anyone who speaks in support of Palestinians, Israel actually works toward making the Holocaust mean less—but in a different way than the event's ontological challenge to meaning.

Moving outside the narrow confines of genocide discourse in this chapter, then, means rearranging the connections between different contexts through an interrelational framework as opposed to a comparative one. This mode of interrelation marks the interruption created by the destruction in each context, specifically, and across differential resonances, often with material entanglements. Rather than closing people off through the notion of an individual case (like Lisa Lowe's archive of historical silos), as with Palestinians right now, violence opens us up to the world and to each other through our collective refusal of it. To understand how the meaning-making of violence has been used to control peoples through our relations to our dead and through narrow conceptions of identification, in this chapter, I explore the historiographic project of *proving* a genocide occurred, what Dylan Rodríguez calls "the discursive regime of genocide."[5] The canonical discourse revolves around the term *genocide* and the question of whether or not the various acts of violence committed by the state and its actors against Indigenous people can be defined by the term. As part of the state's narrative and the discursive production of a scholarly and institutional record, especially considering the lack of material consequences or legal culpability on the part of the settler state, this historiographic project is one whose goal is primarily to make sense of the violence, to give it a story, and to provide an opportunity for the ritual renewal of the state's authority through repentance.

The Coloniality of Disciplinarity

This chapter is focused primarily on the current discourse of genocide in California. I am not concerned, necessarily, with critiquing or engaging genocide deniers or wading into the debate to assert a genocide occurred in California, a debate that is at its core already negationist of the destruction. We need no proofs. Rather, I focus on those who seek to prove or support the claim that a genocide took place using a strict sense of proof in order to understand the force of such meaning-making. The open acknowledgment of the genocidal history of California, evidenced by Governor Gavin Newsom's 2019 apology made via executive order and by the ongoing Truth and Healing Council investigations into the state's treatment of Indigenous people, has shifted California Indian studies and created renewed interest in how we discuss the destruction. Because it is based on an international legal definition and because that legal definition doesn't apply to actions prior to 1948 (or to *cultural genocide,* thanks to U.S. and other settler state interventions in the international legislative process), *genocide* has generally been the domain of historiography related to Native Americans and many other Indigenous populations. The structure of meaning and narrative that had previously made sense of the violence, even if through repression, now no longer seems to hold sway. This shift in public discourse indicates that the articulation between meaning and violence has become somewhat untethered. It presents new opportunities and risks for California Indian peoples.

The first risk is the juridical nature of the term *genocide.* Often considered one of the defining achievements of international human rights legislation, the United Nations Convention on the Prevention and Punishment of the Crime of Genocide was passed in 1948, though it was not ratified by the United States until 1988 and only after adoption of a series of conditions called the Lugar-Helms-Hatch Sovereignty Package. Among other things, the package includes the language that "nothing in the Convention requires or authorizes legislation or other action by the United States prohibited by the Constitution of the United States as interpreted by the United States."[6] For the United States to be tried for genocide as the ICJ requires, according to this *genocide treaty,* "the specific consent of the United States."[7] The law presents a conundrum for Indigenous people in settler states, many of whom turn to the international arena to assert rights outside the authority of those states. Investigations, for instance, even when mandated by an international body, tend to take place through state apparatuses, and the tools of redress tend to be reconciliatory according to state terms, such as reparations.[8] The United States, which effectively made itself immune to international oversight and has continuously asserted its sovereignty over that of the international community, exacerbates this problem. Add to this the machinations of the United States and other settler states in ensuring that *cultural genocide* was removed from the draft legislation and the fact that the law is not retroactive, and one wonders what it even means to declare that the state of California enacted a "genocide" against California Indians.[9] What is the force of the term?

If it is for the sake of truth, one can question the relation between truth and the law as it relates to the destruction. I discuss in this chapter the debates between historians and scholars critical of historiographic claims to empirical truth, specifically why these debates, which took place throughout the 1980s and '90s, revolved around the question of genocide (and the ferocious debates that took place within historiography over the question of comparative genocide in relation to Native Americans and the singularity of the Holocaust), culminating in some ways in the critical field of genocide studies. What is telling is the way that genocide studies relies so rigorously on the international legal definition for a historiographic discourse, using the juridical form for a representational practice to decide the truth without drawing on the performative force of the law. On one hand, this indicates the inherently juridical nature of institutional narratives such as historiography, the good, universal humanism, progressive revelation, settler common sense and reason. It clearly shows the complicity between history as a discipline and the violence of the rule of law, in the name of which genocide was committed anyway, rendering institutional history, as a settler discipline, complicit with genocidal violence. On the other, it opens a conversation about the destruction outside the terms of the law's violence within the realm of study, a rupture in the law's inherent means-and-ends thinking, a perhaps unintended consequence of the discourse that may be worth following.

If it is for the sake of holding states accountable, for justice, for "law and order," beyond even the obvious lack of effectiveness detailed in this chapter, it must be noted that law here takes on a clearly racial-colonial form. Martinican anticolonial poet and scholar Aimé Césaire, in 1950, described the coloniality of the definition of genocide, two years after the law's passage. Naming the law as a response to intra-European violence—and particularly violence against white Europeans—he notes how the law ignores the brutal histories of colonization and the western humanist project that resulted in the deaths and enslavement of hundreds of millions of non-white peoples around the world. Beyond even this horrific empirical and structural challenge to the universal claims of the law, the very idea of appealing to a legal order logically predicated on expansion and territorial acquisition in the name of civilization and law and order, state-formation and western reason, is deeply counterintuitive. Adding to this, Samera Esmeir describes a form of juridical humanism imposed through colonial expansion and the paradoxical ethics of nonviolence that produces extreme amounts of violence done in the name of the law itself.[10] These are the conditions for the monopolization of violence by states that rely on the law as guarantor of this right. The irony, of course, is that the category of genocide was created to place limits on this violence, to create thresholds between humanitarian and inhuman forms of violence by states. But David Kazanjian shows how the category of savagery transmits across a vague temporal threshold as a force of humanization, in which colonized Indigenous populations now hold states accountable for their past savagery. It is a co-constitutive reconciliatory project based in what Kazanjian, citing Louis Althusser, calls an "international of decent feelings" as the ongoing disciplinary practice of making-human.[11]

Across the divide between the savage and the Native, History as a discipline taps into this promise of humanization. It turns the savage into a void as condition for the creation of meaningful oppositions (colonizer/colonized, separation/reconciliation, human/nonhuman, nature/culture) to be overcome. Progress as historical development has always moved by filling this space with meaningful action, with content, with narratives. The savage, as figure of emptiness beyond even the historical a priori conditions of legal categories such as "discovery" and "terra nullius," prepares the way for the Native. Indigeneity is, then, the manageable category of this divide, allowing the work to continue by both being accomplished in it, by definition, and realized in its needs, as developing, such that the emptiness of the savage becomes a certain capacity of and/or for the human. This version of the void is part of the system, a faux discontinuity that works in its service. Such is perhaps the basis of Brendan Hokowhitu's profound critique of Indigenous studies as either a field of universalization through rational development or of opposition that functions as a conflictual dialectic (what he calls "decolonization"), neither being a true discontinuity.[12] These positions are manifest in both the state and the university institutionally by the professional critic who negates in service of the institution, who reforms and manages risk.

History isn't really about time, then; it's about revelation and narrative as the work of making sense and making safe (making sense: making certain people who fulfill the figure of the normative human and the state safe); it's about creating a "global narrative of the universal history of humanity," a mode of knowledge, as Rey Chow reminds us, that is geographically specific with universalizing pretensions and military in origin.[13] History attempts time's redemption, which is necessarily its betrayal. Defined by Walter Mignolo and Catherine E. Walsh (following Anibal Quijano) as the control and management of knowledge by the "universals" of western humanism, eurocentrism, and global capitalism, the coloniality of time subtends History's attempts to control the past and thereby control the present and future.[14] As a mode of western humanist knowledge and practice, History claims to be neutral, universal, and apolitical in its methodology and has led to the erasure of entire Indigenous knowledge systems and frameworks for understanding both time and violence. Further, all the talk about humans and nature, about denaturalization, the critical mastery of what exceeds human control (the inhuman in the form of commodification, technology, and domination), that which places finite limits on human freedom and marks the project of historicity, is what must be redeemed, a nature that precedes and survives history's humanizing force. The dialectical tensions between culture and nature, determination and freedom, presume this force of humanization, what Giorgio Agamben calls the "anthropological machine" that renders the world human, anthropogenic, according to human mastery over nature's forces, including time.[15] For Chow, a visual logic brings this clearly into view, through a combination of technomediated visuality that seeks ultimate reduction and efficiency (the entire world as an accessible picture for human consumption and control) and a form of peace integrated with the visuality of war (world as target). Together these form a knowledge based on information for targeting. Area studies, anthropology, culture as containment, and, specifically, history as a philological discipline of civilizations—disciplines that are complicit with state security and intelligence agencies—contribute to this mode of weaponized knowledge. For Chow, it is representative of a self-reflexive arrogance that produces a "circuit of targeting the other that consolidates the omnipotence and omnipresence of the sovereign [human] self," a knowledge destined to destroy or assimilate, which is another way of describing knowledge as destruction.[16] In this sense, the settler colonial project has always sought to insulate itself from risk (or assimilate it as its own), to take pleasure in the spectacle of the Native, a spectacle that is destructive, without risking anything in the encounter. Historians risk nothing by declaring our genocide or negating it.

Making Meaning Out of Violence

Was it a genocide or not? The various events and forms of violence that mark "the destruction of California Indians," as anthropologist Robert Heizer in 1974 dubbed settler violence during the gold rush era, have invariably become sites of intense investigation and debate in historiography, to the point that the discipline of History has largely claimed the exclusive right to narrate the truth of what happened. This narrative and debate have, at least since the 1990s, often boiled down to the question of whether the violence can be construed as genocide.[17] The narrowness of this question and its institutionalization through historiography and international legal definition operate through what Rodríguez describes as a "discursive regime that attempts to fold an alleged extremity of modern power into an accessible conceptual-juridical artifact. In this sense, 'genocide' invokes, but cannot fully engage, a deep tracing of the violences, exterminations, and fatalities encompassed by the long preceding processes of the global Civilizational project."[18] This regime of genocide discourse, which seeks to make sense of and make "accessible" (one wants to say *consumable*) the destruction, the end of the world, to render it into an articulable truth, is a power made visible by three intertwined discursive contexts that make up the historiographic poetics of genocide in California: (1) the coloniality of disciplinarity as the site of the production of truth as a plot; (2) the crisis that the discipline of History underwent, beginning in the 1990s, in relation to representational politics revolving around the question of writing genocide; and (3) the role California has played as a case study of genocide committed against Native Americans, a role most clearly explicated and argued for by historian Benjamin Madley in his book *An American Genocide* (2016).

The term *genocide,* coined by Raphael Lemkin in 1943, seeks to account for and render legible as a crime mass violence done with the intent to exterminate, or the effect of attempting the extermination of, entire peoples. Defined in the midst of World War II in direct response to German atrocities committed against various peoples but especially the killing of six million Jews and adopted (though in modified form) in the UN Convention on the Prevention and Punishment of the Crime of Genocide in 1948, the coloniality of the term was immediately recognized by members of communities that had been undergoing racial and colonial mass violence for centuries, as evidenced by this passage from Césaire's *Discourse on Colonialism* (1950):

> And they wait, and they hope; and they hide the truth from themselves, that it is barbarism, the supreme barbarism, the crowning barbarism that sums up all the daily barbarisms; that it is Nazism, yes, but that before they were its victims, they were its accomplices; that they tolerated that Nazism before it was inflicted on them, that they absolved it, shut their eyes to it, legitimized it, because, until then, it had been applied only to non-European peoples; that they have cultivated that Nazism, that they are responsible for it, and that before engulfing the whole edifice of Western, Christian civilization in its reddened waters, it oozes, seeps, and trickles from every crack.[19]

David Kazanjian, in his essay "Re-flexion: Genocide in Ruins," in the context of the Armenian catastrophe enacted by the Turkish state in the late nineteenth and early twentieth centuries, describes Lemkin's development of the definition of genocide and relates it to earlier terms he used to define mass violence. Cautioning against the new "international mentality" based on a universal humanist "moral campaign," Kazanjian asks: What is concealed by use of the term? What sociopolitical complexities and realities do not get acknowledged?[20]

Dylan Rodríguez, noting the canonical point of reference that the Holocaust performs for the term *genocide* and "the hegemonic humanist (and thus anti-Black, racial-colonial, juridical and epistemological) assumptions that structure its circulation within the modern global text," offers an answer: "While the (seemingly) exceptional, acute, and temporally discrete character of the Nazi-administered genocide is incommensurate with the epochal violence that structures the formation of Black and Indigenous being in the Civilizational period, the Nazis nonetheless relied on such precedents and coterminous examples of racial-colonial violence to conceive, plan, and actualize their modernist innovations of industrialized killing."[21] Noting that Lemkin, in his 1933 *Madrid Proposal,* used the terms "barbarism" and "vandalism," old European terms for old European crimes, Kazanjian shows how Lemkin's coinage of the term *genocide* combined these two categories. With an appropriately modernizing hybrid of ancient Greek and Latin etymology, this portmanteau, *genocide,* becomes the means to distinguish between legitimate and illegitimate violence along the modernizing and humanizing lines Rodríguez describes.[22] For Lemkin, the crime of genocide is "only new in the civilized world" and therefore needs a coinage to mark the distinction between a "premodern" violence that is understandable if irrational (understandable as irrational) and a modern *crime*, which is a vestige of "uncivilized" irrationality that occasionally irrupts in "civilized" "modern" states.[23] His distinction produces a racialized and civilizationist threshold, especially as it moves into the international institutions of the west. This is most clear in Lemkin's exclusion of imperial and colonial violence from the definition of genocide, forms of violence that contribute to the story of progress, "serv[ing] civilization by clearing inferior races off the earth."[24] Genocide as a concept thereby creates a temporal distinction between a humanizing and an inhuman violence, with modern Euro-American civility cast as the human norm threatened by both the "primitive" inhuman violence of the savage and the excesses of state violence, which channel atavistic savagery; both are an affront to modern civility. As Rodríguez notes, "The logics of genocide, shaped in the material-historical domains of global racialization, thus paradoxically precede the inauguration of 'genocide' as a formal lexicon—in this sense, anti-Blackness and racial-colonial power are the unspoken, illegible preconditions for the term's articulation as a meaningful referent to the intra-racial nadir of (white) modernity (The Holocaust)."[25] As we'll see in this chapter, through the adoption of the legal definition, in whole or in part, the civilizationist line is reproduced by the representational powers and impotencies of historiography and its use of the definition of genocide for the sake of "truth."

According to these terms, "primitive" violence and modern excesses are related under the category of illegitimate violence yet they remain separated/connected by an atavistic, temporal line that marks both of their transgressions as atemporal. Premodern and modern legal and humanizing colonial violence, analogously, are understood as legitimate across the same line but in a linear model of progress, with premodern violence done in the name of monopolizing violence for the state and law and order, seen therefore as necessary. History, in this sense, is the work of legitimating violence, sometimes through retroactive repudiation that serves the present and the capture of the future. Legitimate violence—that which founds and is monopolized by the state (what Walter Benjamin calls "legal violence")—operates through a discourse of nonviolence that is uttered by and supports the state.[26] What connects colonial, imperial, legal, and neocolonial/imperial forms of violence is the self-understanding that they suppress irrational violence and are thereby rational.[27] This configuration is evident in nineteenth-century calls for the extermination or protection of California Indians, framed typically as a disjunction: assimilate or be exterminated. Explicit calls for extermination were framed as calls to end violence, for protection of settlers, and for the institution of the rule of law, a violence done in the name of the law itself.[28] The creation of the definition of genocide, then, places limits on legal violence by deeming its excesses akin to the "irrational" violence of the savage that motivated the colonial violence to begin with. What makes such a reorganization possible is the humanization of the savage and the retroactive recognition of the inhumanity of the settler along temporally progressive lines. This transvaluation occurs through the self-castigation of the state in the form of apology for always "past" events. It calls forth the human voice in testimony through truth and reconciliation projects as the interweaving of trauma narratives with state mediated forms of healing.[29]

This logic of violence, and its relation to the differential and differentiating forces of humanization, operates as a racial and colonial logic that continues to inform how violence registers and gets interpreted. As Rodríguez notes about Césaire's analysis of the category of genocide, "the emergence of Western genocide discourse is animated by a narrative privileging of white death as the instance through which Other peoples' encounters with Western modernity's logics of racial extermination and terror are to be apprehended, calibrated, and conceptually qualified."[30] Genocide discourse not only privileges white death as the interpretive norm, but making sense of violence requires an entire western epistemic infrastructure to enable such recognition: an international human rights regime, modern differentiations of violence from the "savage" past formed in the modernity/coloniality complex (as described by Sylvia Wynter[31]), an emphasis on temporal dimensions of interpretation and the sense of violence as developing or correcting (as opposed to interpretations of violence by the various peoples affected by it), and (especially) the differential categorizations of the human in the colonial racial regime. This categorization includes rendering Indigenous social and political interrelations with all sorts of beings into either beliefs to be tolerated, objects of study, diabolical forms to be eradicated, or nonsense. These together constitute the underpinnings of how western humanism monopolizes and makes sense and use of violence.

But a shattering of the racial-colonial and teleological idea of the state as achievement of (white) rationality—which makes its way into the international basis of human rights and marks the line described by Kazanjian and Rodríguez between a crime against humanity (against the transparent subject) and instrumental colonial violence (against affectable others)—has been made possible, Denise Ferreira da Silva has argued, by racialized and colonized others changing the narrative, not just in content but materially and structurally. "Black activists in Rio, along with graffiti artists in New York, First Nation leaders in Vancouver, and people of color elsewhere had somehow changed knowledge in its production and circulation; black feminist writings in the United States were advancing new statements of 'truth' and 'being,' challenging scientific and literary canons while defending the validity of their local narratives."[32] The narratives produced by these communities stand in stark relief to the western humanist universal narrative that drives the discourse on genocide.

As Rodríguez notes, Israeli indifference to Palestinian death and suffering is more than a psychological effect; it is a matter of the western humanist and civilizationist narrative that undergirds Zionist ideology, a cognitive regime that renders such violence illegible as violence, a reality-making procedure (the "creating facts" on the ground of the Zionist narrative).[33] In contrast, the Palestinians' story of the Nakba, the ongoing catastrophe of colonial violence, challenges the very conditions of truth and historiography on which Zionism depends, not as a contested or relative narrative but onto-epistemologically. Rodríguez cites Loubna Qutami, who describes a Nakba ontology that interrupts the discursive regime of genocide: "Nakba has come to be a persistent condition for Palestinians across time and space. It has come to be a definitive feature of Palestinian insecurity and lack of permanence. It has become a constant experience of displacement, exodus, siege, imprisonment, and death across generations . . . In the end, the Palestinian ontology of Nakba(at) is caused by multiple dimensions of enclosure and annihilation."[34] This proliferation of stories and widening of the sense of the catastrophe, as could be expected, caused a crisis in the discipline of History that has yet to be resolved, one that revolves around the concept of genocide, truth in history, and the reality of the event.

Truth in History

Gavin Newsom's apology to California Indians for the state's "historical mistreatment, violence and neglect" seems finally to openly and officially acknowledge the attempted extermination of California Indian peoples, a hundred seventy years after the state's inception.[35] But how does one understand the implications of such a shift in public perception? What does this mean for California Indian peoples? To answer these questions requires an analysis of how violence gets understood, as the previous lack of acknowledgment of genocide in California was a product of the meaning made of violence. As Mahmood Mamdani writes, "What horrifies modern political sensibility is not violence per se but violence that does not make sense."[36] Settlers, generally speaking, were disturbed more by the perceived inherent violence of Indigenous peoples (the *merciless Indian savages, whose known rule of warfare, is an undistinguished destruction of all sexes, ages, and conditions* we met in the introduction) than they were of state-sanctioned genocide. Settlers considered violence against California Indians unremarkable because it made sense in the context of U.S. settler and imperial conquest and in the securitization of those projects (and for most settlers and settler discourse it still does). Why, then, in the apology does this violence suddenly no longer make sense?

To begin to answer this question, it is important to understand how the use of *genocide* makes meaning out of violence and what the performative force of an apology is. The answer lies in historians' responses to the crisis in representation History underwent in the early 1990s and why this issue concerned specifically the question of genocide. In that moment, historians understood themselves to be facing a wave of historical revisionism and denialism, grounded in antirealist critique, that largely centered on the singularity of the Holocaust as an event.

In his book *The Historiographic Perversion*, Armenian scholar Marc Nichanian draws out the resonances between two conferences held a decade apart on the question of truth in history, one in the domain of philosophy and the other in history, a question ultimately asked in both instances in relation to the definition of genocide. The first, held in France in 1980, was the occasion for a debate between a number of prominent French philosophers over the question of the singularity of the Holocaust, and, more particularly, over the "emblematic name" *Auschwitz*.[37] The debate took place after an early presentation of what later became Jean-François Lyotard's philosophical treatise on this issue, *The Differend*. This debate was to predict a court case in France in 1994, in which historian Bernard Lewis was tried and convicted by the state for denying the Armenian genocide. The second conference, held at UCLA in 1991 under the title "Probing the Limits of Representation," was largely a response by a collective of historians to a perceived threat to their discipline by the crisis in representation. Led by historian Carlo Ginzburg, the conference coalesced as a repudiation of rhetorical and literary analyses of historiography by a number of scholars but especially the work of Hayden White. It was, in essence, a disciplinary reentrenchment in realist representation and augured a series of debates within History over the use of the term *genocide* to define the violence committed against Native Americans by the United States.[38] Reflected in Alan Rosenbaum's collection *Is the Holocaust Unique?* (1995) and summarized by Gavriel Rosenfeld's review "The Politics of Uniqueness" (1999), the UCLA conference and the subsequent debates created the conditions for the development of genocide studies as a field.[39]

Rather than seeing in this narrative an intellectual history for its own sake, these moments and developments and their effects condition discursive production through the demand to make sense of violence—and therefore to measure and make definitions and, ultimately, judgments. Rather than paying close attention to the arguments and getting into the weeds of these debates, I focus here on the forces of production themselves. Taking this position indicates the (unconscious) concerted effort of a discourse that is in constant recalibration and refinement (one too easy to get lost in), a situation in which, as White notes, historians—revisionist and otherwise—all use the same basic criteria of truth and objectivity, all use the same archival and other evidentiary materials, to produce a seemingly contentious debate that in its effect supports existing power relations and their representational forces. Nichanian refers to this condition as the "genocidal will," a circular destruction that destroys not only lives and structures but the very means to measure its destructiveness. The loss of these instruments produces a recursive, if harder or impossible to define, destruction, a black hole of representation in which "the impossibility of quantitatively measuring it does not prohibit, but rather inspires in the minds of the survivors the idea of a great seismic force."[40] We need no proofs because the destruction of representation of violence is the only proof possible. Dian Million describes this situation in the context of an international human rights regime, interwoven with neoliberal modes of multicultural settler colonialism and a reconciliatory politics of recognition, as a paradox in which "the international law that enables Indigenous trauma to appeal for justice is the same sphere in which we articulate political rights as polities with rights to self-determination." In other words, this regime (which has already found us guilty) demands an appeal to the executioner according to *his* terms and through *his* modes of speaking, an epistemic violence felt by those subjected to it as "a great seismic force."[41] Such an impossible condition and its effects maps in the minds of survivors the ongoing destruction.

In this sense, representational and epistemic destruction, for Hayden White, operate through institutional, disciplinary historiography, which acts as a political and colonial domestication of narrative, to render the writing of history into a "comprehensible process . . . to make sense of it one way or another."[42] And this meaning is buttressed by an entire epistemic system of communication and education grounded in such destruction: infrastructures for producing truth, communicating these truths to a public (and thereby defining the public), creating policy based on these truths, and producing, publishing, and teaching them. This is the good history, redemptive of time itself, echoing the goodness of the *friend of the Indian.* It is the fabrication of facts as part of a colonial linguistic mesh, social understanding, and their transparent paths of communication. Such fabrication raises the question of how, why, and when certain facts become safe, recognizable, and incorporated into the historical record.

Jodi Byrd has detailed the cacophonous space of competing discourses around genocide narratives and shown how they make their way into popular consciousness and representation through the generalized cognitive inability to make sense of their entanglements when they rise to the surface. In their piece "'Living My Native Life Deadly,'" they discuss the confluence of media storms that swirled around Jeff Weise, a Red Lake Native teen and self-professed neo-Nazi who shot fellow students at his reservation school for ostensibly acting "too black" before shooting himself; and Ward Churchill, the AIM activist and radical Native studies scholar known for making false claims to Native identity and who at the time was under fire for his anticolonial take on the events of 9/11 and, specifically, his statement that the Twin Towers were full of "little Eichmanns." As Byrd writes, "The provocative enjambment of Native, Nazi, and Holocaust, as well as the two news stories, gestures toward the competition that emerges between US colonialist understandings of Indigenous peoples that perpetually disavow any genocidal conduct on the part of the nation and mainstream media's awareness and sensitivity to the historical significance that the horror of the Holocaust represents."[43] For Byrd, rival narratives of genocide compete at the cost of disavowing the historical experiences and relations of others, particularly Black and Indigenous peoples. The presence of the Holocaust narrative in both instances is amplified by Ward Churchill's centrality (or at least visible presence) in the debate with Holocaust scholars over whether or not U.S. violence against Native Americans can be called genocide. His engagements with Deborah Lipstadt, who had won a legal case against the notorious Holocaust denier David Irving (who had sued her for libel) are noteworthy. In his piece "An American Holocaust?," Churchill makes the argument that not only does Lipstadt uphold the singularity of the Holocaust as reason to deny that U.S. violence constitutes genocide against Native Americans, but also that Lipstadt refuses to acknowledge other groups affected by the Holocaust, such as "Gypsies, Sinti, Roma, Romani."[44] Echoing the argument about instrumental violence common to this discussion, Lipstadt responded, "The Native Americans were seen as 'competitors' for land and resources"; it was not a genocide for her, because "there was a certain logic."[45]

Jeff Weise's antiblackness and embeddedness in white supremacist groups online and in Minnesota open up complex historical connections, for Byrd, between U.S. slavery and Native genocide that the media narratives that Byrd analyzes do not register. The contemporaneity of the Civil War and the Dakota War, for instance, creates the temporal confluence of two seemingly disparate events and histories: Abraham Lincoln signed, during the same week, the Emancipation Proclamation and an order to hang thirty-nine Dakota insurgents.[46] For Byrd, rather than a comparative moment of U.S. violence against different peoples, genocide and slavery, this confluence marks the uneven and rationalized impacts of U.S. imperial logics on different peoples under the same violent system (as we know, the afterlife of slavery continues, as does the afterlife of genocide). These imperial logics and their disavowal of the violence against Indigenous peoples and other groups create difficult double binds.

Churchill and the immense body of work he has done to argue for genocide recognition is, in some ways, representative of this issue for Byrd: "the ambivalence surrounding Churchill and what he represents—a liminal figure who is invalidated or invalidating Indianness through his presence, activism, and scholarship—has created a quagmire in which it is difficult to criticize or support Churchill without reproducing colonialist understandings of Indianness."[47] This quagmire was deepened when Churchill was fired from his position at the University of Colorado after a cadre of conservatives put together a committee to review his teaching and publications for potential academic misconduct and plagiarism.[48] Heightening the cautions they offer against comparison, Byrd describes a tendency in Native studies either to equate Native genocide with the Holocaust (using many of the same arguments, tropes, and metaphors of Holocaust remembrance used by Holocaust scholars) or in many cases simply to borrow the proper name of *Holocaust*, indicating the desire for recognition of violence and an inclusion into the noninstrumental realm of the human. This misuse of Holocaust remembrance by Native scholars is complicated by statements such as that by Holocaust scholar Marthe Robert, who claimed that "to speak of other genocides than the Jewish genocide was to demonstrate 'a very subtle negationism.'"[49] This raises the question of how to confront the disavowal of U.S. imperial violence without falling into the logics of recognition or singularity.

But why genocide? What brings about this confluence of the crisis in representation and the question of whether or not the violence committed against Native Americans can be called genocide? In the previous chapter, we saw how the representational crisis anthropology underwent revolved around the force of representational violence and the presumed disappearance of the Native. The discipline of History assumes for itself a fundamentally juridical nature: taking as its task making meaning of violence committed against Native Americans, it locates this interpretive and semantic project within the frame of its own fitness to judge, its own ability to determine neutrally and objectively if *genocide* happened. That the interpretation of the violence enacted to create the conditions to found the United States becomes the site of a debate over how to name this violence in juridical language indicates clearly the position and power of representation within an institutional and state-funded discourse such as historiography. It is no surprise then that History ended up defining the crisis in representation by the figure of the witness (just as it was defined in anthropology by the figure of the informant). But the identity and position of this witness is a problem. In the United States, what, after all, is the underlying "crime scene" in the nation-state's unconscious (rising at times to the level of preconsciousness)? As discussed in the introduction, this scene is what Byrd indicates by calling often-unrecognized pop cultural manifestations of Indigeneity, as well as those in theoretical discourses, the *return of the repressed.*[50] The scene also forms the confusion of the double bind that underlies Povinelli's governance of the prior.

Historians attacked antirealist critique by conflating it with revisionism/denialism, not understanding that their mode of historiography is more closely related to denialism than antirealist critique is, that it allows denialism in the door. For them, what is on the line is not necessarily the truth of the event but History itself, which acts as the guardian of this truth. The significance of the event is that it is seemingly a nonnegotiable truth and yet, because of this, the event is what has caused the most outrage and conflict in the form of revisionism. Both historical truth and revisionist history boil down to the archive and its interpretation. A quantitative question about the amount of documentation stands in for the presupposed ontology, as if interpretation and a preponderance of evidence can hide the material and epistemo-ontological conditions that define the terms of the debate. Historians claim that what is on the line is reality itself, the facts that hold the discipline together. Critiquing White for his argument that history defines itself as a discipline by expelling the sublime, by actively producing this reality, historians translate this argument into a form of absolute relativism based solely on the discourse of power. But, as Nichanian argues, like historical truth and revisionism, relativism is only the inverse of realism; they are two sides of the same coin.[51] They are not ontologically that different and differ only over their interpretations and what they mean.

For Nichanian, both historical truth and revisionism contribute to the genocidal will, which is the destruction not only of lives but of the fact itself. The genocidal will is a state negation of the Destruction that is only interested in the preservation of the state form and the management of its narrative, hence the shift toward the recognition of genocide that now serves state interests. Once the cognitive regime and the physical threat of oppressed populations are seemingly eliminated by the state, the recognition of genocide absorbs even death and violence into the state narrative. What we see playing out now in Gaza is the fact that a genocidal event can be infinitely documented and still contested. Negationism is built into the system. That is the destruction of the fact. As Nichanian argues, "Historical truth as dominant representation wavers between the constitution of facts as such and the politics of interpretation (power's hold on facts as given)."[52] Everything reduces down to the common plot, which ensures that there is history, facts, historical sense or meaning—in other words, historical truth. The plot bends flexibly, shifting between evidence and its interpretation, organized around a metaphysical belief in the goodness of the system. This is a rhetorical situation that includes an entire linguistic fabric, modes of social understanding, and various paths of communication that nonetheless tie together this embedded network of communicating truth as power.

What is not on the line are these rhetorical conditions on which both the historian's truth and the negationist's lie depend. The difference between the two is that the negationist is on the side of the perpetrator, stubbornly and woodenly. The historian is in a more complex position, seeking to mediate between the perpetrator and the subjects of state violence. The debate in History about genocide and Native Americans and its relation to the crisis in representation indicates the confluence of two anxieties wrapped up in the problematics of the discipline and its poetics: the illegitimacy and insecurity of the geopolitical entity that makes one's work possible (do all historians, in the end, work for the state?) and the illegitimacy and insecurity of the epistemic foundations that justified genocidal violence as the conditions for that geopolitical entity to be founded and to continue to exist, epistemic foundations that also make ones work possible.

Carlo Ginzburg's response to the crisis of representation, "Just One Witness: The Extermination of the Jews and the Principle of Reality," with its title's seeming despairing note of the embattlement of History and reality, implies that reality itself would seem to depend upon the existence of at least one witness. This, of course, is not Ginzburg's argument, which is instead an attempt to engage philosophically the crisis of representation through a mediatory position that accepts the critique of positivism—its "highly problematic relationship with reality"[53]—and calls for attending to the proliferation of viewpoints through what he dubs, elsewhere, "microhistory," a focus on small events and local perceptions, as a last stand against perceived nihilism and skepticism regarding the relationship between historiography and reality. As he asserts, "But reality ('the thing in itself') exists," a sentence that expresses a certain faith and, in the end, perhaps a note of despair.[54] This reality, the *thing in itself,* produces a proliferating series of narratives, as the swarm of possible perspectives offers as many stories, a perhaps convenient and exploitable situation for the discipline. In relation to the destruction, this proliferation creates an impossible ideal, which is the totality of violence and suffering as witnessed, which can never be presented. The lack in the archive itself—what has been recorded, what has not, and what cannot be—as well as the inherent problematics of testimony, which appears distorted, insufficient, fragmentary, create the representational problem; there are too many voices and each is too individualistic. And here we have the problem of the witness and the archive, which, again, History claims as its purview as guardian of the *thing in itself.* The *just one witness* is History, its true assertion: it is sole protector of and witness to the singularity that grounds and stabilizes, institutionalizes and domesticates, the radical proliferation of voices and their materialities, against the coming horde—the fact of reality. To ensure itself of this position and to push back against the swarm of voices, History will take recourse to the law and its fact-making power, even if it has to evacuate the force of both the law and language to do so.

California Indian Studies and Genocide

We are now in a position to understand the roles History and historiography play in both California Indian studies and the discourse on genocide. As non-Native historian Martin Rizzo-Martinez writes in *We Are Not Animals,* "The study of California Indians began in earnest in the mid-twentieth century, when Sherburne F. Cook and others wrote about the terrible attrition and death rates."[55] This beginning is of course across the divide between the study of California Indian *cultures* by salvage ethnographers in the early twentieth century, who selectively and deliberately edited out the impact of colonial violence, as I discuss in the previous chapter, and the study of our destruction as a historical event, generally a demographic approach, as evidenced by Cook's work. This divide, of course, doesn't hold: the need for documentation and, in particular, for the voices of witnesses causes History to begin eventually to slip across the boundary toward the recorded voices of Native "informants," on which ethnography seemingly held a monopoly. In the absence of a chronicle or a collection of testimonies (as found in abundance in relation to some of the twentieth-century genocides), the relatively small number of first-person accounts by California Indians are generally couched within the discourse and semiotics of anthropology, which as part of the destruction of the memory of destruction censored out colonial violence. As we'll see in more detail in the next chapter, California Indians nonetheless often took the opportunity of speaking to a perceived authority in the dominant culture, as well as the anthropologist's tools and methodologies, to record the stories they wanted to tell, despite the narrow scientific purposes of the anthropologists.

Lucy Young, a Wailaki woman who survived the targeted decimation of her people and gave a harrowing account of her life, allowed anthropologist and ethnobotanist Edith Murphey to record her life, offering a case in point. Beginning her narrative under the sign of prophecy and dream, Young describes her grandfather, who died before ever seeing a white person, dreaming the destruction of their people. This is a common occurrence in Native communities who preemptively accounted for the coming destruction through a Native framework of understanding in dreams or prophecy. Leslie Marmon Silko addresses these storying practices in her account of a gathering of and contest between Native witches to see who was the most powerful. The witch who won created white people as a curse and a display of their power, a power that Silko entangles with the dangerous forces of story, as the witch's curse works through the performative force of storying and cannot be taken back.[56] Young's account of her fugitive movements and relations, of the violence and bloodshed she witnessed, of the impossibility of surviving outside of the material and sexual economies of settler colonialism is for her like a dream: "All seem like dream to me."[57] This way of narrating her experiences of the destruction, as if it is of another life, registers the absolute rupture, the turning over of the world, and opens onto the infinite destruction. As Young describes, "white people want our land, want destroy us. Break and burn all our baskets, break our pounding rock. Destroy our ropes. No snares, no deerskin, flint knife, nothing . . . I hear people tell 'bout what Inyan do early days to white man. Nobody ever tell it what white man do to Inyan. That's the reason I tell it. That's history. That's truth. I seen it myself."[58] Young's narration of the event is oddly framed by Murphey as still part of the salvage process of collecting cultural information. Seemingly random cultural information, such as using soaproot to catch fish, interrupt the account of survival.[59] This is amplified by Young's emphasis on the destruction of "cultural items," which indeterminately offers a sense of what Young imagines matters most to Murphey or a broadening of the destruction from a body count. It is likely Young is either offering this information to appease Murphey, as a way to continue telling what she wants to tell, or responding to direct questioning by Murphey. Either way, in this text, the division and awkward conflation of the cultural informant and the witness to genocide is on full display.

Hearkening back to chapter 1, this conflation of informant and witness speaks to how story operates within the allowable cultural terms by History as representation, at best filling in the space of testimony. Within "cases" of genocide, the scientific universality of European enlightenment, which continues to dominate U.S. history (and education in general), operates through an effaced sense of the cultural. We see this most clearly in the discipline's oscillations around the role of story as evidence. As Lisa Lowe notes, culture has "become the medium of the present [and] the site that mediates the past, through which history is grasped as difference, as fragments, shocks, and flashes of disjunction."[60] Native historians, on the other hand, have tended to approach story in ways that reflect this difficult formation of informant/witness: culture/history, one not confined to the role of evidence but part of the form of the text. For example, Wailaki and Konkow historian William Bauer and non-Native historian Damon Akins, have written a location-based history that centers stories specific to places. *We Are the Land* mingles origin and "historical" stories of these locations in a way that centers an Indigenous approach and the lives of Indigenous peoples.

Rizzo-Martinez likewise writes his history of missionary violence and Indigenous resistance in the Santa Cruz area, which centers California Indian accounts and interviews with descendants, under the sign of story tied to place. Beginning with a story about "How They Killed a Serpent That Lived in the Santa Cruz Mountains," Rizzo-Martinez reflects thoughtfully on the ethics of representation and the role of the historian, which he reduces to the practice of listening, a scribe for a collectively told story. He describes being subtly corrected about his interpretation of the serpent story by a tribal collaborator and how this informs his practice of writing and listening. The epigraph for Rizzo-Martinez's book is, appropriately, a description of the force and role of story in history by Maria Ascensión Solórsano de Cervantes, told to John P. Harrington in 1929:

> A story also grows. It never remains the same. Though one wants to tell it the same as one heard it, one always puts in a word more or less. And there are many people in this world who are great gossips, they fix up a story very nice, even if they don't know it. And still more so if it is a story of a religion, they always want to make

> the people believe more. And with time it changes more, so that when a story has passed through the lives of many people surely it is already impossible to tell what story it is, for it is already changed fundamentally, and it is not recognized as the same story that it was earlier. And when the story is written or made into a book, it still is a story and nothing more, they only took the story which was growing, more or less, or took the turns that very various people had given it and gathered them together pruning them off to make a single book. They say that when the story is written it is different, but to me it is the same, it is still a story.[61]

This vision of a headless and tailless story, of its abundance, capaciousness, and interrelationality, its collectivity and confusion of certainty with uncertainty, its many faces as well as its persistence, even when disciplined into a form, a form that it resists, refuses, fails at, is also that of the form the destruction takes in the lives, mouths, and minds of Indigenous people. This description of story by de Cervantes is also a direct commentary on Harrington's ridiculous project of gathering stories, pruning them off from this greater vision to make a book (of all things!), which remains nothing but a story. Rizzo-Martinez seems to be referencing this relation of the book to story in order to reflect on his own project and its limits. One cannot contain story or discipline it. The book is only ever a temporary home. Story has all the force and sociality of gossip and pulls even the serious work of anthropology and history into its realm. We are gossips who tell stories and nothing more.

Story's uncertainty and instability, and yet collective force and endurance, raise the question of how we tell the story of our own death. How do we narrate the destruction? How do we tell the violence underwent by our ancestors? According to historian Michael Magliari, tribal leaders or even Native students who bravely contest genocide denial in a classroom by a teacher should not reproduce the "myth" of scalp bounties in California. Published by the University of California Press (which notoriously publishes very few California Indian scholars), Magliari's 2023 piece "The California Indian Scalp Bounty Myth" traces instances of descriptions of the bounties that were paid for California Indian body parts in scholarship and public discourse (in the accounts of Native people speaking publicly, as well as in documentaries and literature).[62] This tracing is an attempt to *prove* that stories of such bounties are either fully mythical or at best embellishments of a limited number of cases. I should be clear that Magliari is not a genocide denier; he's not in the camp with Gary Clayton Anderson, who has argued strenuously that U.S. settler violence doesn't constitute genocide.[63] Magliari is doing something different: he's shoring up the boundaries of the archive and historiography to protect them from the coming horde of Native gossipers. He's engaged in the protection of truth in history by appealing to the material evidence that exists of genocidal violence and, in the case of scalp bounties, apparently finding very little.

I have no interest in debating Magliari on this issue and thereby contributing to the negationist discourse of history. We need no proofs. I *am* interested in how he approaches the archive, the effects of this approach on the narrative of the past, and what its implications are for California Indian studies. What is the effect of choosing one affectively charged aspect of genocidal violence and analytically pulling it apart? What does it do to our sense of the atmosphere of violence in which our ancestors lived and survived, such as described by Young? How are we to understand a historical narrative that accepts the basic premise that there was a genocide but only under the condition that the narrative remains within the control of history and the law? That genocide only applies to certain California Indian peoples and Native peoples more generally in certain well-defined cases? Challenging the premise that only historians who express outright denial are negationist, Nichanian notes that "the ultimate goal of negationism is to make the qualification of the facts the sole concern."[64] By Magliari's logic—which is the logic of historians—the only scenes or events that become facts and thereby acquire reality are those governed by the archive. And the archive, as we all know, is governed by the state, by the perpetrators. It includes only the voices of killers. It seems, though, that Magliari isn't aware of this condition and that it is, in fact, the destruction of the archive.

Magliari's reduction to the archive through a negation of California Indian voices and the force of story attends to what Rizzo-Martinez calls the "earnest creation of California Indian Studies," and even questions this; he plays a game with the very foundations of historiography and its relation to the archive and the claim to truth. The "not much" evidence he finds is based on witness accounts by settlers, which Magliari assumes must be the source of the public discourse on scalp bounties, ignoring the absolute void of representation of Indigenous voices and representation as well as the networks of story and gossip that exist in spite of that void. Magliari exposes historical truth's severity, and yet his reduction opens up the black hole of negationism that lies beneath all western humanist historiography. It opens up the question of what California Indians mean when we say *genocide* and what we mean is something closer to the Destruction. The scalp bounty story is a collective fact because it registers the destruction better than any historical accounting can. Yes, bounties were given for body parts. Again, we need no proofs. The other side of this equation, of course, is that the most effective evidence in proving a case of genocide is the voices of killers: the official documents that express intent. This is because, on top of the negationism of California Indian voice expressed by Magliari, there is a structural negation that renders all accounts by individuals something other than proof because they fail to show intent.

The criteria put forth in the UN Convention on Genocide represents most clearly the strict form of genocide, and the historical text that employs these criteria the most rigorously in the context of California is Benjamin Madley's *An American Genocide*. As Tony Platt writes in his review of the book,

> Benjamin Madley . . . responds to this challenge as a prosecutor might, building his case on a mountain of evidence until the verdict is undeniable: what happened in California from 1846 to 1873 was a genocide "more lethal and sustained than anywhere else in the United States or its colonial antecedents." By 1880, the Native population had declined by more than ninety percent since the first Europeans arrived in the region.[65]

Madley's text has also garnered the most accolades and has been the most associated with the official recognition of California's violence (always past); among these honors, Madley gave a private reading for former governor Jerry Brown, and received the California Commendation Medal from the Military Department of the State of California. In keeping with the field of genocide studies and its approach, Madley appropriates the international legal definition for genocide as a "powerful analytical tool" to determine historical truth.[66] This use of an abstract definition is a form of positive law that gives Madley a calculus for distinguishing between kinds of violence in order to build a case for the recognition of genocide—that is, to *prove* a genocide occurred, but as positivist history, a positivist history that is at the same time attentive to critical dimensions of historiography. Abdicating the historian's claim to truth based on interpretation and installing an abstract legal definition in its stead, as a recourse to the thing in itself, Madley seeks to give history the form of law without enacting its force.

This use of the definition has a disciplinary quality through its interpretive power, as Madley narrates the realization of his methodology as a literature review that recapitulates the various terms used by historians to describe mass violence in California *(liquidation, extermination)* and the various uses of the term *genocide* (referring to genocides "only briefly or incompletely").[67] Reiterating the civilizationist schema of progress toward law and order described by Kazanjian, Madley reproduces it methodologically as a march toward truth by painstakingly showing how other uses do not stack up to his use of the international legal definition.[68] As he describes, the definition is "more than an academic concept . . . Unlike at least twenty-two alternative definitions proffered since 1959, it has teeth," and yet, as he makes clear, it does not allow for retroactive prosecution.[69] Madley adopts the legal criteria outlined by the UN Convention as a "frame for evaluating the past and comparing events across time," drawing on the international consensus and effectivity of the law to regulate what constitutes the truth of history without enacting any of the law's force. Madley, thereby, presents his book as "the *first* comprehensive, year-by-year history of the California Indian genocide under US rule"; the *only* account to rigorously use the Genocide Convention's definition as a rubric, while others "propose expanding, contracting, or modifying the list of protected groups . . . [or] want to enlarge, reduce, or alter the scope of genocidal acts . . . [or] call for different definitions of intent"; and the most *comprehensive* attempt "to capture the full meaning of genocidal events."[70]

First, only, and *comprehensive.* What Madley is attempting to do with his approach—a rigorous interrogation and categorization of other ways of writing about and understanding mass violence in California—is to transcribe the violence into a case that is fully and finally knowable. It is a "case" in two senses: a historical case as instance of genocide and a case made against the state of California, thereby finding the intersection between the performative charge of genocide by law and the referential truth of history. Lemkin, as Madley notes, had retroactively extended *genocide* into the past in an unfinished historical manuscript on Native American genocide.[71] Madley takes up this project with its implied separation between historical and legal uses of the definition. This separation undoes the civilizing distinction between premodern and modern violences at the definitional level and yet upholds it at the discursive level by distinguishing between historical cases and legal instances across a rift in their respective forces. Madley's use of the legal definition for its "teeth," to ground historiography and establish a truth-making procedure without actually bringing those teeth to bear, is the fulcrum on which the referential and performative dimensions of genocide are balanced. This strange conflation in the form of a "case" makes clear that what is at stake, for Madley, is not proving that the destruction occurred but proving it was *a case of "genocide,"* reducing all language and understanding to the abstract criteria of international law, which adjudicates all other ways of knowing the catastrophe, effectively shackling historiography to the fate of the term *genocide.*

We see this suspension worked out in Madley's critique of the widespread argument (by Sherburne Cook, Hubert Bancroft, John Collier, among others) that lawlessness in the Western frontier led to genocidal atrocity.[72] Madley rightly indicates the legal basis of the violence and has a chapter on how California law itself, including the state constitutional convention held in 1849, contributed to genocide. What he misses is that violence was done in the name of the law's founding and not merely as an effect of specific laws, neglecting thereby the continued production of violence to instate and preserve the law. Because of this, Madley opts for a liberal progressive argument that things could have been different *if only* there had been different laws enacted and *if only* more moderate voices had prevailed.[73] Reiterating the call for law and order by retroactively criminalizing the violence done in its name and by imagining a more perfect institution of law, he thereby presumes the legal norm of a liberal humanized order projected into the past as regulative ideal. This projection anticipates the state apology and Truth and Healing Council. In fact, Madley calls for something like truth and reconciliation in his delimitation of California Indian archival voices from the voices of killers as impossible testimonial evidence, distinguishing evidence from ethnography.

In his attempt to *prove* the case against the state, Madley seeks evidence in the written historical record. When confronted with limitations and erasures performed by the record itself—no forensic or "ethnographic" evidence—Madley opts to build his case using positive archival data/facts found in settler newspapers, state archives, and non-Indian witness accounts, which he transmutes into testimonial confessions highlighting "the voices of killers."[74] This is a decision predetermined by the juridico-historical case for genocide Madley makes, as attending either to archaeological evidence, if it can be found, or to the absence of California Indian voices in the archive would require engaging the question of genocide outside the confines of the fully and finally knowable case. All three approaches, however, raise the problem of voice, offering a comparative site to analyze the construction of voice in relation to violence as it makes meaning. Following Madley's attempt to "dignify the slain and give a voice to the departed," by putting his notion of voice into conversation with theories of the archive, stresses the limits of what can be known and said.[75]

Madley asserts that the "voices of killers" are the only voices available for building a case.[76] As he explains, there are relatively few transcribed Indian voices from the time period, a dearth attributable to a host of reasons: there were not many survivors; laws barred and rarely recorded Indian testimony; authors and journalists did not record the words of Indians; many Indians hid their identities to survive; there were traditional taboos against speaking of the dead; many were removed from land where the violence occurred; Native languages were suppressed; there were intergenerational cuts through the abduction of children; there was compulsory federal boarding education; and there were legal prohibitions against ceremonies and gatherings, including for mourning. This overdetermined silence constitutes the destruction, as not only were California Indian lives destroyed but we were barred from even having any relation to our own deaths.

Madley's response to this silence is to defer and to categorize, as he is clear that his is not an "ethnographic oral-history project," a project he claims is important and needed but not a part of building a case fully and finally knowable.[77] Not only are California Indians asked to depend on the voices of killers to prove their own suffering but Madley's call to solve the absence of Native voices in the archive with an oral-history project that collects the stories of descendants of survivors bumps uncomfortably up against the other silence of the archive: the editorial decisions made by salvage anthropologists to efface the effects of colonial violence by collecting/creating an ethnographic, cultural voice. As we saw with Lucy Young, even the few extant accounts by survivors are almost always written under the sign of culture, because they are collected by anthropologists. This split between the cultural documentation of the "informant" and the testimony of the witness is simultaneously upheld and suspended in Madley's separation of his juridico-historical case from the deferred oral-history project, distinguishing between evidence and ethnography.

As I discussed in the introduction, Saidiya Hartman has described the archive as a power-laden space that discursively makes visible only power itself.[78] The archive is intractable, and, no matter how one reads it, twists it, turns it, it only ever offers up the voice of the killer. This is why Madley's approach abides by the law of the archive, accepts this limit, and seeks to highlight and build a case around it. He exacerbates this limit, though, by asserting that the only "complete" response to the violence in the archive is to instrumentalize it to further call on power in the form of the *recognition* of genocide. Considering the analytic split between the ethnographic voice and the testimonial, the only way recognition can give voice is through a simple transference in which California Indians ventriloquize the voice of power, declaring the state itself to be the savage. We are asked to condemn and judge by speaking in the voices of killers. The discourse on genocide narrows the space of speech and perpetuates the destruction. The discourse also makes demands on our ancestors, asking that their lives and deaths, splayed out in the most vicious language in the archive, be made useful toward this end, naming our ancestors in ways that may have been counter to their own forms of self-identification. The dilemma, as Hartman shows, is that it is, of course, too late.[79] We cannot save our ancestors, and that is the hard truth we must accept and that Madley tramples over in his desire to speak for them and to make a case. The archive shows our ancestors remain in the grasp of the killers and we cannot free them, especially through the construction of a case. Such a painful fact asks us to assess our own desire for some sense of justice or completion and why this desire takes the form of calls for law and order. What if we can never be made whole again and this is the standpoint from which we must approach our relation to the destruction and its ongoing afterlife?

The cultural documentation, absence of testimony, voices of the killers, as well as a limited literature, all indicate the impossibility of creating a voice of genocide. This impossibility calls us to another task, to understand. Our goal then is not to save the dead (give dignity to the slain), transforming their deaths into something positive, or to give a voice to the departed, but to save the destruction itself from the positive denialism inherent in a truthful discourse on genocide. This is not the refusal found in both the recognition of genocide and its denial but rather the refusal of *genocide* itself.

Interlude
How Death Came into This World

One of the most well-versed in reanimation is the trickster, Coyote, who was there at creation, along with Creator, singing it into being, taking part in the salvage process that made the world. He has died countless times in the stories told across tribes and languages, in bookstores, and through the recordings in the archives—stuck on repeat, always coming back to life. Most significantly, Coyote risked his own life in order to bring Death into this world.

Immediately after creation, it is said, he made his intentions clear: "I, Coyote, going along in this world, will ruin it."[1] Establishing his authority as "the First Being of olden times," he claims, "I say let the old people die when they die/Someone who's dead is not going to wake up.... The world is made with Death in it." Challenging Creator's monologue and the intention to create a world consistent throughout, without error or the absence that Death introduces, he says, "it's not going to be just your world," thereby inserting difference into the Creator's sameness and subverting possession in the right of creation.[2] Creator responds with a threat: "'Well, now,' replied Earthmaker, / 'if you talk like that, / you'll not be in this world for long.'"

Creator advised the beings of the world to kill Coyote, so that he could do no more harm, no more mischief, and everyone could live eternally and in peace without Coyote's bringing death into the world. But this was not enough. "'At the same time,' said Earthmaker. / 'All of you go and find every place / where Coyote has pissed or shat! / Don't any of you miss the places / where he has scratched the dirt.'"[3] And they did, seeking out every site marked by Coyote, of which he was both promiscuous and thorough: "He pissed on every kind of thing there was / and scratched up the ground with his hind feet. / He went everywhere, even up toward the land of the Spirit Masters."[4] The beings sought out all of these places, destroying them and rubbing them out, even going so far as to gather together all of his "droppings." Eventually they captured Coyote himself.

Lacking the courage to physically harm Coyote, the beings placed him on an islet in the middle of a very deep and fast-moving stream. "'Here you will die!' they said. 'You who are so clever with words—here you will starve to death!'"[5] The verbal mastery of Coyote is countered with the act of starvation. They waited on the bank of the river for four days to make sure Coyote was dead.

> Meanwhile, Coyote was still on the islet.
> After awhile, he shat. A gopher head crawled out.
> "What shall I do?" Coyote asked the gopher head.
> "Give me good counsel!"
>
> "Well," said the gopher head,
> "if you just stay here like you are you will die!"
>
> "Ah! That's the way you always talk to me," said Coyote.
>
> Then, when he had strained again,
> a bunch of dry grass crawled out.
>
> "What *am* I to do?" asked Coyote.
> "How shall I survive? Advise me well!"
>
> "Why, you must just turn yourself into mist,"
> said the bunch of grass,
> "and then, when the mist rises
> and floats up off the river at dawn,
> it will carry you along with it
> and bring you to shore.
> When you have called out,
> then, from the midst of the high country,
> the places where you have pissed,
> where you have scratched up the ground—
> even where you have lifted your leg against a clump of grass—
> these places will answer you."
>
> "Whenever this bunch of dry grass talks to me,
> it always gives me good advice," exclaimed Coyote.

> He stuck the grass back where it came from
> and plugged it up with the gopher head.[6]

After turning into mist and leaving the islet, Coyote goes on to escape death two more times before Creator and the other beings finally give up, allowing Coyote to his devices. There is always a second chance, a movement of the imagination, where there can be found a *prototype of the collective soul*. It is no accident that the trickster was marooned on an islet, and it is no accident that it was the second time he asked the question, to the second interlocutor, the grass, the rhizome, wherein Coyote receives his second chance at life in the form of mist. Grass, the material of baskets, the hider of bones, the diffuse, gives Coyote his power of dispersion, both through transformation into mist and through the return to Coyote's own diffuse markings—territorial pissings and scratchings. In this way, between the islet and the erased territory, Coyote finds a way.

This way, however, marked as it is by the event of Death, an event made possible by Coyote's own repeated escapes from this event, is a way of nonarrival. The Creator is tricked into allowing Death to enter the world, and it is this death that disturbs ownership through divesting the rights of monologic creation. In seeking to interrupt this event, Creator and the other beings locate the site of contestation in territorialized land, as it is through the erasure of Coyote's own territorial markings that they seek to stop Death's arrival. Death as interruption of eternal life and Life as incessant interruption of Death's arrival are played out as if in a game over ownership of territory, and this ownership is made through either creation of territory or a secondary marking. The land, marked and unmarked, is made to bear the traces of this masculine altercation, and these traces are either erased and ghostly, as in the dispersed voices of Coyote's rubbed-out markings, or they are the footsteps written into the land that mark the path of Creator's passing when he gave up and left the world (mostly in rocks and stream beds).

The arrival of Death is a nonarrival, or perhaps the arrival of nonarrival. In creation, everything has fully arrived, eternal, extending out like points becoming lines on to infinity. And it is only through a killing that occurs before Death has arrived—the killing of Coyote who wills Death's arrival (one that includes a social assemblage of all the other beings in the world: the hunting party)—that the arrival can be maintained and the event of nonarrival can be stopped. To kill before death exists in this world is to not just produce a paradox but to disturb the very foundations of arrival, in the form of creation itself. Coyote, if killed before the arrival of Death, would have gone on dying forever, never released from the starvation feeding off his clever words. Caught between the tongue and the stomach, he would have been *the one exception*, the sacrifice that would have ensured the continued existence of every other being to infinity.

But what happened on that islet? Coyote was given a second chance in response to a second question. Taking the suggestion offered up by grass, the second thing to come out of his anus, he became mist and escaped across the water, calling to and called by the places he had marked, though these markings had been erased. Is this not a new beginning? Does not Coyote re-create the world through transforming into the barely material form of mist, akin to spirit, and splitting time between a world that still bears his mark and one erased and unmarked? Mirroring the forking of the river's path by the islet, a forking of time occurs, allowing Coyote to survive and beat the Creator at his own game. Did Coyote also die on that islet?

Part II
The Destruction

Chapter 4
Bad Indians and the Destruction of Writing

The difficulty and the difference between the usual social historian and me might be my unwillingness to distinguish one suffering from another . . . I feel a desire to feel/link these experiences that is stronger than any knowledge I might have of the value of their historical "specificity."

—Dian Million, "There Is a River in Me: Theory from Life"

If Estéfana's female body is valuable to the colonizer only if "pure" and "legal," then she works to steep that body in as many impurities and illegal activities as possible, thus lowering her value to the Church, and depriving it of a complete victory.

—Deborah Miranda, "They Were Tough, Those Old Women Before Us: The Power of Gossip in Isabel Meadows's Narratives"

The Difficulty and the Difference: Having Bad Feelings in Common

What constitutes the destruction of California Indians is not only the massacres but everything that leads up to, surrounds, and comes after, including state-oriented, institutional forms of redress and reconciliation. The massacres were a frenzied bloodlust, made clear by the descriptions of butchery of the young, old, and everyone in between; instrumental but also vicious and cruel; spectacular in the ways that human rights and historical discourses revel in. The traffic in body parts, bounties, militias and Indian hunting parties, the sheer brutality of actions and language, evince this murderous desire, splayed out conspicuously in the archive and historians' narratives. But the military and juridical executions, forbidding of testimony, legalized abductions, criminalization of freedom, rendering homeless of large swaths of people, forced marches, confinement and starvation, rape and enslavement, removal of children *for their own good* to government schools and to white families, coercion to pray to the wrong god, forbidding of language and ceremony, intentional decimation of Native food sources and relations with other beings, flooding of village and sacred sites, and then forgetting it all happened testify to a will to annihilate completely. Can one wonder, then, at these sorts of descriptions? From the Tuolomne *Courier,* 1858:

> For months past our feelings have been shocked at the condition of the Indians who are located about this neighborhood. There is no sympathizing care extended to these frail relics of humanity, as the storms sweep over their miserable huts and unclad bodies. Their intercourse with civilized communities has been accompanied with *the ordinary results* which other tribes have experienced under similar circumstances: prostitution, intemperance, and vice, in their most revolting aspects. As soon as the grey light of morning appears, they may be seen prowling round in search of miserable offal, for which they must compete with the dogs. At midnight their savage howls may frequently be heard, as they return to their sleeping places, half crazy from the poisonous drink which they have imbibed from some of the low grogeries about the outskirts of town. A few weeks ago, one of their number murdered another in the vicinity of the Catholic Church, while raving with madness from the above cause. But there is no law enforced for these poor wretches. It is no one's business to look after and protect them. Why do not our citizens ask the Legislature to have them removed to one of the reservations, where they will be comfortable, and be afforded an opportunity of learning some of the Christian ways of civilized being.[1]

Here we see the stirrings of, the early conditions and moral sentiments for, reconciliation. All the usual western humanist trappings are here: paternalism; civilizationist white supremacy; calls for law and order, for temperance leading to criminalization, for separation and confinement; isolation of a single violent event in the midst of an unacknowledged genocidal context; mind-numbing ignorance and myopia regarding complicity; liberal outrage and shock and the affected expressed desire to save. Yet, in relation to other accounts in the media and documents from this time, this response is progressive compared to the typical calls for extermination. This writer was a good person. But that, of course, is the rub. What the writer wants are "good" Indians that mirror the writer's own "goodness"—just living elsewhere. A future for all. *We know what storm sweeps over them.*

Sara Ahmed has described the "happiness script," which defines colonial social norms, such as those in the above quote, as social goods to be desired, along with the abjection of anyone who refuses such "gifts."[2] For Ahmed, this form of hegemony seeks to secure the willing participation of the subjected through the language of emotion and the promise of the social: *they will be comfortable, and be afforded an opportunity of learning some of the Christian ways of civilized being.* This script, of course, fails to recognize any other form of sociality that lies outside of such norms and operates by determining in advance the future unhappiness of those who remain outside of it. The problem in the description above and in other colonial contexts is that the "unhappiness" (and here we quickly reach the limits of the term) with the colonial world experienced by Indigenous people is also a refusal of a world that interprets Indigeneity as an inherent source of badness and negative feelings, as if Indigenous people were not perfectly content before colonizers arrived. The plethora of accusations that Indigenous peoples are too emotional, too embodied, throughout the colonial archive, indicate this interpretive double bind; part of colonial public discourse, they also call for an account of colonial affect and of how bad feelings in such scenes authorize, exclude, and otherwise discipline Indigenous responses to violence. This scene, described by the "well-intentioned" colonizer, is not one of a simple absence of goodness and happiness in a miserable people but of a people fundamentally affected by colonial violence where the promise of happiness, goodness, and futurity, according to the colonizer's standards, is itself a continuation of the problem.

But look at the scene again and one begins to see the outline of a different sociality at odds with the writer's vision, one formed along the edge of destitution, the brink of despair. A "crazy" sociality, drunk, fighting, fucking, scavenging, outside the law on the edge of the respectable town, at *the low grogeries.* Uncomfortable, uncivilized, without fellowship, competing with the dogs, both ordinary and revolting, it seethes, bubbles over the edge. How far into the abyss does it push? It is a sociality formed in the crucible of survival, one antithetical to "the social" as conceived by western humanists. Further, the scene isn't an isolated snapshot but a feeling in common *that other tribes have experienced.* Take note of this event as described in the *San Joaquin Republican,* also in 1858: "The Fresno Indians . . . are killing their doctors or medicine-men.

They declare them to be witches, that they cannot cure the sick, and that there will be no more rain or green grass until they are exterminated. Seven or eight of their doctors have in consequence already suffered martyrdom."[3] What would compel a people to kill their connection to the spiritual world and to other beings, to kill their holders of knowledge and health? The same thing that compelled people to refuse white reproductive futurity by calling for the deaths of all mixed-race children as a way to bring back the dead and make the whites disappear.[4] The same thing that compelled people to hand over members of their communities when the Spanish priests and conquistadors cracked down on the Joyas, California Indian third-gendered people.[5] Caused them to make terrible, unforgivable decisions in the face of it: despair.

This chapter is interested in the infrathin distance between—the proximity or imbrication of—despair and emancipation, despair as a fraught emancipation from the demand to be good, as an anticolonial orientation that works itself out through writing. Despair is lived impossibility, a death that exceeds or survives dying. Fundamentally, arriving with the radical destruction of Indigenous worlds, despair is an interruption of temporality, a desperate sense of diminishing future.

Reading Zabel Essayan's description of Armenian survivors of the catastrophe at the hands of the Turkish state gathered in a church in 1911, Marc Nichanian points to the ways the catastrophe turns affective and world-breaking: "with everyone there is discouragement, an extreme despair, they respond with bitter irony to our words of encouragement . . . Anxious and driven mad, they were unwilling to hear any word of consolation. Each person forgot his or her own pain and grief, it was an invincible and collective crowd whose emotions turned at times even against us."[6] Despair produces an unimaginable and unintelligible relation to the world: "This bloodbath, this stream of spilled blood, this despair of a humanity driven mad, caught between fire and blade, all this remained beyond my imagination, and I believe this was the case for everyone involved."[7] Marc Nichanian notes how Essayan expresses a complicated desire to put herself in the place of those who suffered along with an impossibility to do so, creating an aporia of the imagination that she seeks to write (through). Separated by despair, interrupted at the level of imagination, writing here becomes a form of disidentification that, nonetheless, is also general in the assembled group, unmooring the survivors from sense, producing a senseless, invincible collectivity. For Nichanian, this problem for writing is a sign of the interdiction on mourning, of the impossibility of death, which has the effect of bringing literature itself to a halt, replacing the literary imagination, which he associates with mourning, with an archival impetus, a tyranny of the archive to document what happened as the working out of the interdiction. The interruption of the literary imagination and the archival demand for truth together indicate a type of writing founded on destruction and in the throes of despair. From such senselessness derives the demand to make sense of it. The desire to know the sum of what happened, both in terms of the depth of a single experience and the range of experiences, is impossible. For Nichanian, the demand and the impossibility are together the outcome of a genocidal will that places on the survivors the burden of making sense of the violence according to the terms of the executioner. It raises the questions of perception and position through such disidentification and an interrupted and reframed commonality.

Elaborating on the work of Sylvia Wynter, Katherine McKittrick has argued that this aporia—described by Nichanian in the realms of literature and representation—can also be found within archival and scientific metrics that remain forever approximate, plural in their sources and meanings, allowing one to "doubt knowable data and a singular analytic frame."[8] This unknowingness is accumulative and relational, testing the limits of the imagination with too many kinds of death, both past and present, to list and grieve. "It is through conceptualizing weights and measurements as relational to and distinguished from Black Life the promise of the slave ship emerges."[9] Organized around the logistics of the Atlantic slave trade and, in particular, the infamous court case involving the slave ship *Zong*, McKittrick's argument indicates how the various forms of common measure, such as the ledger system, can be read in more complex ways than as forms of dehumanization. These measures exist as "analytical pathways that are beholden to a system of knowledge that descriptively rehearses antiblackness and . . . necessarily refuses decolonial thinking," which, for McKittrick, raises the question of how to engage mathematical and numerical certainties without reprising the violence.[10] For McKittrick, the question isn't about how to get over the brutality but rather how to live with it differently, an imperative that causes her to "move with the numbers" and work out how the discomfort with the "mathematics of Black Life can inform current and future formations of Black Studies."[11] A process of simultaneously noticing, reworking, and mistrusting the archival display of the mutilated body, this alternative hears in the numbers the counting of the whip, to "trust the lie" ("born free") and counts it out differently, because, "as we all know, numbers signify measurable items, but they also invite chaos."[12]

McKittrick references a totalizing maritime metric, deadweight tonnage, which measures the entirety of a ship's weight, "all provisions, crew, fuel, cargo, and so forth," a singular measurement that "erases humanness just as it enacts it" in its very inhumanity. This measurement is a singularity that unfolds infinitely in the face of the complexity of relations and bears unbearably on the unknown dead thrown overboard the ship, translated and made legible as insured loss of cargo.[13] Like Essayan's frustrated desire to record all suffering, *I was unable—despite superhuman efforts—to grasp the totality of their misfortune, and still today I cannot,* loss here is unimaginable as a totality and yet somehow, terribly, quantifiable, the sum of suffering translated into deadweight tonnage.[14] Accounting for loss runs into the dilemma of quantitative or qualitative feelings through the problem of an untranslatable intensity and an unknowable past. Representing numbers beyond sense, this measure makes suffering knowable otherwise, as infinite summation of the death that survives dying and gets recast somehow, somewhat mysteriously, as life. As Dian Million notes, "any official way that . . . knowledge is argued into being is not immune any more to the effects of a radically multiplied field of enunciation."[15]

Together, the sociality founded on despair—that renders literature and mourning impossible, as seen in the "invincible" assemblage of Armenian survivors collectivized by "the feeling of having been trampled collectively, of having been crushed by savage claws"—and the sociality of deadweight tonnage—founded on the infinite undecidability between human and inhuman measure—indicate something about destruction and despair and the limits they place on the social and what sociality looks like across such limits.[16] Despair. Pushed further according to the *more-than-just-killing* that constitutes ongoing destruction and the inhuman relationality of deadweight tonnage, despair is not only inhuman (outside of human control), like all emotions, but also *not just human, competing with dogs searching for miserable offal.* Despair is humanization as terror, reorganizing relational being into a humanized order that trickles down into scraps to be fought over. I am not providing a psychosocial diagnosis (which implies need of a cure) but an attempt to try to understand the political import of this bad feeling, of being on the receiving end of such a humanizing system, including the impossible recuperation of a bad feeling into a political project; to stay with this feeling despite its ugliness or one's own discomfort.[17] Just because despair cannot be recuperated doesn't mean it is without use. This claim is certainly not a prescription, though. In staying with the difficulty of an impossible politics of despair, one ends up perhaps finding a collective orientation. As Jean-François Lyotard notes, "A single referent—say a phenomenon grasped in the field of human history—can be used qua example, to present the object of the discourse of despair, but also qua bit of guiding thread, to present analogically the object of the discourse of emancipation."[18]

In California, genocide socialities sprang up in spaces overrun with despair, what Michael Taussig in another context calls "spaces of death"[19]: the forts where abducted women and children were taken and auctioned into slavery; the missions, including the *monjería* where women were kept and isolated from the men often for the purposes of sexual exploitation; the boarding schools, also segregated by gender for the same purpose; the rez; the places of contact between women sexually enslaved by white men in "marriage" or "concubinage." People gathered together in these spaces: mixed bands of raiders hiding out in the hills, refugees of mass slaughter congregating in the woods, as well as the difficult socialities between California Indians and other abjected groups in nineteenth-century California: Chinese, Mexicans, Hawaiians, enslaved Black people brought to the gold mines by Southern owners escaping the Civil War, and "errant" whites. They are also tied to the radical rupture made in Indigenous socialities with other-than-human beings, an effect of an imposed imperial epistemology that weds capitalist production with secularized theology, creating an ontological hierarchy of terror based on human mastery.[20] As a fundamental part of "the construction of colonial reality . . . these spaces of death blend as common pool signifiers or caption points binding the culture of the conqueror with that of the conquered. The space of death is preeminently a space of transformation."[21] They are also difficult spaces of survival and socialization under extreme duress.

For Taussig, speaking about torture as employed by the Colombian military dictatorship against Indigenous people, that legacy of violence extends directly from the general colonial terrorism employed against Indigenous peoples and enslaved Africans by "an initially far smaller number of [white] Christians."[22] The resources for understanding it, though, flow from Indigenous epistemes and healing practices and the familiarity of Indigenous healers with the space of death. As an "elderly Ingano Indian from the Putumayo" says:

> With the fever I was aware of everything. But after eight days I became unconscious. I know not where I was. Like a madman I wandered, consumed by fever. They had to cover me up where I fell, mouth down. Thus after eight days I was aware of nothing. I was unconscious. Of what people were saying, I remembered nothing. Of the pain of the fever, I remembered nothing; only the space of death—walking in the space of death. Thus, after the noises that spoke, I remained unconscious. Now the world remained behind. Now the world was removed. Well, then I understood. Now the pains were speaking. I knew that I would live no longer. Now I was dead. My sight had gone. Of the world I knew nothing, nor the sound of my ears. Of speech, nothing. Silence. And one knows the space of death, there . . . And this death—the space that I saw, I was in its center, standing. Then I went to the heights. From the heights a star-point seemed my due. I was standing. Then I came down. There I was searching for the five continents of the world, to remain, to find me a place in the five continents of the world—in the space in which I was wandering. But I was not able.[23]

How does one understand this space of death, mediated as it is by the telling of an anthropologist investigating the role of Indigenous healers in colonized spaces of terror? Couched in a story of shamanic vision, a form of experience so desperately sought by colonizers (including anthropologists and avant-garde artists of all stripes), the story/vision is difficult to unpack without contributing to the exoticization and romanticization of Indigenous knowledge and spiritual practices. Its social and historical contexts, specifically in relation to Indigeneity, are essential, and yet this story is about the world's absence, of an absolute disidentification and untethering from earthly coordinates. As Taussig, in another text, explains, context is not "a secure epistemic nest in which our knowledge-eggs are to be safely hatched" but must include the spatially and temporally disorienting juxtapositions and mediations that flow from the destruction, as well as the points of disjuncture and incommensurability.[24] Disorientation, including that caused by or causing of despair, *is the context.* Asserting this position is meant to avoid the trap of employing empirical social and historical descriptions and explanations to enact mastery over both society and history, as well as over our own discourses, according to an expanded western rationality. Such scholarly contextualization is still very much about white, western control, often participating in what anticolonial scholar Dylan Rodríguez calls "white reconstruction," or the reformation of white supremacy along more progressive lines.[25] A complete disorientation, the Indigenous healer's story, rather, encapsulates much of the general disorientation caused by colonization and the destruction of Indigenous worlds, described variously as the world ending, turning over, or having come unstuck. The healer's story precisely indicates the experiences of Indigenous people caught up in the spaces of death and socialities of despair.

The complex array of genocide socialities formed in such a disorientation—what I will refer to from here on out as *(anti)socialities* to mark the ineradicable violence inscribed into their hearts—participate in Dian Million's notion of felt theory in profoundly unsettling ways. This array makes it necessary, in other words, that these genocide socialities become a part of what Stephen Best calls "a collective undoing" through having disaffiliative bad feelings in common.[26] Because, for Million, Indigenous stories are "emotionally empowered," they are "informed with the affective content of the colonial experience," a felt experience that often renders Indigenous stories unrecognizable as theory to western scholarship, relegated to the realm of the personal or traumatic, with its implied justifications for state and institutional interventions and undergirding commitment to humanistic mastery. Indigenous stories, reflective of difficult socialities, don't fit the objectivizing descriptions of Indigenous thought in the cultural narrative, and they don't fit the acceptable social and historical narratives that register colonial violence as knowledge of what happened along with its sociologically determined effects. As a mode of collective, if fraught, theorizing derived from social experience and communicated as story and relation, for Million such theorizing takes the material forms of poetry, memoir, documentary, and, especially, testimony, which are sources for on-the-ground anticolonial theorizing by our ancestors and kin, full of the pain and suffering that incites thought. In the epigraph to this chapter, she relates such theorizing to a common voice, a commonality that can't be anything but a disintegration of individual experience into a common suffering, a commonality that is also a commonness as common disidentification through the antigravity of despair. It is, as she says, *a radically multiplied field of enunciation.*

Million, however, cautions against the desire to seek in these expressive forms of difficult, collective (anti)sociality a recuperative impulse, a too-easy representation of resistance that would merely be a salve for our own bad feelings, an impulse that she locates in a biopolitics that can infuse affect, healing, testimony, and community with power aligned with the neoliberal and reconciliatory forces of the settler state.[27] Million's caution extends to the hegemonic form of representing the destruction of California Indians through the term *genocide,* a term with legal and institutional as well as communal and affective meanings. As seen in the previous chapter, attention to the discourse of genocide and its limits, to history and law (which are its primary productive forces), reveals what Nichanian calls the destitution of the fact, the replacement of the fact with proofs, arguments, evidence—in a word, the archive.[28] Such a notion distorts our readings of and engagements with Million's materialized common voice and raises the question McKittrick asks about how to live with the violence and its material traces. Especially in the current conjuncture, after a state executive order officially recognized genocide in California (though the term is absent from the text, Governor Newsom said "genocide" at a ceremonial apology to Native communities) and in the midst of a Truth and Healing Council's investigations, it is important to try to understand how the tension between a politics of despair and the destitution of the fact (which underlies these developments and is said to provide hope, salve, futurity) interact in the multiplied field of collective voice and bad feelings in common. What happens to the fact? How do the case study, the event (which is always of language), the referent (in the ruins of representation), the ongoing structures of violence, and the afterlives of the destruction relate to the fact, to truth and representation, and to collective voice? What kind of poetics is at work? And what other poetics are possible?

Such questions cannot be asked abstractly as they bear on the positioning of knowledge, writing, and reading as material and interrelational practices in the form of a collective, counterhegemonic perception. Epeli Hau'ofa, in the context of emphasizing a consciousness of the ever-expanding world of Oceania to counteract ideologies of dependence and development, has called for such radical shifts in spatial and temporal perception to ground Indigenous studies.[29] And, following David Lloyd in his call to expand Ngũgĩ wa Thiong'o's challenge to the hegemonic English curriculum in Kenya (to abolish English departments and replace the curriculum with Indigenous African *orature*) to other contexts, these questions must be framed in relation to a demand to center California Indian stories in California.[30] What this demand looks like is of course open, but it would seemingly engage something like the paradox of centering a stubbornly "weak" or "minor" literature and other marginal or minor forms of writing, including in their destroyed, fragmentary, reduced, and absent forms. This demand would also involve engaging noncanonical and a-disciplinary writing, including marginalia, nonliterary and archival documents, minor or niche publications, and everything else that constitutes the expanded text. Beyond the deep oral traditions of Native peoples, this expansive *writing* would include complicated forms of collective voicing and action, such as the antisocialities described in this chapter and the various modes of interrelationality that indicate the absence of distinction between culture and politics and that rearrange social relationships with all kinds of beings. Most important, this challenge to hegemonic English entails a refusal of the English language, where refusal means *everything disclosed without disclosing anything*, that is, writing in English without choice, without commitment, and without ownership.

Esselen and Chumash poet, theorist, and author Deborah Miranda, in the chapter epigraph and in her body of work more generally, outlines the struggle with an absence of choice confronted by California Indian peoples at The End of the World, a struggle that calls on the greatest powers of agency in their most adulterated, inhuman forms. Working in these ruins of representation leads to a problematics of the voice, of how to hear the voice beyond the dilemma of representation and its overcoming. What is the voice in the wake of catastrophe? Of an antisocial sociality? Of a politics of despair? In the next section, I look closely at the poetics of Deborah Miranda's *Bad Indians* in order to understand these questions. In particular, I discuss the lesbian intertextuality that produces poetic relations between Miranda and Konkow Maidu poet Janice Gould in their correspondence and cross-textual references. I also discuss the social and sexual forms of identification and disidentification in the text organized around stories of bad Indians, archival, personal, and beyond. Drawing on the work of Rei Terada, I argue that the text opens a type of "nonway," an original disruption that forgoes the usual dialectic of impasse and transcendence. The nonway creates a poetics that puts into question distinctions between poetics and knowledge, art and truth, performed in Miranda's reuse of archival documents, stories of ancestors, descriptions of violence, and the position of beginning at The End of the World. Miranda argues that the ancestors who braved the destructive production of an ethnographic image of the present in order to use anthropology as a recording device functioned through an aesthetic agency that, for her, takes the form of story as survival, of communal affective and embodied experiences that ground a discontinuous continuity, a lived disruption, communicated across space and time, assimilating destruction itself as part of California Indian perceptual traditions. In this way, centering California Indian writing (literature and history in this chapter) is a specific place-oriented *affair of the various peoples,* peoples caught up in multiple forms of antisociality due to the conditions of violence in its multiple forms *in this place.*

This chapter, then, attends to the gray horizon of what can summarily be called *writing destruction* and its fraught poetics, as part of thinking through what centering California Indian storying might look like. Although, as a problematic and practice, writing destruction has gone by many names in relation to irreducible contexts, and largely should remain nameless in its plurality,[31] here, tentatively, *the destruction of California Indians* opens onto the problem of writing and story.[32] Two questions related to this name orient our attention/intention: *Was Destruction a genocide?* and *Does a California Indian literature exist?*[33] Both questions, when seen as requiring definitive answers with attendant methodologies, risk a certain hegemonic response and approach (in historiography and literary studies, respectively), contributing to the ongoing destruction, as well as a certain retrenchment in genocidal epistemology through disciplinary critical reformulation. And yet, in their difficulty if not impossibility—better yet, their exhaustion and stubborn endurance—they resonate with each other, mapping a certain a-disciplinary space of indetermination where writing can be said to begin or end, to have always been ongoing, to never get started and to have no destination to arrive at. In asking these questions (again and again) without presuming a definitive answer, through an *unmethodical method,* this chapter seeks to inhabit this fraught space of poetics in order to clear away conventional wisdom by following the precarious path of ancestors who lived and wrote the destruction as an open-ended question and by listening to the words of California Indian authors who continue to write this destruction, risking writing's destructive capacity.[34]

Being a Bad Indian: On Lowering Your Value

"I need a song so terrible that the first note splinters like slate, spits shards out into the universe—yes, that's the song I need, the right song to accompany your first steps along the Milky Way, song with serrated edges, burnt red rim slicing into the Pacific—"[35] There's an intertextual moment in Deborah Miranda's *Bad Indians* that functions as a methodology of reparative destruction. It arrives in a scene of uncomfortable affiliation, while she waits in the hospital for her estranged and elderly father, Al Miranda, to have a minor surgery. He is, as the memoir has made clear, both the vessel and product of gendered, colonial violence, has been an inconstant figure in the author's life, bringing both joy and utter pain when he is present; Miranda's father is a connection to her Ohlone and Chumash cultures and a frustrating and insecurity-rending disruption: "It is our father whose body is the source of the most precious part of our identity, and the most damning legacies of our history."[36] This scene, described in the final section of the book, titled "Home," comes at the end of a journey of exploration, of archival research into colonial mission records and documentation by salvage ethnographers, into violent colonial and familial interruptions and relationships through the same sources. Beginning in the profound disorientation of "The End of the World: Missionization" (the first section), the journey moves across "Bridges: Post-Secularization"; follows a mysterious "Light from the Carissa Plains: Reinvention," toward a forgotten creation story; and ends, of course, with "Home." But this isn't a story about an uncomplicated homecoming, just as the resonances between Miranda's ancestors, whose words, stories, images, and lives fill the book, and her more autobiographical moments are not uncomplicated connections. These connections strain across the archival materials, the temporal, spatial, physical, and affective dislocations and violence. At issue is the question of what these connections mean, if they are possible, in the wake of The End of the World. There's a sense of profound brokenness and loss here that disorients (from) the beginning.

In this context, Miranda references a series of letters sent between her and the late Konkow Maidu poet Janice Gould, confessing "I don't have an enrollment number, I don't have stories. All I have is my father's face, my grandmother's hair, these Chumash hands."[37] Taking recourse to the body, it will be to the body, not citizenship or recognizable cultural performance or identity, that Miranda turns over and over again throughout *Bad Indians* as the base materiality of survival and of

Indigenous endurance: "If not of the land, or tribe, or language, or soul, then at least—oh God at least—survival of the body. For just a little while longer, survival."[38] The body, though, is fractured and compartmentalized, not unlike the remains of culture in their own fragmented embodiment or the remains of ancestors murdered and butchered for body part trophies, bounties, and scientific research.[39] The body is the site of the reproduction of colonial violence as well as the terrible song that splinters and makes possible a reassembling of pieces. This reassembling, for Miranda, sometimes takes the form of distant relationships, having spent much of her life in Washington State raised by non-Native relatives, and of sisterhood at a distance. She writes, "I'm impatient too. In my backpack is an unread letter from a woman I recently met at a writing workshop. Living over one thousand miles apart now, we have a rich and voluminous friendship-by-mail. I am anxious to read her response to my last letter, but I don't want to bring it out until I'm alone," and "In my heart, I call her sister. A woman who looks like me, my brother, my son. Like my father. I'm thirty years old; she is the only other California Indian I have met."[40] Miranda documents an impoverishment of culture, of disaffiliation from family and community, tied explicitly to genocidal violence, and an emaciated identity, suddenly nourished by a stream of letters, read when she is alone.

The connection the friends make is through the impoverishment itself, a feeding on emaciation and disaffiliation. Gould writes:

> Mama taught us as kids that we were Konkow Indians, and she was emphatic that we should not be ashamed of this. She could not provide us, however, with a cultural heritage, which had been unraveling in our family for at least two generations as a consequence of intermarriage and the colonial legacy. Understanding our cultural heritage was something we had to do for ourselves: studying the hidden (and overt) "otherness" of our own lives, and tracing our family's being through ethnographic accounts, linguistic data, local histories, folklore, and whatever had not passed out of our relatives' memories.[41]

This impoverishment produces a poetics that, while seemingly initiating an individual project of exploration—*something we had to do for ourselves*—strains the very boundaries of the self, as the reference to the *"otherness" of our own lives* and the repetition of colonial representational forms makes clear. This poetic impoverishment is manifested in Miranda's *Bad Indians* as a self-described and seemingly paradoxical title or form, *A Tribal Memoir.* This is a memoir that spans the end of the world brought on by Spanish missionization to the text's present in 2012, tracing Miranda's ancestors to her federally unrecognized tribe, the Ohlone/Costanoan Esselen Nation, that, as Miranda documents, moves in and out of various states of presence, though always there.

Miranda details this sense of self-otherness in the poem "Correspondence" dedicated to Gould in her book *Indian Cartography:*

> I spend the summer near water:
> McKenzie River, Guemes Island, Birch Bay.
> You spend the summer driving
> From Albuquerque to Santa Fe, back again.
>
> I try to teach my children how to swim.
> You try to raise poetry in adolescents.
> In the evening, crickets scatter
> in the driftwood, sing me to sleep.
>
> You write of mourning dove skies,
> cicada's hypnotic buzz.
> Despite distance we are sisters
> birthed from the same wound.
>
> Half-breeds, we don't know
> our own names, or stories.
> But we can recite the creation myth
> of race, species, inferiority.
>
> We can remember there are others
> like us, unfound.
> They have a certain darkness of face,
> eyes, thought; they move silently
>
> through dry desert towns
> and down the long Pacific coast.
> Maybe they are looking for us.
> I'll leave a small pile of feathers,
>
> shells, and round black stones
> as a sign that I came this way.
> In your classroom you do the same
> With students' words, hearts,
> Jagged-cut poems.[42]

Self-otherness, like the *jagged-cut poem,* is the condition for a sameness across difference, a likeness, *a woman who looks like me, my brother, my son. My father.* Again the body, *a certain darkness* that also qualifies thought and conditions the search for others like oneself, an ambivalent loneliness/desire. An affiliation founded on dis/affiliation from/with the violent father, an entire genealogy of violence, Gould is a sister to Miranda because she is the only other California Indian Miranda has met. As Elaine Marks writes, in her survey of lesbian intertextuality (in French literature), "The I/you opposition remains, but the other is now also familiar, familial—a sister, a friend" for the first time, *birthed from the same wound.*[43]

Moving beyond the pages of *Bad Indians,* the letters between Gould and Miranda open up not only an intertextual relationship through Miranda's reference to them but also a conversation across poems that spans several books. In *Earthquake Weather,* Gould references the letters in her poem "Blood Sisters," dedicated to Miranda.

> I did not know how lonely I was
> till we began to talk.
> You told me of the Mission,
> the Book of Names,
> and the photos you discovered.
> Each offered a remote clue
> about your family,
> Chumash ancestors,
> things you thought permanently lost.
> I told you about the Maidu song my mother sang
> in a scale I could never learn,
> and about the tree on an old dirt road
> where the white men lynched my people.
>
> In our separate childhoods, we each
> read that Indians were stupid,
> lived like swine or dogs.
> Such ignorant lies!
> The Chumash were flogged and tortured,
> the Maidu stolen for slaves,
> and later marched at gunpoint
> to a distant reservation.

We glance at one another,
fall silent.
Americans do not know these things
nor do they want to know.

But each of us knows stories
we have never even whispered.[44]

Sisterhood is here one of being California Indian women in the wake of The End of the World, a difficult sameness (across time and space as will be seen) but also much more. It is a position of knowing—in a certain way—that connects questions of affiliation and identification immediately to the political (as opposed to politics proper). Founded on a not hidden but not entirely known feeling, a previously unacknowledged loneliness, the violent representations, the legacies of settler violence, and the stories *never even whispered*, communicated in a glance, in silence, condition such reparative knowing and complicated association. Loneliness in Gould's poem couples with anxiety-mitigating shared stories of historical violence and disrupted and/or difficult connections to family, tribe, and culture. It is an aloneness that makes relationships of similitude possible, a form of autonomy as *something we had to do for ourselves* that finds in the self the resource of a barely legible self-otherness that prepares the way for a kind of problematic sociality bubbling below the surface of the lonely and divided self.

In loneliness is found a more profound solitude than the isolation of western and settler individualism. It is a loneliness conditioned by an exclusion that makes possible inclusion as an even greater exclusion and dismissal from everyday life. It is a feeling of profound incompleteness, a feeling that, in the end, expresses nothing, a nothingness that appears in the silent glances, in the meandering work of finding others like oneself, alike in feelings, in a shade of darkness. Loneliness is tied to a broken relationality that renders identity only ever a tentative and provisional moment of closure but which ultimately resists definition. It is and conditions a form of communication that operates through feelings.

Like Marks in relation to lesbian writing, Eve Kosofsky Sedgwick locates a form of reparative knowing in gay, lesbian, and queer intertextuality, which she associates with the queer-identified practice of camp, especially, the excessive, plenitudinous nature of its being *too much*, which, according to her, offers resources for a depleted self. These surplus aspects of camp performance, for Sedgwick, include "the startling displays of excess erudition . . . the passionate, often hilarious antiquarianism, the prodigal production of alternative historiographies; the 'over'-attachment to fragmentary, marginal, waste or leftover products; the rich, highly interruptive affective variety; the irrepressible fascination with ventriloquistic experimentation; the disorienting juxtapositions of present with past, and popular with high culture."[45] Exuberant and unsettling, such intertextual and communal explorations of reparative practices, their displays of too much beauty, too much stylistic investment, are also sites of expression for unexplainable "upwellings of threat, contempt, and longing."

Miranda and Gould's intertextual relationship, while related to questions of cultural and racial identity, also resonates with their lesbian identifications in their respective texts as similarly a wellspring. A genocidal relation formed out of feelings of emaciation and loneliness, out of resonant painful family histories and relations, and, especially, out of the violence of the colonial cisheteropatriarchal system of control over their bodies and desires, Miranda and Gould's conversation finds its abundance in these shared negative feelings as well as in the interrupted relations between land and bodies. The landmarks the speaker and interlocutor in Miranda's "Correspondence" left as orienting devices—*I'll leave a small pile of feathers, / shells, and round black stones / as a sign that I came this way. / In your classroom you do the same / With students' words, hearts, / Jagged-cut poems*—mark paths to such abundance, ways of finding each other across the vast wasteland of colonial life and the ongoing aftermath of genocide in a masculine world, even at great distance.

Two poems, "Old Territory. New Maps" by Miranda and "Six Sonnets: Crossing the West" by Gould, map out coordinates of searching, finding, and encountering abundance in distance in recounting a road trip the two took together. In some ways connected to the lesbian literary trope of *awakening*, of an encounter between a more experienced woman and one less experienced (though, as the younger Miranda writes, "she kisses me: lips pursed, trembling, inexperienced for all her boasts"[46]), what Gould and Miranda seemingly chart is a postapocalyptic world traversed by two California Indian lesbians who bear the scars and complex desires forged by colonial violence into other Indigenous lands. In Miranda's poetic accounting, bodies and land hold the tension of desire and distance.

I want my longing to miraculously
bring you through the barrier of your skin
into my blood so that I can possess you
entirely and yet be entirely possessed.
You say no, your face tight with pain, tears
burning your eyes, hands clenching the steering wheel.
I believe you. We drive hundreds of miles
across deserts sculpted by wind and story,
and I learn distance from my hand to your thigh,
your mouth to my mouth, the curve of a collar
along a warm, smooth neck.
You grin as if no one has ever seen you thus:
naked, savage, happy.
That is the beginning of yes.

Ghosts are everywhere.
We hear them singing on that mountain in Ute country,
the cries of your flute pleasuring old spirits.
Like those people whose land we cross,
we don't live by lines drawn on paper.
Instead, we mark the waterfall of shy kisses,
a dry windy town where we exchange secrets in whispers,
the high cliff hollow that shelters us
on the edge of the Uinta forest.
Wildflowers bend beneath our bodies,
cup the trembling weight of touch.
We wander for awhile in a place vast enough
to contain all possibilities.[47]

The possession and dispossession of the self-other is found here in longing, in the desire to absorb a self-same blood that is at same time difference. The desire to be-one-with, which is resisted with a *no*, maps onto the strained sexual relation between the speaker and her desired other: touch and kiss are distance itself. A seduction occurs across that distance, with and through it. Some of the characteristics of lesbian intertextuality and literature that Marks notes are the insistence on physical manifestations of desire, a visceral awareness of the female body, and repetition.[48] These literary figures un-map the female body from heteropatriarchal coordinates and remap through story and poetry an undomesticated body. In Miranda's account of the trip, the liberation of the body is made possible by the movement across land without lines on paper, its vastness. New locations give bearings, *the waterfall of shy kisses, / a dry windy town where we exchange secrets in whispers*, charting a path to a temporary refuge: in both the journey and the poem. As Marks notes, "There, safe temporarily from male intrusion, they indulge in an activity more subversive than love-making: they communicate with each other in woman's language."[49]

Gould offers her own account of the trip that elaborates on the strained relation of desire.

> Her hand on my thigh, my shoulder,
> in my hair. She leans over to kiss my cheek.
> We look at each other, smile. For miles
> we travel this way, nearly silent, point
> with eyes or chins at the circling hawk, the king-
> fisher on the snag above the swollen
> creek. One night I weep in her arms
> as she cries, *"Oh, oh, oh!"* because I have touched
> her scars lightly: throat, belly, breasts.
> In that communion of lovers, thick sobs
> break from me as I think of my love
> back home, all that I have done
> and cannot say. This is the first time
> I have left her so completely, so alone.[50]

A transgression more than of infidelity, the speaker and the lover's connection is through loneliness but of a different kind, through silences that swell with more than just meaning, that dissolve meaning itself. The distance of loneliness here is even greater within the intimacy of sameness, a weeping that alights on scars, scars shared. It is a *communion of lovers* that opens onto something more fundamental than fundament, through scars and weeping, through an Indigenous lesbian encounter with the land outside of colonial heteropatriarchal control.

> Sacred. Sacred. Sacred. Sacred. (Speak
> in a whisper.) We slip into this
> space half cognizant. The land is very
> large indeed: bones of the earth
> worn down, though she is a living thing.
> See how she exposes her grace? Antelopes

graze on the far plain—their high,
white tails—the red soil throbs
its slow heartbeat, and the blue sky
clears so smartly, perfectly, like
radiance. Are the ancestors near?
What can we know? We decide
to wander around this prairie, mistaken
for Utes, buy commodities in little towns.[51]

And while Marks notes that communicating in a woman's language is more subversive than love-making, the abundance of the land, *bones of the earth, red soil throbs,* is unlocked for both Miranda and Gould in the body, in what Monique Wittig lastingly calls *The Lesbian Body*—here the Indigenous lesbian body—its indestructibility outside of colonial heteropatriarchal coordinates and political formations. Finding in the body connection to the land (or perhaps vice versa), Gould describes, "I know / we must be circling Paradise / because the ants enter the fleshy petals / of the roadside flowers with evident / joy and purpose (oh, my dark, pretty one)," rhyming the flesh of sex with that of the land. Miranda also describes the disorientation of this other land found in the body through sexuality.[52]

After twelve hundred miles together
we enter green forest thick along a fearless river.
This dense topography we can't see through,
can't find the horizon to judge distances
or the arc of the sun to know east from west.
There at last you clasp my hand, guide it
to a place beyond maps,
no universe I have ever known.
It is a raw landscape; we are the sojourners
overcome by the perilous shock of arrival.
We stop the car, walk by the river,
clumsy, frightened by desire. I wish
for more than body or soul can bear.[53]

For Miranda, the ecstatic and eccentric deformation of the land, of its violent colonial heteropatriarchal markings, is tied to a desire that is destructive, that is based on destruction, *I wish / for more than body or soul can bear.* In and through desire and its intimacy with destruction, she and Gould find a permanent temporary home in the weave of language, body, and land as a site free from control, unbound, boundless "where every direction took us home / but no place could give us shelter."[54] Errant. Disorienting. Exposed. The disjunctions, though, in the impossible achievement of such a space are hard to bear and deform the lesbian narrative of awakening, "I don't know how to survive awakening / in a woman's body with a child's / broken heart."[55] Interruption. Longing. Loneliness. The body, land, are now permanently marked by loss seeking only a way to express itself, "How can I learn this trick, will your body / back to the other side of my skin? Help me / translate loss the way this land does— / flood, earthquake, landslide— / terrible, and alive."[56]

Mishuana Goeman has written powerfully about the (re)mapping practices that Indigenous women perform in literature, reshaping the creative imaginary of the "settler nation" and what Mary Louise Pratt calls a "European planetary consciousness."[57] As Goeman writes, "(Re)mapping . . . is the labor Native authors and the communities they write within and about undertake, in the simultaneously metaphoric and material capacities of map making, to generate new possibilities," and "(re)mapping is about acknowledging the power of Native epistemologies in defining our moves towards spatial decolonizations."[58] These are mapping practices that, as Indigenous feminists have long acknowledged, confront the shadow of death and violence that haunts Indigenous women: the settler heteropatriarchal state and its structure of femicide.[59] What Miranda and Gould in their intertextual correspondence offer to this discussion is a practice of mapping the Indigenous lesbian body through their overabundance of communication that spills outside the bounds of acceptable text, identity, literature, boundary. It is a mapping practice intractably marked by violence, by layers of violence connected to the Destruction, a profound loss of even the coordinates of culture and Indigenous epistemology, and of the absence of an Indigenous conception of lesbianism. In these absences they find bounty, akin to Pico's *dark part inside,* here translated into the loss of Indigenous sex and gender relational forms. In the inchoate but not really known—manifest in feelings—lies a search toward a space of neutrality as escape from the western colonial grid of cisheteropatriarchal sexuality. Miranda and Gould's movements are ambiguous in relation to what Goeman, borrowing from Diné poet Esther Belin, calls "directional memory."[60] In a postapocalyptic space, their movements invite a certain stillness at the core, direction as a sign, a painful one.

In *Bad Indians,* Miranda traces a process of awakening to this violence and to her desire through the painful encounters she has with men. Using the metaphor of a knife, which she derives from her first memory—of her father holding a knife to her mother's throat, she describes the forging and sharpening and wielding and sheathing and eventually the melting of this blade into lesbian desire as a biography of the trajectory of violence in her life. The knife moves through unspeakable, horrific encounters (her being raped at seven years old by a friend of her mother's; holding a gun to her father's head), mundane manifestations (her inability to stave off her anger toward her children, marrying her high school English teacher), and is eventually melted down in her sexual desire and yet she holds it still in her writing in another form.

> I write these words down with the tip of a pen forged out of grief and violence. I'll send these stories out where other women are waiting, slashed by nightmares and fear. Cutting themselves, their children. Sometimes security is a knife that slits your own wrists. Nothing in my life or world prepared me to suspect such a thing. I kept trying to play by the rules I'd learned: the cure for poverty and loss is property and surety. The remedy for violence and alcoholism is control and cold rationality. The way to fill the gaping hole left by abandonment is to never leave; not even to save your own life. The balm for self-hatred is to marry white skin; or to desire skin so much like your own that scars arise of their own accord out of shared histories left unresolved. It's none of that.[61]

Writing, "Indian languages which originate from the gleaming throats of birds," fear of automatic writing because of its intimacy with mental illness, "writing words that might have the power to take away my children permanently."[62] Through writing, Miranda seeks to ride the wave of destruction, to harness its forces as a reparative practice, to invoke its dangers and risks as a weak violence, through desire, through overabundance, through writing. She seeks to write the lesbian body as survival, in conversation, intertextually, and therefore to rewrite the whole world.

Sedgwick famously locates reparative practices in and as a weak position in analytic (if not actual) opposition to a strong theoretical position of paranoid critique. Critique, in this sense, buttresses the ego (anticipation and avoidance of humiliation) and systematically attempts to account for as many phenomena as possible through critical exposure, what Moten and Harney refer to as the work of the professional critical academic.[63] Critique elucidates and thereby overvalues its object, interested primarily in the value of achievement. But, as Sedgwick reminds us, this will-to-make-visible is complicated by the fact that visibility or making visible is itself a violent act, desire, and epistemology.[64] Interpretive strategies that focus on disciplinary knowledge production bring a world of action and motion into focus in strong forms that overwhelm, suppress, and/or invalidate weak, minor, or otherwise more vulnerable ones. These strategies determine the space of visible antagonism, which often takes the form of historical progress or other types of class conflict, as the only option available. A weak epistemology, on the other hand, is more interested in how things fail in specific and often anticolonial ways, including the space of the failure to be visible that, despite Gould's reference to a hidden otherness, is not the space of the hidden (the hidden is merely the other side of the visible). Outside the discursive formation of objects, of clearly delineated subject-positions, of concepts and strategies, lies a world that often doesn't get perceived as existing but that paradoxically, in its ongoing destruction and perpetual replacement, conditions the colonial world of action and being, which is entirely dependent on the effaced Indigenous world and its perpetuation as merely condition, predecessor, somehow past. Such a site is one of anticolonial struggle.

This is the world Gould references in her description of a song her mother sang in a scale she could never learn, an unlearnable song that nonetheless organizes Gould's poetics into an orientation. In her deliciously anticipated response to Miranda's letter about not having stories, Gould writes, "You do have stories . . . those stories your dad tells are connected with older stories, stories that might not have been passed down to you, but which existed and *maybe even still exist in a world that isn't this one* . . . It is a fragment in one way, but like the shard of a pot that can be restored."[65] Songs, stories, culture, and bodies act as shards, pieces that collectively and in their reparative rearticulation point in the direction of *a world that isn't this one*. This orientation without a clear, untroubled direction informs much of *Bad Indians*, in the stories, through the poetics of the text, and in the book's difficult sociality of being bad Indians and having bad feelings in common. Tom Miranda, Deborah Miranda's grandfather, whose recorded tapes and stories she transcribes, offers Miranda such an orientation. He tells the story of a mysterious light that keeps attracting him, a light seen from afar at night as he sits and ponders. While he "wanted to see . . . where the hell that light was coming from," Miranda understands the light as having a delayed dis/orientation: "His words, spoken when I was still a child, hovered in the air for years, waiting to find me, waiting for me to listen. Waiting for me to look at both the blessing and the genocide."[66] A state of suspension, withdrawn from time, from relations, for generations, the recorded words and thereby this light become forms of absorption, captivation, a leaning toward, an intransitive openness, to be taken (in) by this other world and one's self-otherness, without revelation.

The light, as Miranda later discovers, leads in the direction of Mount Diablo and therefore either toward a creation story or toward the first airplane beacon erected in California, a dilemma Miranda refuses to decide. Following this same direction toward an undecidable destination, along archival paths, Miranda is led to another indeterminate story told by Spanish soldiers about chasing a group of Indian runaways from a mission who took refuge on the mountain and ended up cornered with seemingly no escape. It was too dark for the conquistadors to catch them, so they waited until morning only to find the mountain empty. From the conquistadors' perspective, clearly el Diablo [the Devil] helped them escape. But Miranda imagines the story told among the Indians: "places of power are not tread on lightly; runaway Indians understand the power of the mountain's reputation. Fleeing to the mountain is an act of desperation, perhaps even a call for help. The mountain is a being, infused with the power of creation, from root to cloud. The rocks, soil, meadows, streams, trees, sun—all sacred, sacred, sacred, sacred," echoing Gould.[67] Either way, diabolical or inappropriately associated with other-than-human beings, what is left is a story about bad Indians.

The ambiguity and ambivalence of stories is an opening onto what Rei Terada, following Jacques Derrida, calls the "nonway."[68] More than an impasse, or a slowing down of violent colonial progress, the nonway is neither a path nor its interruption but an original disorientation that foregoes the dialectical tension and development of passage and blockage. There, where the way is not open, is an "other something in the background" unrelated to movement and stillness and yet conditioning both. The ambiguity and ambivalence of stories indicate and orient toward the nonway as unassimilable to choice, to a world of activity in the service of (colonial) life; the nonway is therefore open to the infinite, and stories in their ambivalence are not simply reducible to resistance or powerlessness. "Potentially the largest and most positive [realm], despite its negative name," the nonway lies outside dualities such as rational and irrational, in which "the language of logical argument talks in its sleep about settlement and expropriation, colonialism and racial capitalism in noonday life."[69] If this rational language talks in its sleep, it is a sleep without dreams, of the utterly diurnal that forbids both dream as a strange day in the night and the night in the day that is the nonway itself. More fundamental than critical investigation into and rational argumentation about these violent forces (Sedgwick's strong theory) is the end of the world that has been rendered unthinkable by these very forces. What is the end of the world, as described by Miranda, if not a call to attend to a world that has been rendered irreal? A nonworld that conditions the noonday one of the colonizer. *A world that isn't this one* experienced through a Maidu song one cannot learn or unlearn. This question is the question of story, destruction, and the reparative.

In the introduction to *Bad Indians*, Miranda details the destructive nature of story: being told she isn't a "real Indian," including by other Natives, "because I do not have the language of my ancestors, and much of our culture was literally razed to the ground"; the exclusion of Native Americans from the American literary canon (until, according to Miranda, N. Scott Momaday won the Pulitzer in 1969 for *House Made of Dawn*); education and the suppression of Indigenous voice, because "the gatekeepers of literature have kept us outside by making education and literacy so undesirable and so painful," an effect of the violence of assimilation and the targeted destruction of Indianness; the disparagement of Indigenous storying by rendering it into primitive beliefs to be studied as objects; and the erasure of violence in telling the history of California, including the whitewashing of the history of the missions for generations of fourth graders.[70] As Miranda notes, "this story has done more damage to California Indians than any conquistador, priest, soldado de cuera (leather-jacket soldier), smallpox, measles, or influenza virus" as it has "taught us to kill ourselves and each other with alcohol, domestic violence, horizontal racism, internalized hatred."[71]

Of course, as Miranda makes clear in *Bad Indians*, California Indians, along with other Indigenous peoples of the Americas, had already been dreamed into existence as bad long before the onset of colonization. Our story had preceded us, and that story was something: humungous penises, sex with animals, human-animal offspring, cannibals, mutated monsters, bloodthirsty devils. This is a story that stuck, as Deborah

Miranda describes its persistence: "All my life, I have heard only one story about California Indians: godless, dirty, stupid, primitive, ugly, passive, drunken, immoral, lazy, weak-willed people who might make good workers if properly trained and motivated. What kind of story is this to grow up with?"[72] Highlighting the statement *who might make good workers if properly trained and motivated,* all the other adjectives in that sentence—*godless, dirty, stupid, primitive, ugly, passive, drunken,* and so on—shift and warp in value when their role is considered in promoting something other than work, other than colonial labor or knowledge production, other than western aesthetics and civilizationist conceptions of the human, and other than settler developmental futurity and its presupposed "goodness."

The colonial categories of *the social* and *the political* have both been used, often together, to relegate Indigenous worlds and modes of interrelationality with other beings to the irrational and illegible or, at best, to the realm of apolitical or pre-political belief to be studied and categorized by anthropologists. Marisol de la Cadena has detailed how the coloniality of politics and sociality operates through creating and becoming exclusively a human realm requiring an intellectual disciplinary divide: the humanities, arts, and social sciences study the activities of humans while nature is studied by the hard sciences.[73] Politics, in this project, is explicitly and exclusively a form of human antagonism in social and economic realms, producing an empirical field (the ontic). Drawing on Chantal Mouffe's distinction between politics (ontic) and the political (ontological), de la Cadena notes how the political, on the other hand, attends to the fundamental split that separates humans, now a distinct category, from nature, a split that doesn't exist within Indigenous frameworks (neither does the category of nature).[74] Indigenous worlds and modes of relating, through the colonial ontic categories of human and nature, are thereby rendered unintelligible.

María Josefina Saldaña-Portillo complicates and furthers this discussion by noting that the Spanish understood Indigenous modes of governance and sociality to be invitations to absorb Indigenous peoples into the colonial theological and economic project and worldview.[75] Reflecting on how the encounter with Indigenous peoples of the Americas conditions the historical production of humanism, Saldaña-Portillo analyzes the sixteenth-century debate between Bartolomé de las Casas and Juan Ginés de Sepúlveda, during the Junta de Valladolid, on "just" methods of conquest in the "New World," as two sides of the same humanist coin.[76] Following Jodi Byrd's suggestion that the figure of the Indian was a necessary condition and counterpoint for the production of western humanism in its ongoing colonial form, Saldaña-Portillo locates a productive tension in the different responses during the debate to the question of Indigenous capacity for conversion. De las Casas and Sepúlveda's opposition hinged on the question of whether Indigenous people were intellectually capable of freedom—whether, that is, they are internally enslaved and must come to the Christian faith by force or whether they are able to choose it of their own accord.

Famously, in the context of Christianity's antagonism with the Ottoman Empire, Sepúlveda argued that Indigenous people are enslaved to their passions and unable to come into the Christian fold on their own, necessitating European domination and mastery in the encomienda system as a disciplinary practice. De las Casas, for his part, drew on his experience as a missionary among the Indigenous people of Oaxaca and Chiapas and argued for their agency based on their perceived humanity. In his apologia *En defensa de los indios*, he argued that the "cultivated friendship" and "common fellowship" of the Indigenous peoples are signs of their preparedness for Christian community and unity, a point that echoes Pope Paul III, who defended Indigenous capacity in his papal bull *Sublimis Deus* in 1537 and is echoed later by Pope Benedict XVI, who wrote in 2007 that at the time of conquest the Indians had already been longing for conversion, which had been nonviolent.[77] What is noteworthy is that Sepúlveda and de las Casas agreed on the basic definitions, conditions, and value of human sociality and politics; they tended to emphasize different aspects of Indigenous sociality, however. Sepúlveda highlighted Indigenous peoples' human sacrifice, cannibalism, abortion, incest, and adultery, all tied to the general theme of their diabolical nature and inability to make appropriate distinctions between humans and nonhumans, leading to charges of bestiality and witchcraft. De las Casas saw, on the other hand, a general if primitive or inchoate form of sociality that merely needed to be coaxed into human—that is, Christian—shape through the eradication of the Indian part.

Saldaña-Portillo compellingly argues that the unifying project of converting Indigenous heathens, in which both Sepúlveda and de las Casas were differentially engaged, had the effect of democratizing paternalistic responsibility for Indigenous peoples among colonizers.[78] Such collaborative paternalism created, according to her, the conditions for modern international human rights law based on the unity of humanity and the democratization of responsibility grounded in a shared capacity for reason. Indigenous people had promise but needed to have the Indian beat out of them; if they resisted and therefore died, so much the better. Saldaña-Portillo, referencing the work of the Spanish enlightenment jurist Francisco de Vitoria, details how international modern law weaponized human reason as the base condition of sociality for colonial purposes. "Indians were compelled to allow Spaniards into their dominions," according to Vitoria, because the law of nations compels them to "love" the Spaniards "as they would love any neighbor."[79] These are the conditions for the creation of a singular world through human sociality, "one world, one domain, one geography of humanity" that links Europeans and their fantasied others through a co-constitutive process of making each other human, differentially as determined by proximity to the straight, white, property-owning, cis male norm—as Sylvia Wynter, in her body of work, has thoroughly shown. This humanizing process renders Indigenous worlds and interrelations with other beings, such as Mount Diablo, illegible, nonsensical, perverse through the closure and coloniality of both politics and the social as solely human affairs. As de la Cadena notes, though, at least the interpretation of the freedom of Indians as the work of el Diablo cast them and their relationship to the mountain as being in antagonism with Christian humanity; the western secular interpretation of politics and the social eradicates even this.

The critical call for a stronger politicality or sociality within colonial situations, settler and otherwise, can contribute to the ongoing colonization of Indigenous peoples, lands, and worlds through humanism. And the critical modes for unveiling suppressed political and social energies, as well as supposedly hidden forms of violence, invest those energies into a stronger, more tensile and flexible coloniality. The cultivation of Indigenous humanity has long been a project of colonization, and this undergirds critiques of the notion of dehumanization, which depends on a presupposed humanity as well as critiques of the concept of dispossession. Producing property through a retroactive attribution of ownership to Indigenous peoples as proto-humans, the notion of dispossession replaces Indigenous nonpropertied, nonhuman-centric, and collective interrelations with appropriately human ones.[80] In the same way, the concepts of the political and the social both project a colonial, human-centric mode of relating onto an imagined Indigenous past for the sake of a settler humanized future. Together these different aspects contribute to Povinelli's "governance of the prior," the use of temporal logics and conceptions of prior ownership—for example, through British common law in the context of certain settler states—to paradoxically expropriate land and use land itself as a commodity and resource to manage Indigeneity as a humanistic category.[81]

Arguments about assimilation, development, western humanism, denaturalization and other forms of critical historicism, including the end of history, are based on the basic premise that Indigenous peoples are simultaneously outside of time and also the threshold through which history begins (and sometimes how it ends). It is a logic that must be ritualistically renewed through the repetitive assertion of violent re-beginnings (the forces of recognition, apology, and reconciliation through Indian law and policy), founded on the paradox of Indigeneity as never being fully present (perpetually disappearing, merely occupying, potentially or partially human) and yet ongoing as the framework of settler colonial continuity (settler Indigenizing, the governance of the prior).

This gives us a sense of the extent of the destruction of California Indians, why it is never a complete annihilation or elimination, and how this incompleteness becomes the condition for ongoing destruction through what Jasbir Puar calls "debilitation."[82] It also details the nonway, the delegitimated Indigenous world, as itself the site of struggle. To escape the mode of debilitation, the shards that indicate *a world other than this one* not only open onto a nonway that lies outside of the colonial double bind of the prior, as they merely indicate, but also importantly operate within the ambiguity and ambivalence of story—for Miranda, one that revolves around the question of literature. Literature is an apt form for engaging such a space considering its lack of referentiality and lack of performative force: it is related to the world neither as shelter nor as a set of goals; having receded, goals cease and all falls silent; in it something else speaks.[83] And yet, I have already noted that Miranda discusses the exclusion of Native Americans from "American literature" (what does such a phrase even mean? Does it have the same meaning and double bind as "politics" and "the social"?), an exclusion that doesn't merely take place in the field of representation but operates at a disciplinary and pedagogical level as well. In relation to the coloniality of politics and the social, though, the question of whether or not a California Indian literature exists operates at an even more fundamental level of the destruction. To get there, Miranda traces the destruction in its fragmentary connections to her own story. In writing about her childhood, Miranda asks, "How can I put this into words you'll understand? Armageddon had already happened. I was three years old. My father had been incarcerated at San Quentin . . . My mother had run away. My two older siblings were put into foster care. I had been taken from the apartment we lived in, and I never saw it again . . . Every single familiar thing in the world had disappeared."[84] An atmosphere of threat or dread permeates much of the book: "All my life, I knew I would disappear. I knew my presence here on earth was so tentative that I was in constant danger of being devoured, absorbed, vanished."[85] This threat, this dread is the position and mood through which other stories, archival materials, are experienced. This position and mood is the question of literature for Miranda and produces a fraught poetics.

Bad Indians itself threatens to disappear: into the words of others (colonizers and Indians alike, as well as into the problem of identity) from whom most of the text is taken; into the crevasses between disciplines, in which the text lingers; into the materiality and brutality of the sources it engages; and most fundamentally into the question of literature. This is all to say, into the archive that cultivates and destroys it. The careful selection, textual shaping, and juxtaposition of the words of others—of Spanish priests, anthropologically mediated stories, self-recordings of Miranda's grandfather, along with snippets from newspaper stories, repurposed educational materials about the missions, a novena [prayer] to bad Indians—produces a poetry not of the word or the line but of discourse, of genre, and of the materiality and violence of the archive. It is a mosaic and a problematic embodiment of the text that engages the affective force of what feel like, in some cases, death sentences, the dread of seeing, hearing, and feeling judgments passed. Reading newspaper accounts of the casual violence against Indians, for instance, gives a sense of helplessness, knowing that what is about to come is inevitable, as it has been since the first publication of the article, that nothing about it can be done.

> *San Francisco Bulletin*, May 12, 1859
>
> An old Indian and his squaw
> Were engaged in the harmless occupation
> Of gathering clover

On the land of a Mr. Grigsby
When a man
Named Frank Hamilton

Set Grigsby's dogs upon them
(which, by the way, are three
Very ferocious ones,)

And before the dogs were taken off
Of the Indians, they tore
And mangled the body

Of the squaw
In such a manner that she died
Shortly after. It is said

The dogs
Tore her breasts off her.
The Digger man

Escaped without any serious
Injury, although bitten
Severely. Of course

It was the dogs' fault
Although Hamilton had lived with Grigsby
Over a year and knew full well

The character of the dogs
For this is not the first
Instance of their biting persons.

But he only set them on
For fun
And they were

Only Diggers.
There is talk of having Hamilton
Arrested but no doubt

It is all talk.[86]

We see, hear, and feel this inevitability also in the recast words of Junipero Serra.

Seeing your people come through the fields
We noticed a great flock of birds
Of various and beautifully blended colors
Such as we had never seen before.

We noticed a great flock of birds
Swooping out of the heaven just ahead
Such as we had never seen before
As if they came to welcome our newly arrived guests.

Swooping out of the heavens just ahead
Six or more soldiers set out together on horseback
As if they came to greet their newly acquired hosts
In the far distant rancherias even many leagues away.

Six or more soldiers set out together on horseback.
Both men and women at sight of them took to their heels
In the far distant rancherias even many leagues away,
Fleeing the soldiers, clever as they are at lassoing cows.

Both men and women at sight of them took to their heels
But the women were caught with Spanish ropes.
The soldiers, clever as they are at lassoing cows
Preyed on the women for their unbridled lust.

The women were caught with Spanish ropes
Indian men defended their wives—
Prey for the Spaniards' unbridled lust—
Only to be shot down with bullets.

The Indian men tried to defend their wives
Of various and beautifully blended colors
Only to be shot down with bullets
Seeing your people come through the fields.[87]

Using reports (death sentences) to produce poetry and story, using the words of killers in this way, does two things. First, these words and images are intolerable, and this intolerability pulls the thread of poetry so tight, indicates the impoverishment of language so intensely, tugs on the tongue so viciously, that it puts the very project of literature into question, *from root to cloud*. The distance between the forced/stolen language and the use of form, also forced/stolen, vibrates with the series of negations that excluded California Indians from literature: representation negated before it even exists (giving the sense that the law barring California Indians from testifying against whites in the nineteenth century has become a state of being), literature negated before it exists (oral story's exclusion from literature), language negated (the white supremacist, theocratic, nationalistic, monolingualist project of destroying the more than one hundred distinct languages and more than three hundred dialects spoken in Indigenous California and their replacement with Spanish and then English), and the negation of the world through epistemic means. In relation to language, story takes place, for Miranda, at the third level of the destruction of the Esselen language, a language systematically destroyed by and replaced with Spanish, which was systematically destroyed by and replaced with English. Miranda movingly narrates this deterritorializing relation in recounting two different intensive summer language classes she took, Spanish for graduate school and archival research and a California Indian language revitalization class taken later in life, echoing the temporal inversions of a genealogy of violence.[88] The point, as she notes, is to create a third language "to describe a second language that destroyed my first language . . . blade to slice my tongue," an English that is not of English.[89] To lick the blade along the edge.

Along the thin blade, Miranda puts the descriptions of genocidal sexual violence and killing into poetic form, raising the effect to a point that recasts such destruction and violence in her robust sense of story as reparative destruction. It reinvents these difficult words as a California Indian story, first, foremost, and perhaps solely. It is *our* destruction, emphasizing the ambiguity of the preposition in the phrase *the destruction of California Indians*. The archive, documentation, disciplinary formations, and all the edifices built up to support the western liberal figuration of the human who so casually reduced Indigenous people to violable bodies are turned instead into story. *Bad Indians* uses poetry, uses the destructive aspects of literature itself, to begin to swallow the archive and the voices of killers, assimilating and absorbing them, making *them* disappear. And we don't know where it stops. Miranda has described how her editor at Heyday Books, Malcolm Margolin, told her upon her first submission of the manuscript that it wasn't done yet. It can never be finished as it is a profoundly open text. One that, through its poetics, asks the question: Is everything poetry or is nothing? Makes the selection each time, specifically and poetically, and puts it into form, thereby extending the unanswerable question to infinity. It destroys the archive as proof, as use. And yet, it is a form of research in what Leanne Simpson describes as being both the instrument and the song, a terrible song, *with serrated edges, burnt red rim slicing into the Pacific.*[90]

The theme of rearticulating shards according to a song that one cannot learn describes quite specifically the problem of literature in the wake of destruction. As I noted earlier, the Armenian scholar Marc Nichanian details a condition of the loss of literature in such situations in the turn to the archive, to documentation, to the need to prove what happened as a sort of tyranny of archival logics. For him, this destruction invites further catastrophe: the need to orient all narratives toward making a case, to tell the truth of what happened in organized, temporal order, according to the executioner's own logic and demand, to tell the story in a certain, juridically organized way. While Nichanian sees the death of literature in the logic of the proof, Miranda turns the issue on its head by appealing to the archive, to the stories told and recorded in it, as the site of literary production. This doubling of destruction raises questions: What about stories that don't get acknowledged as being literature? Of peoples defined as nonliterate? What if, rather than a further catastrophe in the death of literature, literature in its western, recognizable form has already deemed the destruction of a people's stories to be unrecognizable? Literature as the destruction and replacement of story. How do you then begin to articulate catastrophe and loss?

To answer this question, it's not only to the words of killers that Miranda turns: "I see Vicenta's story [as told by Isabel Meadows to the salvage ethnographer J. P. Harrington] as a precursor to modern Native literature, a stepping-stone between oral literacy and written literature."[91] While this quote implies a sort of progression from orality to the written as the basis of literature, this movement isn't so clear elsewhere in Miranda's writing. Miranda's intertextual relation to Isabel Meadows and her stories is a case in point. Meadows was born in Carmel Valley in 1846 and was a member of a local Esselen-Rumsen mixed family. A speaker of Rumsen, Esselen, Spanish, and English, with a good amount of knowledge about tribal culture and language, as well as family stories, Meadows became an important resource for the controversial ethnographer J. P. Harrington, who worked with her for several years throughout the 1930s up until her death in 1939, even moving her out to Washington, DC. Miranda engages Meadows's archive significantly for *Bad Indians*, noting both the role of Meadows in producing stories for future generations as well as her role in Miranda's own family: One of Meadows's half brothers married Miranda's great-great-great-grandmother, and she also vouched for many of Miranda's relatives on their BIA applications. A source of many of the stories in *Bad Indians*, including direct language transcribed into the text, as well as a generative site of the production of texts beyond *Bad Indians*, Meadows and her archive elicit an engagement with the question of what constitutes a California Indian literature.[92] "My aim is to restore Meadows to her rightful place as author of her own stories, move those stories from the category of 'social sciences' to the more appropriate category of 'Literature or expressive culture,' and show that Isabel has a clear purpose in depositing these stories with Harrington: to preserve information from Ancestors in ways she knew would provide necessary information for future generations."[93]

Complicating this project is the relationship between literature and what constitutes information in Meadows's archive. The difficult stories I noted in the introduction. In "Extermination of the Joyas," in relation to Meadows's stories Miranda develops a practice of "learning how to re-read the archive through the eyes of a mixed-blood California Indian lesbian poet and scholar."[94] This practice of rereading entails renaming a page from Harrington's field notes "Jotos" and reading it as a petroglyph. "When I touch it, so much else must be known, communicated, and understood to see the power within what looks like a simple inscription, a random bit of Carmel Mission Indian trivia."

Linking this reading practice to an archaeology of gender and sexuality, Miranda understands this Indigenous reading and writing practice as oriented toward *a world that isn't this one*. The term *Joya*, for instance, is intimately associated with grief, as the term refers to third-gendered people who underwent genocidal destruction by the Spanish, who saw in their existence direct evidence of California Indian depravity. The Spanish interpreted the Joyas' perceived inappropriate gendering as a tactic to, for instance, be among the women for the purposes of sexual transgression. Understanding the Joyas' existence the only way the rigid cisheteropatriarchy of the church and state could (with clear resonances with contemporary transphobia), "the priest and soldiers completely misunderstood the situation, and assumed that this man [*sic*] was 'sinning'—that is, sneaking into the women's work area dressed as a woman to flirt or have sex with them."[95] More distressing were the accounts of the soldiers who understood the Joyas to be "sodomites" to be exterminated. Miranda recounts the homophobic words of a Spanish soldier, Pedro Fages, who in 1775 wrote:

> I have substantial evidence that those Indian men who, both here and farther inland, are observed in the dress, clothing, and character of women—there being two or three such in each village—pass as sodomites by profession (it being confirmed that all these Indians are much addicted to this abominable vice) and permit the heathen to practice the execrable, unnatural abuse of their bodies. They are called *joyas*, and are held in great esteem. Let this mention suffice for a matter which could not be omitted,—on account of the bearing it may have on the discussion of the reduction of these natives,—with a promise to revert in another place to an excess so criminal that it seems even forbidden to speak its name. . . . But we place our trust in God and expect that these accursed people will disappear with the growth of the missions. The abominable vice will be eliminated to the extent that the Catholic faith and all the other virtues are firmly implanted there, for the glory of God and the benefit of those poor ignorants.[96]

Miranda details the various forms of terror the Spanish unleashed on the Joyas as well as the devastating decision by many tribal peoples to turn against the Joyas for their own survival. On top of the direct forms of torture and murder, Miranda notes the violences of renaming (replacing with Spanish interpretations) and regendering through discipline and shame, to conform with Spanish conceptions of cisheteropatriarchy. She also notes the complex roles that the Joyas held in California Indian communities, of great esteem, including spiritual ones, as mourners and mediators to the dead. The gendercide committed by the Spanish created a need in California Indian communities that was initially filled by 'aqui [post-menopausal women] and then eventually the Catholic Church. Direct murder, renaming, regendering, and replacement all contributed to what Miranda calls gendercide.

The field note/petroglyph that opens the discussion of the sexual and spiritual or interrelational convergence in the Joyas and the destruction of this relationality is primarily about a distant cousin of Miranda's, Victor Acedo, whose sexuality moves in a relational direction toward the women who raised him.[97] Called Joteras in the note, they are central figures in Isabel Meadows's stories of women who resisted in the missions, had sex with whomever they wanted, had many children with many men, and who were interpreted by Spanish mores to be a mix of masculine and feminine, but it was their relation to Victor Acedo, who was gay, that caused them to be dubbed Joteras. Such a notion of relation is deeper than association or affiliation, as it ties directly to the syntax of many California Indian languages that decentralizes the subject, emphasizes positionality, and associates relationships through existential categories and not possession: it's never "my child is gay," but "I am gay in respect to [child's name]."[98] Gayness is the mediation of kinship. In terms of the coloniality of politics and the social, these actions by bad Indians are apolitical (in the colonial sense) and antisocial on many levels. The fundamental Indigenous interrelationality deemed diabolical by the colonizer links the modes of sexuality with relationships to all sorts of beings as part of the same epistemic conditions, what Kim Tallbear calls an Indigenous critical polyamory, an opening onto a world lived otherwise.[99]

The poetics associated with this world, that orient one toward it, operate within what Deleuze and Guattari refer to as a hatred of "all literature of masters" (perhaps meant doubly, both aesthetic masters and colonial masters).[100] Story, in this sense, sweeps away all difference between the language and theory of the everyday and that of the elite. It's an interruption of systems of value. We see this destruction and its possibilities in an anecdote by Harrington, relayed in *Bad Indians* in the section titled "Gonaway Tribe."[101] Harrington sets the scene in the typical ethnographic arrival description: "Arrived here amidst mud and rain. There are twenty-one Indians left. Very few of them old and wise! The ones I have found are living with the younger Indians near town. This is *bad* because the young Indians tell the old ones to ask for money, but I get around that by telling them that I am to pay a certain price and no more."[102] Immediately placing the anecdote under the sign of value, Harrington replaces Indigenous protocols and modes of interrelation with the secular demand for Indigenous stories for research and the calculating work of ethnographic collection. When "the old woman, Sadie, says that [he is] fortunate in coming here in the wintertime because it is against the law of her people to tell these stories she told me in the summertime. She says if she told a story like this in the summer a rattlesnake would bite her," Harrington insists upon an economy of scarcity in which Indigenous people are always impoverished: "But I bet with a dollar bill or two flashing in her face, she would forget her law."[103] Fretting over the standard perceived disappearance of

Indigenous people, Harrington refuses to let the inclement weather and consideration for others, including his "informants," get in the way of his task: "These Indians are altogether too civilized . . . they keep saying I should come back when the sun is out, that I mess up their houses and track mud in."[104] Yet, the value of these stories, perceived by Harrington through an economy of scarcity and a logic of authenticity, is offset by their translation into valueless objects of study according to the coloniality of politics and the social: "Susie says that white people do not pay enough but I told her that there is no work to this, all she would have to do is talk."[105] *Just talk*, no work at all. The highly valued "work" of literature is nowhere to be seen. In its place is the workless work of story, just talk. The anecdote ends, quite appropriately, with the hatred of masters: "My, how the Petie Simpsons hate white people—they could not use too many words in telling me. It is a good thing they don't know that this research is for the Smithsonian."[106]

Remember: Indians don't work. Too natural, therefore unproductive, unable to own and master property; full of bad behavior and qualities, *godless, dirty, stupid, primitive, ugly, passive, drunken, immoral, lazy, weak-willed people who might make good workers if properly trained and motivated.* "Bad Indians" means all of this. Poor quality, unpleasant, harmful, without virtue, offensive, unwell, putrid, negative feelings, worthless. For Harrington these were *bad* Indians, disruptive of his research, wanting too much money, not authentic enough, hating white people. The bad Indians connected to each other through bad feelings: hatred, grief, loneliness, anger, resentment. They are excluded from, in opposition to, the work of the master, which attains its ultimate form not just in the work of art or scholarship but in the gradual achievement of human mastery and freedom: a total realization of a liberatory process.

In a context in which English departments are still dominated by American and British literature, by the work in the sense of the literary object and of the gradual achievement of human mastery and freedom—the humanities buttressed by a general historicity—Miranda's workless work *Bad Indians: A Tribal Memoir* calls us to another task through the question of literature. *Does a California Indian literature exist?* bears both on literature in general and its pedagogy, as well as the centralizing of American and British canons through a tie that can only ever be temporal. *American* and *British* literatures are historical only in the sense that Vine Deloria describes in *God Is Red:* "The very essence of

Western European identity involves the assumption that time proceeds in a linear fashion; further it assumes that at a particular point in the unraveling of this sequence, the peoples of Western Europe became the guardians of the world. The same ideology that sparked the Crusades, the Age of Exploration, the Age of Imperialism, and the recent crusade against Communism all involve the affirmation that time is peculiarly related to the destiny of Western Europe. And later, of course, the United States."[107]

Note the resonance between this quote and the following, written by the head of a Department of English in Nairobi, as related by Ngũgĩ wa Thiong'o, in his chapter "Quest for Relevance": "The English Department . . . has built up a strong syllabus which by its study of the historic continuity of a single culture throughout the period of emergence of the modern west makes it an important companion to History and Philosophy and Religious Studies. However, it is bound to become less British, more open to other writing in English (American, Caribbean, African, Commonwealth) and also to continental writing, for comparative purposes."[108] Ignoring the murderous history of the British in Kenya, the chair seamlessly aligns the national project of Kenyan independence and education with European coloniality. David Lloyd, in his reflection on the continuing significance of Ngũgĩ's engagement with this problem, notes how this description "gradually synthesizes its disparate strands and influences into a single, unfolding whole."[109] The unification of national literature through canonicity, developing temporality (through epochal arrangements), development of the individual as heroic center of literary narrative, and the pedagogical reproduction of this unity in the student "who becomes its pedagogical object in the form of an ideal of fully cultivated selfhood" accurately depicts the coloniality of English and, more broadly, humanist education.

Ngũgĩ's response to this situation was to forgo discussions about the problem of inclusion of Kenyan or African literature into the curriculum and to instead call for the abolition of Departments of English: "Here then, is our main question: if there is a need for a 'study of the historic continuity of a single culture,' why can't this be African? Why can't African literature be at the centre so that we can view other cultures in relationship to it?"[110] Lloyd interprets this robust response as a turn away from temporal colonial consistency, as described by Deloria, and toward a spatial model of organization that privileges regional and often neglected, suppressed, or actively destroyed forms of literature, or, more accurately in relation to Ngũgĩ's project, forms of "orature," eliding the temporally and colonially structured divide between orality and literacy.[111] To the question, then, of whether a California Indian literature exists must be added the question *does an American literature exist?* This question is especially relevant considering how much the American literary tradition has stolen from Native Americans without acknowledgment (Emerson and Thoreau immediately come to mind), but it's also an epistemological question in terms of the angle of perception from which literature is viewed. Outside of U.S. perceptions and narratives of temporal progress and unified history, what holds American literature together as some sort of center? It certainly cannot be national, as there's nothing natal about it. Lloyd suggests, rather, a mode of interrelationality that attends to geographic locality first, not as a center but, following Ngũgĩ, as "networks of cultures, exchanging or 'interweaving' with one another without passing through centers."[112] This is a differential relationality that nonetheless begins with Indigenous orature.

Bad Indians indicates that perhaps a California Indian "literature" is not just impossible but already exhausted in the question, akin to Indigenous lesbian literature. From a weak position that destructively disrupts the consolidation of centers of power in each case, California Indian lesbian "orature" as weak literature seeks reparatively to open onto the nonway of the nonworld that isn't this one in a complementary nonpoetics, and does so by listening to a song one cannot learn and to the Indigenous lesbian body as orienting devices. *Bad Indians* as orature is radically open and hinges on the ambiguity of disappearance and absence, mobilizing the intertextuality of the archive for this and other queer purposes. Antisocial, apolitical, tenuously held together by bad feelings, by revenge, it maps for us story and a necessary coming to writing that never arrives and yet grounds us in endurance. As Miranda says:

> So from the time I could hold a crayon, I scribbled. I scrawled. My hand grew cramped and tired, calluses formed . . . Couldn't stop, because if I did, I would disappear. Everyone I loved had disappeared. I knew I was next . . . I remember the first word I ever wrote. On a brown paper bag, with a red crayon. D E B Y. I sat at my grandmother's kitchen counter in a red cabin with white trim, high in the Tehachapi Mountains . . . [Miranda shows her grandmother the writing] that's when I made a transformative leap in my understanding of being. It was as if, when I wrote those letters, made a written

> record of myself, my name, my existence, those letters grew roots and plowed down through the Formica countertop, into the wooden floor, beams, and concrete foundation of the cabin, deep into the heart of the Tehachapi Mountains themselves.[113]

This description comes near the end of the book, in the last chapter, which, in a sense, bookends *Bad Indians* as beginning with the end of the world and nearly ending with an Armageddon that has already happened, rhyming the destruction of Miranda's world as a child with that of the destruction of her peoples' world. The format of *Bad Indians* indicates the difficult process of storying, which takes on an isomorphism with both culture and strained and broken family relationships: "[To survive her father] You had to want to survive more than you wanted to be good. As we sat there in sudden silence by the fire, our faces hot, [her sister, whom she met much later in life] Louise's clapperstick mute in her lap, I felt as if I'd put together all the pieces of a mirror that had broken into thousands of shards: *This is how our ancestors survived the missions.*"[114] Using the mirror shards as a recursive, yet fragmentary, reflection on the genealogy of violence, Miranda locates the bad actions and feelings of Native peoples in both the family and the archive as being one and the same. As I noted earlier, the relation between violence in the family and the history of violence is not an uncomplicated identification with her ancestors and the things they did to survive but a sociality across and outside of time through disaffiliation as a form of survival. The layers of these statements in their work across the sinewy and resistant archive creates a recombinant effect—a mosaic, as Miranda describes culture. Neither literature nor discourse on literature but perhaps a bit of both, *Bad Indians* shows us the intimate, and necessary, entanglement of writing and research, of what it means to be Bad Indians in the archive and the university. To understand the layered and difficult complications of the many meanings of the statement Miranda makes: in order to survive, we became destroyers.

Miranda's writing is a challenge to historical authority, a refusal in the nonoppositional sense that Audra Simpson offers in her explication of the representational force of the term, as delineating the edge of the text and discourse through attention to what is not said or sayable, like a black hole that absorbs all light and whose existence is only known by its effects on what is seen.[115] It's a form of discursive wrestling, an open, multivalent struggle with power and its material effects, engaging global and world destroying forces in the everyday struggle of living under ongoing genocidal conditions at the thin edge of multiple sovereignties and their failures and limitations, *blade to slice my tongue.* It's an acknowledgment of the impossibility for California Indians to hold a privileged position outside of representation in a way in which our very lives wouldn't be at stake, in the way most historians of California genocide can, and the need therefore to continue to work within/without its terms. In this context, Miranda discursively risks the very question of survival in terms that exacerbate that risk through the vulnerability of the lesbian body, as well as its complex stabilities, securities, and openings onto violence according to the terms of survival. Another way of saying this is that Miranda writes from and with the discomfort of collective bad feelings that organize the fragmented body of the expanded text as an antisociality across disaffiliative and disidentificatory gaps that paradoxically make continuities and collectivities possible as threads of survival and the stickiness of having bad feelings in common. As Madley made clear in the previous chapter, there is no such thing as a voice of genocide. Through writing and study, Miranda offers instead a voice of the Destruction, a way for the ancestors to continue to speak.

Ancestors

In 2019, after a battle with cancer, Janice Gould began her four-day dance at Kahkini Kumme (the spirit dance house) in Estobisim Yamani (the center of the mountain) before embarking on her journey along the feather road.[116] Gould and Miranda had not been in contact for many years, likely in large part due to the difficult emotions and complex experiences of their road trip together, but when Miranda found out about Gould's diagnosis she sent her the following poem:

Dear Friend,

If your body wakes you,
if night is a restless dream
wondering
        what's to come,

let comfort come to you,
touch your cheek,
smooth your forehead
        the way your mother did.

Some kinds of love
are older than blood.
Listen, tonight
your ancestors sit with you.

Sleep safe.
They see you, friend—
no walls, no miles,
no years

between generations.
Close your eyes.
Hear those old songs,
a rattling joy—

remember bright rivers,
how beauty flows and circles,
how shining currents
        shape the rock—

fight as long as you must.
Hold all the sweetness you can.
Rise up when you are ready.
It won't be the first time

you've had to brave
switchbacks, rockslides,
the hard way home,
but this time

you have gifts
of moonrise, twinflowers,
trilliums, sunrise—
        sturdy medicines,

all the companionship
        you'll need.

A direct address, but to the familiar but generic denomination "friend." How much weight does that word carry? How many referents are sheltered within it? Which emotions does it stir? Does it harbor? Sister, lover, muse, addressee. A secret, intertextual correspondence written through poetry over the years. The pain and healing, excitement and frustration, joy and dread, as well as the calm of time, intermingled in a moment, collapsed in a word. "Friend." The form of the address calls back to Gould and Miranda's correspondence and to the question of what companionship means in a postapocalyptic setting, a connection across shared wounds, one that was impossible, made im/possible by a colonial loneliness. *Dear Friend.* Written at the end and at the beginning, "friend" barely holds it all together. And yet what carries through is love, care, a certain sweetness, a touch of the cheek, a smoothing of the forehead. Written under the conditional "if," the poem is a hypothetical, *if your body wakes you / if night is a restless dream / wondering / what's to come,* marking the distance of space and time between speaker and addressee but also the more fundamental ambiguity of the source of anxiety: *what's to come.* Wittig's lesbian body becomes here a source of mystery, vulnerability, and an opening onto ambiguity itself, lastingly. The speaker cannot know if the addressee's body wakes her, because of the distance. But she imagines across space and time and outside of both a moment and an intimacy to caress and reassure. Reversing the earlier relationship between lovers, younger and older, indirectly through comfort the addressee is now daughter, *the way your mother did.* Though, as in the comfort offered by Miranda in Gould's poetic recounting of their road trip, we are brought once again to a scene of Gould's head gently cradled in Miranda's lap.

What follows is a series of soft commands, perhaps whispered to the addressee: listen, sleep safe, close your eyes, hear, remember, fight, hold, rise up. An exercise in the reflex of agency and its release, the speaker eases the addressee's transition to the other, more infinite, journey. Walls collapse, distances of time and space disappear: the addressee is in the presence of her ancestors. Pure immediacy. The veil between worlds is worn thin. The mosaic is pieced together. And her mother's song, heard but not learned, is present once again, *a rattling joy.* The speaker encourages the addressee to fight as long as she must and to hold onto as much sweetness as possible, to grasp onto life before rising up, the most ambiguous and profound phrase of the poem. *Rise up when you are ready.* And begin your journey home. The nonway, full of rockslides, switchbacks, a hard way home, is a path the addressee has braved before (the nonway is always there; the other world always present, neither passage nor blockage). This time, though, relations to the land and cosmos, flowers and the rhythms of celestial bodies, act as sturdy medicines, gifts to help her along her journey. Gifts: the Koyangk'auwi way of ensuring that their relatives arrive where they need to and do so happily with all that they need. Yet *rise up* is not an action and therefore no longer a command; it is the cessation of all action and nonaction. It is readiness in its most pure form. Arrival as non-arrival caught in the infinity of nondeparture. *All the companionship / you'll need.*

In response, Gould wrote one of her last poems shortly after receiving Miranda's email with the above poem. Miranda's message arrived a day before Gould received the news that she was no longer in remission and treatment would no longer help.

Ancestors

Are they near?
Do only the
Koyangk'auwi
show up?
Only those
brown-skinned
women in tule skirts
and caps woven
like baskets
in sedge, red bud,
and maidenhair
fern? The men
bend toward me.
Like the women,
they are bare-chested,
but wear headdresses
decorated in bright
flicker feathers.
Some hold
in their hands
rattles or clappers.
They are singing,
I hear that now,
where I sit
on the rock
hillside above
the North Fork
of the Feather River,

a morning in July
or September,
blue sky above,
far off cloud,
white and puffy,
wind in treetops,
a grosbeak calling,
river rushing by
over hard stones.
Yonder are
the others,
the French and Irish,
who made their way—
such long journeys—
to end up in this
terroir of red soil,
this granite, schist,
and serpentine
country. The French
with moustaches,
the Irish with beards,
their mixedblood
children playing
at their booted
feet, their Indian wives
nearby, gathering
elderberries.
Great-grandfather Beatty
produces a fiddle
and begins a jig,
while the Frenchman,
Orcier, claps,
tapping his sabots
on the rock,
ooh-la, c'est
magnifique!
And now
the English appear,
late-comers

with ruddy faces
and upright postures,
carting among them
bricks and mortar,
insurance forms, a whiff
of superiority, all
except my father,
who ambles slowly
up the trail
with my mother—
they are holding hands
and smiling at the first
of their daughters
to arrive home
safely, no judgment,
just happiness,
and I stand, tears
streaming down my face
to greet them,
the terrible longing
to see them again
diminishing,
like the sudden
gust of warm air that
fingers my black hair -
and departs.

A long thread of a poem, in it every line is enjambed across long sentences with multiple enjambments. The last sentence is strewn across twenty-nine lines. Enacting a discontinuous continuity between the first and last words, *Ancestors, departs,* Gould has pulled the English language taut; like the string of a guitar it vibrates, holds some kind of space, resonates. She is tuning the language. *Jagged-cut poems,* it is a map, but one that turns tightly, a narrow, winding passage, everything cut roughly urging the reader on and down, twisting in the mouth/mind, and yet somehow smoothed, like the forehead. Such jaggedness is pushed past its form. Not quite poetry. Almost an extended haiku, form pushed past its limit, it breaks with rules of content by gesturing to something beyond this world. But still breaches meaning. Read aloud or internally, it reads breathlessly. Cadence abrupt, rhythm broken. The story flows down like water over rocks, smoothing the rough edges, burbling at the breaks. The rocks mumble; language speaks. A certain force of gravity. A cliff's edge. Things stick for a moment and then flow on, a reflex of life. The speaker hangs onto each word, like a sweet goodbye, but also quickly lets them go, lets them tumble on without grasping. Especially the single word carried over from the above line, or left dangling above the rest of the idea, tasting it in the mouth, urging it softly. The speaker tells a story, describes a scene, but there is no complete thought per line; a fact that makes every line a line, and nothing more, and every sentence an opening onto the nonway. Switchbacks. Rockslides. Fragments. Glimpses of images. Like a string of scintillating shards. This path is the hard way home. Time drawn out, holding on as long as one can, cherishing, without possessing, letting go. An exercise in readiness. The most "concrete" of the series of images is a description of sitting on a rock hill above the Feather River (in Northern California, in the homelands of her people) with sketches of images that approach haiku, its lack of image, its effect of reality, is nonetheless the most clearly uncertain, *a morning in July / or September.* Does it matter which? A brief speculation of a moment. *What's to come.* Remaining in the speculative without meaning or weight. Followed by the temporally deep and malleably soft but insistent tension referenced in Miranda's poem, of stones shaped by the flow of water in rivers. What flows beside the river? Ancestors arrive with songs, *a rattling joy.*

The beautiful un/certainty of the questions that begin the poem—*Are they near? / Do only the / Koyangk'auwi / show up?*—questions without answers, points not to an afterlife but to a beside life, around it on all sides, not as its meaning but its absolute lack. Meaning is a momentary refuge, utterly human, and the poem has no time for that, is of another time. Ancestors, who call these questions forward, are the very disturbance of meaning, of closure. They are an opening onto the underlying void. Who is an ancestor? Which ancestors show up? Along the flow of the poem is the dissonance, the distortion of the frayed thread of identity that calls back to Gould's assurances to Miranda about the persistence of connections through absence as well as to her own anxieties about being raised without her Native culture. It is an Indigenizing of death and of the difficult relations most California Indians have in their ancestral lines conditioned by genocide. In Gould's poem ancestors arrive in a phantasmagoric manner, almost as signs of their origins, arriving briefly without becoming "real." They fracture the real, opening onto another world *that isn't this one.* Only in the Creator's absence, an absence as well as a plurality—creation being always a matter of multiple beings—can ancestors return in such a manner, without the fullness of being, without the leaden weight of western meaning and its logocentric god. California Indian relations to the Creator tend toward a certain godlessness.

Echoing Miranda's difficult "homecoming" in *Bad Indians,* land and place appear in the poem in the uncertainty of time, *July / or September.* Though strung along a string of moments, the long thread of the poem offers a series of instantaneous events in incredibly vivid detail, yet tenuous, sweet. The freshness of matter-of-fact descriptions in brief, abbreviated form, *blue sky above, / far off cloud, / white and puffy, / wind in treetops, / a grosbeak calling, / river rushing by / over hard stones,* almost a list, offers an image without settling, without its fully taking shape, conditioning the (non)arrival of the ancestors. Non-Indigenous ancestors are "yonder," within eyesight but full of that infinite distance that vision, time, and genocidal histories produce, marked by the out-of-placeness, the formality, of the term "yonder." An intimate distance. The poem forgoes judgment and commentary, just describes these other ancestors, white colonizers, in succession, a parade of sorts, of scenes of everyday music and dancing, *Great-grandfather Beatty / produces a fiddle / and begins a jig, / while the Frenchman, / Orcier, claps, / tapping his sabots / on the rock, / ooh-la, c'est / magnifique!* All except the English, who arrive without music, *late-comers / with ruddy faces / and upright postures, / carting among them / bricks and mortar, / insurance forms, a whiff / of superiority,* no judgment, still matter-of-fact. It is a mixed-blood genealogy that dissipates the violence of form, liberates language from the rhetorical labor of meaning-making and capture, collapses an entire genocidal history into an instantaneous moment, for the parade is all at once. There is something a bit carnivalesque about it without the spectacle, without the heavy political meaning of "the people" at odds with the ruling class. While seemingly offering up a scene of afterlife relations, it throws off the shackles of expectations, of Native "spirituality," of critical form. Recalling that Miranda initiated this conversation between poems with a conditional under the sign of dream, *If your body wakes you, / if night is a restless dream / wondering / what's to come,* is Gould's poem a dream? It has the intensity, the strangeness and vividness, of a fever dream, somewhere between waking and sleep, mind and body in intense, inextricable interaction. Is she dancing in a circle without moving? Going everywhere and nowhere all at once? Has her body brought her into the presence of the ancestors through dreaming? What speaks through the poem?

The poem ends on two notes: a reunion with her parents, marked by the dissolving of a terrible longing to see them again, *they are holding hands / and smiling at the first / of their daughters / to arrive home / safely, no judgment, / just happiness, / and I stand, tears / streaming down my face / to greet them,* and an analogy, *like the sudden / gust of warm air that / fingers my black hair - / and departs.* The distance of time and the terrible longing rhymes these two notes. And I cannot help but hear the resonance between *fingers my black hair*—marking a time shift perhaps based on age—and Gould's description of the road trip that she took with Miranda decades earlier, *Her hand on my thigh, my shoulder, / in my hair.* The brevity of their relationship, the distance of space and time, and the sudden (re)emergence, then and now, like a gust of warm air, (re)activates a certain loneliness, a terrible longing, that existed before the speaker even knew these feelings were there and that continues as a mode of difficult sociality, only dissipating along the feather road, along the infinite path, what some might call the moment of death.

In these two poems, the ancestral relationship is a form of study, a practiced exercise in writing the word "ancestors," together. Miranda begins her poem with the conditional if-then and gives assurance of the presence of ancestors, erases distance, eliciting the questions Gould opens her poem with, the uncertainty of their presence, of who or what they are, and her reinstating of distance. In conversation, Miranda's and Gould's poems produce an unsettled relation, unresolved, finding resolution through irresolution. Inverting the question and answer exercise, Miranda answers, though in the form of the conditional, before Gould asks the question. Are ancestors near? If your body wakes you, ancestors are near. Miranda's invitation to uncertainty is taken up by Gould with questions that anticipate and challenge Miranda's answer followed by the fleeting images of nonanswers. Together Miranda and Gould exercise the word "ancestors," the ancestral relation, flexing and releasing, past the point of meaning. No resolution, no absence of resolution; a different kind of carrying on happens in this conversation, a collaborative praxis that jams the colonial language and empties it. The gust of warm air is anything but spirit. In a sense, it is everything not spirit. *Some kinds of love / are older than blood.*

Chapter 5
Atlas for a Destroyed World

Once in a while I take up color and paint a little bit, because, if I do not do this, all things will be forgotten. It's good enough all right to sing and talk and explain things on these broadcasts here or especially on tape recording or in records, but it's also nice to have someone who's able to print this or illustrate by color upon a chart. And then it would remain that way. You cannot change it then. And then you've got to be honest and true about it, and not copying from anybody else. But just translating the language, the Maidu language, and putting it up on a chart. And this shows exactly how the Maidu people had been doing before the coming of the white man.

—Frank Day, self-recording, 1975

All the things that I have illustrated here by drawings, paintings, is true because I went to see it. I'm able to take you back to it.

—Frank Day, interview, 1963

All Things Will Be Forgotten

Outside of California Indian communities and art and academic circles, Frank Day is largely unknown. His obscurity is compounded by the still mostly unacknowledged catastrophic conditions of his people, the Kóyo•mkàwi Maidu.[1] Born in 1902 in the Northern California Sierra Nevada foothills, by Day's own account, he saw the end of a way of life, the end of a world. His grandparents' generation experienced massacres, abductions, sexual violence, enslavement, removals, and confinement. Day himself was taken as a child and placed in a federal boarding school for forced assimilation. An overdetermined silence on the destruction was created by few survivors; laws barring Indian testimony; settler-centric media; interdictions on speaking of the dead; suppression of languages; abduction of children; and legal prohibitions against ceremonies and gatherings, including for mourning. The continuing pressures of land loss, extreme poverty, lack of political representation, enforced western culture and epistemology, and racism compounded these initial conditions, foreclosing the Maidu relationship to death in an ongoing catastrophe. Dying in 1976 in the midst of such disaster, Day spent the last sixteen or so years of his life documenting the Maidu world in paint and on audiotape so that things would not be forgotten.

As the epigraphs make clear, Day's project of anamnesis is a matter of Indigenous informatics and cartography. Day used paint and tape, images and words, to code information and map the (destruction of the) Maidu world in order to transmit information across space and time. The politics of information in this context is fraught, thanks in part to the early twentieth-century anthropological project of salvage ethnography and the critiques it has provoked. Salvage ethnography has emphasized the separation between those who had direct experience with "traditional" ways of life and those with *mere* memories. Much scholarship also reframes and sometimes reclaims the work of so-called informants outside such a notion of salvage. This is especially true of Day's generation, who were represented as a bridge between those who lived more traditional lifestyles and post-assimilation generations. These ancestors have, of course, left us an amazing gift in the information they provided, risking the dangers of colonial knowledge-making enterprises to sow the seeds for revitalization projects.

The claims of our ancestors to provide access to their worlds are not often taken at face value, with a critical ethics intervening to oppose evaluations of authenticity.[2] Focusing on authenticity and its critique, however, risks overemphasizing problematics set out by fields such as anthropology and art history, predetermining how we hear the words and see the images of our ancestors and leaving us circling around these knowledge formations in a critical posture, fascinated and revulsed. On the other hand, hearing and seeing our ancestors' mediations too literally, with an ear and eye for realism, couches their often-subtle strategies and our Indigenous modes of being in a western metaphysical formalism that consolidates Indigenous subjects and an Indigenous world as stable identities easily transmitted and known. In approaching Day's obscurity and his claim that the Maidu world has come to an end—the unknown and the unsayable—I prefer to take Day's words and images at face value. I attempt to listen to how he frames problems, trying to understand his artwork in response. Due to the complex mediations at play in Day's representational practice, such intensive listening requires delinking from the false dilemma between antirealist critique and realist assertions of positive knowledge. Navigating around these two intimately related aspects of western knowledge formation—assertion and critique—is made easier by attending to California Indian epistemologies and metaphysics that outstrip their western counterparts. I draw much of this knowledge from Day himself, who not only emphasized the mediation of his knowledge in a distinctly California Indian epistemology but also used this mediation to invoke and transmit a disrupted way of being and an interrelationality that constitute the essence of the Maidu world.

As Day describes in one of his recordings, as part of his research he spent years looking for the "central point in Maidu territory," a journey that led him to all the different regions through which he "slept, crawled, walked," never finding an answer.[3] But, he reports, while painting the four points of a leaf from a tree, "as I was illustrating, it came to me." In a detouring exposition on Maidu patterns and designs, Day links these four points of a leaf to different periods of time, such as the "half-mourning" performed during severe drought; the spiritual realm; the significance of geographic shapes, especially straight lines, curves, circles, and points; the celestial sphere; the use of indelible roots for designs in basket weaving; and the existence of petrified monsters. Following this detouring path requires one to emulate the tempo and halting movements of Day's failed pilgrimage. It further requires shifts between times, levels of abstraction, and categories of knowledge across representational practices. This complex episode hints at how Day maps the missing center of the Maidu world in paint and on tape. Together, Day's words and images chart a detouring path back that is oriented around this central emptiness, one made possible by its very difficulty.

To add to this difficulty, Day was distrusted by many of the academics he contacted in his attempts to have his knowledge recorded and by many members of his own community, who referred to him as a criminal, cheat, and fraud.[4] This biographical wrinkle has implications for understanding how to hear and see Day's words and images. That Day was ostensibly a liar exposes cracks in the knowledge edifice and its modes of stabilizing and transmitting information. Day's lying also draws attention to the intricate and foreclosed networks between being a witness to atrocity and being a cultural informant. Within a California Indian framework, lying is accepted as a legitimate way to confront radically incommensurate forms of power, such as the forces that destroyed Day's world. These forces threaten further destruction through forgetting and silencing the catastrophe and carve out institutionalized forms of memorialization based on a discourse of truth. The lack of veracity in Day's words and images, from this perspective, short-circuits the demand to be a *real Indian* by offering a path outside of aesthetic and veridical forms of recognition without falling back into a critique of the Indian as ideological figure covering over the real Native.

Along this path, Day made nearly two hundred paintings and spent the last year of his life producing more than seventy hours of self-recordings, from which the first two epigraphs of this chapter are taken. How do we hear his claim that he is simply transmitting information through painting? That this information is coded in the Maidu language, which he charts with images? What does this statement say about painting and art more generally in the context of Native California, Native America, and Indigeneity more broadly? How does the claim to transparent information transmission help us understand the relation between Day's images and the hours of recordings he made, as well as the recorded explanations he gives for his paintings? Day's stated problem is to preserve what he fears is being lost, yet to travel over distance or time requires being in a form, hence paintings, stories, and songs. Day's work in these media raises these questions, which are obscured by disciplinary knowledge formations such as art history, anthropology, and other social sciences, which have their own institutional and epistemological investments. What is needed instead is careful consideration of Day's informatics and cartography through mediation, as well as the difficulties and interruptions he confronts in the recording and transmission of information. Archival issues, catastrophic foreclosures of relations to death, violences of representation, disciplinary and discursive captures in truth-making procedures are all impediments to conveying knowledge for Indigenous people. If the medium is the message, what do these interruptions say about the Indigenous message?

On the significance of recording, Day notes: "It may come in mighty handy . . . especially to the young Konkow people who may listen to it at a later period of time."[5] The dilemma for Day is how both to transmit the information he seeks to preserve under these perilous conditions and to create the conditions for the revitalization of a kind of personhood and its concomitant world. This personhood, I argue, resists western conceptions of person, subject, and the human. Transmitting information and personhood are not opposed, though they generally imply different forms of mediation: the first is interested in smooth transference without interruption—clear communication—while the second lingers in the interval, in ethical breaks. Day, I argue, destabilizes any consolidation of mediatory processes into this difference (information/personhood) and finds the point of intersection between them. He outstrips both reference to a stable identity and world through knowledge *and* the performative force of an ethical transference of personhood.

To transmit information and create the conditions for revitalization, Day creates through his paintings and words an atlas for the Maidu world. Following Day down this path, we are helped by a number of elements that constitute a map key. Stated here in preliminary and condensed form, rather than rendering meaning more transparent, the elements of the map key may appear inaccessible. But this difficulty is part of the means of transmission: only by following Day on his errant journey and in his halting time can one access the map. What is carried over is not the world itself, whatever that might mean; rather, Day begins with the enigmatic violence of suspending the usual ways of seeing and interpreting painting, culture, and meaning. Clearing the ground, he similarly resists evaluations that privilege the western epistemological distinction between the vital and the mechanical, personhood and information, opting instead for an Indigenous, nonvital sense of the eye and the ear as material mediations. This nonvital approach opens onto a uniquely California Indian theory of power in the form of luck and a sense of the interrelationality of all things. Drawing on this theory, Day achieves a force of suspension by emphasizing the indexicality of painting as nonvital and interrelational, pointing both toward the world and toward the mediation of painting itself in a form of representation that is ambiguously pictorial and discursive. Distributed throughout Day's oeuvre, these indexical elements mark a metaphysical investment in the complexity and permanence of a uniquely Indigenous form of image-making: the petroglyph. Day represents and produces this complexity as what is to be transmitted and the means of such transmission. Through paint and tape, Day creates an atlas to a destroyed world by transmitting with and transmitting an undone petroglyph in images and words.

Enigmatic Violence

We enter the path through Day's paintings. Nonvital, immobilizing, fragmentary, his series of images represent a force of suspension. This static movement is not entirely obvious at first glance, considering the wide array of beings, elements, relations, and actions that make up the

Kóyo•mkàwi Maidu world Day represents. Bodies and trees are locked in a tension between preservation and decay; stones manifest on a continuum from the most general to textured and colored particularity to petrified monsters that connect the land to time immemorial (storied time); wind is caught for a moment in violent spirals; water is always potentially poisonous (from shamans or earthquakes); smoke curls and rises, cutting across variously hued skies to carry prayers, to cleanse; there is fume, mist, and fire. Every figure, including that of the landscape, which never settles, is in arrested motion: wrestling, jumping, falling, killing, cooking, gathering. Animals and monsters are engaged in life-and-death struggles with their natural adversaries. The sick, dead, and dying lie somewhere between healing and decay, buried and disinterred. The land is riven with crevices, marked by impressions and petroglyphs, littered with bone and tree fragments, gathered and released in earth and stone forms, smooth and flat spaces, a proliferation and spilling of particulates. It rises up violently. The landscape is, further, visually partitioned by rocks and fallen trees that carve internal frames, fracturing the scene. Day certainly represents violence in his images, both the violence of bound and tortured bodies and the violence associated with life, activity, supported by his ethnographic representations of village life, but, *at its heart,* Day's painting commits a very different kind of violence against vitality itself through employing representational powers of suspension.[6]

What are they, these "strange, sensuous, mystical paintings"?[7] They are not art—they are too "cultural" for such a designation. They are not cultural documentation—painting was not made for such work. Are they even true? Are they even good? These questions have little bearing. Despite Lucy Lippard's claim that Day is a "consummate artist," he himself deferred that designation, preferring to see himself as a documentarian, at best an illustrator, and yet it is generally agreed that his information left much to be desired.[8] His paintings have been variously interpreted as folk or outsider art due to his lack of training, cultural content, and ambiguous narratives, with the paintings being shown at the influential 1986 exhibition *Cat and Ball on a Waterfall: 200 Years of California Folk Painting and Sculpture;* as a type of autoethnography, due to his use of western aesthetic and representational practices to document his culture for his and his people's purposes, which is the primary lens through which his main biographer, Rebecca Dobkins, interprets his work; and, of course, as an Indian artist, with his work historicized as a precursor to the California Indian painting movement, which began in the late twentieth century. All these interpretations, though, fail to capture the radical rupture Day's paintings make in the field of the image as these interpretations seek *to make something* of them. They make meaning and/or knowledge by finding in his work critical vitalist tendencies that render visible his life, culture, and imagination at the margins.

The first thing one must contend with in viewing Day's images is this desire to want his paintings to be more, for them to make something visible. This desire raises an anxiety and a palliative such that Day's work seems to be a pale imitation of western painting—to signify that practice by failing at it—yet supersedes it on so many levels. The question of how to read Day's paintings is thus exacerbated: as paintings, as cultural documents, as spells of some sort? The discomfort this ambiguity raises for many viewers is that Day's paintings offer us nothing to hold on to while indexing so much more and so much less than western art—both the absolute and "just something," as we will see—by using painting's representational capacities inappropriately to transparently represent, as if a science. Day instrumentalizes this desire to make visible and yet inverts and frustrates it by making nothing clear, by failing. Suspending the play of visible and invisible by disrupting the power to make visible at its source, its representational power—being more and less than—Day's images carry the suggestion that western art and knowledge are a farce. "Painting deceives the eyes in so far as they admire the painter's art" and not the replication of a thing, yet what cannot be shaken in Day's context is that the catastrophic loss of what is replicated occurs through the very force of its representation.[9] This is a dangerous game that Day gladly enters, the power of his work hinging on this fulcrum.

I have struggled with the desire to make something of Day's work in trying to write near his images, to see in his work a form of intellectual sovereignty and the performance of a gesture of survivance. I have finally, as much as I can, tried to let go of this desire after my realization that Day was engaged in a much stickier problem: the impossibility of visibility itself under catastrophic conditions. This problem brings refusal—Day's refusal to paint something recognizable and my refusal to make positive knowledge about it—into an uncomfortable intimacy with failure.[10] Because of this problem, Day's paintings and words are better understood in the context of the archive in general, issues of vitalism in western metaphysics, and the unsayable in the face of genocidal violence and the intractability of the archive. In this sense, biographical, historical, cultural, and any other contextual frames need to be explained by Day's work and the problems he addresses as much as the other way around.

Tear of the Visible

Day's movement of suspension can be seen in the untitled painting that is part of a series of images by Day that show Maidu people skinning deer (Figure 9). It is a good example to demonstrate how Day's paintings have generally been read. As a dramatic scene of Maidu life, of the reproduction of Maidu life, of relationships between human and nonhuman bodies, of cultural information of the variety sought vigorously by salvage ethnographers, as well as by some of the anthropologists with whom Day was in direct contact throughout the 1960s and 1970s, this image seems heavily coded in the discourse of cultural anthropology. In its aesthetic presentation, the image appears to be clearly a figurative painting, representing a narrative cultural scene in as truthful a manner as possible. But the image cannot be *only* a figurative painting, because the relationship to "real life" is complicated by the disruption caused by catastrophic violence, and it cannot be *fully* narrative, as the function of story gets repurposed by Day through a complex relationship to truth and the archive.

Day likely never experienced this scene as presented, yet such a rupture is already implied by the mechanism of painting: "The art of painting as mimesis, with all its technique and science, is made to deceive the eyes by an innocuous magic which makes a picture display things that do not exist."[11] Through variance in resemblance, painting suggests what it represents without ever representing anything at all, yet this force of suggestion is only possible because of the representational promise. In the practice of painting, Day finds a strange destructive power that fails precisely where it draws its force, making painting a paradoxically appropriate medium to register catastrophe. Two things emphasize the enigmatic aspect of this weak (and/or self-) destructive capacity: the use of painting to scientifically document and the role of documentation in contributing to the catastrophic function of the archive.

To understand the dilemma, we can turn to the inherent absurdity of a project like anthropology, with which Day was intimately familiar, which asked people to record knowledge of their culture in the face of

FIGURE 9. Frank Day, *Untitled*, ca. 1967. Destroyed in the 1991 Oakland Hills fire. Photograph courtesy of Rebecca J. Dobkins.

their own disappearance both after catastrophe and in response to its always imminent arrival as an extension of murder. To contribute to one's own disaster as an informant was the condition for having a share in the visible world. Herein lies the destruction of visibility as such. It is one that carries over to the current moment in which an overdetermined invisibility that has long held sway, like a shroud over California Indian peoples and our worlds, has seemingly begun to disintegrate, raising the need to attend to the question and politics of visibility anew. The well-documented logic of disappearance tied to definitions of blood quantum and property production is seemingly losing its hold; it is a logic that was exacerbated during the institution of the state of California by removals of Indigenous peoples and direct genocidal violence—widely documented as an "extermination" project bluntly summed up by the generic use of the term *Indian* to refer to all Indigenous peoples during the indiscriminate violence of "punitive" raids (they are all "Indians" and therefore culpable)—and followed by ex-nominations by state officials of tribal names and replacement with the terms *mission* or *digger*

Indian, along with termination of tribal designation. Such a violent process of ex-nomination, which conditions these naming practices by settlers, renaming land, animals, and peoples, has been directly called into question in numerous contexts through the activism of California Indian people demanding attention to these histories and names. To understand this challenge to invisibility requires moving beyond the superficial politics of representation, particularly a simple claim for more visibility, to understand the conditions and coloniality of visibility itself.

The invisibility and seeming disappearance such renaming presumes is a broad-ranging project that has been documented in other contexts as part of a structural settler apparatus (see Jean O'Brien's discussion of "firsting" and "lasting" narratives, for an example[12]), but, as we saw in chapter 2, in California took a particular form as an organized epistemic and pedagogical project during the salvage ethnographic surveys of the early twentieth century. Metaphorized as a "snapshot" taken at the moment of disappearance, a frozen moment that both captures and initiates a sense of the destruction, these surveys coincided with the development of anthropology in California and the infrastructural and material "development" of the land and resources, a point of intersection made by the vast ethnographic and archaeological collections still held by institutions. The anthropological Ur-image produced by these surveys of language, performance, and material and immaterial culture was set in contrast to the western metaphysics of development that undergirds the settler project. Anthropology's impetus to preserve what was presumed to be disappearing before the onslaught of a naturalized and inexorable civilizing process produced well-documented effects such as a timeless sense of culture and an impossible ethics of authenticity. At bottom, though, is a very specific archival logic based on a supposedly inexorable destructive force that conditions vanishing.

It's a well-known distinction that bears repeating: the spatial and temporal differences between oral cultures and literate cultures are discursively sedimented in the disciplines of anthropology and history across a profound epistemic difference, one that continues to condition interpretations of Indigenous cultural production even when, in fact, Indigenous people are literate. According to this evaluation, oral story on its own doesn't constitute knowledge but requires an outside interpretation. Anthropology is then the work of outsiders who travel to Indigenous homelands to interpret, to make visible, while history is an immanent discourse. Indigenous people, by this thinking, do not separate knowledge from its medium; knowledge is immediate. Indigenous people are their own archive. "Ethnological knowledge is [thereby] rendered possible by the armed hand of Western humanism and by its phenomenal power of extension and expansion, that is to say, by colonialism."[13] Knowledge that comes from dreams, from the sacred, is, according to this colonial perception, only knowledge if it is interpreted, made visible, placing it in an episteme of secrecy and invisibility. And secrets only remain secret as long as they are not revealed, dissipating as soon as they touch air. Such is the law of the archive imposed on Indigenous peoples through a structure of vanishing.

This archival structure produces an undecidable dilemma between the dream of a society without archive and the irreducible archive as a general structure. Are dreams, as experienced as prophecy, positive facts, definitive modes of reality, or are they what get excluded from the general archive, an exclusion perpetuated as the archive's and therefore truth's guarantee? What's at stake in this question is western liberal humanism's monopoly on reality effected through material colonization and discursive education. But it is a false dilemma. Based on a force of revelation (the real meaning of apocalypse),[14] the dilemma itself turns everything not visible into the merely not-yet-visible based on a decision about reason and the irrational, with the savage figured as the epitome of irrationality. In this sense, dreams as prophecy become beliefs to be tolerated or eradicated, or, as we saw in the introduction, a new form of theory for western and settler scholars to try on, but something to be made known as part of an archival impetus. Marc Nichanian has noted how this profound distinction has produced a difference between the "savage" and the "Native," with the savage being the absolute abject figure who is one with their knowledge, a figure of disappearance and the dream of anthropology, and the Native being the threshold figure of a developing humanity, the promise of civilization in inchoate form, the dream of history. As mentioned, the split between the savage and the Native is one that has organized the colonial project from its inception. It is founded on the question of the humanity of the indigene.

Jean-François Lyotard has argued that the western definition of the human is the realization of the savage in its promise of humanity, in its inhumanity.[15] The inhumanity of the savage, for Lyotard, is an obscure mixture of being determined (not free, held hostage by desires, drives, and a lack of reason) and yet radically indeterminate in the struggle with human-made institutions, a remainder of the failures of pedagogical training and the "infinitely secret" conditions that "hold the soul hostage."[16] One of these secret conditions would, of course, be language in its quasi agency and in the tension between its radical freedom (in theory, we can use any word to indicate anything arbitrarily) and its conservative nature (it is impossible to change the linguistic system as a whole due to its semiotic and collective structure). Language is a condition of human freedom and yet completely outside of individual human control. One can fill in various other structures that hold the soul hostage in a similar manner: technology, rights, culture, citizenship. These produce a split in western humanism between "native indetermination" and "self-instituting reason,"[17] between failure and accomplishment, a split that cannot be reconciled or made sense of. This is because, for Lyotard, the inhuman as condition for the human, as that which is perpetually expelled through a definitional procedure as not proper to the human and yet creates the conditions for the human's emergence, is likewise split between the inhuman violence of the western system's developmental metaphysics and the infinitely secret otherness that "holds the soul hostage." This produces a dialectic between the humanism of civil society as rational system and the disciplinary training of the individual to be made into a rational citizen. Together, these are the engines of a western metaphysics that disavows itself as metaphysical and thereby institutes itself as reality.

For Lyotard, such a system assimilates challenges through its developmental force, feeding on a dynamics of complexity and rigidity, depending upon the current conditions, which might explain the seemingly extreme swings between multicultural neoliberalism and fascism in a number of western, particularly settler, countries. "The richer—i.e. itself mediated—the mediating term, the more numerous the possible modifications, the suppler the regulation, the more floating the rate of exchange between the elements, the more permissive the mode of relation."[18] Development, thereby, assimilates risks, mobilizes informational value, and turns its challenges into new mediations through which it continues to function. It initiates an absolute destruction of alternatives by turning all alternatives into its various facets and toward its purpose. As Lyotard further notes, "What else remains of 'politics' except resistance to this inhuman? What is left to resist with but the debt which each soul has contracted with the miserable and admirable indetermination from which it was born and does not cease to be born?—which is to say with the other inhuman?" That is, with failure.

In its critical, self-reflexive form, anthropology has manifested the developmental logic of western humanism through institutionalizing knowledge-production based on the mining of Indigenous knowledge and then the disavowal of its own procedures and material collections. The field has passed through an activist phase of attempting to advocate for Indigenous peoples and then attempted to "give them voice." It has interrogated the political and historical conditions of its own coloniality. It has since sought to get out of the Native's way by turning toward other concerns, ironically adopting the savage philosopher's position in producing anthropologies of all sorts of beings through a strategic anthropomorphization. The field as a whole has become very adept at taking domination into account, but it cannot take into account the fundamentally destructive aspect of its archival logics, its production of a force of vanishing knowledge that destroys itself, and this is because its critical position is more invested in reforming and recreating the discipline. It is utterly institutional. To do so would require it to undermine the institution that houses it and the western episteme that lies at its foundation.

There remains in anthropology's heart a racialized exhibition value of the naked savage tied to detestable histories of display of non-white bodies, what in museum studies is referred to as the "human zoo." There remains a trace of destruction through its fundamentally preservative spirit, even in, and really through, its turn away from representation.[19] These traces continue to crop up time and time again in overt fashion through the field's series of controversies (which are clearly not anomalies, as more progressive representatives of the field would have you believe), but the subtler, more malleable forms of knowledge production are equally laced with these traces. This is in part because anthropology is and always has been a visual discipline whether we are talking about race, land, culture, or body. The discipline has disciplined the conditions of sight, even and especially when it presents itself as a textual and discursive project (this includes ethnomusicology and sound studies). Understanding, then, the shift in visibility for California Indian peoples means understanding these conditions of the visible and going beyond them to the realm of the avisual, by engaging the struggle within the realm of the inhuman.

The *savage*, from this perspective, was always understood to be concomitant with the archive, to be their own archive without distance. Hence the impossibility of an Indigenous archive through technological mediation and the need for ethnographic transcription and translation. Rendering the savage visible was therefore a destructive act, leading to the crisis anthropology underwent in the recognition of the murder of its own referent.

In the opening epigraph, Day insists that he can hold this catastrophe at bay with just color and a little bit of painting. Such a claim marks a confluence of humility and the absolute, which characterizes much of Day's life. While seemingly echoing the destructive anthropological gesture, it instead marks a refusal/failure to make visible. This interruption emphasizes the force from which anthropology's dangerous powers are drawn but in an ambiguous medium with its own destructive powers. In the untitled painting, instead of depicting a truthful cultural scene or a history of painterly gestures, Day simultaneously employs and maps the destructive powers of representation in both representation's pictorial and discursive senses. A response to what Nichanian calls the "tear of the gaze"—the impossible desire to render the catastrophe visible through aesthetic means and/or representational practices—Day's refusal/failure to make visible brings the viewer to the limit of the image and employs the limit itself for preservation.[20]

Day's painting turns away from the aggressive exigency to make visible without recourse to the invisible or hidden, what is merely not yet visible. He hides nothing. He instead suspends the question of visibility in order to make other arrangements of the senses available in his images. Day's words, for instance, as we will see, are difficult to follow because they fail to uncover what is hidden, unlike the language of anthropology or the formal language of exposition. Yet they also do not hide anything, which would merely be a call to be deciphered. His words are open to enter into interrelation with his images in a way that holds the viewer suspended between visibility and invisibility, sound and silence, ear and eye. Day paints the impossibility of representing the catastrophe by not showing it and not hiding it, by painting the nothingness left in the wake of the world's destruction as refusal/failure to make visible: "To show the most terrible images is always possible, but to show who or what kills every possibility of the image is impossible, except by recreating the gesture of the murderer."[21]

The various elements represented in the untitled painting demonstrate how this suspended action produces an orientation through avisuality. Together, the elements offer an impression of Day's cartographic strategy, though in inchoate and barely adumbrated form. I list them here to coax them into a precariously held shape: the toes of a petrified monster poking into the frame on the right; the differently shaped and individuated stones littering the landscape; the circle of the dance ground; the jagged, broken form of a log or large rock; the floating quality of the figures involved in deer skinning; and, finally, the enigmatic symbols drawn onto/above the painting near Day's signature. Each of these elements will be addressed in more detail but here can be enigmatically highlighted as an ensemble lying somewhere between a discourse and a picture. These distributed elements suggest representational powers while drawing out the more dangerous aspects of representation by resisting categorization or clear organization. The ensemble suggests a world and orients the viewer through suspension and preservation of its possibility.

By addressing this tear in/of the visible through its impossibility, Day is not intentionally being evasive, as Sascha Scott reads the paintings of Awa Tsireh, the early twentieth-century Pueblo painter who became well known for his striking minimalist renderings of Pueblo imagery.[22] Scott carefully interprets the evasive strategies Tsireh employed to sell his paintings on the substantial Southwest Indian art market without revealing any sensitive knowledge and to cleverly manipulate the desires of Pueblo art aficionados. But the Indian art market did not want Day's work. Or, at least, there was not much of a market for California Indian art during the time he was painting. He did have collectors—the usual hodgepodge of local anthropologists, Native art enthusiasts, public historians, and some academics, as well as a few Indians. And he did eventually find a venue at Pacific Western Traders in Folsom, California, where he became a fixture for the last three years of his life. But Day's story must ultimately be understood as one of failure and not one of resistance. Day's paintings are not a fully intentional and masterful coding of information but rather a failure to communicate and to communicate by that very failure. As Nomtipom Wintu scholar, cultural leader, and artist Frank LaPena writes, "Sometimes Frank's stories were so strange, or the point of view so unfamiliar, that one was unsure whether one was listening to Frank's personal creative inventions or stories representing events from another time and place. For instance, his explanation of several paintings dealing with the time when there were once 'monster beasts' in the beginning of creation was better understood if one knew the Maidu tradition or had a chance to actually see what he was talking about."[23] This ambivalence not only does not resolve in Day's transmission of information but also becomes the very means of charting itself.

Real Indians Don't Lie

Specifics of Day's life contribute to the ambiguity. By some accounts, Day was a trickster, a coyote slinking around the outskirts of the community, a "con man"; by others, he was a central and important figure of Maidu cultural renewal. These accounts are not mutually exclusive, and their concomitance in Day strikes at the heart of presumptions about cultural authenticity and the figure of the witness. Day's dual positioning challenges conventional forms of analysis and representation, including the critically examined figures of the anthropological "informant" and the market-based "Indian artist," not to mention the historicist tendencies within biographical, social, and political contexts. Day, however, positioned himself as a bulwark at the threshold of the disappearance of the Maidu world, drawing on the waning powers of western figurative painting and salvage ethnography to engage the catastrophe on other terms for the sake of preservation: "If I do not do this, all things will be forgotten."

Day was raised as the son of one of the last headmen of the Bald Rock band of the Kóyo•mkàwi Maidu, the people of the meadows. His mother died when he was two. A Northern California tribe whose homelands are in the Sierra Nevada foothills, the Kóyo•mkàwi were devastated by the gold rush, including mass murder; many of their people were marched (often to death) in the Maidu Trail of Tears in 1863, as well as in the earlier 1854 removal. The Maidu homelands were flooded in the 1960s by the Oroville Dam project, with several village, ceremonial, and cultural sites now underwater. Day attended the Greenville Indian Industrial Boarding School, a coercive federal project to humanize the savage by destroying their cultural life and severing their ties to Indigenous modes of interrelationality by taking away language, ceremony, and knowledge. At the same time, his father, Twoboe (a.k.a. Billy Day), a well-respected political, cultural, and spiritual leader, was sought out by anthropologists as an informant, something Day would have been very aware of as a child, leading to an early understanding of the significance of the production of an archive and the need for cultural preservation. Frank Day was also raised around the last generation of elders to structure their lives around the time of the roundhouse, the ceremonial house at the center of Maidu life, and was therefore exposed to ceremonial singing "all day and night."[24] So Day from a very early age had a sense of the catastrophe, the one that had already occurred, the one ongoing during his life, and the impending one prophesied through the night singing of these elders.

Rebecca Dobkins, who wrote her dissertation on Frank Day in the 1990s, curated an art exhibit and edited a catalog based on his paintings. She also produced an account of Day's early life that indicates the holes in knowledge and the limitations of biography, particularly under the extreme conditions of poverty, colonization, and U.S. hegemony. Conducting interviews with Kóyo•mkàwi elders who knew Day, reconstructing his biography and genealogy using spotty and problematic census records, and engaging with Day's shifting autobiographical accounts, Dobkins indicates the slippages between different narratives and the unlikeliness of producing an authoritative or coherent biography for him. Day, for instance, suffered a severe injury when he was a child that limited the use of his legs. For years, it seems, he used tin cans tied to his hands for mobility, dragging himself around. Explaining this injury, Day says that he was thrown from a horse, but several other accounts, including one by Day himself, state that he was beaten severely by his grandmother when he was three years old for running through acorn soup that she was leaching (a primary food source that requires significant labor), to the point that one witness thought he was dead. Day's explanation for how he regained the use of his legs recounts a miracle: "One day while sitting in a vineyard, Frank decided to take hold of a vine. A radiant light came out of the dawn and gave him the power to pull himself upright. Immediately he was made 'whole.' So from that time forth he has carried the name Ly•dam•lilly, which in Maidu signifies 'fading Morningstar.'"[25] Day elsewhere gave as the reason he received his Maidu name that he was born in the early morning hours.[26] He apparently suffered numerous injuries throughout his life, including breaking both of his knees in a farming accident that left one leg permanently shorter than the other. According to one account, Day took up painting while recovering from this last injury, but Day also claims to have taught painting while traveling throughout the country as an itinerant laborer during his early twenties.[27] He also claims to have taught "spiritual ministry" during this time and to have attended a number of religious colleges, though there are no records of his enrollment. Enigmatically, in the same recording where Day discusses the loss of the use of his legs and miraculous recovery, he recalls that an "enemy later destroyed me, but I'm not going to talk about that; I'm going to sing you a song."[28]

This refusal to talk about his personal destruction by an enemy all while giving competing personal narratives that sound fantastical to the skeptical ear is a complex play of power. Dobkins, for instance, cites an account by Day of how his two older brothers died from wearing stone caps that were part of "spiritual warfare."[29] Expressing that initially she found the story to be fantastical, she was surprised to have it corroborated both in interviews with the Kóyo•mkàwi community and in earlier anthropological literature that documented ku'kinim to'ni (spirit or pain baskets), portable mortars "used by shamans as receptacles in which to keep their most powerful and precious charms, especially the 'pains' which they shot at people to cause disease or death."[30] At the same time, California Indian power is tricky and dangerous, affecting not only the ways people behave but also the very structures of many California Indian languages, which only indirectly reference it.[31] In a description of California Indian power, another anthropologist notes that while it is accepted that it is generally wise to be honest, moderate, and reciprocal with others in order to not offend power and bring about your own destruction, as well as acquire power yourself, "honesty is qualified by the understanding that deceit can be used by the weak when dealing with powerful beings or persons who have an unfair advantage."[32] In this realm of the indeterminacy of truth and lying, of power and weakness, Day engages the dangerous colonial tools of representation in order to transmit information without truth, a nonpatriarchal transmission and use of authority.

To ensure such transmission within a treacherous context, Day leverages his authority on his very failure to be an authority: "I'm not a doctor, I'm not a soothsayer, I'm not a shaman, I'm not a spiritual man, I'm not a medicine man. I'm just an ordinary man who by my constant listening and . . . my business . . . was . . . to be around older folks to listen, to learn. It's been my business to prepare myself for the spiritual course in the Indian tradition, and then the way of life came to an end when I was just nine or ten years old. And things have changed."[33] This complex authority distinguishes between the ordinary and extraordinary while conflating the two within a discourse of catastrophe. Day's use of this authority is augmented by his outsider position in relation to his community. While Day might have been the son of an important leader, his decision to leave the community to travel around the country after performing a burning ceremony for his father's death created distrust. Returning after twelve years, Day was somewhat excluded, although his vast knowledge was welcomed, as evidenced by his performance of a mourning ceremony promptly upon his return.[34] In a type of quasi exile without full exclusion, Day returned home without ever fully returning, his travels appropriately bookended by mourning.

Yet Day was responsible for bringing songs and dances back to his people. Frank LaPena led a dance troupe, the Maidu Dancers and Traditionalists, who studied under Day. LaPena describes the experience of performing for the Kóyo•mkàwi at Bald Rock: "In order to appreciate the moment, you must imagine the power of words, Maidu words sung on a public occasion, in Maidu territory where Indians were not always acknowledged, and Frank Day as a Maidu elder bringing their dance back to them."[35] What Day returned with was the journey itself. The dances and songs had traveled with Day, a traveling that did not end with his return to Northern California. Neither entirely welcomed back nor excluded: this contradictory and suspended movement of Day's life is transcribed into his work, making it difficult to position him. Indeed, Day was not to be trusted, because he took it upon himself to live the dissonant rhythms of power and knowledge at the limits of two different and genocidally structured cultures. This dissonance has been transcribed into and has made possible the recording of a type of Maidu visuality and visual theory in paint.

Subterranean Vision

In Frank Day's painting *The Mushroom Picker*, a relationship is implied between the Kóyo•mkàwi man picking mushrooms and the ants in the bottom-left corner of the image, but it is a subtle one mediated by a transverse decaying fallen tree that separates the top of the human figure from his legs and acts as a dark tunnel of activity for the ants, an extension of their mound (Figure 10). The other trees in the background are on a continuum of life and death, reflecting the stakes of survival through the mirrored bending of the man's figure, draped over the fallen tree, and the bending of the lightest-colored tree out of the left side of the frame. The figure's lean musculature and protruding spinal column and ribs echo the bone color of the left-leaning tree, which fades in brightness and deforms, suggesting an indeterminacy between flesh and bone. A dead gray spire splits both this mirrored image and the evergreens in the background, with a black bird of some sort perched

FIGURE 10. Frank Day, *Cycle of Life*, ca. 1965. Oil on board, 23 3/4 × 29 7/8 in. Crocker Art Museum, 2017.62.5. Gift of the Aeschliman McGreal Collection.

on a branch near the top. Two deer run up the hillside. As with most of Day's paintings, the landscape is complexly textured and full of tensions, ridges or rifts, and various states of solidity. Everything in the image, from a certain standpoint, has an organic quality to it; from another standpoint, everything tends toward a subtle deformation that resists the organic/inorganic distinction (which in a Maidu sense means it is charmed, imbued with power). In several of Day's paintings, like this one, a vista is naturally framed; the transverse tree resting on a rock or earth formation makes up the frame, creating a triangle shape replicated by the figure's bent arm. Through this vista runs a creek and then a valley that seem compressed and distorted. The vista disciplines the eye with texture and other earthly elements, enfolded into the layered interplay of environmental forces, just like the horizon itself.

The fungal, though, is the essence. Mushrooms pervade the scene, insinuating themselves into the crevices, where they populate the darker spaces, moving from textural affect to figure and back. They are mediators between decay and life, the darkness of the earth and the cool night sky, soil and digestion, rootedness and floating spores, unseen underground rhizomes and aboveground fruit. Life and death are in an oscillating series of tensions. This painting is (about) employing the forces of death, the earth, and darkness for the sake of preservation. The status of death, though, is up in the air. Another title recorded for this painting, *Cycle of Life*, represents an organic vision, yet death in Day's work and practice pushes beyond the organic cycle toward another kind of death outside of the life-and-death divide. Though it appears to be daytime, the day is strongly interrupted by the forces of the night. Trees are both bone and decaying flesh, structure and meat, just like the human body. Using these qualities in paint, Day has sealed in the essence of fungus, which infuses the painting itself, insinuating itself, like the ants, between the paint and the canvas, the image and the neutral toward which it always leans.[36] As Day explains, the ants are horticulturalists who plant mushrooms in the dead tree, harnessing the forces of the earth, of death and decay, to bear fruit, just as Day uses the decaying corpses of art and anthropology to preserve the Maidu world.[37] By sprouting, this painting takes us underground in the full light of day.

What kind of vision is this? It is not stratigraphic, a form of vision detailed by Jason Weems in his discussion of subterranean mapping as an expansionist force that reshapes the landscape of the "American" West, making the invisible visible, particularly through geology and archaeology.[38] It is, in fact, the inverse. In the former, rationality, action, clarity, abstraction—all the instrumental forces of the day in the service of "life"—are brought to bear on the hidden recesses of the earth. It is a kind of vision that Trinh T. Minh-ha notes "seek[s] to perforate meaning by forcing . . . entry or breaking it open to dissipate what is thought to be its secrets," an action that "is typical of a mentality that proves incapable of touching the living thing without crushing its delicateness," a mentality that, ironically, presents itself as being in the service of life.[39] In Day's vision, one does not pry open the earth to reveal its secrets, exposing it to the light of day; instead, one entreats the forces of the earth for the purposes of survival, going into the ground like a corpse in order to deform the visible landscape itself with an opaque sight, that of painting. Rock and earth fold, contract, and dilate. Trees and land take on monstrous forms. The darkness of the earth, of night, of death otherwise, of what Day refers to as "the Great Mystery" of the West, is brought to bear on the California landscape, so well-known in colonial terms with its two kinds of light in landscape painting (northern and southern) and history of visual and epistemological representation and capture.[40]

Nonvital Interrelationality

By employing a subterranean vision, Day's representational practice seeks to step into the realm Kim TallBear locates beyond the life/nonlife binary, where Indigenous interrelationality challenges the life-and-death distinction.[41] For TallBear, what she calls an Indigenous metaphysics precedes and exceeds the biological or carbon-based metaphysics that subtends western and colonial forms of governance. Drawing on the work of both Vine Deloria Jr. and Charles Eastman, she argues that the sociopolitical interrelationality that includes humans and animals, as well as energy, spirits, rocks, and stars, upends the slow division that occurred between the human and other-than-human worlds that has marked colonization and the enforcement of an imperial epistemology.[42] It also shifts the position of the human in relation to ontological hierarchies that alter the human constitution, which can be understood in more complex ways than in simply biological terms.[43]

Contesting the scientific "molecular definition of life," founded on the presumed extinction of Indigenous populations and the study of their cell lines, TallBear notes how DNA becomes a proxy for bodies and life in such a way that it exposes a contradiction in the desire for western genomic futures.[44] Not only are Indigenous peoples persistently narrated in discourses of endangerment and death, but, as we saw in the introduction, nationalist coherence requires their preservation as guarantee. As Jasbir Puar might frame it, U.S. sovereignty requires stunting the Indigenous body (politic and otherwise), not its death.[45] This perversion of power, for TallBear, is part of the way that death is brought into power and biopolitically managed. Indigeneity is held back from the brink of extinction through an epistemological form of recognition that ultimately destroys Indigenous identity, and the settler is thereby granted eternal life in the reservoir of Indigenous half-life.

TallBear analyzes two western theoretical fields located broadly under the umbrella of posthumanism that seek to reflexively subvert this power-laden conception of life and death by focusing on a broader notion of vitality, and she finds both lacking in relation to Indigenous metaphysics. In the first, multi- and inter-species fields such as animal studies get close to Indigenous emphases on "complex forms of relatedness of peoples and nonhumans in particular places" but ultimately fall short by limiting relationality and "life" to the organismically defined.[46] In the second, new materialism extends understanding of how both organic and inorganic nonhuman lives "press into and are co-constituted with human lives," emphasizing the vitality of all things in a world of quasi agents and forces.[47] This co-constitution comes close, for TallBear, to Deloria's ethical metaphysics, in which there is a realization that "the world, and all its possible experiences, constitute a social reality, a fabric of life in which everything [has] the possibility of intimate knowing relationships because, ultimately everything is related."[48] Here the issue is the secular nature of the discourse that discounts Indigenous emphases on the co-constitution of the material world and immaterial realms and beings. This immaterial realm is sometimes described as spirit or the sacred, but, referencing David Shorter's important critique of the use of spirituality to define Indigenous practices, TallBear makes clear that material and immaterial beings are all part of the social fabric described by Deloria.[49]

A sense of interrelationality can certainly be seen within Day's images, including relations with petrified monsters, vengeful whirlwinds, smoke for prayer and healing, and coyotes that mourn an old man who has died. Moving to the level of representation, however, requires care in how vitality gets understood beyond the life and nonlife divide, because the move risks reinstating a critical mode based on privileging vitality in a way that can be too easily co-opted. TallBear makes this clear in her critique of new materialism, a discourse that furtively borrows Indigenous perspectives and universalizes and secularizes them as a form of vitalist critique. Such a sense of critique amounts to a disavowal of death, of all that is inert and nonagential, tending toward a flattening ontology that renders representation transparent/inconsequential and equalizes in a manner counter to California Indian interrelations, which can be very particular and have more complex relations to vitality and animacy. Not all rocks are alive, but some are (and some have power and are good for gambling, but some might kill you). To the decisively animist question "Are rocks alive?," the appropriate nonvitalist response is "Which rock?"

Indigenous sociopolitical interrelations do not imbue everything with vitality, which would expand biopower exponentially. Life and death are not managed according to what Elizabeth Povinelli calls a "biontological enclosure," in which "Western ontologies are covert biontologies" and "Western metaphysics [acts] as a measure of all forms of existence by the qualities of one form of existence, [Life]."[50] Like TallBear, Povinelli is concerned with the way these new vitalisms impose the qualities of one of western metaphysics' categories (Life) onto its concept of existence (Being), raising the question: "How does this ascription of the qualities we cherish in one form of existence to all forms of existences reestablish, covertly or overtly, the hierarchy of life?"[51] Instead, the particularity of Indigenous interrelations is part of a distinctly and differentially interested (and oftentimes threatening) world, and the concept of vitality offers little in the way of understanding it or operating within it.

The disruption of the biontological enclosure can also be understood in relation to California Indian conceptions of power, which are not simple and which open up onto a nonvital field. In a number of California Indian frameworks, along with the material and immaterial beings and realms that, according to TallBear, make up the social fabric, there is a third realm generally translated as "luck." Power has two valences, then. There is a positive valence, which humans and other beings can gather and harness, as evidenced by the work of healers, who can use this power for good or bad. In some conceptions, this power is a remnant of the creative energies employed during the formation of the world, which both explains its dissemination into all types of beings and its specific and unequal measures, as this form of power is entropic. But the realm of luck is of another order and is entirely negative in valence in the sense that one cannot control it, curry its favor, or approach it directly: "The natural, reached through luck, is impersonal; it cannot be known or sensed, and it is never addressed; but not so the supernatural."[52] Luck has the effect of bending the very structure of language, which contorts to take on a humility and indirectness in relation to luck. It also bends behaviors, relationships, and the entire world around it and its unknownness, placing an infinite distance through distortion and deformation within interrelation itself. Yet one can play within its purview, which explains the significance of gambling in California Indian cultures (hand game, grass game, walnut dice). Such is the force of enigma, which opens onto the impersonality of catastrophe, as the loss of luck can be catastrophic and is therefore linked to the prophetic.

Charting the Maidu Language

The Maidu language is where Day locates the greatest archive and site of preservation, as it is through language and ultimately song that the world takes form. Day's name for his people, Tay•yee, for instance, means westward, not just in the sense of being located in the West but as a people that tend toward the mystery of the great expanse of the Pacific Ocean, Mon•dow•wi (big waters), where darkness falls and toward which everything leans: sun, moon, land, streams, tall grass, wind, cold.[53] Day's vision (theory, speculation) is, then, westward leaning, conditioned by enigma, both that of the water and that of the earth. In a thirty-minute self-recording made toward the end of his life, Day explains the name Tay•yee, which he links, seemingly haphazardly, to an imperative to never talk fast (as it makes it seem like one is running from something), different types of ground (burial, crying, drying, hunting), the displacement of his people through "legal" means, the disappearance of a world and "the last of the Tay•yee," identity through language, relation between song and story, his encounter with Ishi before Ishi was captured, the importance of a life of study trying to "understand these things," the reason why he paints "pictures" (to encode the Maidu language in images), and how one learns how to sing. What possible connection can there be between these (other than the tape on which they are recorded)? It is too much. And when one finds out that the tape is part of a series of self-recordings that go on for over seventy hours in a similarly meandering style, it is overwhelming.

This excess is perhaps why Day's commentators have largely limited their words to his paintings. Though the paintings are also complex, they seem to hold together more consistently in terms of their content and developing realist style. But Day is clear that he is transmitting information/personhood through his paintings to future generations, and for that reason one must pay attention to the surreptitious and often subterranean networks of connections between what he says and what he shows. What are the elements he is putting into play in each, and how do they resonate with each other? Day was interested in painting not as painting but as a mode of communication (though a problematic and outdated one) that he saw as a visual archiving of the Maidu language: "just translating the language, the Maidu language, and putting it up on a chart. And this shows exactly how the Maidu people had been doing before the coming of the white man." Similarly, the Maidu language for him was encapsulated by individual words and their meanings, which were condensed forms of stories together with an analogy to environmental sounds. Explaining the meaning of a word such as ko•pak, or "deer in a jump trouncing a snake," necessarily leads to an

FIGURE 11. Frank Day, *Deer Protecting Her Fawn*, ca. 1970. Image used for publication by permission of Sage LaPena.

extended, detouring interweaving of story, explanation, and description of the moment a deer jumps on a snake, followed by a song about the event (Figure 11).[54]

The telescoping that Day performs when unpacking Maidu words leads ultimately to "song-stories," which he performs on his recordings: "These songs seem to comprise exactly what the Maidu language is in itself."[55] Further, across the various tapes, Day makes little distinction between biographical details, ethnographic facts, tales of monsters, descriptions of sacred practices, sermonizing, and ethical imperatives, which all blend into each other and are organized into an ensemble around the gravitational pull of the song-story. This is not surprising, considering that most California Indian origin stories begin with the world being sung into being, which places rhythm and resonance at the heart of all things, linking story, sound, and song. Not only was the world sung into being, but words, which derive from the world, were also originally sung: language comes out of singing. What is perhaps surprising is how individualistic these songs can be. Even while everything has its song and there are songs for every action (hand game songs, fishing songs, bubbling acorn soup song, acorn grinding song, hunter song, night songs, doctor songs, different bird songs, bee song, butterfly song, rippling water song, mole song, snake song, snail song, cry song, midnight songs, morning songs, evening songs, fire song, hummingbird song, glowing leaf song, bear song, deer hoof song, gopher song, squirrel song, different dance songs . . . "so numerous"), the economy of songs is based on both the acquisition of personal power and the pedagogical relationship with the world.[56] One learns songs by watching and listening intently, and one gathers songs and makes them one's own for personal luck, protection, power against others, and prestige. There are thus prohibitions on using someone else's song, which Day abides by. But some songs are also about the things other beings have taught Indians, including how to survive, and are sung communally. Some songs are meant to be purely for delight.[57]

In one of his recordings, Day offers up to the listener song as "a foundation that you may build upon for the future."[58] Here he is using song as a way "back to the period of time I'm talking about." This is a precarious path, as songs, according to him, are no longer sung correctly. In a post-vernacular way, they are sung without understanding and under the wrong circumstances, usually without awareness of their origin or who they might belong to, which, Day claims, can lead to one's destruction.[59] While this is a warning, it is not entirely a reproval, as Day also repeatedly talks about the importance of younger generations *just going on ahead*. It is this balance between imminent danger and necessary risk that Day navigates in his own relaying of songs, stories, and information. Careful to ascribe these things to their owners and originators, Day nonetheless "borrows" them and sings them before an unknowable audience, using a recording technology that has been widely understood to efface the kind of authority and presence that Day is asserting.[60] But it is precisely this authority and presence that is at stake.

The complexity of this authority can be heard in another recording, in which Day meditates on the notion of preservation as it relates to California Indian pedagogical relationships with ants.[61] Noting that rosin (pine pitch) acts as a form of congealed darkness, harnessing the forces of the earth in times of imminent danger, he states that it was by watching ants that Indians learned how to preserve food by encasing it in rosin for the purposes of survival. He goes so far as to equate Indians and ants: "We were known as wild Indians. Ants are still wild."

A reference to wildness in an Indigenous context is certainly a risk. Day nonetheless explicitly links the problem of survival to the kinship between his people and ants: the organization of ant mounds mapped onto Kóyo•mkàwi dwellings around the central round house; a tendency toward silent movements; the ant's ability to sense danger, which he links to night singing (a Maidu prophetic tradition); and the use made of the underground for both dwelling and food storage ("[like the ants,] we tried to go beneath the ground"[62]).

It is impossible to parse out cleanly from a series the concepts Day offers in his explanation: dwelling, security, survival, preservation, pedagogy, interrelations of beings and environment, darkness, storm, rosin. The explanation goes on for thirty minutes, weaving these ideas together (the length of the recording tape he was using). Day, however, offers clues as to how to hear these ideas. He structures the explanation around a song-story about "how the ants fit in with the life of a Konkow Indian." Just before singing the song, he makes a distinction between two Maidu words for ant: bo•le•sa, which refers to the ants we are in intimate relation with today, and ne•non, which refers to ants during the time of creation stories. This sense of difference between experience and time immemorial, of beings with whom one socializes and beings whose actions made such sociability possible, conditions the performative reenactment through singing. The time immemorial is neither a belief nor a simple empirical fact; it is the condition for the world. To sing is to hear the ants' song interrelationally, and this song is necessarily one that resonates (with) these very conditions themselves. For Day, the song-story functions as a set of instructions, "like 2 + 2 = 4," linking singing and hearing to the first beings and to the pedagogical relations humans have with the rest of the world. In this sense, how might paint and recording tape act like rosin for the sake of preservation but in a Native pedagogical way? And how can the images inscribed on them be made to carry such resonance?

While expressing urgency, even emergency, about the need for preservation, Day, however, does not demand immediate action or the speeding up of activity. This is because, rather than a call to action, his response to destruction is the imperative to slow down, to take one's time. He gives cautions about the temporality at stake, with perhaps the most poignant example being his repeated assertions of the need to sing gambling songs slowly so that one can sing all throughout the night, as opposed to the sped-up singing that he hears California Indians doing and that he laments. This is a warning offered at the threshold and under the sign of disappearance: *You are about to die. Slow down and make it last. And by so doing, maybe you will outlast death.* It is also a practical suggestion in that California Indian gambling often includes singing as a way to hide patterns from those guessing, and slow singing creates more opacity.

Watching the painted environment, in the same way that Day describes watching ants all day long in order to learn from them, we learn from such intensive watching that we can no longer simply read or view the painting in an art historical or visual cultural sense. We must learn from it how to endure, hearing it as a song-story or singing it in a way that creates opacity. The painting is a complex niche of its own framed in a way that implicates us. It is a vision, certainly, but one brought down to the ground: "Now I want to come down a little bit in altitude to a thousand feet, between a thousand and three thousand feet."[63] Day's own traditional Indigenous knowledge of his tribal homeland encodes and is encoded in the painting in a way akin to how survival from time immemorial encodes and is encoded in the earthwork performed by ants. As Day puts it, "Maybe that was one of our maps."

Painting the Charmed Landscape

Day's theories of language and image, evidenced in the recordings and paintings he produces, rely upon a notion of petrification that contrasts with settler memory. Day archives language with certain terminology that he claims is ancient or original, maps the landscape with the location of petrified monsters, and represents impressions in stones, indexing in exploded form a petroglyph. The petroglyph, as carving in/on stone, already functions in an ambiguous manner, marking the land as Indigenous, communicating a message across time, lying somewhere between image and text, and functioning as a visionary and interrelational space in conversation with the land itself, not just writing on stone but writing stone. Day represents petroglyphs directly in four forms: as preexisting (moving heavily through time), as being made (creating a message), as embodied by figures (which take the form of glyphs, inverting referentiality), and as floating glyphic signifiers abstracted from stone and inscribed in/on the painting or image, like in/on the untitled painting of the deer skinners (Figure 9, which makes every stone a surface of inscription and the painting a stone).

Rather than emphasizing motion, implied, for instance, by Gerald

Vizenor's neologism "pictomyth," a concept inflected with humanist and vitalist natural philosophical tendencies, Day emphasizes in the petroglyph the ambiguity of human or inhuman materialized memory by representing a process of petrification as nonvital and im/mobile preservation. Vizenor would most likely use the term "transmotion" to refer to pictomyths: "The figures painted on stone, on the face of granite, are more fantastic than any representations of natural motion or naturalism."[64] But this distinguishes between natural motion/presence and graphic motion/sense of presence in a way that implies the ability to transmit the essence of motion itself, to carry it across mediations (trans-late) through a privileging of liveliness. The distinction is made emblematic by the difference between Vizenor's descriptions of nature and his sense of the totemic as gesture. From this perspective, reductively, motion is good, stasis is bad.

Day's paintings not only indicate the immobility and permanence of images carved in/on stone but also represent motion in a manner that is distinctly unnatural, such that the very concept of the "natural" implodes. Suspicious whirlwinds; forces that act on bodies in the form of breath, whistling, vision, and the light from the sun; but, most important, the figures who act in the images and take on the graceful, uncanny movements and poses associated with marionettes all represent this unnatural motion.[65] Day describes this awkward gracefulness in terms of the wind, in which "straight wind is a broken up whirlwind," a line that always tends toward a curve.[66] Such is the impression of Day's figures as moving effortlessly and without gravity or center, even as they are at times embroiled in life-and-death struggles, lending them the inhuman effect of an immobility that moves more than any "natural" movement. This sense of unnaturalness represents movement differently outside of the stasis/motion binary. Memory, preservation, and revitalization must then be thought in different terms. What Day preserves is not a vitalist sense of motion but an orientation. This orientation, however, is not entirely intentional and, like marionettes, has an inhuman, nonvital "life" of its own.

Note the left hand of the figure in the painting *E-nom-oe, or Dancing Girl and Whirling Snake* (Figure 12). The dancing woman is pointing at the petrified remains of a large creature that blends into the granite hills in the background or forms out of them. Her head is turned facing the opposite direction, looking out of the frame of the painting. The line of the eye and the line of the index finger form a nearly symmetri-

FIGURE 12. Frank Day, *E-nom-oe* or *Dancing Girl and Whirling Snake*, 1973. Collection of the Shingle Springs Band of Miwok Indians.

cal horizon, yet they immediately break the usual connection between pointing and seeing. Her finger points at the mountainous rock remains of a large creature, and this behind-the-back index of the remains of the immemorial, of a time when gigantic beings roamed the land, as told in stories, is further displaced, as it is not entirely clear by perspective that she is pointing at the remains. Yet she is, as two-dimensionally her finger is almost close enough to touch them, nearly interrupted by the spire of a tree that attempts to recover perspective but fails. *This*, her finger seems to say, *look at this*, or perhaps, *look there*. Yet she is dancing. What are we as viewers to make of this silent gesture, caught in arrested motion?

The dancing woman is both within a landscape and indicating something about that landscape. This seems rather straightforward as a representation of a closed-circuit sign system: landscape as background, woman as figure, index as representation of a sign, rock formation as ground becoming figure through signification. The viewer's gaze is directed by a sign to an image of a rock, which we are told is the remains of a large creature. But this sign lacks the usual force of indexicality for two obvious reasons: the figure pointing is dancing, and she cannot know what she is pointing at. The fact that she is dancing disrupts the force of meaning-making because we cannot be sure that this pose is not a randomly arrested posture. Maidu dance also offers its own symbolic system based in gestures, movements, and postures that have mimetic qualities and interrelational acts. Frank LaPena remarks of Day's painting of a deer dancer, *Toto Dance at Bloomer Hill* (1973):

> In my interpretation of this painting, I see the deer dancer at the primordial time when he begins his dance, moving and dancing steps that create the hills and mountains and valleys that became the natural world with which we are familiar. The vitality of toto (dance) is used to explain this moment of cultural consciousness raised to a time of energy, a time of sparkle and fire. If creation is wonderful and dynamic, then I, as a dancer, would present creation as a dance. I can think of no more wonderful thing to do: every time we dance, we recreate the original moment as a conscious act of renewal.[67]

A strict referential gesture interrupts the performative renewal of an original moment just as much as performativity disrupts the transmission of meaning in a strict representation. Such a complex and suspended indexical function documents in its failure to indicate a charmed landscape in an appropriately California Indian oblique gesture.

The dancing woman is part of an assemblage of more-or-less distinct beings that include the creature/rock formation; a shell or distinct stone of some sort that leaves a trace of movement; "resemblance(s) . . . of a fish, angleworm, deer, high-flying bird, a track, [and] grizzly bear"; a wind snake; sky; and a separated and disjointed landscape of differential colors, textures, dynamics, shading, variably recognizable representations, including hills, forest, and a number of crevices, rifts, and boundaries.[68] The painting represents variable motions and variable states of presence and absence (traces), as well as variable times: is she indicating the creature now or the creature during the time when it was alive? While seeming to privilege the human figure, the painting raises the question of her position within such an unstable landscape. In a literal circle, she is centrally caught in the motion of a whirlwind—in a California Indian epistemology, associated with obscure power—as the wind loses distinction with her own motion of dance, giving one the sense that she is spinning, or the world is spinning about her stillness.

This is a variable world of force and fragility in roughly and beautifully formed fragments.

The indeterminacy of the index proliferates indexicals throughout the image. The impressions in the stone circle can be seen to indicate other beings and worlds in a manner similar to what Elizabeth Povinelli, in the context of the Belyuen Aboriginal community in Australia, describes as "manifesting." Manifestations, for Povinelli, are an indicative dimension of existence that "discloses itself as comment on the coordination, orientation, and obligation of local existents and makes a demand on persons to actively and properly respond."[69] These manifestations present as either unknown or demanding, which, in a California Indian context, means they present either as deformed things, manifesting their nonvitalism through resistance to form and connection to power, or as linkages to another time through a logic of trace. Much of what constitutes human engagement in such interrelations is the ability to interpret these signs, not to understand them in themselves but to understand changes in the overall interrelationality, particularly for Day as warning signs. There is also the possibility in certain situations, as Povinelli describes, "to lure, seduce, and bait a part of the world to reorient itself toward you in order to care for you," and, indeed, in Day's description of *E-nom-oe*, he explains that the woman has come to this place of power to try to have a child.[70]

Indexicality extends to the roundness in the center of the image, which isolates the figure and connects to the roundness of other prominent images in Day's paintings: his series of round houses; his series of burial images, with the dead enclosed in large circular baskets and curled into fetal postures (a nonvital, crosscut vision of the womb); his images of whirlwinds; the central fire. Many of these circles are, of course, well-known aspects of the notion of dwelling.[71] These circles are also openings through which a subterranean vision can be achieved. Dwelling, in this sense, is linked to preservation, as it, like the mapping performed by ants, takes the viewer underground. Day's well-known crosscut image of a roundhouse, read in some cases as the epitome of the ethnographic present, can instead be seen as a map that preserves, bringing the image closer to the notion of manifestation than to the salvage ethnographic image. Subterranean vision has the effect of turning the landscape inside out to show how form, as an organizing principle of reality itself in many California Indian epistemologies, becomes the differential force behind interrelationality.[72] The roundness of the image links to the roundness of the eye and the field of vision, which open up to the nonvital forces of the subterranean, which deform. The manifestation and the circle are the points of indeterminacy between land and figure, raising the entire painting to the level of the index, imploring the viewer to listen attentively with their eyes.

Day emphasizes the indeterminacy of painting with two senses of indexicality: as represented (he represents indexing in the woman who points) and as performed (he himself is indicating with the image). This double aspect of indexicality has three simultaneous functions for Day that cannot be understood through a simple framework of visible/invisible//information/personhood: preserving, referencing, and pointing in the direction of a path. A formal matter, indexicality here is neither purely human (in the mind as perception) nor in the world waiting to be discovered. Neither showing nor hiding, to compound the complexity, because of its interruption in the image (Figure 12), as well as in Day's inappropriate use of painting to document, a broken indexicality opens onto the third realm of interrelationality, which includes the reciprocity between the many different beings Day paints and is based on a California Indian theory of mediated formalism where referential signs and the performative force of sign-making become ambiguous. Interrelational indexicality gives us an idea of how to read the elements Day uses in his paintings in conversation with the material media that transmits them in their colonial context, while these elements and materials point us in the right direction. Interrelational indexicality also places Day's work within the category of re-representation, or the charting of elements from an earlier representation to be conveyed. The world has always been mediated. The Maidu elements Day transmits by paint and tape are the very forces of interrelationality and indexicality *themselves*, which together offer a powerful pathway toward re-revitalization.

The interrupted indexicality of the painting leads to the last and most obscure point regarding this image. There is a direct image of sound represented in the form of a line originating from the wind snake. According to Day, these creatures live between crevices in rocks and trees and come out to dance, whirling, when wind passes through.[73] The most important feature of the ecology of the wind snake, though, is its whistle. The whistle functions as a powerful index, linking it to the discourse on warning and danger in which Day is invested. In fact, most creatures, according to Day, have the ability to whistle in this manner (such as ground squirrels, birds, raccoons, deer, bear, and elk), but the whistle of this snake indexes the mysteries of prophecy, particularly that of Maidu night singing. Night singing is a powerful practice of communal vision that addresses pressing questions that range across the luck involved in hunting; prognostications of danger; the approaching conquest; "sickness in or among the people"; and the ability to dance well. For Day, these different aspects of prophecy are "all enclosed and answered by that little snake whirling around in a circle."

Like the compression of image as language and song, here Day uses the silent image of the sound of the whistle to condense an entire prophetic tradition, connecting the range of manifestations depicted in the image in a complex diagram across which the interrupted indexicality represented *in* the painting and the difficult indexicality *of* the painting itself take on an isomorphism. An exploded mnemotechnology, Day's images and recordings create an atlas of a destroyed world in order to point the viewer in the right direction, like a set of instructions. Yet this is a broken path, raising the question of how broken one needs to be to traverse it. *All the things that I have illustrated here by drawings, paintings, is true because I went to see it. I'm able to take you back to it.*

The Undone Petroglyph

If one can read this in/determinate index as applying to the medium of painting itself, it also raises a number of questions about the efficacy of the image and brings us back to the question of the figurative: Is this a representation of an actual creature (Day's painting of the wind snake and/or the dancing woman's rock creature)? Does it point to a precise geographical location? As evinced by the following narrative about Day by anthropology student Bernard Fontana, what the dancing woman points at, in fact, does exist, though its status is contested: "I drove to Frank's Oroville home and spent a day with him, his young son [Billy], and his wife [Marian]. Frank, his son, and I visited a site in the Plumas National Forest where there was a peculiar (but natural) rock formation which did, indeed, resemble an animal of some kind. Frank told a fairly elaborate story about the monster represented in the formation. Whether it was a traditional Concow tale or a Frank Day original I cannot say with any degree of confidence."[74] The uncertainty that Fontana expresses has to do with Day's reliability as an informant echoing those who questioned Day's trustworthiness. The identity of the rock formation, however, is not in question, as, although it *resembles an animal of some kind*, it is nonetheless definitively *natural*. In other words, the rock formation is in the domain of a hard science, like geology, and not one of a human science like anthropology or even archaeology. And it is certainly not a remainder of the time when such creatures roamed the land. The anthropologist, regarding the petrified remains, reaches the limit of interest in the storied landscape at the line between natural rock formation and the monstrous. He draws a hard distinction between image and reality through a logic of resemblance that upholds western conceptions of truth. The land is already known. Not only has it been mapped geopolitically in a process co-constitutive with the displacement of California Indians, but its processes and effects have been surveyed temporally and spatially through the strict delineation of discourses and what counts as evidence. Further, Indigenous interrelations have already been rendered as belief and therefore are outside of either the sociopolitical realm of humans or the hard scientific realm of nature, moving petrified monsters into the nonsensical. While the rock formation may resemble a large creature of some kind, resemblance is merely accidental, explainable, and, at best, perhaps aesthetic.

During his visit with Day, Fontana took pictures of the head, vertebrae, and paw of the monster that he and Day had hiked up to see.[75] Day painted the monsters, representing them as petrified figures and as he imagined them alive. In his painting *Playful Creatures* (1964), he depicts two of these monsters entangled with each other. Another anthropology student and a collector of Day's art, Lyle Scott, summarizes Day's explanation of the painting:

> This scene is of two large prehistoric creatures playing. The serpent-like creature, with the head of a deer, is called "Hickey." The other creature is called "Hum-hum." By the Maidu language it sets the time of this scene as several thousand years ago. In the trees at the left can be seen a young "Hum-hum." In the foreground is an Indian with a bolo weapon used to hunt game with, but too small to use on these large creatures. The "Hickey" is said still to be found in the Oroville area, while the "Hum-hum" are found only in petrified form.[76]

This painting pits adversaries, one a living species and the other extinct, in a playful contest. It is this vision, of a time when two creatures of gigantic proportions—one now petrified and part of the landscape and the other having receded into rumor and/or hiding—could play freely and in open sight, that Day seeks to preserve in paint. The intertwining of petrification and the hidden with rumor and resemblance in an image of living, wrestling creatures reaches across the divide of time immemorial and the present circumstances of Native peoples surviving under the conditions of settler colonialism and its effacement of our presence. Like the trees around which each creature wraps, used for leverage, this temporal polarity snaps from the tension and we are left to contend with the amorphous, gray wash of an absent/present (unfinished?) ground, over which the coiled, taut duo are precariously poised. A shadow rises in this mist, taking form; a human and a young creature watch the struggle from the other side of a rift in the ground, too small to enter the contest; bands of color radiate out from this empty center eventually making the blue mountains of the Sierra Nevadas, eventually making the pale wash of the horizon and then the darker stratosphere.

Fontana's photographs and Day's vivid, archival paintings stand in direct contrast in terms of their representational techniques, stances toward the truth, modes of transmission, liveness of contents, semiotic-material articulations, and distances from the realities whose absences they indicate. Yet, both do indicate an absent reality. And both offer us a transcendence from the setting in which we are immersed. Yet they each encounter the disaster differently as fact. The ease and seeming immediacy with which Fontana's photographs document the resemblance the stones have to a "fabled" or "invented" creature seeks to efface the trip, the encounter, the storied and politically agonistic landscape, and the other mediations at play. It positions the stones squarely on a virtual and visual map of the Northern California landscape—one pieced together from all the various discourses about the land. From afar, both temporally and spatially, one can always go back to the images in order to indicate where one had been and where and what the stones are. This is a clear and seemingly unproblematic transmission of photographic contents. Whereas, the difficulty Day's paintings have documenting the seemingly same landscape, like the perilous finger of the dancing woman in *E-nom-oe,* pointing ambiguously at ambiguous remains/form, creates a gesture that does double work: pointing toward the represented landscape and pointing away from it toward the very act of mediation itself, toward absence. This is a difficult and hard-won presence. And, yet, Day can still always take us back to it.

Frank LaPena gives a very different interpretation in his narrative of having also gone with Day to see the petrified monsters:

> On one exploration trip done in the spring along with students from D-Q University near Davis [a tribal university that was in operation from 1971–2005], we went into the Bloomer Hill area. After scrambling around the brush all day, sometimes on hands and knees, Frank and I were the only two to show up at the petrified "remains" of a huge snake, about seventy-five feet long. I had brought my dancing gear because we had talked about the possibility of doing a dedication dance at this special place. What was amazing about this whole trip was a chance to see the "animals" Frank had been talking about and painting for so long. Seeing the stone forms confirmed for me both the paintings and the stories about them.[77]

Here, dancing is mapping an interrelational place, recreating the original moment as a conscious act of renewal, and scrambling and crawling are in order to *see.* Such a viewpoint confirmed for LaPena Day's paintings and stories. This because it is part of a materialized interrelational geography.

LaPena takes the reader on his own path of exploration. He describes Day's painting *Petroglyphs,* in which Day "shows a man using petroglyphic figures to create a message" (Figure 13).[78] Because the painting depicts the use of glyphs to create lasting messages and, therefore, issues of variance and permanence in interpretation, it is difficult to get at the meaning of the painting: "Petroglyphs have the ability to capture both the abstract and the prosaic, and the painting conveys this complexity."[79] LaPena emphasizes that what is "conveyed" is the complexity itself, that of being both abstract and prosaic. The conveyance indicates a sort of isomorphic structure between the conveyance performed by the petroglyph and the conveyance performed by a painting representing the making of a petroglyph. What is carried over is enigma, difficulty, even failure to communicate. This transmission is made possible through the conflation of the ordinary with the extraordinary. The cool, bloodless, ordinary act of carving on stone is renewed in its very simplicity, heaviness, and atemporality. The prosaic, outside of any distinction between the ordinary and extraordinary, is thereby preserved. Meaning, then, is not the point for either the petroglyph or the painting. The act of carving the petroglyph, like the less-than-heroic act of painting, is an indexical one that points to the very suspension of meaning itself, not as a simple reference but as what is conveyed and as the form of conveyance.

FIGURE 13. Frank Day, *Indian Carving Petroglyphs*, 1962. Collection of the Museum of Anthropology, California State University, Sacramento.

Rock art is such that one cannot separate the images from the material surface without undoing the petroglyph itself. The particular rocks used seem to be chosen for this reason and therefore must be taken into consideration when discussing the interpretation of the symbols/figures. This is, of course, radically different from the sense of inscription commonly assumed in communication theory for alphabetic language. It is precisely the fungibility and mobility of printing surfaces that gives writing its unique technological force. Rocks, particularly large ones, don't move, and print, in its many forms, doesn't ever really settle down. And yet the materiality of print/language has been mobilized to critique this notion and its assumption of an ever-more-powerful means of transmitting information. For instance, Jacques Derrida famously noted that the term *communication* also refers to the material transmission of a force, such as a shock or tremor.[80] The petroglyph, then, has a distinct role in relating signs to materiality as the glyph tends toward the petro- along a material continuum in a way that implies a near permanence and yet also communicates via the physical force of the earth itself. Citationality, as the material force of dissemination, would lie on one side of a spectrum that includes the petroglyph on the other, as certainly one can cite, and thereby lift, both the transmitted force and meaning from the rock, moving from one medium to the next. And yet the glyph will always tend back toward the site of the rock. Cite and site lie in a complex interrelation in this way across the difference of sound and sight. As Day describes, "I talk my paintings, say them, sing them, and then paint them."

A rock, then, can never simply be a surface of inscription. Image and meaning carry the weight of materiality. Material, as understood in Eurocentric theories, generally says nothing but waits passively for inscription; and when one begins to read or interpret a sign, one is generally lifted away from the material. This is a standard hierarchization that also organizes the relationship between image and language, with one generally subordinating the other. If discourse is dominating the image, then the image falls back into material that conforms to the knowledge-shape that articulates it; and, on the other hand, when the movement is from image to discourse, then the image organizes the materiality of language for its own purposes. This is not the case for Day's paintings and helps us understand the obscure statement that he is simply diagramming the Maidu language in them. It is not a form of linguisticism or linguistic determination, but rather indicates the deep connection between image and sound as mediated across a textural environment rooted in a specific place. The dispersion across Day's paintings of impressions in rock and figures in stone, shows that archaeology, petrified monsters, and petroglyphs meet in a space of textured impression and petrification. When such a transformation or undoing of the figure/ground relationship occurs, placing them on the same haptic plane, the subordinations must shift, and eye and ear enter into new relations according to both material specificity and interrelations with other beings.

Atlas for a Destroyed World

This is to say that Day has produced in his paintings a map of interrelational geography through a hidden petroglyph that dis/re/organizes all of his images, hinted at through his representation of the creation of a petroglyphic message, as described by LaPena. This hidden, undone petroglyph is one that intertwines images, sounds, and materials but, ironically, through the separation of eye and ear produced by other media: paint and recording tape. Day's paintings document this via representations of liminal beings—monsters, petrified remains, impressions—thereby preserving both the separation and the momentum of rearticulation. This is a treacherous map that connects past and future through speculation. The way back is by following this represented and unknown message in stone, and it is marked out along a granular path perilously indicated by the dancing woman's silent, in/determinate gesture. Across the broken index lies the connection of impressions and stone monsters as the force of petrification. As something akin to both salvage ethnography and figurative painting, in their respective destructions, this movement is in conversation with a prior isotopism between language, image, and reality that has been rendered broken, like a language that refers to a world that no longer exists. The in/determination of sign and gesture, rock and creature, shows that Day, like the dancing woman, is doing double work: he strives to reclaim and rigorously rejects this priority by pointing both toward and away from it, indicating the making of a message and the material and being on which it is inscribed. This is a radical suspension of the vitality of the image under catastrophic conditions, the endurance of a dying world in the form of luck that will outlast colonial death.

Conclusion
Bad Writing, Bad Art

The self-published "source book" *The Destruction of the People*, by the pseudonymous collective author, coyote man (most likely Maidu cultural leaders, Tom Epperson and Leland Scott with amateur ethnographer and scribe, Tom Rathbun), was published in 1973 by Brother William Press in Berkeley, California, one year before Robert Heizer's similarly titled and more well-known *The Destruction of California Indians*. Coyote man's book offers a California Indian theory of violence to contest the western liberal humanist one. Part of a grassroots, local history market, this idiosyncratic text, which masquerades as an (auto)ethnography, tells the story of the Destruction but in an ambiguous voice, placing "the white man's story" in the appendix and foregrounding stories of violent encounters between California Indian peoples, told from the perspective of the Maidu. A flawed, convoluted, problematic text that mixes amateurism with authenticity in an undecidable manner, a troubling mix of good and bad ethics, it is nonetheless a "people's book" that was sold at social gatherings and ceremonies for years (though it is now out of print and in limited supply—the persistent problem of the disappearing archive outside of mainstream history and its maintenance). It is bad writing, transcription, or a collage, a mingling of voices that move through origin stories of violence; prophecies of coming destruction; accounts of forced removal; strife and negotiation between different Native peoples, including calculations to pay off the debt of having killed someone from another tribe or family (a fair trade of people, generally; the live for the dead, but also sometimes with beads).[1] As well as a discourse on western violence and genocide.[2] It often lets colonizers off the hook but moves narratively toward an unstable collective of tribes who have negotiated peace among themselves under threat of extermination, emphasizing Indigenous plural politics and sociality through an affect of exhaustion. A tenuous way forward. Read through a prophetic lens, attuned to antisociality and despair (staying with its troubling aspects), it narrates a becoming (anti)social through violence and its mode of relationality and a (re)turn of sorts to an interrelational collective that has anticolonial prophetic undertones. It raises the question of what constitutes "a people," and therefore a people's voice, in terms that refuse consolidation into any sort of nationalism or easy oppositional stance.

With *Indigenous Inhumanities* I have tried to capture something of this intricate and indeterminate voice in its fraught response to the Destruction that continues to affect our people. I have attempted to attend to colonial and imperial violence through a California Indian angle of perception in an interrelational mode or to at least prepare the way for one, to prepare the dance grounds. This was not and should never be an easy task as it is the difficulty of the task—the bad feelings shared in common, the double binds of coloniality against which we bang our heads—that provides a way through, a way to keep going, to outlast the difficulty itself. And yet, as with the stories in *The Destruction of the People* and the figures in Frank Day's paintings, there should also be a certain effortlessness, an absence of the strict morality of labor and its accomplishments with their heavy movements, both internal and external. This worklessness, if and when it is present in *Indigenous Inhumanities,* is meant to engage what coyote man called our people's "complex and subtle system of thought."[3] Difficulty need not mean burden or weight.

The weight here is the burden of the human, its violence and enticements. I have sought to find in the un/work, the theory and praxis, of activists, artists, authors, elders, and ancestors a way outside of this burden, an Indigenous antihumanism, if you will, that orients us in a different, anticolonial direction. For me, this path has been indicated often by aesthetics, its failures and refusals, particularly in its eccentric and anti-institutional mode. An enigmatic violence, this is an aesthetics that is an extension, not a sublimation or expression, of the violence, giving us a way to reorient the Destruction. Miranda's writing of a layered destruction of lesbian intertextuality and the absence of California Indian literature, in turning to the archive that supposedly destroys Indigenous voice, points in such a direction. As does Day's mapping of the forces of the destruction through image and language, in outmoded and dangerous forms of representation understood to possess a certain amount of the neutral, of luck. From my vantage point, both offer us a distinctly

California Indian approach to implementing the inhuman forces of the Destruction against the colonial present.

This is especially true for the hidden/not hidden text that, like a blade of bear grass, weaves throughout this book tying the chapters together, Tommy Pico's *IRL*. In this long poem, Pico engages the impoverishment that is the English language but through excess, through overabundance. Written as a Kumeeyay epic story in the vein of a birdsong cycle but also in the form of an extended text message or social media post, with their vernacular and abbreviations as well as concomitant oversharing, *IRL* mourns the loss of Indigenous language by destroying the limits of poetic form and the boundaries between the literary and the everyday, online life and the "real" world.

Throughout the poem, Teebs, Pico's poetic persona, strains against the limits imposed by a language forced onto him and his people, "the English fucking language with its high beams in my face," a language that is both his, his innermost self, and yet radically foreign, an impersonal personality that perpetually limns the ambiguity of public and private, a conflict that takes the form of complex expressions of rules and boundaries overthrown.[4] Against the control of death employed by the colonizer, Teebs offers information about protocols concerning death and peoples' names by breaking the protocols, appealing to the names of those who have died, because he can't be alone. He puts their names into the poem, giving everything away, just like his email password, because, in a postapocalyptic sense of revelation, and because of anthropology's incessant gaze, *there are no more secrets*. The epic story follows Teebs, moving from boy to boy, chasing Muse, a pulsing light that flits from one person to the next, as unreliable as desire and the incredibly nuanced as well as banal emotions of Teebs, drifting and surging from irritation, loneliness to elation. Like language, sex is also a reflection on genocide, described by Teebs as having one's land crammed full of brawny English men and still being unable to get laid. *Flirting*, Teebs describes to his date how he stares into fires at wakes because so many people on the reservation die; his date's response: "I'm not looking for anything serious." Teebs connects everything in the poem immediately to some amalgamation of the political, epistemological, and ontological. The loss of the name of a god he doesn't believe in is connected directly to his description of growing his poems long as an extension of and replacement for cutting his hair in mourning, a third form of the poem, which slams into, through enjambment, the anticolonial discourse that weaves throughout. In this situation of language, art is never safe or enough: "Art is not very kidneys. / Your dialysis is not very well / composed."

The use of Grindr messages, engagements with pop culture that keep crashing into genocide, the destruction of the distinction between truth and fiction, are due to, as we've seen, what Teebs calls "a dark part inside of me" formed by having a sense of what is lost but having no access to it.[5] This conditions a type of bad writing, as Pico notes in an interview:

> I recently did my birth chart and it basically said I enjoy bending the truth to a certain extent, and that's kind of true because I will stretch the shit out of the truth if it's in service of a punchline. That's kind of all writing is. I don't lie to my friends, I don't lie to my family or other loved ones, but when it comes to writing I see that as the opportunity to chop and screw a lot of things I've learned and thought I knew.[6]

In part this is an intentional lack of commitment to an ethics or politics of clarity that would make what one says or writes easily believable or understandable. As Trinh T. Minh-ha notes, "Clear expression, often equated with correct expression, has long been the criterion set forth in treatises on rhetoric, whose aim was to order discourse so as to persuade."[7] She continues, "The language of Taoism and Zen, for example, which is perfectly accessible but rife with paradox does not qualify as clear (paradox is illogical and nonsensical to many Westerners), for its intent lies outside the realm of persuasion. The same holds true for vernacular speech, which is not acquired through institutions and therefore not repressed by either grammatical rules, technical terms, or key words." And the same can be said for the expression of many Indigenous concepts that have historically been treated as nonsensical, as mere belief, or even as dangerous and diabolical. To take this further, sometimes one *needs to write badly* in order to break through what Mark Rifkin calls settler common sense, which he defines as "the ways the legal and political structures that enable non-native access to Indigenous territories come to be lived as given, as simply the unmarked, generic conditions of possibility for occupancy, association, history, and personhood."[8] The imposition of clarity and disciplinary force of good writing carry around connections to this position in its assumptions of privileged occupancy, a sense of progressive history, as well as the reproduction of a certain organization of the social through subjectivity and personhood. It is a structure of writing that especially affects bad subjects or those who don't live up to the ideals of western humanist literacy, and, in a settler colonial context, places Indigenous people in the complex position to choose between assimilation or exclusion.

This is an issue for evaluation that affects creative forms in general. Eric Michaels, for instance, in speaking about aboriginal art on the international market in the late 1980s, makes the observation that none of the work that is sold is ever designated as "bad," which he quickly and logically asserts also means that none of the work can ever be seen as especially good.[9] More than a problem for just the market, this is an issue that gets to the heart of the problem of aesthetic evaluation and something like cultural authenticity in relation to Indigenous creation. This observation about the resistance of Indigenous art to western, nationalistic, market-oriented evaluations and recognition offers a sense of a different force or perhaps trajectory that Indigenous making presents. In Michaels's analysis of the situation, he quickly eschews the racist and, as he deems it, "vulgar" interpretation that *all aboriginal art is bad*, and yet, he also opts to suspend judgment and refrains from offering any criteria through which to judge aboriginal art.[10] This is a rhetorical move, done because Indigenous making is already the product of too many discourses, the site of too much colonial knowledge production. Rather than being negated or absent, Indigenous creation is overloaded with meaning, has too much presence but of the wrong kind, as do the voices of Indigenous people.

Onondaga and Mi'kmaq artist and scholar Gail Tremblay describes the situation in which "pressures about 'authenticity' and indigenous art tend to be a struggle between outsiders who want indigenous art to be traditional and other outsiders who pressure indigenous artists to make work that is 'universal' and not related to indigenous culture, history, and politics."[11] For Michaels, this leads to a form of negative dialectics as the contradictions presented by the many competing discourses, for instance art or tradition, individual or collective, and so on, have no apparent resolution, and so he sits in the space of ambivalence about the value of the art while indicating the social and political conditions under which the art is produced and to which the art and artists are subjected.[12]

Returning to the observation that Indigenous making seemingly has a nonstick surface in terms of its value, perhaps Indigenous art *is all bad*, not in the sense of aesthetic value but rather in its behavior. One could read this as a kind of refusal or failure inherent to the art work, as well as the work of the artists, in their relation. To see this, it is important to understand the dilemma in which Indigenous creators and work find themselves. Caught between the intentional destruction of "traditional" modes of authority, a term that acts as a corrective to the anthropological evaluation of authenticity, and the inherently political position of being colonized and surviving destruction, Indigenous creators confront a discursive space of meaning that is overflowing with coloniality. In Native California, this issue manifests in both the amazing number of California Indian and other Indigenous creators and their substantial collective body of work, together with the absence of these artists from places of value in dominant discourses. This is in part because they have already been "explained," made known by a knowledge production industry that seeks to wring every little bit of value out of them as possible.

In this sense, as we saw, Miranda's notion and use of story as praxis acts as an inversion that reorders the relations of power, diminishing and redistributing the accumulation of esteem and privilege through knowledge constructs. Stories are not owned; they are acts of relation and collectivity. They invite imagination but not in opposition to the truth. They are situational, elicit critical thought, often operate through ambiguity. Stories are fragments that never stop interacting, sometimes go on for months, and, as in Pico's use of the internet abbreviation for meeting up in real life, IRL, can confuse story with life itself. Stories don't have an absolute end or point, a fact that, as Trinh T. Minh-ha notes, "keeps the mind puzzling."[13]

Story without the weight of literature or art and their heavy infrastructures of value and meaning can then be seen as liberated. The characteristics of writing and story as seen in the works of California Indian artists are freed to be workless through their very badness. This extends to the importance of bad feelings. In discussing the difficulty of writing about difficult emotions in art, Jennifer Doyle provides a profound analysis of how depression functions in the performance art of Payómkawichum and Mexican American artist James Luna as a sort of antihistory.[14] Focusing on Luna's "The History of the Luiseño People (Christmas, La Jolla reservation 1990)" and a 2009 performance of the piece at an event organized by her, Doyle describes Luna's work as engaging in a form of "political depression" that pushes back against the desires of a settler audience to mourn through imperialist nostalgia, to "weep over the bodies it has buried,"[15] in a cathartic manner often associated with theater and performance art. During the performance, Luna performs depression in a living room scene in which he drunkenly calls family members, friends, and an ex on Christmas night, speaking a "depressed talk" to them with a clearly unsettlingly detached and unsatisfyingly forced intimacy. For Doyle, Luna is creating a radical estrangement from the audience who continue to try to enlist him in a romantic fantasy about a traumatic past, to want to hear him speak his trauma sincerely as a type of witnessing, which is a biopolitical, state-oriented project of reconciliatory healing, as described by Dian Million.[16]

This estrangement is heightened, for Doyle, in the 2009 performance, which includes a prelude of Luna and his friends drinking in the parking lot and then a preparatory smudging of the room with sage. During this performance, Luna is more hostile and angry, creating a palpable and then unbearable awkwardness for most of the audience, who begin to leave. As more and more people leave, the demand on those remaining, to bear witness to the exodus, causes even more people to leave. For Doyle, Luna was experimenting with the audience, something that he has done with other performances (see "Take a Picture with a Real Indian," for example). The performance asked audience members to shift from being passive members of an audience to "something more challenging, [to] keeping company with a difficult and drunk man."[17] This highlights the role of depression as "a crisis in affect in which all forms of relationality become unbearable" and asks of the audience what it means to be in relation to a certain political and affective negativity associated with the afterlife of genocide. "Luna does not present history and depression as knowable, as a straight forward narrative of cause and effect (history makes us sad). Nor does he position his work as a compensatory form of healing, in which talking through the historical trauma of settler colonialism will make him and his audiences feel right."[18] Rather, Luna performs a refusal to heal, to seek a whole self and happiness, to adjust, to, at the very least, find some connection with the audience, who are increasingly placed in an awkward situation.

This alienating of the audience is, however, not a critical operation, à la Bertolt Brecht's distancing effect, which focuses on a certain consciousness raising, a rationalization and display of the artifices of theater toward critical judgment and revolutionary consciousness. As I discussed in chapter 5, one of the hallmarks of California Indian refusals of settler discourses and epistemes is the co-opting of destructive western powers to be turned against the settler and other colonial projects, but from a position of weakness. This working with dangerous forces is part of California Indian conceptions of power. In this case, Luna is adopting the forces of alienation and connecting them to the destructive side of the inhuman and its effects, alcoholism, depression and other negative feelings, the spectacle, as well as the impossible settler desire for an origin, which is easily exploitable and the source of much Native humor and poking fun. This is definitively not a critical denaturalization, which would seek to dispel these effects toward some sort of liberated reconciliation, but rather a roll of the dice, playing with forbidden affects and materials. It is a much more humble endeavor while also being much more profound. Doyle puns that Luna's performance is "moving" in that it moves the audience to leave, which I think is precisely the point. The dream of the performance is the disappearing audience. And we know that Luna, in his most well-known performance/installation, "The Artifact Piece (1987)," which he sedated himself for, has trafficked with the dead, work that continued with his engagement with Ishi's photographic archive in "Ishi: The Archive Performance" (2016). Luna initially draws the audience in with the promise of fulfillment where only a violent lack exists, drawing them into a void. By playing on the ir/reality of the savage, with various technologies and their attempts to tame these powers through rationality, such as estrangement, Luna is seeking to make the audience disappear into their own in/security, into their lack of risk in the encounter. And into their tepid western humanism and aesthetics.

At bottom, this is the question of/for California Indian art. How does it engage what David Lloyd calls the "lure of western aesthetics," the formation of subjects of the state through an aesthetic project that "performs its ideological function through its claim to compensate for the fragmentation of humans by the division of labor and social conflicts with an exemplary experience of wholeness and harmonization"?[19] I would argue that it does so with a distinctly California Indian strategy of turning the lure back on itself, weaponizing the fragmentation of the "human," the very forces of the inhuman, according to a California Indian conception of power and for anticolonial purposes. This is a movement that calls the very project of western art into question. There is a fundamental ambivalence in western aesthetics where this struggle takes place. In it, literature and art maintain the separation necessary for development to occur by holding the western division between art and knowledge, and between the human and nature, stable along disciplinary lines and providing opportunity for the pedagogical project of making human, making subjects of the state (with severe repercussions for education). And yet, this relation between aesthetics and knowledge also becomes the site for anticolonial struggle and refusal, as the emphasis on the empirical and its rejection are merely two sides of western humanism. Lloyd makes clear that the racial-colonial foundations of western aesthetic philosophy offer up the promise of a certain liberation, a form of freedom that both undergirds western liberal conceptions, including those legally enshrined, and imposes a "regime of representation" that creates differential determinations of humanity based on proximity to this concept of freedom and distance from a "natural" state of necessity, in effect the savage.[20] This is a historical movement of development from a state of nature to a humanized order of freedom that produces an immanently racial schema. Again, the distinction between the savage and the Native functions as the engine of progress, as the "threshold that divides the Savage into the latent or protohuman and the outcast, the latter being discarded to the realm of mere affectability."[21]

Luna didn't seek to correct this racial-colonial error but to weaponize it by turning it toward a more fundamental movement of error. In the struggle over the inhuman, what else would an anticolonial position look like? In doing so, he acknowledges and refuses the profound fact that the western conception of art is connected intimately to its conception of critique in which, as described by Lloyd, "art cancels and preserves its magical antecedent" in a movement away from necessity toward liberation that "preserves and opposes the irrational moment of rationality itself." Akin to Bracken's concept of the savage philosopher, art becomes for Lloyd, citing Theodor Adorno, a "deinstrumentalized magic" that "generates the historical from the threshold condition of prehistory by inaugurating the development of the human out of the Savage through reflective representation."[22] In part, this explains the dual projects of anthropology and history and their interests in the savage and the native, respectively. Together, through preservation and critical reform, they create an abstraction of the savage/native into both a conception of aesthetics that guarantees their "scientific" projects and a notion of radical critique they differentially employ toward their own institutionalization (anthropology is much more "critical" in this sense) while simultaneously "liquidating" actual Indigenous peoples' ways of thinking and living by circumscribing them to the realm of belief or depoliticized culture in a genocidal logic of developmental humanization. One can begin to understand, then, the double bind that Luna was confronted with in engaging art practice. Following Luna and other California Indian artists, confronting this double bind is what *Indigenous Inhumanities* has sought to do.

> I can't sing the part in
> that Beyoncé song at
> karaoke where the music
> gets all soft and I try
> to croon *ooh baby, kiss me*-
> Maud has to take
> the mic be the feeling gets
> bigger than my voice n
> the feeling I think it's her My God
> 's shadow walking down a hall-
> way away but like I said I
> lost my voice n don't know
> her name Maybe it's
> Wa'ashi or Pemu,
> says this clairaudient
> to me apropos of nothing
> But I'll never know 4
> sure So I can't call after her
> n then I'm like, crying
> at a Beyoncé song
> *r u kidding me Teebs get*
> *it together bitch* My dad grows
> his hair long Black waves
> cascade down his back Bc knives
> crop the ceremony of his
> grandfather's hair at the NDN boarding school
> I cut mine in mourning
> for the old life but I grow
> my poems long. A dark
> reminder on white pages.
> A new ceremony. I grab
> the mic back from

Maud Flip for a new song to
flash across the karaoke
screen Fist breath low

n ready James
is finally following me
back on Insta so I take a
somewhat *risque*
selfie send it DM
n right after message
OOOPS! omg I
meant to send that
to someone else gosh
so embarrassed oops!
He responds w/
a pic of his computer
screen His phone #
on it so we
text n he's like
come over n I'm like
do u have A/C he says
Yes n I just straight up drop the mic
n Leave.[23]

In the end, we're punk first.

—Dead Pioneers

Acknowledgments

I owe an infinite debt that I can never repay to my teachers and mentors, past and present: Trinh T. Minh-ha, Judith Butler, Tom Biolsi, Michael Wintroub, Samera Esmeir, Kehaulani Kauanui, Lisa Lowe, Michelle Raheja, and Mishuana Goeman. I especially want to thank my mentor David Lloyd, whose own work and attention to this book has marked it indelibly. I'd also like to thank the many others who have taken time with me and my work in both big and small ways: Audra Simpson, Sarita See, Tammy Ho, Sherryl Vint, Jennifer Doyle, Dylan Rodríguez, Jason Weems, Kat Whiteley, Cj Jackson, Amrah Salomón, Hannah Appel, Nancy Marie Mithlo, David Shorter, Jessica Cattelino, Clare Counihan, Rana Barakat, Terri Castaneda, Sigrid Benson, Carlos Dimas, Long Bui, Laura Grappo, Matthew Garrett, Patricia R. Hill, Joel Pfister, Mark Slobin, Kris Manjapra, Kamran Rastegar, Khury Petersen-Smith, Anna Cruz, Nidhi Mahajan, Alexandra Chreiteh, Tom Abowd, Kareem Khubchandani, Alex Blanchette, and Matt Hooley, to name a few.

I'd like to thank my former writing crew: Hyaesin Yoon, Keerthi Potluri, and Katherine Brewer Ball. I miss our collaborations.

I am deeply grateful to the CISSA collective, especially Katie Keliiaa, Cutcha Risling Baldy, Vanessa Esquivido, Melissa Leal, Annette Reed, Stephanie Lumsden, Brittani Orona, Kat Whiteley, Bayley Marquez, and Olivia Chilcote. I have developed this book alongside our project to reorient California Indian studies for our communities.

I am delighted to be part of such a supportive, brilliant, and committed group of colleagues in the English Department at UCR and am grateful to our faculty and staff. I am also very appreciative of my other UCR colleagues, especially my collaborations with the Memory and Resistance Lab (Latipa and Crystal Baik) and the support I have received from the California Center for Native Nations (CCNN), the Performing Difference and Reclamation and Native American Communities Faculty Commons groups, the Center for Ideas and Society, and the Costo Chair of American Indian Affairs.

I am indebted to the many students who I have taught and discussed these ideas with over the years. I have learned as much if not more from them as the other way around.

This book has benefited from presentations at or support and interest by the following organizations: the Native American and Indigenous Studies Association (NAISA); the American Studies Association (ASA); the Native American Cultural Center at Yale University; the Wong Forum on Art and the Immigrant Experience; American Indian Studies at California State University Long Beach; Alberta University of the Arts; the Consortium of Studies in Race, Colonialism, and Diaspora at Tufts; Indigenous Choreographers at Riverside; the Palestinian American Research Center (PARC); the Association for Study of the Arts of the Present (ASAP); the Association for Study of Literature and the Environment (ASLE); the Shingle Springs Band of Miwok Indians; San Diego State American Indian Studies Department; the International Consortium of Critical Theory Programs (ICCTP); the UC Retreat on Experiments in Critical Theory; the Pembroke Center at Brown University; and the UCLA American Indian Studies Center.

I want to thank the authors, artists, their relatives, and the institutions that have given me permission to reproduce the work that I discuss in this book, which would be nothing without it: Marie-Elise (Mimi) Wheatwind on behalf of Janice Gould, Gregg Deal (and Dead Pioneers), Karen Murphy on behalf of Rick Bartow, Rebecca J. Dobkins, Sage Lapena on behalf of Frank LaPena, Crocker Art Museum, Shingle Springs Band of Miwok Indians, and the Museum of Anthropology at the California State University Sacramento. Thanks to the *NAIS Journal* for allowing me to reprint my article "Atlas for a Destroyed World: Frank Day's Painting as Work of Nonvital Revitalization."

Deborah Miranda, I owe you a special debt as I couldn't have done this work without your example and without your words.

Janice Gould chaired a panel I organized for the NAISA conference in Los Angeles in 2018 where I delivered a paper that became the first draft of chapter 3. Janice was incredibly generous with her time and wisdom. Through our email communications leading up to and after the conference, she offered suggestions for thinking about how to approach the discourse on genocide from a California Indian and especially artistic perspective. She also expressed support for holding, and interest in attending, a gathering of California Indian scholars, artists, and cultural workers that I was considering organizing, which would later become the initial meeting of CISSA. I only later found out she was battling cancer at the time. Janice passed on June 28, 2019.

Frank LaPena was the dance captain for the Maidu Dancers and Traditionalists who led the Bear Dance that I attended while growing up. We had a number of conversations about Frank Day and his work while I was working on the article that became chapter 5. Frank LaPena's work and vision have deeply influenced the writing of this book.

I am grateful to the other authors, artists, and cultural bearers (theorists one and all) whose work I discuss in the book: James Luna, Gerald Vizenor, Dugan Aguilar, L. Frank, Tommy Pico, Beth Piatote, Tom Epperson, Leland Scott, and Lucy Young. I also admire the Ghost Dancers for your bravery and infinite commitment.

Thanks so much to the University of Minnesota Press for publishing my work and to everyone who worked on it, especially Jason Weidemann, Robert Warrior, Zenyse Miller, and the anonymous readers for your attention to it. It is an honor to have it be among the amazing collection of books in the Indigenous Americas series.

I am deeply appreciative for the support I received from the Andrew W. Mellon Postdoctoral Fellowship in Native American Studies and everyone at the Center for the Americas at Wesleyan University; the Mellon Sawyer Postdoctoral Fellowship and everyone at the Center for the Humanities at Tufts; the Hellman Foundation; the University of California Humanities Research Institute; and UCLA's Institute for American Cultures.

Susanville Indian Rancheria, thank you for your support.

Camaraderie and comradeship with Hannah Appel and James Crosby, as well as our shared childcare duties during the beginning of the pandemic, have given much to this book. Whiskey Wednesdays with James and our discussions of art, politics, and life are woven into its sociality.

Susan Campbell (Mom) has been an important guiding star, in her work as a cultural bearer and in the random phone calls from me when I was trying to track down some information. There's no better archivist than an Indian mom.

Rocelyn de Leon-Minch and Mikaela Ysabel de Leon-Minch, what I owe you is too great to comprehend; our endless and boundless love and care have made so much more than just this book possible. Through you I see the stirrings of another world.

To the Ancestors. This book is for you.

Notes

Prologue

1. Cora Du Bois, *1870 Ghost Dance* (Lincoln: University of Nebraska Press, 2007), 26, 10.
2. Du Bois, *1870 Ghost Dance*, 15.
3. Du Bois, 26.
4. Du Bois, 16.
5. Du Bois, 13.
6. Du Bois, 10.
7. "The Ghost Dance challenged industrialization in California. A Wintu and Yana man named Norelputus adapted the Ghost Dance into the Earth Lodge Religion, whereby dancing in subterranean houses protected participants from the end of the world. Near Grindstone, a Pomo prophet named Santiago McDaniel heard the Earth Lodge Religion. McDaniel may have been an indentured servant [slave] as a young boy, but he was reclaimed by his community. After hearing the Ghost Dance, McDaniel traveled throughout Mendocino County, preaching the message," and "McDaniel made labor and economic relations central to the message be brought to the reservation. . . . Indigenous People carried these hopeful messages to workplaces during the following decades" (Damon B. Akins and William J. Bauer, *We Are the Land: A History of Native California* [Berkeley: University of California Press, 2022], e172–73, 173–74).
8. Du Bois, *1870 Ghost Dance*, 20.
9. Du Bois, 19.
10. Du Bois, 20.
11. Du Bois, 24.
12. Du Bois, 25.
13. Du Bois, 15.
14. Trinh T. Minh-ha, *Elsewhere, Within Here: Immigration, Refugeeism and the Boundary Event* (New York: Routledge, 2010).
15. Du Bois, *1870 Ghost Dance*, 17.
16. Du Bois, 9.
17. Du Bois, 20.
18. Du Bois, 16.
19. Du Bois, 17.
20. William Shipley, *Maidu Indian Myths and Stories of Hanc'ibyjim* (Berkeley, Calif.: Heyday Books, 1991), 50–52.
21. Du Bois, *1870 Ghost Dance*, 22.
22. From Maurice Blanchot's *The Space of Literature*, trans. Ann Smock

(Lincoln: University of Nebraska Press, 1982): "One does not proceed from day to night. Whoever follows this route finds only sleep—sleep which ends the day but in order to make the next day possible; sleep which is the downward bending that verifies the rising curve; sleep which is, granted, a lack, a silence, but one imbued with intentions and through which duties, goals, and real action speak for us. In this sense the dream is closer than sleep to the nocturnal region. If day survives itself in the night, if it exceeds its term, if it becomes that which cannot be interrupted, then already it is no longer the day. It is the uninterrupted and the incessant. Notwithstanding events that seem to belong to time, and even though it is peopled with beings that seem to be those of the world, this interminable 'day' is the approach of time's absence, the threat of the outside where the world lacks" (267).

23. Du Bois, *1870 Ghost Dance*, 17.

24. Du Bois, 24.

25. Du Bois, 25.

26. Du Bois, 23.

27. Du Bois, 10.

28. Du Bois, 11.

29. Du Bois, 9.

30. Du Bois, 15.

31. Du Bois, 6.

32. Du Bois, 20.

33. Du Bois, 10.

34. Du Bois, 10. I am riffing on Fred Moten and Stefano Harney's concept of the surround: "In films like *Drums Along the Mohawk* (1939) or *Shaka Zulu* (1987), the settler is portrayed as surrounded by 'natives,' inverting, in Parenti's view, the role of aggressor so that colonialism is made to look like self-defense. Indeed, aggression and self-defense are reversed in these movies, but the image of a surrounded fort is not false. Instead, the false image is what emerges when a critique of militarised life is predicated on the forgetting of the life that surrounds it. The fort really was surrounded, is besieged by what still surrounds it, the common beyond and beneath—before and before—enclosure." *The Undercommons: Fugitive Planning & Black Study* (Wivenhoe: Minor Compositions, 2013), 17.

35. Damon B. Akins and William J. Bauer Jr., *We Are the Land: A History of Native California* (Oakland: University of California Press, 2021), e172–73.

36. Elizabeth Povinelli, *Geontologies: A Requiem to Late Liberalism* (Durham, N.C.: Duke University Press, 2016), e12, https://doi.org/10.1215/9780822373810.

37. Cutcha Risling Blady, "Why I Teach 'The Walking Dead' in My Native Studies Classes," Nerds of Color, April 24, 2014, https://thenerdsofcolor.org/2014/04/24/why-i-teach-the-walking-dead-in-my-native-studies-classes/.

38. Tommy Pico, *IRL* (Austin: Birds, 2016).

39. Abigail Boggs and Nick Mitchell, "Critical University Studies and the Crisis of Consensus," *Feminist Studies* 44, no. 2 (2018): 435.

40. On aesthetic humanism, see David Lloyd, *Under Representation: The Racial Regime of Aesthetics* (New York: Fordham University Press, 2019).

41. Fred Moten, "Blackness and Nothingness (Mysticism in the Flesh)," *South Atlantic Quarterly* 112, no. 4 (2013): 740.

42. Franz Fanon, *The Wretched of the Earth,* trans. Constance Farrington (New York: Grove Press, 1993), 93.

43. Dead Pioneers, "Bad Indian," released November 18, 2021, Bandcamp, https://deadpioneers.bandcamp.com/track/bad-indian-single.

44. Lowell Bean, "Power and Its Applications in Native California," *Journal of California Anthropology* 2, no. 1 (1975): 25–33.

45. This is an adaptation of Paul Celan's configuration of the "angle of reflection" from which the poet speaks who reflects their existence and physical nature in their language that becomes shape and presence. He writes, "The poem holds its ground, if you will permit yet another extreme formulation, the poem holds its ground on its own margin. In order to endure, it constantly calls and pulls itself back from an 'already-no-more' into a 'still-here.'" This "still-here" is the strangeness of the edge of nonexistence. Paul Celan, "The Meridian," in *Collected Prose,* trans. Rosemarie Waldrop (New York: Routledge, 2003), 49.

46. Jonathan Lear, *Radical Hope: Ethics in the Face of Cultural Devastation* (Cambridge, Mass.: Harvard University Press, 2006).

47. Blanchot, *The Space of Literature,* 103.

48. Deborah Miranda, "'They Were Tough Those Old Women Before Us': The Power of Gossip in Isabel Meadows's Narratives," *Biography* 39, no. 3 (2016): 375.

49. Miranda, "'They Were Tough,'" 379.

50. Fanon, *Wretched of the Earth,* 14.

51. Miranda, "'They Were Tough,'" 380.

52. David Hearst Thomas, *Skull Wars: Kennewick Man, Archaeology, and the Battle for Native American Identity* (New York: Basic Books, 2000), xvi–xvii.

53. Deborah Miranda, *Bad Indians: A Tribal Memoir* (Berkeley, Calif.: Heyday Books, 2013), e40–42.

54. See Jodi Byrd et al., "Rage, Indigenous Feminisms, and the Politics of Survival," *Signs: Journal of Women in Culture and Society* 46, no. 4 (2021): 1057–71.

55. Sandy Grande, "Refusing the University," in *Toward What Justice,* ed. Eve Tuck and K. Wayne Yang (New York: Routledge, 2018), 61.

56. Epeli Hau'ofa, "Our Sea of Islands" *The Contemporary Pacific* 6, no. 1 (1994): 147–61.

57. Jaime de Angulo, *Indians in Overalls* (San Francisco: City Lights Books, 1950/1990); Dorothy Lee, "Linguistic Reflections of Wintu Thought," *International Journal of American Linguistics* 10, no. 4 (1944): 181–97.

58. Jack Halberstam, *The Queer Art of Failure* (Durham, N.C.: Duke University Press, 2011), 3.

59. Halberstam, *Queer Art,* 2.

60. Halberstam, 5.

61. Moten and Harney, *Undercommons,* 74.

62. Jodi Byrd, "'in the city of blinding lights': Indigeneity, Cultural Studies, and the Errants of Colonial Nostalgia," *Cultural Studies Review* 15, no. 2 (2009): 19.

63. Byrd, "'in the city of blinding lights,'" 26.

64. Jodi Byrd, "Still Waiting for the 'Post' to Arrive: Elizabeth Cook-Lynn and the Imponderables of American Indian Postcoloniality," *Wicazo Sa Review* 31, no. 1 (2016): 75–89.

65. Note the significance of earth lodges.

66. Glen Sean Coulthard, *Red Skin, White Masks: Rejecting the Colonial Politics of Recognition* (Minneapolis: University of Minnesota Press, 2014), 13.

67. William J. Bauer, *California Through Native Eyes: Reclaiming History* (Seattle: University of Washington Press, 2016), 135; Akins and Bauer, *We Are the Land*, 154.

68. Michelle Raheja, *Reservation Reelism: Redfacing, Visual Sovereignty, and Representations of Native Americans in Film* (Lincoln: University of Nebraska Press, 2010), 180.

69. On the killing of doctors, see Robert Heizer, *They Were Only Diggers: A Collection of Articles from California Newspapers, 1851–1866, on Indian and White Relations* (Ramona: Ballena Press, 1974), 113–14. On the killing of mixed-race children and dogs, see Du Bois, *1870 Ghost Dance*, 7, 20, 22. On killing Joyas, see Deborah Miranda, "Extermination of the Joyas: Gendercide in Spanish California," *GLQ: A Journal of Lesbian and Gay Studies* 16, no. 1–2 (2010): 259.

70. Nick Estes, *Our History Is the Future: Standing Rock versus the Dakota Access Pipeline, and the Long Tradition of Indigenous Resistance* (London: Verso, 2019).

71. Estes, *Our History*, e166.

72. Estes, e165.

73. Dian Million, "There Is a River in Me: Theory from Life," in *Theorizing Native Studies*, ed. by Audra Simpson and Andrea Smith (Durham, N.C.: Duke University Press, 2014), 32.

74. Moten, "Blackness and Nothingness," 746.

75. Dian Million, *Therapeutic Nations: Healing in an Age of Indigenous Human Rights* (Tucson: University of Arizona Press, 2013), 57.

76. Estes, *Our History*, e166.

77. Dian Million, "Intense Dreaming: Theories, Narratives, and Our Search for Home," *The American Indian Quarterly* 35, no. 3 (2011): 321.

78. Estes, *Our History*, e166.

79. See Marcel Mauss, *The Gift: The Form and Reason for Exchange in Archaic Societies* (London: Routledge, 1990); Pierre Clastres, *Society Against the State* (New York: Urzone, 1987); and Georges Bataille, *The Accursed Share: An Essay on General Economy*, Vol. 1: *Consumption*, trans. Robert Hurley (Brooklyn: Zone Books, 1991), for a few examples of such "borrowing."

80. Estes, *Our History*, e169.

81. Estes, e167.

82. Estes, e168.

83. Elizabeth Povinelli, "Governance of the Prior," *Interventions: International Journal of Postcolonial Studies* 13, no. 1 (2011): 13–30.

84. Robert Nichols, "Theft Is Property! The Recursive Logic of Dispossession," *Political Theory* 46, no. 1 (2017): 3–28.

85. Patrick Wolfe, "Settler Colonialism and the Elimination of the Native," *Journal of Genocide Research* 8, no. 4 (2006): 392.

86. Walter Benjamin, "Critique of Violence," in *Walter Benjamin Reflections: Essays, Aphorisms, Autobiographical Writings*, ed. Peter Demetz, trans. Edmund Jephcott (New York: Schocken Books, 1986). The police, in this sense, can only ever function in a genocidal manner as they, as Benjamin describes, simultaneously preserve and make in the moment the law's violence. And the law will always be willing to enact extreme forms of violence to preserve and extend itself.

87. A project that has never ended, as made clear by the contemporary evangelical political movement in the United States, one that echoes the Zionist movement in Israel and supports it.

88. Fanon, quoted in Coulthard, *Red Skin, White Masks*, 141.

89. Moten, "Blackness and Nothingness," 739.

90. Moten, 776; my italics.

91. Jack Halberstam, "To the Wild Beyond: With and for the Undercommons" [introduction], in *The Undercommons*, 8.

92. Moten, quoted in Halberstam, "To the Wild Beyond," 8.

93. Moten, "Blackness and Nothingness," 737.

94. Estes, *Our History*, e167.

Introduction

1. Audra Simpson, "On Ethnographic Refusal: Indigeneity, 'Voice' and Colonial Citizenship," *Junctures: The Journal for Thematic Dialogue* 9 (2007): 67. See also her *Mohawk Interruptus: Political Life across the Borders of Settler States* (Durham, N.C.: Duke University Press, 2014).

2. Simpson, "On Ethnographic Refusal," 69.

3. Simpson, 69.

4. Simpson, 69.

5. Simpson, 75.

6. Simpson, 74.

7. Simpson, 70.

8. Simpson, 74.

9. Audra Simpson, "The Ruse of Consent and the Anatomy of 'Refusal': Cases from Indigenous North America and Australia," *Postcolonial Studies* 20, no. 1 (2017): 20.

10. Gilberto Rosas, *Barrio Libre: Criminalizing States and Delinquent Refusals of the New Frontier* (Durham, N.C.: Duke University Press, 2012).

11. Simpson, "The Ruse of Consent," 27–28.

12. Simpson, 27.

13. Trinh T. Minh-ha, *Elsewhere, Within Here: Immigration, Refugeeism and the Boundary Event* (New York: Routledge, 2010), 48.

14. Fred Moten and Stefano Harney, *The Undercommons: Fugitive Planning & Black Study.* (Wivenhoe, Eng.: Minor Compositions, 2013), 96, 98.

15. Moten and Harney, *The Undercommons*, 124.

16. Walter Benjamin, "Critique of Violence," in *Walter Benjamin Reflections: Essays, Aphorisms, Autobiographical Writings*, ed. Peter Demetz and trans. Edmund Jephcott (New York: Schocken, 1986), 290, 291–92. "When this nationalist reformist movement, often a caricature of trade unionism, decides to act, it does so using extremely peaceful methods: organizing work stoppages in the few factories located in the towns, mass demonstrations to cheer a leader, and a boycott of the buses or imported commodities. All these methods not only put pressure on the colonial authorities but also allow people to let off steam." Fanon, *Wretched*, 27–28; "This tendency of law [to prohibit the use of wholly nonviolent means] has also played a part in the concession of the right to strike, which contradicts the interest of the state. It grants this right because it forestalls violent actions the state is afraid to oppose." "While the first form of interruption of work is violent [the limited labor strike] since it causes only an external modification of labor conditions, the second, as a pure means, is nonviolent. For it takes place not in readiness to resume work following external concessions and this or that modification to working conditions, but in the determination to resume only a wholly transformed work, no longer enforced by the state, an upheaval that this kind of strike not so much causes as consummates."

17. Trinh T. Minh-ha, *Woman, Native, Other: Writing Postcoloniality and Feminism* (Bloomington: Indiana University Press, 1990), 7, 47, 127.

18. Vine Deloria, "American Indian Metaphysics," in *Power and Place: Indian Education in America*, ed. Vine Deloria and Daniel R. Wildcat (Golden, Col.: Fulcrum Publishing, 2001), 2.

19. Vanessa Watts, "Indigenous Place-Thought & Agency amongst Humans and Non-Humans (First Woman and Sky Woman Go on a European World Tour!)," *Decolonization: Indigeneity, Education & Society* 2, no. 1 (2013): 27.

20. Watts, "Indigenous Place-Thought," 21.

21. Watts, 21.

22. Watts, 23.

23. Marisol de la Cadena, "Indigenous Cosmopolitics in the Andes: Conceptual Reflections beyond 'Politics,'" *Cultural Anthropology* 25, no. 2 (2010): 355.

24. Christopher Bracken, *Magical Criticism: The Recourse of Savage Philosophy* (Chicago: University of Chicago Press, 2007), 2.

25. Bracken, *Magical Criticism*, 7.

26. Bracken, 7.

27. Jodi Byrd, *The Transit of Empire: Indigenous Critiques of Colonialism* (Minneapolis: University of Minnesota Press, 2011), 19.

28. Byrd, *Transit*, 17.

29. Byrd, 9.

30. Byrd, 10.

31. Bruno Latour, *We Have Never Been Modern*, trans. Catherine Porter (Cambridge, Mass.: Harvard University Press, 1993).

32. Jane Bennett, *Vibrant Matter: A Political Ecology of Things* (Durham, N.C.: Duke University Press, 2010).

33. Eduardo Viveiros de Castro, *Cannibal Metaphysics: For a Post-Structural Anthropology*, trans. Peter Skafish (Minneapolis: Univocal Publishing, 2009/2014).

34. De Castro, *Cannibal Metaphysics*, 47.

35. De Castro, 47.

36. De Castro, 48.

37. See, for example, James Clifford's introduction "Partial Truths" to James Clifford and George E. Marcus, *Writing Culture: The Poetics and Politics of Ethnography* (Berkeley: University of California Press, 1986). In it, he discusses the resuscitation of anthropology that is, referencing Rodney Needham, facing its intellectual disintegration and redistribution into neighboring disciplines. As a last resort, anthropology turns to a reinvestment in a renewed ethnographical practice as a bulwark against its disappearance in "an iridescent metamorphosis." The new ethnographic field at the time sought to perform the voice of the Indigenous subject but at the very least invested itself with the plural energy of Indigenous thought and ways of being, anticipating de Castro's argument that does away with the ethical consideration of representational tact for which Clifford, Marcus, and the authors in the collection argue.

38. De Castro, *Cannibal Metaphysics*, 48, my italics.

39. Vanessa Watts, "Indigenous Place-Thought," 29. Watts notes Stacy Alaimo's discussion of the agency of dirt as an example: "In this relationship with dirt, humans are responsible to land the way an owner might be responsible for a pet," as Alaimo describes dirt as "something worthy of proper care and feeding."

40. Byrd, *Transit*, 16.

41. Byrd, 17.

42. Mark Minch-de Leon, "Race and the Limitations of 'the Human,'" in *After the Human: Culture, Theory, and Criticism in the 21st Century*, ed. Sherryl Vint (Cambridge: Cambridge University Press, 2020), 206–19.

43. Tiffany Lethabo King, "Where We Intend to Meet after the 'Turn,'" in "*The Black Shoals* Dossier," Tiffany Lethabo King, Stephanie Latty, Stephanie Lumsden, Karyn Recollet, and Megan Scribe, and ed. Beenash Jafri, *Lateral* 12, no. 1 (2023), https://csalateral.org/issue/12-1/black-shoals-dossier/; Deborah Miranda, *Bad Indians: A Tribal Memoir* (Berkeley: Heyday Books, 2013), 203.

44. Tiffany Lethabo King, "Where We Intend to Meet." See also King, *The Black Shoals: Offshore Formations of Black and Native Studies* (Durham, N.C.: Duke University Press, 2019).

45. King, "Where We Intend to Meet."

46. Tiffany Lethabo King, "Humans Involved: Lurking in the Lines of Posthumanist Flight," *Journal of Critical Ethnic Studies* 3, no. 1 (2017): 180.

47. King, "Humans Involved," 180.

48. A comment made during the Otherwise Worlds conference, referenced in Tiffany Lethabo King et al., eds., *Otherwise Worlds: Against Settler-Colonialism and Anti-Blackness* (Durham, N.C.: Duke University Press, 2020), 6.

49. Against Womack, Pulitano argued instead for a superior hybridity that

was (no surprise) less exclusionary of non-Native viewpoints and more reconciliatory; in this sense, her book breaks down to an evaluation of good and bad Indigenous theorists, not qualitatively but based on how they relate to her intellectual agenda. Warrior argued against the hegemony of the western canon as colonial tool, the progressive historical narrative of the novel as cultural achievement, and the "preoccupations of literary studies" with the cutting edge of theory.

50. King, "Humans Involved," 164–65.

51. King, 164–65.

52. King, 163.

53. King, 178.

54. King, 165.

55. King, 165–66.

56. King, 166.

57. Lisa Lowe, *The Intimacies of Four Continents* (Durham, N.C.: Duke University Press, 2015).

58. Fanon, *Wretched*, 57.

59. Peter Burnett, "State of the State Address," delivered January 6, 1851.

60. Lowe, *Intimacies.*

61. Saidiya Hartman, "Venus in Two Acts," *Small Axe* 26 (2008): 2.

62. Hartman, "Venus," 10.

63. Hartman, 13.

64. Hartman, 13.

65. Hartman, 14.

66. Eve Kosofsky Sedgwick, *Touching Feeling: Affect, Pedagogy, Performativity* (Durham, N.C.: Duke University Press, 2003).

67. Byrd writes, "Deleuze and Guattari re/deterritorialize America as the world, coming full circle to find its west in its east and its east in its west, a worlding anew, in Gayatri Spivak's terms, that decenters all static, grounded belongings and locates them instead in becomings: becoming-Indian, becoming-woman, becoming-America." Byrd, *Transit*, 13.

68. The Sequoya League, Mission Indian Federation, Northern California Indian Association, Indian Board of Cooperation, and the California Indian Brotherhood are a few examples. Some of these were complex, run by non-Natives, or were used to exploit California Indian people for dues or governmental grants, but they all express the coalitional energies of California Indian communities.

69. Brendan Hokowhitu, "Indigenous Existentialism and the Body," *Cultural Studies Review* 15, no. (2009): 101–18.

70. Ngũgĩ wa Thiong'o writes, "If there is need for a 'study of the historic continuity of a single culture', why can't this be African? Why can't African literature be at the centre so that we can view other cultures in relationship to it?" Ngũgĩ wa Thiong'o, *Decolonising the Mind: The Politics of Language in African Literature* (Nairobi: East African Educational Publishers, 1986), 439. David Lloyd has highlighted the shift to a spatial mode of literary analysis Ngũgĩ's

anticolonial work calls for in his chapter "Ngũgĩ: Decolonizing the Curriculum," in *Ngũgĩ in the American Imperium,* ed. Timothy J. Reiss (Trenton, N.J.: Africa World Press, 2021): 325–44. Lloyd notes that, against some interpretations of Ngũgĩ's call to abolish English departments in Kenya as identitarian along the colonial model, "On the contrary, the mode of spatialization is not merely the replacement of Africa as the originating centre, with the 'development' of an African literature being traced from its origins to its apex in independent national existence. The structure of the proposed curriculum performs a far more radical and displacing break with the norms of curricular formation." This break takes the forms of orature—"the oral forms of poetry, storytelling, and performance that are absolutely contemporary with the university," a centering of the student and community as collaborator, a concentric model or relationality between specific locations (as opposed to a singular line of historical development), and a recentering or differential, relational, and plural understanding of the networks of cultural forms against the centrality of Europe and its categories and disciplines. See chapter 4 for more.

71. See chapter 5.

1. The California Indian Bone Game

1. Colleen Flaherty, "Anthropologist Says She's Being Punished for Views on Bones," *Inside Higher Ed,* February 14, 2022, https://www.insidehighered.com/news/2022/02/15/anthropologist-says-shes-being-punished-views-bones.

2. Ryan Quinn, "San José State Anthropologist Against Reburying Bones Retires," *Inside Higher Ed,* July 5, 2023.

3. Chairs' Report to the SAA Board of Directors, "SAA Statement Concerning the Treatment of Human Remains Follow-up Report," https://documents.saa.org/container/docs/default-source/catf/cnar-repat-report-on-statement-final-edition.pdf.

4. Indigenous Archaeology Collective, "Open Letter from the Indigenous Archaeology Collective," News From Native California, June 29, 2020. https://newsfromnativecalifornia.com/open-letter-from-the-indigenous-archaeology-collective/.

5. Indigenous Archeology Collective, "Open Letter."

6. I borrow this somewhat tongue-in-cheek definition of *rhetoric* from Marianne Constable: "Rhetoricians don't just read the lines . . . They read between the lines; they read around the lines. They read parentheticals. (They read so carefully that they even read signs that are not there . . .) They love words and silences—and libraries, but they don't usually say anything about that. More often they say outrageous things about the scholarship of more serious disciplines—like anthropology, history, sociology, law, philosophy—while claiming that these caricatures are based on their own careful readings . . . A rhetorician, after a careful reading of texts of and about law, might suggest that there are many more interesting ways of talking about law and justice than as a dichotomous conflict between natural law and legal positivism, between ought and is, divine and human. To the rhetorician, jurisprudence appears less a

debate as to the meaning of 'law' than an inquiry into complicated relations between law and justice around particular questions of action or of what to do . . . precisely the questions that philosophy does not answer." *Just Silences: The Limits and Possibilities of Modern Law* (Princeton, N.J.: Princeton University Press, 2005), 25.

7. Elizabeth Povinelli, "Governance of the Prior," *Interventions: International Journal of Postcolonial Studies* 13, no. 1 (2011): 13–30.

8. James May, "New California Repatriation Law Includes Enforcement Teeth," *Indian Country Today*, October 31, 2001.

9. Note CalNAGPRA's (2001) focus on California Indians and inclusion of a mechanism for nonfederally recognized California tribes to file claims as well as authorization of the imposition of civil penalties for failure to comply, and National NAGPRA's code of regulations passed in 1995 and amended in 1997, 2003, 2005, 2006, 2007, and 2010, including the rule for the disposition of the "culturally unidentifiable" (43 C.F.R. 10.11).

10. Audra Simpson, "On Ethnographic Refusal: Indigeneity, 'Voice,' and Colonial Citizenship," *Junctures: The Journal for Thematic Dialogue* 9 (2007): 78.

11. Gerald Vizenor, *Wordarrows: Native States of Literary Sovereignty* (Lincoln: University of Nebraska Press, 2003).

12. Tommy Pico, *IRL* (Austin: Birds, 2016).

13. Glen Coulthard, "Subjects of Empire: Indigenous Peoples and the 'Politics of Recognition' in Canada," *Contemporary Political Theory* 6 (2007): 452.

14. Simpson, "On Ethnographic Refusal," 19.

15. Tony Bennett, *The Birth of the Museum: History, Theory, Politics* (New York: Routledge, 1995), 60–61.

16. Winona LaDuke, *Recovering the Sacred: The Power of Naming and Claiming* (Chicago: Haymarket Books, 2005), 77.

17. Quoted in Jim Watson, "Exhibition Explores the Life of Amateur Archaeologist Ralph Glidden," *Catalina Islander*, April 12, 2013, https://thecatalinaislander.com/exhibition-explores-the-life-of-amateur-archaeologist-ralph-glidden/.

18. Sarita See, *The Filipino Primitive: Accumulation and Resistance in the American Museum* (New York: NYU Press, 2017).

19. Gayatri Chakravorty Spivak, "Acting Bits/Identity Talk," *Critical Inquiry* 18, no. 4 (1992): 776.

20. Spivak, "Acting Bits/Identity Talk," 776.

21. UCOP, NAGPRA Policy (1991), 2.

22. This work is now largely done by a repatriation coordinator on each campus.

23. Lalo Franco, California Senate Hearing, February 27, 2008. Morningstar Gali reports, "On February 26, 2008, Native American Tribal Leaders, Cultural Heritage Directors, Native American Graves Protection and Repatriation Act (NAGPRA) experts, and UC Berkeley administrators testified at a Senate hearing held at the State Capitol. The hearing was held following Tribal protests of UC Berkeley's violations of federal law, the Native American Graves Protection and Repatriation Act. Tribal leaders and representatives have voiced concern

that UC Berkeley has denied the Tribes' right to bring to rest hundreds of thousands of sacred objects and ancestral remains. UC Berkeley also eliminated their special NAGPRA unit that was created for the purposes of ensuring compliance with the laws. The hearing room was full with 60 Tribal Officials, Native American supporters, and less than a handful of UC Berkeley Administrators and Officials. Senator Dean Florez, Chairman of the Committee on Government Organization facilitated the informational hearing as an intervention to the ongoing eight-month battle between Native American Tribal Representatives and UC Berkeley officials and administrators, including Chancellor Birgeneau."

24. Tony Platt tells some of this story in his book *The Scandal of Cal: Land Grabs, White Supremacy, and Miseducation at UC Berkeley* (Berkeley: Heyday Books, 2023).

25. Clare Counihan notes in a personal conversation about land grant universities: "[The Morrill Act] is also connected to post-civil war segregation; the Morrill act required that land grant institutions—all public and focused on vocational/technical training—be accessible to Black peoples; in the south, rather than desegregate, states created separate institutions, establishing at least part of the foundation for the HBCU system."

26. Robert Nichols, "Theft Is Property! The Recursive Logic of Dispossession," *Political Theory* 46, no. 1 (2017): 3–28.

27. Roderick Ferguson, *The Reorder of Things: The University and Its Pedagogies of Minority Difference* (Minneapolis: University of Minnesota Press, 2012).

28. Gerald Vizenor, *Crossbloods: Bone Courts, Bingo, and Other Reports* (Minneapolis: University of Minnesota Press, 1990), 75.

29. Larri Fredericks, California Senate Hearing, February 27, 2008.

30. Joanne Barker, "The Recognition of NAGPRA: A Human Rights Promise Deferred," in *Recognition, Sovereignty Struggles, and Indigenous Rights in the United States*, ed. Jean O'Brien and Amy E. Den Ouden (Chapel Hill: University of North Carolina Press, 2013), 107.

31. Barker, "Recognition," 102–103.

32. Barker, 95–96.

33. Barker, 105.

34. Larri Fredericks, email correspondence to AIGSA, 2007.

35. Barker, "Recognition," 104.

36. Lee Maracle, "Oratory on Oratory," in *Trans.Can.Lit: Resituating the Study of Canadian Literature*, ed. Smaro Kamboureli and Roy Miki (Waterloo, Ont.: Wilfrid Laurier University Press, 2007), 57.

37. Maracle, "Oratory," 59.

38. Maracle, 58.

39. Maracle, 68.

40. Constable, *Just Silences*, 75.

41. Constable, 75.

42. Constable, 75.

43. Constable, 85.

44. Constable, 85, 87.

45. Constable, 25.

46. Constable, 89.

47. Dian Million, *Therapeutic Nations: Healing in an Age of Indigenous Human Rights* (Tucson: University of Arizona Press, 2013), 10.

48. Million, *Therapeutic Nations*, 10.

49. Million, 12.

50. Million, 19.

51. Nikolas Rose, quoted in Million, 18.

52. Joanne Barker, introduction to *Critically Sovereign: Indigenous Gender, Sexuality, and Feminist Studies*, ed. Joanne Barker (Durham, N.C.: Duke University Press, 2017), 3.

53. Million, *Therapeutic Nations*, 8.

54. Million, 8.

55. Brittani Orona and Vanessa Esquivido, "Continued Disembodiment: NAGPRA, Cal NAGPRA, and Recognition," *Humboldt Journal of Social Relations* 1, no. 42 (2020): 50–68, 56.

56. Orona and Esquivido, "Continued Disembodiment," 57.

57. Orona and Esquivido, 58.

58. Aileen Moreton-Robinson, quoted in Orona and Esquivido, 61.

59. Jack Norton, *Genocide in Northwestern California: When Our Worlds Cried* (San Francisco: The Indian Historian Press, 1979).

60. Orona and Esquivido, "Continued Disembodiment," 54.

61. Pheng Cheah, *Inhuman Conditions: On Cosmopolitanism and Human Rights* (Cambridge, Mass.: Harvard University Press, 2006), 2.

62. Related to Lowe's *Intimacies of Four Continents* (Durham, N.C.: Duke University Press, 2015), it is also necessary to connect the museumizing practices being discussed in this chapter to their impact on other communities and peoples within the history of what became known as California and U.S. imperialism and how this process structures the very formation of the state and yet makes possible coalitional and relational possibilities.

63. Cheah, *Inhuman Conditions*, 3.

64. Vizenor, *Crossbloods*, 78.

65. The original title of Vizenor's research project was "The Woodland Tribal Trickster as a Compassionate Mixblood."

66. See the chapter "Shadow Survivance" in Gerald Vizenor, *Manifest Manners: Narratives on Postindian Survivance* (Lincoln: University of Nebraska Press, 1994).

67. School for Advanced Research, "History of SAR," School for Advanced Research, https://sarweb.org/about/history-of-sar/.

68. David Lloyd, *Under Representation: The Racial Regime of Aesthetics* (New York: Fordham University Press, 2019), e12–14, https://www.fordhampress.com/9780823282371/under-representation/.

69. School for Advanced Research, "Mission," School for Advanced Research, https://sarweb.org/about/mission-2/.

70. Vizenor, *Crossbloods*, 63.

71. Vizenor, 64.

72. Vizenor, 63.
73. Vizenor, 64.
74. Vizenor, 66, 67.
75. Vine Deloria Jr., *Custer Died for Your Sins* (Norman: University of Oklahoma Press, 1988), 78.
76. Gerald Vizenor, *Earthdivers: Tribal Narratives on Mixed Descent* (Minneapolis: University of Minnesota Press, 1981), xv.
77. Lee Edelman, *No Future: Queer Theory and the Death Drive* (Durham, N.C.: Duke University Press, 2004).
78. Vizenor, *Crossbloods*, 66.
79. Vizenor, 66.
80. Vizenor, 71.
81. Eyal Weizman, "Forensic Architecture: Notes From the Field and Forums," *documenta* 13 (2012): 5–6.
82. Weizman, "Forensic," 9.
83. Weizman, 16.
84. Weizman, 16.
85. Quoted in Weizman, 9.
86. Vizenor, *Crossbloods*, 66.
87. Beth Piatote, *Antíkoni*, in *The Beadworkers* (Berkeley: Counterpoint, 2019), e124.
88. Piatote, *Beadworkers*, e159.
89. Piatote, e159.
90. Piatote, e161.
91. Gerald Vizenor, "Aesthetics of Survivance," in *Native Liberty: Natural Reason and Cultural Survivance* (Lincoln: University of Nebraska Press, 2009), 87.
92. Vizenor, *Native Liberty*, 87.
93. Vizenor, 88.
94. Vizenor, 88.
95. Piatote, *Beadworkers*, e147.
96. Quoted in Vizenor, *Crossbloods*, 65.
97. Robert H. McLaughlin, "Refracting Rights through Material Culture: Implementing the Native American Graves Protection and Repatriation Act," paper prepared for the Cultural Policy Workshop, University of Chicago, 2000.
98. Coyote Man, *Songs of the California Indians Vol 1: Mountain Maidu* (Recording) Pacific Western Traders (Berkeley: Heyday Books, 1975).

2. The Postapocalyptic Imaginary

1. Allan Sekula, "The Body and the Archive," *October* 39 (1986): 18.
2. Sekula, "The Body and the Archive," 50.
3. Sekula, 22.
4. Audra Simpson, "On Ethnographic Refusal: Indigeneity, 'Voice' and Colonial Citizenship," *Junctures: The Journal for Thematic Dialogue* 9 (2007): 67. See also her *Mohawk Interruptus: Political Life across the Borders of Settler States* (Durham, N.C.: Duke University Press, 2014), 74.
5. Simpson, "On Ethnographic Refusal," 67.

6. Simpson, 67.

7. Edward Said, *Orientalism* (New York: Vintage, 1979).

8. Tony Bennett, "Cultural Studies and the Culture Concept," *Cultural Studies* 29, no. 4 (2015).

9. Boas, quoted in Bennett, "Cultural Studies," 551, 551–52.

10. See the American transcendentalists for a similar strategy but in literature, or note the number of Native stories that have been translated into "American folklore."

11. Richard Haller, quoted in Bennett, "Cultural Studies," 552.

12. Bennett, "Cultural Studies," 551–52.

13. Eduardo Viveiros de Castro, *Cannibal Metaphysics*, ed. and trans. Peter Skafish (Minneapolis: Univocal Publishing, 2014), 43.

14. De Castro, *Cannibal Metaphysics*, 42.

15. De Castro, 42.

16. De Castro, 55.

17. De Castro, 91.

18. Eve Tuck and K. Wayne Yang, "Decolonization Is Not a Metaphor," *Decolonization: Indigeneity, Education & Society* 1, no. 1 (2012): 1–40.

19. Denise Ferreira da Silva, *Toward a Global Idea of Race* (Minneapolis: University of Minnesota Press, 2007), xl.

20. Bennett, "Cultural Studies," 552.

21. Bennett, 553.

22. From an Achumawi story about the creation of light.

23. Tommy Pico, *IRL* (Austin: Birds, 2016).

24. Jean Baudrillard, quoted in Jodi Byrd, *Transit of Empire* (Minneapolis: University of Minnesota Press, 2011), 221.

25. Pico, *IRL*.

26. Pico.

27. Pico.

28. Pico.

29. Pico.

30. Akira Mizuta Lippit, *Atomic Light (Shadow Optics)* (Minneapolis: University of Minnesota Press, 2005), 83.

31. Patrick Wolfe, "After the Frontier: Separation and Absorption in US Indian Policy," *Settler Colonial Studies* 1, no. 1 (2013): 22.

32. See Glen Sean Coulthard, *Red Skin, White Masks: Rejecting the Colonial Politics of Recognition* (Minneapolis: University of Minnesota Press, 2014).

33. Jean Baudrillard, *Simulacra and Simulation*, trans. Sheila Maria Glaser (Ann Arbor: University of Michigan Press, 1994), 5.

34. Maurice Blanchot, *The Space of Literature*, trans. Ann Smock (Lincoln: University of Nebraska Press, 1982), 257.

35. Roland Barthes, *Camera Lucida: Reflections on Photography*, trans. Richard Howard (New York: Hill and Wang, 1981), 6.

36. Paul Chaat Smith, *Everything You Know about Indians Is Wrong* (Minneapolis: University of Minnesota Press, 2009), 4.

37. Smith, *Everything*, 4.

38. Gerald Vizenor, *Native Liberty: Natural Reason and Cultural Survivance* (Lincoln: University of Nebraska Press, 2009), 182.

39. Vizenor, *Native Liberty*, 182.

40. Smith, *Everything*, 6.

41. Gerald Vizenor, *Crossbloods: Bone Courts, Bingo, and Other Reports* (Minneapolis: University of Minnesota Press, 1990), 90.

42. Vizenor, *Crossbloods*, 86; *Native Liberty*, 167.

43. Vizenor, *Crossbloods*, 86.

44. Pauline Wakeham, *Taxidermic Signs: Reconstructing Aboriginality* (Minneapolis: University of Minnesota Press, 2008), 94.

45. Wakeham, *Taxidermic Signs*, 93.

46. Wakeham, 88.

47. Patrick Wolfe, "Settler Colonialism and the Elimination of the Native," *Journal of Genocide Research* 8, no. 4 (2006): 387–409.

48. Roland Barthes, *Mythologies*, trans. Richard Howard and Jonathan Cape (New York: Hill and Wang, 2012), 132.

49. Gerald Vizenor, "Edward Curtis," in *Native Liberty*, 206.

50. For example, see Pheng Cheah's analysis of Karl Marx's organismic philosophy in "The Rationality of Life: On the Organismic Metaphor of the State," *Radical Philosophy* 112 (Mar./Apr. 2002).

51. Vizenor, *Crossbloods*, 90.

52. Vizenor, 89.

53. Vizenor, 89.

54. Barthes, *Mythologies*, 165, 84.

55. Barthes, 86.

56. Also see Rey Chow, *The Age of the World Target: Self-Referentiality in War, Theory, and Comparative Work* (Durham, N.C.: Duke University Press, 2006), https://www.dukeupress.edu/the-age-of-the-world-target.

57. Friedrich Nietzsche, "On Truth and Lying in an Extramoral Sense," in *Friedrich Nietzsche on Rhetoric and Language*, trans. Sander L. Gilman, Carole Blair, and David J. Parent (Oxford: Oxford University Press, 1989), 252.

58. Ishi was a Yahi Indian who spent the majority of his life in the Sierra Nevada foothills as a refugee from settler violence. His tribe was massacred in successive attacks, until Ishi and his family went into hiding. With the exception of an encounter with a group of surveyors, in which the surveyors took everything of value from the camp, including the blanket in which Ishi's sickly and elderly mother was hiding, the tribe was considered extinct for nearly forty years. In 1911, Ishi came into the Northern California town of Oroville looking for food. He had burnt off his hair, a sign of mourning, and it is thought that he had outlived everyone in both his tribe and his family. He was at first arrested for "thievery" and then taken by anthropologists to live in the University of California Berkeley Museum of Anthropology as both a research assistant and a display until his death in 1916 from tuberculosis. During this time, he befriended Kroeber, calling him affectionately "Big Chiep." His presence had also caught

the imagination of the American public as "the Last Wild Indian." The recovery of his remains from the Smithsonian and subsequent burial is a controversial case of repatriation detailed in Orin Starn's *Ishi's Brain: In Search of America's Last "Wild" Indian* (New York: W. W. Norton, 2004).

59. Vizenor, *Crossbloods,* 93.

60. Robert Bellah, quoted in Vizenor, 95.

61. Vizenor, 95.

62. Vizenor, 95.

63. Barthes, *Camera Lucida.*

64. Paul Virilio, quoted in Chow, *Age of the World Target,* e5–e6.

65. Chow, e5–e6.

66. Chow, e6–e8.

67. Baudrillard, *Simulacra,* 4.

68. Barthes, *Camera Lucida,* 118–19.

69. De Castro, *Cannibal Metaphysics.*

70. Paul Virilio, *The Vision Machine,* trans. Julie Rose (Bloomington: Indiana University Press, 1994).

71. Shelbi Nahwilet Meissner, "The Moral Fabric of Linguicide: Un-Weaving Trauma Narratives and Dependency Relationships in Indigenous Language Reclamation," *Journal of Global Ethics* 14, no. 2 (2018): 266–76.

72. Cutcha Risling Baldy, *We Are Dancing For You: Native Feminisms and the Revitalization of Women's Coming-of-Age Ceremonies* (Seattle: University of Washington Press, 2018).

73. Don Hankins, "Restoring Indigenous Prescribed Fires to California Oak Woodlands," in *Proceedings of the Seventh California Oak Symposium: Managing Oak Woodlands in a Dynamic World,* ed. Richard B. Standiford and Kathryn L. Purcell (Berkeley: US Department of Agriculture, Forest Service, Pacific Southwest Research Station, 2015).

74. Save California Salmon, https://www.californiasalmon.org/about.

75. Vanessa Esquivido, "The Social Life of Basket Caps: Repatriation Under the Native American Graves Protection and Repatriation Act, in Hopes of Cultural Revitalization," *McNair Scholars Journal* 11 (2007): 51–70; Carolyn Smith, "Weaving pikyav (to-fix-it): Karuk Basket Weaving in-Relation-with the Everyday World" (PhD diss., UC Berkeley, 2016).

76. Ira Jacknis, "Alfred Kroeber and the Photographic Representation of California Indians," *American Indian Culture and Research Journal* 20, no. 3 (1996): 4.

77. See introduction.

78. Jacknis, "Alfred Kroeber," 7.

79. Barthes, *Camera Lucida,* 14.

80. Barthes, 7.

81. Barthes, 7, 31, 52, 88.

82. Bennett, "Cultural Studies," 556.

83. Bennett, 557.

84. Bennett, 557.

85. Jenny Reardon and Kim TallBear, "'Your DNA Is Our History': Genomics,

Anthropology, and the Construction of Whiteness as Property," *Current Anthropology* 53, no. S5 (2012): S234.

86. Bennett, "Cultural Studies," 557.

87. Bennett, 557.

88. Edward Winslow Gifford, *Californian Anthropometry* (Berkeley: University of California Press, 1926), 298.

89. See, for example, Geertje Mak, "A Colonial-Scientific Interface: The Construction, Viewing, and Circulation of Faces via a 1906 German Racial Atlas," *American Anthropologist* 122, no. 2 (2020): 327–41.

90. See Mark Rifkin, *When Did Indians Become Straight? Kinship, the History of Sexuality, and Native Sovereignty* (Oxford: Oxford University Press, 2011); and Scott Lauria Morgensen, *Spaces Between Us: Queer Settler Colonialism and Indigenous Decolonization* (Minneapolis: University of Minnesota Press, 2011).

91. Judith Lowry (illus.), with Chiori Santiago (auth.), *Home to Medicine Mountain* (New York: Children's Book Press, 2002); Chag Lowry (auth.) with Rahsan Ekedak (illus.), *Soldiers Unknown* (Temecula, Calif.: Great Oak Press, 2019); Michelle LeBeau, "A Healing Process," *Frontiers: A Journal of Women's Studies* 23, no. 2 (2002): 109–16, the oral history of my great-uncle, Leonard Lowry.

92. Theresa Harlan, *She Sang Me a Good Luck Song: The California Indian Photographs of Dugan Aguilar* (Berkeley: Heyday Press, 2015).

93. Harlan, *She Sang.*

94. L. Frank and Kim Hogeland, *First Families: A Photographic History of California Indians* (Berkeley: Heyday Books, 2007).

95. Frank and Hogeland, *First Families*, xi.

96. Of this last one, titled, "Modesta Avila (Ajachamem), prison photo, 1889," the caption explains, "Angered by the noise and filth of the Santa Fe railroad running through her mother's land and that they had never paid for the right of way, Modesta Avila protested: locals said she hung her laundry on a clothesline across the tracks; Santa Fe said she placed a railroad tie across the tracks. Either way, a railroad agent removed it before the train came. Four months later Modesta Avila was arrested and charged with attempting to obstruct a train. She was sentenced to three years in San Quentin. She died, at the age of twenty-two, after serving two years of her sentence." Frank and Hogeland, *First Families*, 119.

97. Frank and Hogeland, xi.

98. Frank and Hogeland, 184.

99. Frank and Hogeland, xi.

100. Susan Sontag, *On Photography* (New York: Rosetta Books, 2005), 4.

101. Barthes, *Camera Lucida*, 96.

102. Barthes, 6.

103. Achumawi, The Creation of Light.

3. Refusing Genocide

1. And, yes, I'm including the Holocaust, which did have a similar force, but largely for a western audience—Gaza is a global and globalizing event in a different way.

2. Marc Nichanian, *The Historiographic Perversion*, trans. Gil Anidjar (New York: Columbia University, 2009), 83–84.

3. Though the efficacy of the IOF is also in question, as Hamas's successes make evident.

4. Nichanian, *Historiographic Perversion*, 49.

5. Dylan Rodríguez, *White Reconstruction: Domestic Warfare and the Logics of Genocide* (New York: Fordham University Press, 2021), 135.

6. Lawrence J. LeBlanc, *The United States and the Genocide Convention* (Durham, N.C.: Duke University Press, 1991). As LeBlanc describes: "[Senators] Helms, Hatch, and a few other outspoken critics of the convention in the Senate were left with no practical alternative but to work for ratification under conditions that would reduce the convention to no more than a symbol of opposition to genocide. The Sovereignty Package was intended to accomplish that objective." Note 6, above 241.

7. Quoted in Lawrence J. LeBlanc, "The ICJ, The Genocide Convention, and the United States," *Wisconsin International Law Journal* 6 (1987): 43–74, 43.

8. See Guatemala's Commission for Historical Clarification and Canada's Truth and Reconciliation Committee for two of many examples.

9. "During the drafting of the Genocide Convention, the United States opposed the inclusion of a proposed article that would have broadened the definition of genocide to encompass acts targeting the cultural identity of a protected group, stating: In the first place, the new and far-reaching concept of cultural genocide, i.e., the destruction of a culture, had no connection with the better known conception of genocide as the physical destruction of members of a human group. For the inclusion of cultural genocide in the convention on genocide, it was not enough to say the acts enumerated in [the proposed article] shocked the conscience of mankind. In the second place, [the proposed article], as it now stood or in any amended form, would not meet the wishes of those who favoured its retention . . . If the objective were to preserve the culture of a group, then it was primarily freedom of thought and expression for the members of the group which needed protection. Such protection came within the sphere of human rights. If the individual's fundamental right to use his own language, to practice his own religion and to attend the school of his choice were protected, that would be tantamount to protecting the group of which the individual was a member. GAOR, 3rd session, Pa11 I, Sixth Comm. (83rd meeting), at 203, 25 Oct. 1948. 29 Genocide Convention art. III-IV." International Court of Justice, "Declaration of intervention of the United States of America," Document Number 182-20220907-WRI-01-00-EN.

10. Samera Esmeir, "The Violence of Non-Violence: Law and War in Iraq." *Journal of Law and Society* 34, no. 1 (2007): 99–115.

11. David Kazanjian, "Re-flexion: Genocide in Ruins," *Discourse* 33, no. 3 (2011): 367.

12. Brendan Hokowhitu, "Indigenous Existentialism and the Body," *Cultural Studies Review* 15, no. 2 (2009): 101–118.

13. Rey Chow, *The Age of the World Target: Self-Referentiality in War, Theory, and Comparative Work* (Durham, N.C.: Duke University Press, 2006), e13–e14.

14. Walter Mignolo and Catherine E. Walsh, *On Decoloniality: Concepts, Analytics, Praxis* (Durham, N.C.: Duke University Press, 2018).

15. Giorgio Agamben, *The Open: Man and Animal*, trans. Kevin Attell (Stanford, Calif.: Stanford University Press, 2004), 33.

16. Chow, *Age of the World Target*, e17–18.

17. Hupa scholar Jack Norton is likely the first historian in the context of California to use rigorously the term *genocide* as defined by the United Nations. He did so to claim that a genocide was committed against his people in *Genocide in Northwestern California: When Our Worlds Cried* (San Francisco: Indian Historian Press, 1979). This is an important point to keep in mind when discussing the racial and colonial regime of genocide discourse, especially since non-Native historians have generally erased or minimized Norton's contribution. Brendan Lindsay is an exception to this racist and colonial trend.

18. Rodríguez, *White Reconstruction*, 135.

19. Aimé Césaire, *Discourse on Colonialism*, trans. Joan Pinkham (New York: Monthly Review Press, 1972), 36.

20. Kazanjian, "Re-flexion," 368.

21. Rodríguez, *White Reconstruction*, 135, 139.

22. Kazanjian, "Re-flexion," 369.

23. Kazanjian, 369.

24. Mahmood Mamdani, "Making Sense of Political Violence in Postcolonial Africa," *Identity, Culture and Politics* 3, no. 2 (2002): 3.

25. Rodríguez, *White Reconstruction*, 139.

26. Walter Benjamin, "Critique of Violence," in *Walter Benjamin Reflections: Essays, Aphorisms, Autobiographical Writings*, edited by Peter Demetz and translated by Edmund Jephcott (New York: Schocken Books, 1986).

27. See Esmeir, "Violence of Non-Violence."

28. Samera Esmeir has analyzed this violence done in the name of the law describing it in its performative force as the institution of juridical humanity.

29. See Dian Million, *Therapeutic Nations: Healing in an Age of Indigenous Human Rights* (Tucson: University of Arizona Press, 2013).

30. Rodríguez, *White Reconstruction*, 135.

31. Sylvia Wynter, "Unsettling the Coloniality of Being/Power/Truth/Freedom: Towards the Human, After Man, Its Overrepresentation—An Argument," *The New Centennial Review* 3, no. 3 (2003): 282.

32. Denise Ferreira da Silva, *Toward a Global Idea of Race* (Minneapolis: University of Minnesota Press, 2007), xxi.

33. Norman Finkelstein, "History's Verdict: The Cherokee Case," *Journal of Palestine Studies* 24 no. 4 (1996): 32–45, 36.

34. Quoted in Rodríguez, *White Reconstruction*, 138.

35. Gavin Newsom, California Governor, "Executive Order N-15-19 of June 18, 2019 [apology to California Indians]," Office of the Governor, https://www.gov.ca.gov/wp-content/uploads/2019/06/6.18.19-Executive-Order.pdf.

36. Mamdani, "Making Sense," 2.

37. Nichanian, *Historiographic Perversion,* 5. Along with Lyotard, Jacques Derrida, Jean-Luc Nancy, and Philippe Lacoue-Labarthe participated.

38. David Stannard, Norman Finkelstein, and Cherokee-identifying non-Native scholar Ward Churchill have critiqued the works of a number of historians of the Holocaust for their claims about its singularity and their refusals to acknowledge genocide against Native Americans, including Deborah Lipstadt, Steven Katz, and Daniel Goldhagen. More recently, Gary Clayton Anderson's *Ethnic Cleansing and the Indian: The Crime That Should Haunt America* (2014) and his refusal to acknowledge that the United States committed genocide against Native Americans has set off another round of debates over the use of the term *genocide* in the Native American context, taken up by Roxanne Dunbar-Ortiz, Benjamin Madley, and Jeffrey Ostler, among others.

39. Alan Rosenbaum, ed., *Is the Holocaust Unique? Perspectives on Comparative Genocide* (New York: Routledge, 1995); Gavriel Rosenfeld, "The Politics of Uniqueness: Reflection on the Recent Polemical Turn in Holocaust and Genocide Scholarship," *Holocaust and Genocide Studies* 13, no. 1 (Spring 1999): 28–61.

40. Nichanian, *Historiographic Perversion,* 81.

41. Million, *Therapeutic Nations,* 3.

42. Nichanian, *Historiographic Perversion,* 62.

43. Jodi Byrd, "'Living My Native Life Deadly': Red Lake, Ward Churchill, and the Discourses of Competing Genocides," *American Indian Quarterly* 31, no. 2 (2007): 311.

44. Ward Churchill, "An American Holocaust? The Structure of Denial," *Socialism and Democracy* 17, no. 1 (2003): 29–30.

45. Quoted in Byrd, "'Living My Native Life Deadly,'" 328.

46. One of the captives was released, and thirty-eight Dakota men were hanged, the largest mass execution in U.S. history.

47. Byrd, "'Living My Native Life Deadly,'" 327.

48. Churchill's ouster echoes the circumstances around ex–Harvard University president Claudine Gay in the current moment of Israel's genocide in Gaza. There are differences, however: Gay's actions were far less principled than Churchill's, who has remained steadfast in his support of Palestinians, and her position far more powerful. She is also the first Black woman to be president of Harvard while Churchill is a white man pretending to be Native.

49. Nichanian, *Historiographic Perversion,* chapter 2.

50. See Jodi Byrd, "'in the city of blinding lights': Indigeneity, Cultural Studies, and the Errants of Colonial Nostalgia," *Cultural Studies Review* 15, no. 2 (2009): 13–28.

51. Nichanian, *Historiographic Perversion,* 78.

52. Nichanian, 70.

53. Carlo Ginzburg, "Just One Witness: The Extermination of the Jews and the Principle of Reality," in *Threads and Traces: True False Fictive,* trans. Anne C. Tedeschi and John Tedeschi (Berkeley, Calif.: University of California Press, 2012), 178.

54. Ginzburg, "Just One Witness," 178. See also Carlo Ginzburg, *The Cheese*

and the Worms: The Cosmos of a Sixteenth-Century Miller (Baltimore: Johns Hopkins University Press, 2013); the turn to oral history, ethnohistory, memory, and now the forensic approach to other-than-human narratives are all part of this general problematic.

55. Martin Rizzo-Martinez, *We Are Not Animals: Indigenous Politics of Survival, Rebellion, and Reconstitution in Nineteenth-Century California* (Lincoln: University of Nebraska Press, 2022), 6.

56. Leslie Marmon Silko, *Storyteller* (New York: Little, Brown, 1981), 133.

57. Lucy Young, as told to Edith V. A. Murphy, "Out of the Past: A True Indian Story Told by Lucy Young, of Round Valley Indian Reservation," *California Historical Society Quarterly* 20, no. 4 (1941): 350.

58. Young, "Out of the Past," 358.

59. Young, 353.

60. Lisa Lowe, *Immigrant Acts: Asian American Cultural Politics* (Durham, N.C.: Duke University Press, 1996), 6.

61. Quoted in Rizzo-Martinez writes in *We Are Not Animals*, epigraph.

62. Michael F. Magliari, "The California Indian Scalp Bounty Myth: Evidence of Genocide or Just Faulty Scholarship?," *California History* 100, no. 2 (2023): 4–30.

63. Gary Clayton Anderson, *Ethnic Cleansing and the Indian: The Crime That Should Haunt America* (Norman: University of Oklahoma Press, 2014).

64. Nichanian, *Historiographic Perversion*, 51.

65. Tony Platt, "When Our Worlds Cried: California's Genocide," review of *An American Genocide: The United States and the California Indian Catastrophe, 1846–1873*, by Benjamin Madley, *News from Native California* 29, no. 4 (2016).

66. Benjamin Madley, *An American Genocide: The United States and the California Indian Catastrophe, 1846–1873* (New Haven, Conn.: Yale University Press, 2016), 5.

67. Madley, *An American Genocide*, 7.

68. Madley, 6.

69. Madley, 5.

70. Madley, 13, 5, 6; emphasis added.

71. Madley, 5.

72. Madley, 3.

73. Madley, 2, 124, 146, 171, 203.

74. Madley, 10.

75. Madley, 13.

76. Madley, 10.

77. Madley, 11.

78. Saidiya Hartman, "Venus in Two Acts," *Small Axe* 26 (2008): 1–14, 2.

79. Hartman, "Venus," 14.

Interlude

1. William Shipley, The Maidu Indian Myths and Stories of Hanc'ibyjim (Berkeley, Calif.: Heyday Books, 1991), 31.

2. Shipley, *Maidu Indian Myths*, 32.
3. Shipley, 34.
4. Shipley, 35.
5. Shipley, 36.
6. Shipley, 37–38.

4. *Bad Indians* and the Destruction of Writing

1. Quoted in Robert Heizer, *The Destruction of the California Indians: A Collection of Documents from the Period 1847 to 1865 in which Are Described Some of the Things That Happened to Some of the Indians of California* (Lincoln: University of Nebraska, 1993), 37, my italics.

2. Sara Ahmed, *The Promise of Happiness* (Durham, N.C.: Duke University Press, 2010), 59.

3. Robert Heizer, They Were Only Diggers: A Collection of Articles from California Newspapers, 1851–1866, on Indian and White Relations (Ramona: Ballena Press, 1974), 113–14.

4. Cora Du Bois, *1870 Ghost Dance* (Lincoln: University of Nebraska Press, 2007), 7.

5. Deborah Miranda, "Extermination of the Joyas: Gendercide in Spanish California," *GLQ: A Journal of Lesbian and Gay Studies* 16, no. 1–2 (2010): 253–84, 259.

6. Marc Nichanian, "Catastrophic Mourning," in *Loss: The Politics of Mourning*, ed. David L. Eng and David Kazanjian (Berkeley: University of California Press, 2003), 108.

7. Nichanian, "Catastrophic Mourning," 111.

8. Katherine McKittrick, "Diachronic Loops/Deadweight Tonnage/Bad Made Measure," *Cultural Geographies* 23, no. 1 (2015): 11.

9. McKittrick, "Diachronic Loops," 12.

10. Katherine McKittrick, "Mathematics Black Life," *The Black Scholar* 44, no. 2 (2014): 18.

11. McKittrick, "Mathematics Black Life," 19.

12. McKittrick, 23.

13. If there is any doubt that such structures remain the same, Sandy Grande, in an excellent piece titled "Aging, Precarity, and the Struggle for Indigenous Elsewheres" (*International Journal of Qualitative Studies in Education* 31, no. 3 [2018]: 168–76), discusses the financialization of aging and other "social ills" through social impact bonds that allow governments to harness private capital to fund social programs in which investors invest money and receive dividends based on rates of success, on things such as recidivism.

14. Nichanian, "Catastrophic Mourning," 110.

15. Dian Million, "Intense Dreaming: Theories, Narratives, and Our Search for Home," *The American Indian Quarterly* 3, no. 3 (2011): 313–33, 36.

16. Nichanian, "Catastrophic Mourning," 114.

17. See Sianne Ngai, *Ugly Feelings* (Cambridge, Mass.: Harvard University Press, 2005).

18. Quoted in Marc Nichanian, *The Historiographic Perversion*, trans. Gil Anidjar (New York: Columbia University Press, 2009), 88–89.

19. Michael Taussig, "Culture of Terror—Space of Death: Roger Casement's Putumayo Report and the Explanation of Torture," *Comparative Studies in Society and History* 26, no. 3 (1984): 467–97.

20. I take up this issue in the next chapter.

21. Taussig, "Culture of Terror," 468.

22. Taussig, 468.

23. Taussig, 469. Taussig, the anthropologist, predictably excludes the healer's name.

24. Taussig, "Violence and Resistance in the Americas: The Legacy of Conquest," in *The Nervous System* (New York: Routledge, 1992), 44.

25. Dylan Rodríguez, *White Reconstruction: Domestic Warfare and the Logics of Genocide* (New York: Fordham University Press, 2021).

26. Stephen Best, *None Like Us: Blackness, Belonging, Aesthetic Life* (Durham, N.C.: Duke University Press, 2018), 2.

27. Million, *Therapeutic Nations*. See introduction.

28. Nichanian, *The Historiographic Perversion*. See previous chapter.

29. Hau'ofa, "Our Sea of Islands," *The Contemporary Pacific* 6, no. 1 (1994): 147–61.

30. David Lloyd, "Ngũgĩ: Decolonizing the Curriculum," in *Ngũgĩ in the American Imperium*, ed. Timothy J. Reiss (Trenton, N.J.: Africa World Press, 2021).

31. Related concepts to writing destruction: Marc Nichanian's writing catastrophe; Saidiya Hartman's critical fabulation; Christina Sharpe's in the wake; Maurice Blanchot's writing of disaster; Deborah Miranda's writing at/from the end of the world; Giorgio Agamben's remnants of Auschwitz; Sara Dowling's translingual poetics; and Deleuze and Guattari's minor literature.

32. There is a venerable tradition of anthologies of the destruction of California Indians. Such collections of archival documents, compiled in order to sketch an image of a topic, constitute a genre that produces what Michel Foucault, in his meditation on the archive of criminality calls a "kind of herbarium." Michel Foucault, "Lives of Infamous Men," in *The Essential Foucault*, ed. Paul Rabinow and Nikolas Rose (New York: New Press, 2003). Decidedly not books of history, these collections are, following Saidiya Hartman, "a death sentence, a tomb, a display of the violated body" ("Venus," 2). A small sample of titles include Robert Heizer, *The Destruction of California Indians* (1974); Heizer, *They Were Only Diggers: A Collection of Articles from California Newspapers, 1851–1866, on Indian and White Relations* (1974); Heizer and John E. Mills, *The Four Ages of Tsurai: A Documentary History of the Indian Village on Trinidad Bay* (Berkeley: University of California Press, 1952); Alan J. Almquist and Heizer, *The Other Californians: Prejudice and Discrimination under Spain, Mexico, and the United States to 1920* (Berkeley: University of California Press, 1971); Clifford Trafzer and Joel Hyer, *Exterminate Them! Written Accounts of the Murder, Rape, and Enslavement of Native Americans During the California Gold Rush* (Lansing: Michigan State University Press, 1999); and Madley's nearly two-hundred-page-long eight appendices

to *An American Genocide: The United States and the California Indian Catastrophe* (New Haven, Conn.: Yale University Press, 2017).

33. These questions bear on more fundamental questions about the referential and/or performative dimensions of the phrase *California Indian* as well as *literature*, not to mention *existence*.

34. See Theodor Adorno, "The Essay as Form," in *Notes to Literature*, vol. 1, ed. Rolf Tiedemann, trans. Shierry Weber Nicholsen (New York: Columbia University Press, 1991); and Gerald Vizenor, "Penenative Rumors," in *Fugitive Poses: Native American Indian Scenes of Absence and Presence* (Lincoln: University of Nebraska, 2000).

35. Miranda, *Bad Indians:* A Tribal Memoir (Berkeley: Heyday Books, 2013), e176.

36. Miranda, *Bad Indians*, e171.

37. Miranda, e132.

38. Miranda, e50.

39. Miranda, e101. See the section "Juan Justo's Bones."

40. Miranda, e129, e132.

41. Janice Gould, *Earthquake Weather* (Tucson: University of Arizona Press, 1996), xii.

42. Deborah Miranda, *Indian Cartography* (Greenfield: Greenfield Review Press, 1998).

43. Elaine Marks, "Lesbian Intertextuality," in *Homosexualities and French Literature: Cultural Contexts/Critical Texts*, ed. Elaine Marks and George Stambolian (New York: Cornell University Press, 1979), 370.

44. Gould, *Earthquake Weather*, 7.

45. Eve Kosofsky Sedgwick, *Touching Feeling: Affect, Pedagogy, Performativity* (Durham, N.C.: Duke University Press, 2003), 149.

46. Miranda, *Bad Indians*, e117.

47. From Deborah Miranda, "Old Territory. New Maps," in *The Zen of La Llorona* (Cromer, Eng.: Salt Publishing, 2005).

48. Marks, "Lesbian Intertextuality," 372.

49. Marks, 366.

50. From Janice Gould, "Six Sonnets: Crossing the West," in *Doubters and Dreamers* (Tucson: University of Arizona Press, 2011).

51. From Gould, "Six Sonnets."

52. Miranda, "Old Territory."

53. From Miranda, "Old Territory."

54. Miranda.

55. Miranda.

56. Miranda.

57. Mary Louise Pratt as cited in Mishuana Goeman, *Mark My Words: Native Women Mapping Our Nations* (Minneapolis: University of Minnesota Press, 2013), 2.

58. Goeman, *Mark My Words*, 3, 4.

59. For examples, see Simpson, "The State Is a Man"; Risling Baldy, *We Are Dancing for You;* Sarah Deer, *The Beginning and End of Rape: Confronting Sexual*

Violence in Native America (Minneapolis: University of Minnesota Press, 2015); and Paula Gunn Allen, *Grandmothers of the Light: A Medicine Woman's Source Book* (Boston: Beacon Press, 1991).

60. Goeman, *Mark My Words*, 7.

61. Miranda, *Bad Indians*, e117.

62. Miranda, e117.

63. Fred Moten and Stefano Harney, *The Undercommons: Fugitive Planning & Black Study* (Wivenhoe: Minor Compositions, 2013).

64. Eve Kosofsky Sedgwick, *Touching Feeling: Affect, Pedagogy, Performativity* (Durham, N.C.: Duke University Press, 2003), 139.

65. Miranda, *Bad Indians*, e131–32, my italics.

66. Miranda, e195–96.

67. Miranda, e197.

68. Rei Terada, "Impasse as a Figure of Political Space," *Comparative Literature* 72, no. 2 (2020): 146.

69. Terada, "Impasse," 147.

70. Miranda, *Bad Indians*, e114, e125.

71. Miranda, e187.

72. Miranda, e136.

73. Marisol de la Cadena, "Indigenous Cosmopolitics in the Andes: Conceptual Reflections beyond 'Politics,'" *Cultural Anthropology* 25, no. 2 (2010): 334–70.

74. De la Cadena, "Indigenous Cosmopolitics," 343.

75. María Josefina Saldaña-Portillo, *Indian Given: Racial Geographies Across Mexico and the United States* (Durham, N.C.: Duke University Press, 2016), e57–e58, https://doi-org.proxy.lib.duke.edu/10.1215/9780822374923.

76. Saldaña-Portillo, *Indian Given*, e43–e44.

77. Saldaña-Portillo, e46–e48.

78. Saldaña-Portillo, e58–e59.

79. Saldaña-Portillo, e59–e61.

80. On the point about a presupposed humanity, see Mel Chen, *Animacies: Biopolitics, Racial Mattering, and Queer Affect* (Durham, N.C.: Duke University Press, 2012); on retroactive attribution of ownership, see Robert Nichols, "Theft Is Property! The Recursive Logic of Dispossession," *Political Theory* 46, no. 1 (2017): 3–28.

81. Elizabeth Povinelli, "The Governance of the Prior," *Interventions: International Journal of Postcolonial Studies* 13, no. 1 (2011): 13–30.

82. Jasbir Puar, *The Right to Maim: Debility, Capacity, Disability* (Durham, N.C.: Duke University Press, 2017).

83. Echoes Blanchot's definition of literature in *Space of Literature*.

84. Miranda, *Bad Indians*, e119.

85. Miranda, e118.

86. Miranda, e58–e59.

87. Miranda, e3.

88. Miranda, e136–46.

89. Miranda, e138.

90. Leanne Betasamosake Simpson, *As We Have Always Done: Indigenous*

Freedom Through Radical Resistance (Minneapolis: University of Minnesota Press, 2017), 19.

91. Miranda, e27.

92. Miranda published several essays based on her engagement with Meadows's archive and references a planned book, *The Hidden Stories of Isabel Meadows*, in one of the essays.

93. Miranda, "'They Were Tough Those Old Women Before Us': The Power of Gossip in Isabel Meadows's Narratives," *Biography* 39, no. 3 (2016): 373–401, 374.

94. Deborah Miranda, "Extermination of the Joyas: Gendercide in Spanish California," *GLQ: A Journal of Lesbian and Gay Studies* 16, no. 1–2 (2010): 253–84, 255.

95. Miranda, "Extermination of the Joyas," 265.

96. Miranda, 256–57.

97. Miranda, 255.

98. See Dorothy Lee, "Linguistic Reflections of Wintu Thought," *International Journal of American Linguistics* 10, no. 4 (1944): 181–97.

99. Kim Tallbear, *The Critical Polyamorist* (blog), http://www.criticalpolyamorist.com.

100. Gilles Deleuze and Félix Guattari, "What Is a Minor Literature?," *Mississippi Review* 11, no. 3 (1983): 26.

101. Miranda, *Bad Indians*, e99–101.

102. Miranda, e100. Emphasis added.

103. Miranda, e100.

104. Miranda, e100.

105. Miranda, e101.

106. Miranda, e101.

107. Vine Deloria, *God Is Red: A Native View of Religion* (Golden, Col.: Fulcrum Publishing, 1992), 62.

108. Ngũgĩ wa Thiong'o, *Decolonizing the Mind: The Politics of Language in African Literature* (London: James Currey, 1986), 89.

109. Lloyd, "Ngũgĩ," 327.

110. Thiong'o, *Decolonizing the Mind*, 89.

111. See both Thiong'o, *Decolonizing the Mind;* and Lloyd, "Ngũgĩ."

112. Lloyd, "Ngũgĩ," 332.

113. Miranda, *Bad Indians*, e119.

114. Miranda, e172.

115. Audra Simpson, "On Ethnographic Refusal: Indigeneity, 'Voice,' and Colonial Citizenship," *Junctures* 9 (2007): 67–80.

116. The two poems discussed in this section, Deborah Miranda's "Dear Friend" and Janice Gould's "Ancestors," were shared with me by Deborah Miranda while I was seeking permissions for the other poems discussed in this chapter. Gould's "Ancestors" is going to be published in a forthcoming, posthumous memoir being edited by a number of Gould's associates, including her

partner, Mimi Wheatwind, and Deborah Miranda. "Dear Friend" was published in Miranda's *Altar for Broken Things: poems* (Kansas City: BkMk Press, 2020).

5. Atlas for a Destroyed World

1. This condition of obscurity of the catastrophe has undergone revision recently with California governor Gavin Newsom's 2019 executive order apologizing to California Indians and the creation of the Truth and Healing Council.

2. In my own case, this access is mediated through the massive salvage ethnographic survey that took place in California during the early twentieth century.

3. LA186.042. I take Frank Day's words from the *Survey of California and Other Indian Languages*, an online archive hosted by the University of California, Berkeley, https://cla.berkeley.edu.

4. Rebecca Dobkins, "From Vanishing to Visible: Maidu Indian Arts and the Uses of Tradition" (PhD diss., UC Berkeley, 1995), 119. I cite from this dissertation because, while Dobkins has a few short publications drawn from its materials, the bulk of it remains unpublished. Due to the paucity of commentary on Day's work and the extensive and Dobkins's exceptional research, this dissertation is one of the best resources for his work and life.

5. LA186.034. Konkow and later Concow are colonial transliterations of Kóyo•mkàwi.

6. Day's images depicting violence against women deserve special consideration, which I do not have space to address here.

7. Peter Nabokov, "Pacific Western Traders," *News from Native California* 25, no. 2 (2011/2012).

8. Lucy Lippard, "Frank Day: Inside Place, Inside Art," *Museum Anthropology* 24, no. 2–3 (2001): 30.

9. Louis Marin, "Opacity and Transparence in Pictorial Representation," *Est: grunnlagsproblemer I estetisk forskning* 2 (1991): 55–66.

10. I borrow and adapt this notion of refusal from Audra Simpson's important concept of "ethnographic refusal"; see more detailed discussion in the introduction and chapter 1.

11. Marin, "Opacity and Transparence," 57.

12. Jean M. O'Brien, *Firsting and Lasting: Writing Indians out of Existence in New England* (Minneapolis: University of Minnesota Press, 2010).

13. Nichanian, "On the Archive."

14. Byrd, *Transit of Empire: Indigenous Critiques of Colonialism* (Minneapolis: University of Minnesota Press, 2011), 221. Jodi Byrd begins the conclusion to her book *Transit of Empire* on Zombie imperialism, with an epigraph by Jean Baudrillard: "The apocalypse is the end of secrecy. Literally, it is the discovery, the revelation when everything is said. It is the end of metaphors and secrets. The nuclear bomb is the Sun cast on the Earth, of the end of the Sun as a metaphor, as distance. It is the Sun materialized on Earth: the end."

15. Jean-François Lyotard, *The Inhuman: Reflections on Time*, trans. Geoffrey Bennington and Rachel Bowlby (Cambridge: Polity Press, 1991).

16. Lyotard, *The Inhuman*, 2.

17. Lyotard, 4.

18. Lyotard, 6.

19. Eduardo Viveiros de Castro, *Cannibal Metaphysics*, ed. and trans. Peter Skafish (Minneapolis: Univocal Publishing, 2014).

20. Marc Nichanian, *The Historiographic Perversion*, trans. Gil Anidjar (New York: Columbia University, 2009), 98.

21. Jean-Luc Nancy, quoted in Nichanian, *The Historiographic Perversion*, 102.

22. Sascha Scott, "Awa Tsireh and the Art of Subtle Resistance," *Art Bulletin* 95, no. 4 (2013): 597–622.

23. Frank LaPena, quoted in Dobkins et al., *Memory and Imagination: The Legacy of Maidu Indian Artist Frank Day* (Oakland: Oakland Museum of California, 1997), 29.

24. Dobkins, "From Vanishing to Visible," 93.

25. Dobkins, 97–98.

26. LA186.013.

27. Dobkins, "From Vanishing to Visible," 115.

28. Dobkins, 115.

29. Dobkins, 92.

30. Roland Dixon, quoted in Dobkins, 92.

31. See Dorothy Lee, "Linguistic Reflections of Wintu Thought," *International Journal of American Linguistics* 10, no. 4 (1944): 181–97.

32. Lowell Bean, "Power and Its Applications in Native California," *Journal of California Anthropology* 2, no. 1 (1975): 28.

33. LA186.005.

34. LA186.015.

35. Dobkins et al., *Memory and Imagination*, 28.

36. The *neutral* is the space of indetermination. Theories of the image often indicate a sort of vanishing point or disappearance of the image itself in its very function of representing and also its power to make disappear that which it represents by risking replacing it. The neutral is often used as a way to indicate this space of indetermination and nonmeaning that images, in their difference from what they represent, evade by creating meaning through separation, but it also points to the fact that everything does disappear, leaving only the image. Day's paintings, for me, operate in this space of the neutral in complex ways related to his conception of preservation through image.

37. Transcribed explanation of the painting from Rebecca Dobkins's dissertation archive, provided by Dobkins.

38. In his article "Stratifying the West: Clarence King, Timothy O'Sullivan, and History" (*American Art* 29, no. 2 [2015]: 34–41), Jason Weems notes that more than the epistemological effect of making what is obstinately invisible visible, stratigraphy makes it possible to visualize time differently, connecting it to a much more shallow sense of human history in relation to the catastro-

phist rhythms of geological eras. It also enables both intellectual and economic resource extraction, which together facilitated colonial expansion.

39. Trinh T. Minh-ha, *Woman, Native, Other: Writing Postcoloniality and Feminism* (Bloomington: Indiana University Press, 1990), 48–49.

40. LA186.031.

41. Kim TallBear, "Beyond the Life/Not-Life Binary: A Feminist-Indigenous Reading of Cryopreservation, Interspecies Thinking, and the New Materialisms," in *Cryopolitics: Frozen Life in a Melting World,* ed. Joanna Radin and Emma Kowal (Cambridge, Mass.: MIT Press, 2017), 181.

42. For a historical analysis of the slow banishment of other than human beings from Indigenous political worlds to the realm of belief, see Marisol de la Cadena, "Indigenous Cosmopolitics: Conceptual Reflections beyond 'Politics,'" *Cultural Anthropology* 25, no. 2 (2010): 334–70.

43. TallBear, "Beyond the Life/Not-Life Binary," 191.

44. TallBear, 180.

45. See Jasbir Puar, *The Right to Maim: Debility, Capacity, Disability* (Durham, N.C.: Duke University Press, 2017).

46. TallBear, "Beyond the Life/Not-Life Binary," 185.

47. TallBear, 189.

48. Vine Deloria Jr. quoted in TallBear, "Beyond the Life/Not-Life Binary," 188.

49. See David Shorter, "Spirituality," in *The Oxford Handbook of American Indian History,* ed. Frederick E. Hoxie (New York: Oxford University Press, 2016), 1–24, https://doi.org/10.1093/oxfordhb/9780199858897.013.20.

50. Elizabeth Povinelli, *Geontologies: A Requiem to Late Liberalism* (Durham, N.C.: Duke University Press, 2016), e12, https://doi-org.proxy.lib.duke.edu/10.1215/9780822373810.

51. Povinelli, *Geontologies,* e26.

52. Lee, "Linguistic Reflections," 186.

53. LA186.031. Day claims that Tay•yee is an older name for Kóyo•mkàwi.

54. LA186.024.

55. LA186.042.

56. LA186.005.

57. LA186.026.

58. LA186.009.

59. LA186.005.

60. In discussions of audio recording technology, a distinction is sometimes made between a commodified form of presence that comes about through production quality, something that encourages consumption, and the generally edited-out presence of the body and/or environment, which ambient and experimental projects will seek to capture. But at a technical level, the recording of sound and the nearly unlimited capabilities of copying and disseminating it produces cut the relationship to the site and moment of performance or necessity

of being there. The sense of presence that Day is asserting is intimately linked to the song-stories he is relaying, which always tend toward and indicate an origin, but one only known through a resonance that dissipates and brings out of phase through dissonance the play of absence and presence that western metaphysics continues to return to and attempts to escape.

61. LA186.034.

62. LA186.034.

63. LA186.034.

64. Gerald Vizenor, "Anishinaabe Pictomyths," in *Native Liberty: Natural Reason and Cultural Survivance* (Lincoln: University of Nebraska Press, 2009), 180.

65. See Heinrich von Kleist, "On the Marionette Theater," trans. Thomas G. Neumiller, *TDR: The Drama Review* 16, no. 3 (1972): 22–26.

66. LA186.042.

67. LaPena, "Frank Day, a Remembrance," in Dobkins et al., *Memory and Imagination*, 30. From a description of the painting: "In the practice of Maidu dance, dancers experience spiritual and physical transformation, becoming representative of the spirit of the animal they impersonate in their regalia. In this painting, a deer dancer leaves his footprints, as well as the deer's hoof prints, in the earth as he dances. He is joined by a centipede, which similarly leaves marks upon the earth. This toto, a frequently performed dance, is taking place at Bloomer Hill, the area where Frank Day's father Billy had a round house" (84). LaPena further comments: "While the deer dancer begins to cause the mountains and valleys to take shape, one can see that it is his own dancing feet and the deer toe staffs that are helping break down and shape the earth and stone. As the pressure from the earth escapes, it is seen that a cloud personifying some 'being' is formed in the sky" (103n47).

68. LaPena, "Frank Day, a Remembrance," 83. The wind snake is a creature that Day explains in detail in one of his recordings, discussed later in this chapter.

69. Povinelli, *Geontologies*, e63.

70. Dobkins et al., *Memory and Imagination*, 83.

71. For one powerful example, see Trinh T. Minh-ha's film *Naked Spaces—Living Is Round* (1985).

72. Lee, "Linguistic Reflections," 182.

73. LA186.046.

74. Letter to Rebecca Dobkins, 1/12/93, as cited in her dissertation.

75. Dobkins, "From Vanishing to Visible," 140.

76. Dobkins, 143.

77. LaPena, "Frank Day, a Remembrance," 29.

78. LaPena, 28.

79. LaPena, 28.

80. Jacques Derrida, "Signature, Event, Context," in *Limited, Inc.*, ed. Gerald Graff, trans. Jeffrey Mehlman and Samuel Weber (Evanston, Ill.: Northwestern University Press, 1988), 1.

Conclusion

1. This includes debts unpaid between different groups of people outside of Native communities. "The Chinese stole some cattle and accused the People of doing it. The White men then hung four people. The People never liked the Chinese because of this. They felt as though the Chinese owed them four." Coyote Man, *The Destruction of the People* (Berkeley: Brother William Press, 1973), 87. Here we see the genocidal logics of racial competition in relation to white supremacy but from a different angle of perception through a Maidu calculus of violence that treats Chinese migrants as a tribe. Four of their people would have settled the dispute.

2. Coyote Man, *Destruction*, 3–4.

3. Coyote Man, 1.

4. Tommy Pico, *IRL* (Austin: Birds, 2016).

5. Pico, *IRL*.

6. Tommy Pico, interview by Tobias Carroll, "'I Said What I Had to Say': An Interview with Tommy Pico," *Vol. 1 Brooklyn*, June 14, 2017, https://vol1brooklyn.com/2017/06/14/i-said-what-i-had-to-say-an-interview-with-tommy-pico/.

7. Trinh T. Minh-ha, Woman, Native, Other: Writing Postcoloniality and Feminism (Bloomington: Indiana University Press, 1990), 16.

8. Mark Rifkin, *Settler Common Sense: Queerness and Everyday Colonialism in the American Renaissance* (Minneapolis: University of Minnesota Press, 2014), xvi.

9. Eric Michaels, *Bad Aboriginal Art: Tradition, Media, and Technological Horizons* (Minneapolis: University of Minnesota Press, 1994), 143.

10. Michaels, *Bad Aboriginal Art*, 144.

11. Gail Tremblay, "Issues in Contemporary American Indian Art: An Iroquois Example," Native Case Studies, The Evergreen State College, https://nativecases.evergreen.edu/sites/default/files/case-studies/TremblayIssuesincontAmIndian_Art.pdf, 5.

12. Michaels, *Bad Aboriginal Art*, 147.

13. Trinh, *Woman, Native, Other*, 150.

14. Jennifer Doyle, *Hold It Against Me: Difficulty and Emotion in Contemporary Art* (Durham, N.C.: Duke University Press, 2013), 98–104.

15. Doyle, 103.

16. Dian Million, *Therapeutic Nations: Healing in an Age of Indigenous Human Rights* (Tucson: University of Arizona Press, 2013).

17. Doyle, *Hold It Against Me*, 103.

18. Doyle, 103–4.

19. David Lloyd, *Under Representation: The Racial Regime of Aesthetics* (New York: Fordham University Press, 2019), e26.

20. Lloyd, e212.

21. Lloyd, e35–e37.

22. Lloyd, e249.

23. Pico, *IRL*.

Index

(continued from page ii)

Jean M. O'Brien, *Firsting and Lasting: Writing Indians out of Existence in New England*

Jamaica Heolimeleikalani Osorio, *Remembering Our Intimacies: Moʻolelo, Aloha ʻĀina, and Ea*

Shiri Pasternak, *Grounded Authority: The Algonquins of Barriere Lake against the State*

Steven Salaita, *Inter/Nationalism: Decolonizing Native America and Palestine*

Leanne Betasamosake Simpson, *As We Have Always Done: Indigenous Freedom through Radical Resistance*

Leanne Betasamosake Simpson, *Noopiming: The Cure for White Ladies*

Paul Chaat Smith, *Everything You Know about Indians Is Wrong*

Lisa Tatonetti, *The Queerness of Native American Literatures*

Lisa Tatonetti, *Written by the Body: Gender Expansiveness and Indigenous Non-Cis Masculinities*

Gerald Vizenor, *Bear Island: The War at Sugar Point*

Robert Warrior, *The People and the Word: Reading Native Nonfiction*

Robert A. Williams Jr., *Like a Loaded Weapon: The Rehnquist Court, Indian Rights, and the Legal History of Racism in America*

MARK MINCH-DE LEON is assistant professor of Indigenous studies in the Department of English at UC Riverside. Minch-de Leon is an enrolled member of the Susanville Indian Rancheria.